6⁰⁰

A Think Tank for Liberty

A personal history of Reason Foundation,

America's most influential libertarian think tank

A Think Tank for Liberty

A personal history of Reason Foundation,

America's most influential libertarian think tank

Robert W. Poole, Jr.,

Founder and CEO, 1978–2001

Jameson Books, Inc.
Ottawa, Illinois

Titles from Jameson Books, Inc., and its imprints are available at special discounts for bulk purchases, for sales promotions, premiums, fund raising or educational use.

For information and other requests please contact:

Jameson Books, Inc.
722 Columbus Street
Ottawa, Illinois 61350

jamesonbooks@yahoo.com
https://jbooksinc.com

815-434-7905
800-426-1357 for mail and bulk orders.

Printed in the United States of America.
ISBN: 978-0-89803-184-3
 5   4   3   2   1   21   20   19   18

Library of Congress Control Number: 2018944667

Contents

Dedication

For Lou, without whose love, support, advice,

and assistance this improbable story might not

have had a happy ending

Chapter 1

Origins of a Policy Entrepreneur

Introduction

In June 2016, I took part in the fiftieth reunion of my MIT Class of 1966. The reunion planning committee decided to invite five or six classmates who had pursued "unusual" career paths to give presentations on their accomplishments. Thanks to committee member Ralph Schmitt, a long-time subscriber to *Reason* magazine and fan of Reason Foundation, I was one of those invited. When Ralph pitched me on this, I mulled it over and decided that doing this would be good publicity for Reason Foundation. Putting the huge (graphics-intensive) PowerPoint together was a lot more work than I'd imagined. It also led me to consider explicitly several questions that had only lurked on the periphery of my thinking over the years.

First and foremost, how did a nerdy young introvert, channeled into science and engineering in the aftermath of the Soviet Sputnik launch, get interested in politics, economics, and public policy? And how did that interest evolve into publishing what became the country's leading libertarian magazine, and subsequently building one of America's most effective public-policy think tanks? It's a long and unlikely path that I managed to condense into that forty-five-minute talk at the reunion: "Changing the World: My Career as a Think-Tank Entrepreneur."

Secondly, I was sure my MIT audience wanted to know whether my background as an engineer (BS and MS in mechanical engineering, jobs at Sikorsky Aircraft and at General Research Corp.) influenced the kind of public policy think tank I ended up creating. Among the points I included in my presentation were these:

- The first print magazine to use computerized page layout;
- Among the first with an online version of the print magazine;
- A pioneer with "virtual employees," working full-time from home offices across the country, connected electronically;
- The world's first individually personalized magazine, with an aerial photo of each subscriber's residence on the cover; and,
- The first full-time think-tank video division, *Reason TV*.

As you will see in this book, Reason Foundation developed a very results-oriented approach to policy change. Instead of measuring success by the number of media appearances or legislative testimonies given (though of course we tracked those as partial indicators), our real measure of success is policy ideas that get implemented. During the twenty-three years when I was CEO, I often explained to donors that while our free-market/limited-government perspective set the course and helped define policy goals, the real work of policy change required finding "customers" in the public sector—people who saw the need for change and were willing to draw on the thinking and policy proposals of an independent think tank. In the early years, some libertarians criticized Reason as being "gradualist"—as opposed to radicals who would settle for nothing less than total abolition of an agency or program. By contrast, we developed an MO as pragmatic libertarians, getting serious reforms implemented on which we or others could subsequently build.

Over the years, the educational efforts of our think magazine and its online partners have helped bring libertarian ideas into the national debate on issues, aided by recruiting national figures such as John Stossel and Drew Carey to our cause. And our policy research has led to a large array of changes in city and state service delivery, transportation infrastructure, school choice, public pension reform, and a number of other areas.

As I write this book, *Reason* magazine is in its forty-ninth year, with fiftieth anniversary celebrations planned for 2018. The budget for fiscal year 2017 was $12.6 million, up from $5.2 million in 2001, my last year as CEO. Our Washington, DC, office (leased space), on Connecticut Avenue just north of Dupont Circle, opened in 2007, and has greatly increased our presence in the nation's capital. Reason Foundation's new headquarters in Los Angeles is a two-story office building on the west side of Los Angeles, acquired in 2013 and fully paid for by 2016.

I stepped down as CEO in 2001, because the entrepreneurial phase of Reason's growth was over, and I realized that I was tired of managing a large and growing organization and spending increasing amounts of time on the road, fundraising. I wanted to get back to hands-on policy research, in which I'd already helped popularize competitive contracting of municipal services in the 1980s and privatized infrastructure in the 1990s. I was sure I could do much better work in transportation policy as a full-time policy researcher—and that has proved to be the case.

My successor as CEO, David Nott, is also an engineer (Stanford University). He has transformed the organization I created, increasing its budget, breadth, and funding base substantially and launching new efforts, including the DC office, *Reason TV*, and the LA headquarters building. And I have gone on to do the best and most effective policy work of my career, as you will see in the book's last two chapters.

But to return to the original question, how did this unlikely career choice come about? In these chapters, I have tried to focus on the influences that shaped my values and decisions over the years, leading first to writing for a fledgling libertarian periodical, later turning it into an unprofitable business, and subsequently creating a national think tank to house it. It's an unlikely story, but it happened.

Earliest Years and Influences

I was raised in a small three-bedroom house in a subdivision in Hialeah, Florida, near Miami International Airport. My family was part of a large post-World War II migration from the Northeast to South Florida.

Dad was a science graduate of Syracuse University and had taught high school science in his first job. He apparently didn't like it much, and having always worked on cars and done some small-plane flying, he became aircraft engine mechanic at Caldwell-Wright Airport in New Jersey. Our move to Florida was motivated by wanting to escape frigid winters and facilitated by a job offer from the engine overhaul department of Eastern Air Lines, which had its main base in Miami.

Mom was a full-time housewife who taught my younger sisters and me the alphabet using flash cards, followed by teaching us to read. I remember my first day of school at Hialeah Elementary when I read words out loud that had been posted above the blackboard, surprising the teacher. After the first semester they moved me to a class of more-advanced students; apparently they had some kind of ability grouping in those days.

Although Mom seemed very protective of us, my sisters and I grew up as what would today be called free-range kids. After the first few weeks of elementary school, I walked the four blocks to and from school alone, and when I finally got a bicycle in fourth grade, I biked to school from then on. As a member of the school's Safety Patrol, I got a free weekly movie pass to the nearby Essex Theater, so nearly every Thursday or Friday after school I biked over there and saw a movie, getting home in time for dinner.

Sunday school and church were an important part of my growing-up years. Dad had been raised Unitarian, but my parents weren't churchgoers in my earliest years. But when I was nine or ten, they were introduced to a Lutheran church near Coral Gables, whose minister was a very dynamic preacher. They "got religion," so from then on we kids went to Sunday school every week, followed by church service. Dad and Mom joined the choir, and for several years Dad served on the church council. I ended up with many years of perfect Sunday school attendance.

Aviation was an early part of my life. As an Eastern family, we had pass privileges to fly anywhere the airline flew for vacation trips, on a space-available basis. In those days, when airlines were regulated and there was little or no competition, load factors were about 50 percent, so there were nearly always seats available for us when we wanted to go somewhere. In those days, flying was a luxury that most middle-class people could not afford, so we felt like pioneers on our flying vacations.

One of my best memories of Hialeah Elementary is the library. I devoured books on American historical figures and then discovered the library's great collection of juvenile and young-adult science fiction. My favorites were Robert Heinlein's dozen or more juvenile science fiction novels, such as *Space Cadet*, *Red Planet*, and *Citizen of the Galaxy*. I started on these in fourth or fifth grade and read the rest of them (as they were published) in junior high. I didn't realize it at the time, but what I was getting from Heinlein—in addition to great stories—were values of rationality, competence, individualism, and questioning authority. I also enjoyed reading the photo captions in Dad's college science textbooks, especially one on dinosaurs and the classic Baker astronomy text.

Like most boys of that era, I loved building model airplanes and ships, and ended up with a large collection of each, especially air force fighter planes. But my main hobby was model railroading (which has persisted to this day). For Christmas when I was ten, I got my first Lionel electric train—a steam locomotive and a set of freight cars. Dad built me a layout in my bedroom eventually extending the length of two of the room's four walls. I spent years adding buildings, streets, automobiles, scenery, etc., to make it as realistic as I could.

But with a tiny allowance, it was not possible to purchase additional freight cars or accessories, let alone an additional locomotive. So I got myself a job doing yard work in the neighborhood on Saturdays. I also had a small newspaper route—about two dozen customers of the weekly *Hialeah Home News*.

My cousin Tom Yorke lived up the street, and we shared the model-building and model railroad hobbies. We would go on periodic scavenging expeditions on our bikes. About six blocks east of us, the Seaboard Railroad line went through, with an array of light industries along the tracks. We scrounged various things from their scrap piles, including a sink cutout from a Formica countertop that I used as a cutting board for model-making.

Tom and I also shared a warped sense of humor, loving novelty records, satire, and parody. Late in our elementary school years, we created a newspaper parody, including news articles and numerous ads. One of Tom's brilliant product ads was for "Spray-On Dust—for the housewife who doesn't know what to do with herself"—a preview of Betty Friedan's *The Feminine Mystique*.

In the mid-1950s, like millions of other kids, I discovered rock & roll. Leading the field initially was Bill Haley & the Comets, whose number-one hit was "Rock Around the Clock." Haley was soon eclipsed by Elvis, and then an avalanche of others—the Everly Brothers, Little Richard, Chuck Berry, the Coasters, etc. Interestingly, despite this being the still-segregated South, nobody seemed to care that many of our rock stars were black. I've often wondered if our generation's enthusiasm for performers like Chuck Berry, et al., helped the civil rights movement to change hearts and minds.

Getting More Serious: Junior and Senior High School

In those days, elementary school was grades first through sixth, followed by three years of junior high and three years of high school. Kids from our neighborhood were assigned to Miami Springs Junior High, just across the Miami River in the neighborhood that abutted Miami International Airport. The distance was just under two miles from our house, which meant school bus service was not available. So a group of us, who'd all gone to Hialeah Elementary, rode our bikes together each morning to our new school. (Due to various afterschool activities, there was usually not such a convoy going home.)

Junior high was a bit of a culture shock. While the Hialeah kids were mostly from working class families, many of the Miami Springs kids had parents who were doctors, pilots, or other professionals. This created something of a divide, despite these kids mostly being friendly. And with the shift to this larger school, my thoughts turned to what I expected would be a struggle to get into a high-end college with enough scholarship support to be able to afford to go. So I approached junior high with a determination to excel.

The Soviet Union launched the world's first artificial satellite, Sputnik 1, in 1957, when I was thirteen. That set off a national educational fervor to channel bright kids into science and engineering, which created a climate that influenced the rest of my pre-college years. I soon became friends with the brightest kid in our seventh grade cohort—Peter Gullotta. We were in several classes together, including an eighth- or ninth-grade science class taught by a very smart and tough Dr. Leo Boles. He tried hard to get us to think, rather than simply memorizing stuff.) Boles organized the school's science fair, and in 1959, I won a second-place ribbon (for a project on factors influencing bean growth), while Peter got a first place ribbon for his construction of a Geiger counter. We both then took part in the subsequent South Florida Science Fair.

Junior high was not all science and math, though. I benefitted from an art class, a crafts class, and a speech class. The latter was my first introduction to public speaking—at least in front of a class of thirty fellow students. A further step in that direction was eighth- and ninth-grade chorus. I discovered that I loved singing in four-part harmony, and was one of the few kids in the chorus who could read music (thanks to about four years of guitar lessons). I was selected to be part of an eight-member "ensemble" that did some numbers separate from the rest of the chorus when we performed—first at school events in the auditorium and then on several South Florida tours. To my surprise (given my self-perception as an introverted bookworm), I found that I loved performing. And my love of vocal harmony has grown over the years.

I was confronted more directly with racial segregation during a seventh-grade civics class project. I decided my project would be to investigate the supposedly "separate but equal" public schools for non-whites in South Florida. I got a list of "colored" schools that were within biking distance and set out on my bike one Saturday morning, lugging my little Brownie Hawkeye black-and-white camera. I found that the schools I visited and photographed were anything but equal in terms of facilities. Instead of the modern, concrete-block buildings with landscaping and playgrounds or athletic fields that I attended, what I photographed were old frame buildings, many of them just portables, with little or no landscaping. I should not have been surprised, since until recently there had been "colored" and "white" drinking fountains in the supermarkets, and blacks were still required to sit in the back of the city buses. And, of course, for all twelve years of my enrollment in the Dade County School system, the schools were legally segregated.

Hialeah High School (HHS) was located a few blocks east of the Hialeah Race Track—and too far to bike. Fortunately, the school bus stopped a half block from our house, so that's how I got to and from high school. But when I had afterschool activities, I learned to ride the city transit bus down Palm Avenue and then east on Hialeah Drive, to a stop five blocks from home on 5th Street.

HHS's culture was very sports-dominated—the jock culture. Time was taken away from classes for everyone's required attendance at "pep rallies" prior to each football game. The relatively small number of us who were interested in academics felt marginalized by the overwhelming focus on sports teams.

Peter and I remained friends (and academic rivals) throughout high school, but I developed some other good friendships, as well. Eight or ten of us, all part of the relatively small academic portion of our nearly thousand-strong class, formed "the Clique," which socialized at school and at some members' homes, discussing books and ideas, listening to classical music, and bad-mouthing the much larger jock faction of the student body. We also made periodic excursions to the only decent book store in the area—a quite large and well-stocked store in the huge new terminal building that had just opened at Miami International Airport. There we found challenging books like physicist George Gamow's *One, Two, Three . . . Infinity*, serious adult fiction, and even books on sex.

There was a partial overlap of this group with a somewhat more organized group historically called the Loafers Club—open only to male members of the senior class (remember, this was the late 1950s!) with a straight-A average. By the time my friends and I were "tapped" for membership late in our junior year, the administration had cracked down, requiring that if we wanted to be accepted on campus and have a page in the yearbook, we had to come up with a more respectable *name*. Given that the long-accepted logo was an L in a circle, I came up with "Literati," and that became the group's official name. We did get our page in the yearbook.

In these post-Sputnik years, national groups were working hard to beef up public schools' science and math curricula. I was not subjected to "new math," but in tenth-grade biology HHS was one of the test schools for a new biology textbook developed by the Biological Sciences Curriculum Study. The large-format paperback book arrived a bit later than the start of the school year, and we soon discovered why. In the section on reproduction, a full page that showed profile views of the human male and female reproductive systems was blacked out. Apparently the facts of life were too much for the Dade County School Board, which caused much laughter among my classmates and me. We also had an experimental (PSSC) physics text in twelfth grade, but there was nothing controversial enough to be censored.

Perhaps also inspired by the post-Sputnik panic, HHS had a class open to juniors and seniors called Science Research. It focused on teaching us to design and carry out projects that could be entered in the local science fair, and hopefully be good enough to get selected for the state science fair. My junior year project, "predicting the population curve of fruit flies with an analog computer," was something of a dud. The damned *Drosophila melanogaster* flies kept dying, and I never did really master the analog computer. My friends and I attended HHS football home games—because Science Research had the concession to sell soft drinks, to raise money for science fair travel. The only one excused was my friend Lee Mendez, who was a member of the marching band.

In the summer between my junior and senior years, I got a summer job at the University of Miami medical research building near downtown Miami. Working in a biochemistry lab under Dr. Alfred Krall, with a group of fun-loving medical students, I worked on a project involving uptake of carbon monoxide, in similar fashion by bell peppers and Portuguese man-of-war. I managed to turn that into a winning science fair project, and a number of my Science Research classmates and I were selected to take our projects to the state science fair. (I worked two more summers in Dr. Krall's lab, carrying on further biochemistry research.)

The most important HHS experience for my intellectual development was a senior-year class called Math Analysis (which I took in addition to the normal one semester of trigonometry and one of solid geometry). While not new math, it did introduce us to things like set theory, number systems other than base 10, etc.—although it did not include calculus, which put me at a disadvantage when I got to MIT. The course was taught by Darryl Johnson, who was also the school's debate coach. And he was something of a classical liberal, with values stressing limited government and free markets. One day per month instead of teaching us math he taught us political economy. I found these ideas really engaging. My parents were moderate Republicans, and I'd read several anti-communist books by the time I got to this class. But I'd never really been exposed to political philosophy before.

Around this same time, I came across a paperback edition of Barry Goldwater's *Conscience of a Conservative* (1960), which I read avidly, especially his critique of big government and his advocacy of something much closer to the vision of Jefferson, Madison, and other Founding Fathers. This passage in particular struck a chord with me:

> I have little interest in streamlining government or in making it more efficient, for I mean to reduce its size. I do not undertake to promote welfare, for I propose to extend freedom. My aim is not to pass laws but to repeal them. It is not to inaugurate new programs but to cancel old ones that do violence to the Constitution, or that have failed in their purpose, or that impose on people an unwarranted financial

burden. I will not attempt to discover whether legislation is "needed" before I have first discovered whether it is constitutional. And if I should later be attacked for neglecting my constituents' "interests," I shall reply that I was informed that their main interest is liberty, and that in that cause I am doing the very best I can.

Before my graduation, I asked Mr. Johnson if he could recommend any periodicals I could subscribe to, to help me through my college years. As a result, I entered college with subscriptions to *The Freeman* (published by the Foundation for Economic Education) and *National Review*, as well as membership in the Intercollegiate Society of Individualists (ISI, later to be renamed the Intercollegiate Studies Institute).

On the advice of my guidance counselor, I decided early on that to maximize my college/scholarship chances, I needed to build a resume of success. So I got myself elected to the Key Club, and became vice president of the National Honor Society chapter and president of Junior Scientists (basically the Science Research students). That plus my science fair project award, test scores, and grades ended up gaining me five scholarship offers from an array of good to excellent universities. Fortunately, MIT (my first choice) offered enough financial aid that my parents could afford to accept their offer. I had not applied to Cal Tech, since any school I attended had to be reachable on passes by Eastern Air Lines (which Los Angeles was not), since my parents would not have been able to afford to pay for several airline trips per year.

I also ended up as co-valedictorian, along with Peter Gullotta. Co-salutatorians were my Science Research classmates Lynn Kinsky and Dan Smith. Dan was a member of the Clique and of Science Research, and had been a classmate since Hialeah Elementary. Lynn was also a Clique member and a Science Research classmate. Peter and I gave the two graduation speeches. I had to fight with the administration over what I planned to say, and was required to make it "non-political." Thanks to my junior high speech class, I was able to give the speech tolerably well, though it was something of an ordeal.

Flying down for my graduation was my uncle, Col. Theodore Poole, a career army officer and also my godfather. While I was growing up, Uncle Ted was my window on a larger world than Hialeah, having been stationed in South Korea and Germany at various points in his career. (He was also an active model railroader.) By this point in his career, he was commanding officer of the army's Transportation Combat Developments Agency at Ft. Eustis, Virginia. He occasionally sent me articles on some of the things they were exploring there, including rocket belts, hovercraft, and other advanced technologies. I was honored by his being at the graduation in his dress-whites uniform.

MIT, a Whole New Ballgame

If junior high had been a minor culture shock, MIT was more like an earthquake. First, I had never lived anywhere apart from my family, not even summer camp. Second, I was unprepared for hundred-year-old buildings in Cambridge and Back Bay across the river in Boston; to me, they all looked like slums, at first. Third, I knew I had to be prepared for cold winters (since I had no recollection of playing in the snow when I was two or three years old in New Jersey), but the winters were still a shock.

But more than that was the fierce competition. I had pretty much coasted through twelve years of school, and all of a sudden I was in the midst of hundreds of other freshmen *at least* as smart as I was, many of whom had already had some calculus or had gone to elite public or private schools (e.g., Bronx High School of Science). Fortunately, the institute—or at least my new dorm, Baker House—provided advisors to help us each get oriented. These were seniors who agreed to begin their school year a few days early. The pair assigned to me gave me an orientation to the campus, explained how student housing worked, and took me into Boston to buy suitable winter clothes.

They also explained to me that everything at MIT (except dorms) has a number in addition to a name, and most everyday usage is by number, not name. Every building has a number—the building under the Great Dome is Building 10, and its main lecture hall is 10–250. Each course has a number; e.g., physics is Course VIII, and first-semester freshman physics is 8.01, second-semester is 8.02. So you could hear someone tell a friend, "I have an 8:30 5.02 in 26–100," and everyone would understand exactly what that meant.

The initial coursework didn't seem too bad. Freshman year was pretty standard for everyone—calculus, chemistry, physics, humanities, and an elective (intermediate German in my case)—plus a required swimming and diving class first semester and an elective sport second semester (I took tennis). There was a huge amount of homework—far more time doing readings and problem sets than time spent in class. Still, I did fine on my first quizzes in calculus and chemistry—but flunked my first physics quiz. The difference was that physics quizzes required the student to apply principles learned in class to actual problems, and this was something I was completely unprepared for. Having never flunked anything in my life, I was devastated, and sought help from the in-house counselor/coach in Baker House. He overcame my panic, and then helped me to grasp what was needed to do this kind of problem-solving. That was very fortunate, because all my engineering classes from sophomore year onward required the same approach. I did get the hang of it by the second physics quiz, and ended up with a B for first semester physics (with all the rest A's). These were real grades; there was no such thing as grade inflation in the 1960s, at least not at MIT.

Freshman year I had two roommates, Peter Wolfe from Encino, California, and a fellow from Vermont who later dropped out or flunked out. Peter was very much into classical music and high-fidelity stereo equipment, so our dorm room was well-equipped. I learned a lot about both topics from Peter, especially coming to appreciate composers beyond the standard Bach, Beethoven, Rachmaninoff, and Tchaikovsky. New favorites thanks to Peter included Elgar, Franck, Poulenc, Saint-Saens, and Vaughn Williams. I've often said, only half in jest, that two of the best things I took away from my years at MIT were learning how to swim (as opposed to dog-paddling) and a much deeper appreciation for classical music.

Toward the end of freshman year, everyone had to decide on a major. I'd entered MIT with the post-Sputnik idea of physics as the pinnacle of science and therefore what I should aim at. But I soon realized that I didn't really want an academic career, so pure science was out. Since I loved aviation, I took advantage of a letter of introduction from Uncle Ted to Prof. Rene Miller of the Department of Aeronautics and Astronautics and had a long discussion with him about that as a major. I ended up concluding that the risk in that choice was ending up too narrowly educated for anything but aerospace. The best bet for something like a *general* engineering education appeared to be Course II (mechanical engineering). So that's what I chose.

I enjoyed the engineering courses, including the introduction to machine tools that gave us hands-on experience making castings, machining aluminum test specimens and testing them to destruction, and writing reports on what we did. Since I was the only one in our small project group who'd been in honors English in high school, I was elected to write the report, and it won some kind of minor prize for clear exposition.

I especially enjoyed the required second-year humanities sequence, called Modern Western Ideas and Values. Freshman year had covered Thucydides, Homer, Plato, Aristotle, Augustine, and other ancients. But the second year had us reading Locke, Rousseau, Voltaire, Smith, Hume, Mill, Marx, and a host of others. I discovered the Enlightenment—basically, the overthrow of tradition and its replacement by a new stress on individualism and rationality—and also Classical Liberalism: limited government, religious freedom, and free markets. In subsequent years there was enough course flexibility that I was able to take macro and micro economics, the history of engineering, business law, and marketing, nicely rounding out my engineering education.

Interestingly, one third-year engineering course was devoted to a major transportation project that some of the professors had been studying. Under the rubric of "Project Transport," the idea was high-speed ground transportation in an evacuated tube, using linear induction motor propulsion, with the initial application being the Northeast Corridor between Boston and

Washington, DC. It sounds a lot like Elon Musk's Hyperloop—but this was in 1964!

A new experience for me, after growing up in whites-only Hialeah, was to make friends with students of other ethnicities. During my twelve pre-college school years, I had only one Jewish friend, Fred Mohel—but MIT had large numbers of Jewish students, many of them coming from elite high schools. My freshman dorm room had Orthodox Jewish guys on one side and a Chinese-American guy on the other side. And one of my lasting friendships from MIT is Adam Powell, son of the famous congressman from Harlem. With his droll sense of humor, Adam became part of a group of us who palled around on weekends.

Adam, who later went into broadcasting, was involved with student radio station WTBS (whose call letters were later purchased by Ted Turner for his Turner Broadcasting System). I enjoyed listening to the WTBS Saturday "Rock & Roll Memory Time," featuring "oldies" from our junior and senior high years. Our driving around music was often new tunes from the Beach Boys and the Supremes, later supplemented by the Beatles and the Rolling Stones. In my senior year, the Beach Boys gave a free concert on campus, which cemented a life-long fandom for me, based not only on their sun-and-fun California images but also on their wonderful harmonies.

My weird sense of humor was shared by many MIT friends, and we especially loved the song creations of Tom Lehrer, spoofing politics, religion, and culture. I learned that Lehrer was a mathematician teaching courses at both Harvard and MIT. One of my great regrets is that I never audited a math class that he taught several days a week at MIT—at 8 a.m. In those days of studying ("tooling") till midnight or later, I avoided 8 a.m. classes—a big mistake in this case. Lehrer even created a song that he performed on WTBS—a piece incorporating the names of the MTA Red Line stations from Harvard Square to downtown Boston, based on the "M-O-T-H-E-R" song. It was never commercially recorded, but I have a copy saved on my computer.

In my third year, a small number of us were offered the

opportunity to enter an honors program, under which we could take the graduate versions of certain courses and end up with both a BS and an MS at the end of five years. Though my scholarship was only for four years, my counselor said there was a good chance I could get some kind of fellowship for the fifth year (which I did, thanks to the National Science Foundation), so I decided to go for it.

So did my fellow Course II classmate Jim Weigl. We'd shared a number of classes and been lab partners our sophomore year, so we decided to become quasi-roommates for our junior year. By that point we were high enough in the Baker House pecking order that we could get single rooms, and we ended up with almost-adjacent rooms, with just one single room in between our two rooms. We became friends with its occupant, a Course VI (electrical engineering) student from West Virginia, Aaron Snyder. Aaron was also a classical music lover, and he played the most amazing symphonies. I learned that they were all by Gustav Mahler (whom I'd never heard of) but who soon became my favorite composer. Jim, Aaron, Sandy Sawchuk, Adam, and I drove around on weekends in Jim's huge '57 Chrysler which we nicknamed Dino.

MIT's Baker House dorm is a modernist six-story, wave-shaped building designed by Finnish architect Alvar Aalto. It is all brick, with linoleum floors and built-in blonde wood desks, with freestanding blonde wardrobe cabinets. The rooms were very gloomy, which many of us found depressing. Jim discovered that the MIT maintenance people replaced all the fluorescent tubes in classrooms and labs on a regular schedule, whether they were burned out or not. We gathered up a whole supply of them that tested positive and brought them back to Baker House. Jim bought ballasts and starters at an electronics supply place in Cambridge, and we assembled fluorescent light fixtures on top of our wardrobes, bouncing their light off the white ceilings. This transformed the gloomy rooms into bright, inviting living spaces. We ended up starting a little business, with Xeroxed flyers saying, "Tired of living in the gloom? Why not brighten up your room?" After we'd sold a number of these kits, when you walked past Baker House at night, the difference among the rooms was striking. (And since we had no idea how much life was left in any bulb, we offered free replacements for any that burned out.)

Those were still the days of the Ma Bell telephone monopoly, so getting a private phone in a dorm room cost an arm and a leg. Jim had had a summer job with the phone company, and had obtained a large supply of surplus relays. He cobbled together a switching system so that with one telephone line, the three of us (Jim, Aaron, and I) could each have access. We called the kludge that did the switching the Interociter, after the communications device from the cult science fiction film *This Island Earth*.

In 1963 or '64, Jim and I were among a group of mechanical engineering students invited to test drive the Chrysler Turbine Car. The company had spent years of research coming up with this car, producing fifty-five to be tested in the field—including letting selected engineering students drive them. It had a cool, space-age look, thanks to styling by Ghia in Turin, Italy. And while it was fun to drive, we noticed a predictable phenomenon: turbine lag. When you tried for fast acceleration, it took a second or two for the gas turbine to speed up enough to produce the expected speed increase. This could have been fixed by having the turbine drive electric motors at the wheels, but nobody was thinking of such hybrid propulsion in those days. Despite providing some great PR, the cars were not ready for production, and Chrysler ended up scrapping all but a handful, which ended up in auto museums (except for one that was acquired by Jay Leno).

Political and Intellectual Activity

MIT was not completely all work and no play, though studying ("tooling") was a seven-days-a-week activity. The student-run Lecture Series Committee (LSC) ran a regular movie program on Friday and Saturday nights, with nearly first-run films, always preceded by a Road Runner cartoon (which we appreciated for the coyote's hair-brained engineering projects). LSC also brought interesting speakers to campus. Though I went to a movie almost every week, I attended only a few of the guest speaker events. The two that stand out are *National Review*'s William Buckley and a man named Willis Stone. Buckley's appeal is obvious (though part of his talk was over my head), but who, you might ask, was Willis Stone? He was the founder and president of the Liberty Amendment Committee, a group working to repeal the Sixteenth Amendment (authorizing the federal income tax). He gave a fascinating talk, not just on how great it would be for the economy to not have the income tax but how the budget numbers could work if it were repealed. His program called not just for eliminating some costly ongoing federal programs but also for selling off major assets and using the proceeds to pay down the national debt. That was my first exposure to what we later called "privatization" of government assets.

After hearing Buckley speak, I decided to read several of his books. During a summer job at the medical research building, I read his *Up from Liberalism*, and was dismayed by some aspects of his thinking. He strongly defended "states' rights," which in those days meant denying that the Fourteenth Amendment applied to deprivations of liberty by state governments. Courts had often upheld such interpretations, the impact of which was to leave in place the discriminatory Jim Crow laws in the South. These views seemed fairly widespread in the conservative movement of the 1960s—and riding the segregated city buses to and from that job much of the time brought me face to face with this kind of discrimination.

The fellow MIT student who'd arranged for Willis Stone to speak was David F. Nolan, Class of '65. Like me, Dave was a Goldwater supporter, and by 1963 there was an active effort going on to "draft" Goldwater to run for president. Dave decided to launch "MIT Students for Goldwater," and I agreed to serve as its literature director. In 1963–64, we staffed a regular literature table in Building 10, and grew the membership to about two hundred, which turned out to be the largest campus Goldwater group in New England by far. Nearly all of us joined Massachusetts Young Republicans, in order to go to its state nominating convention in 1964 to endorse Goldwater over Nelson Rockefeller. By sheer weight of numbers, we prevailed, to the great surprise of YR's national office.

Jim Weigl was part of this effort, and he came up with the idea of us becoming the campus distributor of the "Gold Water" soft drink that was available in 12-oz. cans, produced quietly by a major soft-drink bottler. Since my room had the refrigerator Jim and I shared, it became the point of sale. We bought many cases, and offered both cases and cold individual cans during that year. I don't recall how many we sold, but it was definitely thousands of cans. I still have one can that I use as a pen and pencil holder on my office desk.

The large majority of our Goldwater group, which overlapped considerably with the MIT chapter of Young Americans for Freedom (YAF), were libertarian/Objectivists as opposed to traditional conservatives. And it seemed as if most of the former had read and been inspired by the fiction and non-fiction of Ayn Rand. I'd never read Rand, though some of the members of the Clique in high school were fans and had tried to get me to do so. With Rand's ideas coming up so often in our political discussions (and especially after I learned that a railroad was an important part of the story in *Atlas Shrugged*), I decided I had to read it. So on my summer job in 1964, working for Southern Bell Telephone Company in Miami, I lugged around a 1,084-page paperback of the novel, reading it on breaks, at lunch, and in the evening (on nights when I was not going door-to-door handing out Goldwater literature in various Miami neighborhoods).

I would have been unprepared for Rand's ideas in high school. But after having read key works by the thinkers of the Enlightenment (including Hume's devastating critique of the idea of miracles) and coming to understand the rationality of the scientific method, I was ready. And the ideas really took. I very clearly identified not just with Rand's individualism and free markets, but also with the idea that rational self-interest is morally right, and therefore that capitalism is morally right, in addition to being economically productive and beneficial. Jim also read Rand, and we had many discussions of the implications of her ideas for politics, government, and making one's way in the world.

One direct implication for me was that I stopped going to church. Between the ideas of Heinlein, the Enlightenment,

Classical Liberalism, and Rand, I could no longer believe what now seemed to be the simplistic religious teachings of my youth. My parents, needless to say, were not happy about this, but did not hassle me about it (though I'm sure they prayed for me). Some years later, Uncle Ted confided in me that he'd always thought it strange that his Unitarian brother had gotten so caught up in churchgoing.

Back at school in autumn 1964, many of my colleagues and I signed up to be Republican poll watchers on Election Day. And we took part in a motorcade when Goldwater came to Boston and spoke at Fenway Park. But dismay was already in the air. First, we libertarian/Objectivists were very turned off that the national party had decided not to run a strongly issues-based campaign, but were going forward with the wishy-washy slogan "In your heart you know he's right." Second, someone high up in the organization had quietly passed the word that polls predicted a major loss, but that for the sake of changing the future of the GOP we needed to press on. So we did, but we were still crushed by the magnitude of Goldwater's loss.

An interesting footnote to the Goldwater campaign is something I learned only in 2015. At that year's FreedomFest conference in Las Vegas, I talked with Goldwater biographer Lee Edwards. After I told him my MIT Students for Goldwater story, he told me that two other long-time think-tank presidents had had similar experiences. Both Ed Crane of Cato Institute and Ed Feulner of Heritage Foundation had been student Goldwater activists; Crane at UC Berkeley and Feulner at the University of Pennsylvania.

The summer of 1965 was my last one living at home. Dad had arranged for me to work in the engineering office at Eastern in Miami, to which he had been promoted from the engine overhaul shop some years before. Much of my summer work was pretty boring, plotting thousands of data points from jet engine tests, by hand, onto graph paper. That left my mind free to wander, pondering America's future in light of the Goldwater debacle. Rand had written that this showed that the intellectual groundwork had not really been prepared—that it was "too early" for politics. I thought about how great it would be to be paid to do work on ideas, building a serious case for what I thought of as a free society, true to the principles of the Enlightenment and the limited-government vision of our Founding Fathers.

Many of my MIT colleagues had dropped out of YAF after Goldwater's defeat, leaving me to pick up the pieces as I accepted the presidency of the much smaller chapter in spring 1965. But I was now having doubts over whether that kind of political effort was worthwhile. I decided to attend the 1965 YAF National Convention later that summer in Washington, DC, to get a better feel for where YAF was headed. I could fly for free on an Eastern pass, just as I'd been doing for three years back and forth between Miami and Boston.

I attended sessions at the convention for several days, capped off by the closing banquet. The featured speaker was Sen. Strom Thurmond from South Carolina, who had switched from Democrat to Republican during the Goldwater campaign. But I was disgusted—there was no evidence that Thurmond had stopped being a segregationist, and given my firsthand exposure to the reality of segregation growing up, I thought it was a travesty for an organization supposedly dedicated to liberty to laud such a figure. I remained seated during the standing ovation, gaining the requisite dirty looks. And after I got home, I wrote a letter to the national office resigning as president of the MIT chapter and YAF itself, telling them why. (Six years later, at YAF's 1969 National Convention in St. Louis, the remaining libertarian delegates walked out, with some of them going on to found a libertarian counterpart, the Society for Individual Liberty.)

Back at MIT for our senior year and graduate school, Jim and I joined a newly created on-campus Objectivist group, Radicals for Capitalism. We were not in its leadership, but we arranged a very well-attended showing of the film version of Rand's novel *The Fountainhead* on campus. RadCaps went on to publish a weekly libertarian campus newspaper called *Ergo*, which lasted for fifteen or twenty years.

The summer of 1966 was my first summer job away from home. From several attractive offers, I chose the Advanced Vehicle Concepts division of Ford Motor Company in Dearborn,

Michigan. A month or so before the end of the spring semester, I bought my first car: a 1962 Plymouth Valiant with pushbutton automatic transmission. One of the fun things of working at Ford was that my summer friend Ken and I had access to the junkyard, where crash-test vehicles were stored. In addition to salvaging a few usable parts for company projects, we were allowed to salvage parts we could use for our own cars. Since I planned to do my master's thesis on auto safety, I was motivated to make my own car safer. In addition to buying and installing seat belts (they'd been optional on the '62 model), I scrounged door lamps from a wreck and installed them in the left and right doors, so they would light up when the doors were opened. (I'd driven over to a Chrysler facility and purchased a service manual for the '62 Valiant.) I'd planned to add padded sun visors, but could not find any that fit.

It was an enjoyable summer, driving around listening to the Beach Boys singing "I Get Around" and "Fun, Fun, Fun," in my own car. Ken and I took part in a weekend road rally, and I went to a Saturday night drag race (pretty boring). We worked on interesting design projects, too, but as the summer progressed I realized that although Dearborn was lovely in the summer, it would be cold and miserable in the winter, and the only real industry for engineers was the auto industry. That did not seem like a good career choice, despite the excitement of "advanced vehicle concepts."

One of the books I read that summer was Betty Friedan's *The Feminine Mystique*. It made a big impression, bringing me face to face with what had been my (typically) condescending attitude toward the handful of "Tech co-eds" on campus, despite having admired the strong female characters of Heinlein and Rand. On a lighter note, I was also enjoying the "Modesty Blaise" series of thriller novels, starring an amazingly competent woman.

That summer I'd been corresponding with HHS friend Lynn Kinsky, who had graduated from the University of Wisconsin in chemistry and was headed to grad school as one of the first female students at Dartmouth. So we would be within driving distance when I was back in Cambridge for my grad school year at MIT. After learning that my sister Kristi was planning to get married, I reflected on the fact that, at age twenty-two, I'd been on exactly two dates in my whole life, with a girl I knew from high school when we were both home for the summer in Hialeah. Maybe I should try dating Lynn, I thought. She had been one of those in the Clique who'd encouraged me to read Rand, to no avail. She seemed very pleased that I'd now done so. I decided I'd visit her in the autumn at Dartmouth and see what happened.

My chosen master's thesis topic was a cost-effectiveness model of an array of possible auto safety improvements. Ralph Nader had published his book criticizing the Chevy Corvair as *Unsafe at Any Speed* in 1965, and though he was somewhat off-base technically, General Motors had embarrassed itself by hiring private detectives to dig up dirt on him, instead of hiring independent engineers to contest his claims. GM's financial settlement included a large grant to MIT for auto safety research, one of whose projects was my thesis. I assembled reams of data on the estimated costs and benefits of various possible safety improvements to (1) cars and (2) roadways. I then wrote a computer program to take a pot of money and allocate it to safety improvements, in order of bang for the buck, starting with the one that had the highest benefit/cost ratio. The broadest general finding was that there were more cost-beneficial opportunities to save lives sooner by fixing the worst hazards on roadways than by equipping all new cars with various individual safety improvements. This was largely because the hot spots on the roadways would yield immediate safety benefits, while it would take many years for improvements made only to new cars to produce many benefits. The grant also paid for a trip to Detroit for my advisor and me to present the results to GM.

I visited Lynn at Dartmouth one weekend that fall, and we seemed to hit it off. So despite the usual heavy load of grad school courses and my thesis work, we managed to spend occasional weekends together during that year. With graduation on the horizon for June, my other preoccupation was job hunting. MIT's placement office had no trouble attracting companies to do brief introductory interviews on campus, and when they found somebody promising, the next step was to arrange a trip for the prospect for detailed interviews. I made about a dozen such trips that school year and ended up dropping several courses that I did not need in order to graduate, so that I could keep up with my school work, despite all this travel.

The most elaborate trip was to Boeing in Seattle for several days of being pitched to by the company (along with a few dozen others), including plant tours and a salmon barbecue on a nearby island. The project they would have hired me for was the federally subsidized supersonic transport (SST). I had several concerns— that the project might get cancelled (as it later did), that Boeing was the only aerospace company in the area, and that I really hated the gloomy weather (one Boeing engineer told me the sun had not come out for twenty-nine days, as of my visit). Another noteworthy trip was to Southern Pacific Railroad headquarters in San Francisco. Their management training program would have had me do six-month stints in half-a-dozen portions of the business. While there, my MIT friend Sandy Sawchuk (who'd gone on to grad school at Stanford) gave me a guided tour of the City. But I did not accept SP's interesting job offer, because there was no way they could obtain a draft deferment for me. This was 1966–67, the height of the Vietnam War.

The draft problem ended up limiting my choices to aero-space/defense companies. Though I really wanted to escape New England winters, and had offers from several companies in California, the budding relationship with Lynn led me to accept the offer from Sikorsky Aircraft in Stratford, Connecticut. That was still within (longer) driving distance from Dartmouth, so we could see where that relationship would go.

Chapter 2

Young Engineer and Fledgling Policy Analyst

Sikorsky Aircraft

In late June 1967, I reported for work at Sikorsky Aircraft in Stratford, Connecticut. I'd rented a one-bedroom apartment in West Haven. Thanks to a BankAmericard helpfully provided to new MIT graduates by State Street Bank, I was able to furnish the place prior to receiving my first paycheck.

My job at Sikorsky was in the Systems Analysis Branch of the Engineering Department. We engineers sat in a large open space with rows of desks side-by-side, with our supervisor in a glassed-in cubicle at the back, with a secretary's position beside it. I was part of a whole crop of new hires fresh out of school, so Sikorsky gave us several days' worth of orientation, including a tour of the helicopter assembly area on the ground floor of this headquarters plant (on the bank of the Housatonic River, with a small landing field adjoining the river). We also got a hands-on tour of the nearby plant in Bridgeport, at which we briefly learned riveting.

As a systems analyst, my job consisted mostly of doing cost-effectiveness analysis of possible improvements to existing helicopters. Since this was during the war in Vietnam, most of these analyses involved military missions. I found in my archives one such report, undated but with a contract number implying 1968. I had constructed a model to quantify the costs (initial and operating) and benefits (in terms of increased mission effectiveness) of potential improvements to the HH-53C night rescue helicopter. The paper is filled with equations, which I could probably re-create today, given enough time.

This kind of work was part of the systems engineering/systems analysis efforts developed by the team of "whiz kids" brought to the Department of Defense by Robert McNamara in the 1960s. The basic idea was to do a better job of figuring out "how much is enough" in terms of defense hardware, also known as how much bang do you get for each buck spent. The intent was certainly worthwhile, but it ended up generating mountains of paperwork, and could get mind-numbingly detailed.

Part of what kept the work interesting for a few years was the opportunity to interact with other parts of the organization. The advanced-concepts engineers were looking into some quite different configurations, such as a helicopter with two main rotors, stacked one atop the other and rotating in opposite directions, to permit faster speeds and eliminate the need for a tail rotor. (Only in the last decade or so has Sikorsky seriously promoted this idea via several flying prototypes.) When I got assigned to do some analysis of anti-submarine warfare (ASW) helicopters, I got a familiarization ride in the standard navy ASW helicopter, flying out over nearby Long Island Sound, hovering, and dipping the sonar into the water.

Sikorsky offered to pay for additional graduate work at New York University's campus in the Bronx, about an hour's drive from Stratford. So several of us signed up for the engineering department's basic course on helicopter engineering, and I went on from there to study operations research, intending to get a second master's degree.

As a budding libertarian/Objectivist, I was desperate for intellectual stimulation. The organization that was promoting Ayn Rand's philosophy, the Nathaniel Branden Institute (NBI), offered a whole series of taped lecture courses in Objectivism around the country, usually in the homes of authorized NBI representatives. During my summer 1966 job at Ford in Dearborn, I had taken one such course. In Connecticut, the nearest NBI rep was in West Hartford, about an hour away. I signed up and took one weekly evening course there. As with the one in Michigan, I did not find the attendees to be very friendly, so although I learned the material, my objective of finding friends to discuss the ideas with (as I'd done at MIT) came to naught. I did manage to engage a few of my young Sikorsky colleagues in such discussions, including one recent graduate from England who'd grown up in a Labor household but proved to be intrigued by free-market economics.

Finding *Reason* Magazine

Somehow I stumbled on a small California-based libertarian newsletter called *Liberal Innovator*, and immediately subscribed. It introduced me to new ideas and to thinkers I'd never heard of. A small classified ad in one issue for what sounded like an Objectivist publication called *Reason* caught my eye, so I subscribed to that as well. It had been launched in the spring of 1968 by a Boston University student named Lanny Friedlander. It was produced on a typewriter and duplicated by mimeograph, a defunct low-volume copying technique, which suggested *Reason*'s quite small (a few hundred) circulation. But the content was surprisingly good, written almost entirely by Friedlander himself. My quest for intellectual stimulation also involved joining the Conservative Book Club—not because I was a conservative, but because its offerings included books written from free-market and limited-government perspectives.

But my primary discussions of issues and ideas, including Objectivism and libertarianism, were with Lynn Kinsky. We spent a growing number of weekends together, either me driving up to Hanover, New Hampshire, or her driving down to West Haven. We were each other's best friend, and by autumn 1967 Lynn had decided she wanted us to get married. That was not what I'd expected or desired at that time, having never had a serious relationship before this and feeling not really ready for such a big step. But she was persistent, and by the end of the year she'd talked me into it.

We told our families and planned a June 1968 wedding. We insisted on a civil ceremony, we wrote our own vows, and the families accepted that. We planned for an outdoor wedding, beside the lighthouse on Key Biscayne, but it started to rain just as everyone arrived there, so we all drove back to Lynn's parents' home in South Miami and did the honors there. My best man was MIT Course II friend and fellow Objectivist Lyall Morrill. Lynn's matron of honor was our high school friend and Clique member Anna Tiberi Appleby (whose husband, Jon, was on duty in Vietnam). After the wedding, we honeymooned on one of the Out Islands in the Bahamas.

Back in Connecticut, we found an apartment in New Canaan, west of my job in Stratford and east of Lynn's new job at the Geigy pharmaceutical company in Westchester County, New York. As a now married couple, we became part of a small group of similar young couples at Sikorsky, so we had something of a local social life. Around this time, Adam Powell got married, and we were invited. It was a big-deal Washington, DC, wedding with Adam's father, "Big Powell," and his mother, singer Hazel Scott. Adam and Beryl settled down in New York City, so they became part of our social circle.

Lyall was in grad school at Columbia in New York City. He told us that NBI was beginning regular social events in New York, in addition to the live lectures we had started attending. Lynn and I enjoyed the new social evenings where we could drink wine, converse with a whole array of like-minded people, and dance. Compared with the rather rigid atmosphere of the taped NBI lectures I'd attended, these events were a breath of fresh air. We really felt like part of a large and growing community of individualist thinkers.

But later that fall (1968) this happy world was shattered. Lyall called us to say that "Mr. Branden" had done something terribly wrong and that NBI would be closing. He expected us to automatically side with Ayn Rand and accept, with no evidence, Branden's evil, which neither Lynn nor I could do. So Lyall decided he could no longer be our friend. A month or two later, Ayn Rand's magazine, *The Objectivist*, carried her non-specific denunciation of Branden, again without specifying what he had done. Lynn's perceptive response was that "this sounds like it was written by a woman scorned"—which was right on the money, though it was many years before the truth came out.

The near-term damage to the rapidly growing Objectivist movement was profound. It split into opposing camps, those accepting Rand's assertions without evidence and those like us who withheld judgement in the absence of facts. With no NBI, the growth of the Objectivist movement stalled, leaving the field open for other libertarian organizations and publications to fill the intellectual and social void.

In June 1969, Lynn and I took a two-week vacation to explore California as a future place to live. We took a northerly route going west, so we could see places like the Grand Tetons and the famous Wall Drug Store in South Dakota. We stayed several days with my former MIT roommate Jim Weigl, now in grad school at Stanford and living in Palo Alto. In addition to showing us around the peninsula (it was not yet called Silicon Valley), he drove with us to Yosemite National Park, and we had a great time there. Next Lynn and I drove down US 101 to Los Angeles, visiting Anna and Jon (who'd returned from Vietnam) in the Playa Vista part of Los Angeles. We did a lot of driving around to get a feel for LA, noticing with dismay how bad the smog was, especially inland in otherwise lovely places like Pasadena, home of CalTech. Anna fixed tacos for us for dinner—the first time either of us had had Mexican food.

On our drive back to the east we talked about how much nicer California seemed than Connecticut, and how great it would be to move there, especially with friends like those we'd just visited living there. We didn't make a specific plan, but figured that once I no longer needed a draft deferment, the way would be cleared for such a move.

"Fly the Frenzied Skies"

Earlier in 1969, I had gotten in touch with *Reason*'s Lanny Friedlander, by letter and occasional phone call (since there was no email in those days). When he learned that I was an aerospace engineer and Lynn was a pharmaceutical chemist, he urged us to try writing articles for *Reason*. We each gave this some thought; Lynn proposed a piece on how FDA regulation was stifling new drug development, and I decided to research and write an article calling for an end to economic regulation of airlines.

At Sikorsky one of the fringe benefits was reading *Aviation Week*, which I hadn't seen since high school when Dad brought home copies from Eastern. As a child growing up, I had been made painfully aware of the fact that airlines could not fly wherever they thought there was demand—but only where the Civil Aeronautics Board (CAB) allowed them to fly. Most routes had only two airlines, and new routes typically had a monopoly carrier. In the mid-1950s, there was no airline service from Miami to Los Angeles, but with the newest airliners able to fly that route non-stop, the CAB decided to pick an airline to begin that service. Eastern applied, and so did its smaller competitor, National. After a long CAB proceeding, National was awarded the route. And that meant that my cousin Tom (and his brother Davey) could visit newly opened Disneyland, since Uncle Tony worked for National. My sisters and I, in an Eastern family, could not.

That episode still rankled, so I took advantage of the Sikorsky library to research the history of airlines and the government's economic regulation of them. The premise was that airlines were like utilities, with large "economies of scale" such that it was more efficient to have a single provider rather than multiple providers, at least in new markets. And even where demand could support more than one airline, the thinking was that government regulation was necessary to prevent destructive price competition and ensure good service. The practical result was cozy monopolies or duopolies, with airlines competing not on price (forbidden) but on drinks, meals, seats, etc.—all of which made flying a luxury good, not the affordable, accessible service it is today (albeit with fewer amenities). I also learned, partly from *Aviation Week*, that CAB regulation only applied to routes between states; routes entirely within a large state (such as Texas and California) were exempt. So there was a natural experiment going on—real price competition in California and Texas, resulting in lots of service and low fares, versus limited, high-priced service wherever the CAB called the shots.

I put all this together into an article and sent it to Lanny in August 1969, and Lynn sent hers at the same time. Lanny decided that Lynn's needed more work, but accepted mine. He told me nothing about his publication plans, but on October 10 the mail brought a huge surprise. The September 1969 issue of *Reason* was no longer an amateurish mimeographed publication, but a typeset and offset-printed real magazine. And my article was the cover story, which Lanny had titled "Fly the Frenzied Skies" (a take-off on United Airlines' advertising line, "Fly the Friendly Skies"). I was blown away.

That November Lynn and I drove to Boston to meet Lanny and discuss the future of *Reason*. He lived with his mother in a rather unkempt house in the Brighton neighborhood of Boston. In my journal after the visit, I wrote: "What a character—not the stereotyped Objectivist but certainly an individual—longish unruly hair, sloppy old clothes, sloppy room, rambling mind— but very intelligent." We had brought along a Nathaniel Branden tape, and after dinner about fifteen local Objectivists/libertarians came over to listen to it and talk. Among them was Jim Meginnis and others from the MIT Radicals for Capitalism. We spent more time with Lanny the next day, partly focused on needed revisions to Lynn's FDA article and partly on the future of *Reason*.

It became clear to me then that Lanny had no head for business, despite being a good writer and editor, with an excellent design sense. He'd spent time hanging around at MIT Press, from which he got many of his graphic design ideas, including the use of Helvetica type and of ragged-right margins. In deciding to visit Lanny, I'd had the vague idea of getting involved to help build *Reason* into a business, but I came away very doubtful that a viable business could be created.

The following month we had several more phone conversations with Lanny. He was making contacts with other writers, thinkers, and editors who had generally free-market or Objectivist leanings. He said the editor of *Chemical Engineering* was something of an Objectivist, and that he'd been impressed by my *Reason* aviation article. He'd also made contact with two drug company officials whom he said would be happy to assist Lynn with her FDA article. He was enthusiastic about a young philosopher in California named Tibor Machan, and also about an "underground" libertarian 'zine called the *Libertarian Connection*, one of whose contributors was a creative thinker called Skye D'Aureous.

I agreed to do another article for *Reason*, this time on international efforts to regulate seabed mining. And I told Lanny I'd sent copies of the issue with my aviation cover story to F. Lee Bailey (then counsel to the air traffic controllers union PATCO) and to the chairman of the CAB, Secor Browne, hoping to get some reaction. But I didn't hear from either of them.

Around this same time, I had also embarked on a policy-related project. In addition to being a member of the American Society of Mechanical Engineers, I was also in the Society of Automotive Engineers (SAE), whose scope had broadened over the years to include aircraft. When SAE announced that in response to increasing moves by the federal government to impose new safety regulations on the auto industry, the members of SAE should be seen as "a valuable resource at the disposal of the government," I was outraged. I sent the organization a letter of resignation, arguing that this stance would hasten a de-facto takeover of automotive design by the government. To my surprise, I received a letter from SAE's president inviting me to reconsider and become a member of their relatively new Public Interest Advisory Committee (PIAC). After some back and forth, I accepted, and Sikorsky even agreed to cover my travel expenses to attend PIAC meetings.

My basic idea was that rather than helping formulate new federal safety regulations, SAE should develop its own set of safety standards and promulgate them for voluntary adoption by auto manufacturers. Adopting the model of Underwriters Laboratories, it could publicize an SAE seal of approval, which those companies in full compliance could display in their advertising. This would allow niche companies (for which the cost of certain regulations would be prohibitive) to opt out. And companies agreeing to comply and be certified by SAE would not violate antitrust laws, since they would not be colluding with one another but would merely be accepting a set of well-respected engineering standards, as with electrical appliance makers and the UL symbol.

I wrote a seven-page concept paper outlining this approach, and engaged in extensive correspondence with other PIAC members prior to the one meeting I attended, in Detroit in January 1970. Alas, the effort fell flat. Basically, the auto companies had already decided that their best bet was to work with the feds to try to make sure the resulting regulations were not too costly or unworkable, rather than trying to stave off what I predicted would be increasing government control of vehicle design (as did occur). So I gave up, and resigned from the PIAC (and SAE) later in 1970. In hindsight, reviewing my memos and letters forty-five years later, I can see that even though my message was a pragmatic one, my rhetoric was highly ideological, and likely turned off the business leaders who made up most of the PIAC's membership.

Time for a Career Change

By autumn 1969, I'd grown quite dissatisfied with Sikorsky—and thereby with large aerospace companies as a category. First, it was big and bureaucratic, and treated engineers like cogs in a machine. As a government contractor, it pushed hard for 100 percent participation in payroll deductions to buy US Savings Bonds and make United Way contributions—neither of which appealed to me as an individualist making my own decisions about investments and charitable giving, so I pointedly refused to comply. I was also increasingly dismayed by the huge cost in tax money and lives of the seemingly endless Vietnam war, and felt uncomfortable being, in effect, part of the war effort. On one day of protest (National Moratorium Day) I stayed home from work. I also worried that in such a huge organization, unless I wanted to be on the management track, I could end up knowing more and more about less and less (e.g., the design of landing gear struts). None of this seemed like a challenging and satisfying career path.

Thanks again to the Sikorsky library, I discovered the RAND Corporation—a think tank in Santa Monica, California, that mostly did research for the air force, but had recently launched a civil division to do public policy research. I'd seen a summary of that division's assessment of the negative consequences of rent control in New York City. That kind of work sounded far more interesting than remaining in a huge aerospace bureaucracy for most of my career.

So I did some research on think tanks and discovered about half a dozen of them located in California, all with some connection to defense research. Besides RAND, they included GE Tempo, General Research Corp. (GRC), and Stanford Research Institute. I sent query letters to all of them, figuring that even though my goal was civil public policy work, their overall links to defense work might still make possible a draft deferment. I got a positive response from GRC, which (like GE Tempo) was located in Santa Barbara but also had a branch office in New Jersey. I was invited to that branch office for an initial interview and evidently passed muster. The next step was an invitation to meet two of the leaders of GRC's new civil division, Public Safety Systems, Inc., (PSSI) when they came east.

In November 1969, PSSI Vice President Bill Hanna invited me to dinner at a French restaurant in New York. He and his colleagues explained why PSSI had been started (within the past year). The initial mission was to apply the relatively new mini-computer technology to do real-time dispatching of police, fire, and other public safety services. Besides the availability of this new computer technology, far less costly than traditional mainframes, the other new factor was the coming implementation of 9-1-1 as the universal emergency phone number. That meant cities and counties would need to create consolidated dispatch centers, with trained dispatchers able to size up the emergency, get its precise location, and dispatch the relevant first responders (police, fire, or ambulance) from the relevant agency or agencies. PSSI's mission was to help implement these new capabilities.

That sounded far more interesting to me than being enmeshed in an aerospace bureaucracy, and what they told me about Santa Barbara sounded especially attractive. (On our California trip, Lynn and I had simply driven through Santa Barbara on US 101 without stopping.) I evidently gave a good interview, because by the end of the dinner they had basically decided to hire me, but promised a trip to Santa Barbara so I could meet other staff members and get a feel for the place before making it official. So in late November I flew to Los Angeles, staying overnight with Jim Weigl (who'd left Stanford and taken a job in or near

Santa Monica) and then driving up to Santa Barbara for the day. I was very impressed by beautiful, small-town Santa Barbara and grateful for GRC's offer to pay full moving expenses, including moving one of our two cars. We agreed I would start work in early February 1970.

In December, the Nixon administration held its first draft lottery, randomly drawing numbers from 1 to 365, and announcing that those drawn in the first batch (indicating which day of the year they'd been born) would be the first drafted. My number was near the tail end, so my need for a deferment from GRC basically vanished.

Lynn was happy that we had found a way to relocate to California, but worried about finding a job in chemistry in Santa Barbara. We tentatively decided to look for a place to live midway between Los Angeles and Santa Barbara, commuting in opposite directions, as we'd been doing in Connecticut. But during my Santa Barbara visit, GRC promised to find a suitable job for her there, so that we could live in Santa Barbara instead. We should have been more skeptical, but accepted this assurance in good faith. We were eager to be on the same coast with Jim and with our friends Anna and Jon, and also to be done with winter, which was particularly harsh in December 1969/January 1970.

After a farewell lunch for me at Sikorsky, the movers came and loaded up our furniture and boxes of stuff, plus Lynn's car, and we spent the night in a nearby Holiday Inn. And on January 31 we began our long drive across the country, heading south to avoid the worst winter weather and hitting I-10 near New Orleans for the rest of the trek. Our new California lives were about to begin.

Chapter 3

Reason Enterprises (1970–1977)

A New Job and New Friends

Santa Barbara was like another world—a beautiful, laid-back Spanish/Mediterranean city of about seventy thousand people on the California coast. PSSI put us up in a hotel on the waterfront while we looked for a place to rent. Getting up our first morning there, we were dumbfounded to see the sun rising out of the ocean. It took looking at a map to realize that Santa Barbara is on a part of the California coast that runs east–west, so we were actually looking south, and in January the sun is very far to the south. We found a two-story townhouse to rent, less than a mile from General Research Corp. and its PSSI subsidiary, close enough that I occasionally bicycled to work.

My first day on the job that February was a revelation: everyone had a private office! What a great change from the enormous sea of engineers at Sikorsky! My initial assignment, for orientation, was to rewrite the technical development plan for PSSI's first major contract: the computer-based dispatching system for the huge Los Angeles Fire Department. I would remain at PSSI as a full-time staffer through the end of 1974, working on projects in public safety and criminal justice in a considerable number of cities and counties in California, Arizona, Nevada, and Oregon. That experience led me to discover privatized delivery of municipal services, which I will recount in Chapter 5.

We reconnected with our libertarian friends in Los Angeles right away, visiting Jim Weigl and calling Jon and Anna. In the latter case, we were surprised to learn that they had just split up, with Anna moving back east with their young daughter. Given the way in which libertarians tended to find one another, later that year Jon and Jim became roommates.

The year 1970 turned out to be a big one for libertarian

conferences in Los Angeles, with the University of Southern California (USC) as the center of a large student libertarian movement. The first weekend in March was the "Left–Right Festival of Mind Liberation" at USC, with an array of speakers including Prof. John Hospers, head of the USC philosophy department, who was at that point finishing up his book *Libertarianism: A Political Philosophy for Tomorrow*. Also on the program was libertarian troubadour Dana Rohrabacher, singing an array of anti-state folk songs. Other speakers included anarchist Karl Hess, ex-communist Philip Abbott Luce, and Skye D'Aureous. Skye (real name Durk Pearson) was a regular contributor to the photocopied underground 'zine *The Libertarian Connection*. A number of its contributors used nom de plumes to avoid possible harassment by the government; in Durk's case, I found out later, it was because he worked at TRW, an aerospace company, and was worried about having his security clearance revoked.

The conference was exhilarating, as was the experience of being together with several hundred libertarians and Objectivists for a whole weekend. I wrote in my journal the next day, "Somewhere along the line I've got to figure out how to make what I like (researching and writing libertarian articles) and want to do (promoting cultural change in a major, effective way) profitable, so that I can make a living at it."

Thanks to an introduction from Lanny Friedlander, Lynn and I met Tibor Machan and his wife, Marilyn Walther. We went to their house on a Santa Barbara hillside and spent a stimulating evening discussing ideas with a half dozen Objectivists. A week later we invited Tibor and Marilyn over for dinner and discussed our experiences of becoming libertarians and the ups and downs of the Objectivist movement.

Lanny had announced a special issue of *Reason* devoted to the newly trendy subject of ecology, with the first Earth Day coming up that April. So Tibor and I spent several evenings brainstorming that topic, and Tibor's friend Mike Etchison in Los Angeles arranged a colloquium on the subject, which we attended. There we met two people who would have important roles to play in *Reason*'s future: a young attorney named Manny Klausner and a

USC student named Leon Kaspersky. Leon published a libertarian student newspaper called *Protos*.

Late in April, I got five author copies of the latest issue of *The Freeman*, published by the Foundation for Economic Education (FEE). They had reprinted my "Fly the Frenzied Skies" article from *Reason*, and I was already getting letters about it from serious people. What a difference it makes to be published in a periodical with forty thousand subscribers, compared with *Reason*'s four hundred! And that soon became a topic that Tibor and I became excited about: making *Reason* into a "real magazine" that could compete in the marketplace of ideas.

Lynn and I agreed to help Leon distribute *Protos* on the UC Santa Barbara campus, so he drove up with about a thousand copies. We stayed up until 2:30 a.m., talking about publishing: typesetting, printing, selling ads, renting mailing lists in order to market subscriptions, etc. I wrote Lanny a long letter about these ideas. And about that time—the end of April—the December(!) issue of *Reason* finally arrived in the mail. It was clear that Lanny could not get it out on any kind of regular schedule, partly due to lack of organization and partly due to lack of money. That *Reason* had kept coming out at all was due in part to Boston-area high school student Mark Frazier, whom Lanny had spotted due to Mark's student publication, *Thought*. Mark volunteered on weekends doing typesetting and paste-up (and Lanny listed him as publisher) starting in late 1969 and for most of 1970, until he enrolled in Harvard that September. After that, he became a contributing editor, focusing on interviews and articles.

Rescuing *Reason* Magazine

Tibor and I had long discussions about *Reason*'s problems, and in mid-May we called Lanny and talked for about an hour. We asked him to write up general goals for an expanded *Reason*, with the idea of developing a business proposal to pitch to a local Objectivist-oriented businessman, Phil Goldman, whom Tibor knew.

Jim Weigl drove up to have dinner with us late in May, and we filled him in on the *Reason* brainstorming. We took him over to Tibor and Marilyn's and spent the evening discussing Jim's interest in becoming the magazine's business manager. We reviewed Lanny's written objectives and decided they were too narrowly focused. The magazine should be geared to "young professionals," we decided, not just to self-identified libertarians. In my journal I noted that "young professionals have large incomes and are good ad prospects, and they are probably more influential." We thought there was an untapped market for a think magazine that was pro-individual liberty and pro-market, neither liberal nor conservative.

Tibor and I took our pitch to Phil Goldman, but there was no meeting of the minds. Phil wanted serious control, and he also had a peculiar view (which he'd somehow derived from Ayn Rand's argument that a woman should not be president of the country) that women should not be part of the management of a company. Given that both Lynn and Marilyn by that point intended to be part of this effort, there was no way to make this work with Phil (though he stayed friendly with us and eventually became a Reason Foundation supporter).

So we decided to draft a serious business plan and use whatever network of contacts we each had to raise money to launch our *Reason* makeover. Tibor wrote most of the idea content while I focused on the business model, drawing on what I'd learned from Leon about direct-mail marketing. The initial forty-four-page proposal was finished by the end of July. It began by explaining the rationale for such a magazine, described the kind of content we intended, analyzed the near-term competition (the plethora of small libertarian and Objectivist periodicals then extant or recently defunct), and defined what we considered the market to be. In introducing the marketing plan, I wrote, "Our basic premise is that among young college-educated professional people there exists a large number of people who do not accept the collectivist premises of the mass media but who say very little about their own views because they have little or no intellectually respectable support for them."

Our marketing plan was based largely on direct-mail subscription promotion. The plan called for a Phase 1 target of six thousand subscribers, recruited mostly from lists of self-identified libertarians. A second phase would begin marketing beyond that core group. The Phase 1 plan laid out a twenty-four-month budget, with no paid staff but forty hours/month of contract editorial work (at $5/hour) and forty hours/month of contracted office work (at $2.50/hour). On that bare-bones budget, the losses in the first eighteen months would be recouped in the last six months—which was wildly over-optimistic. Manny read the proposal and liked it, and we recruited him as one of the principals and as our legal advisor.

Tibor had the largest number of contacts whom we thought might be willing to "invest" in our project. Among them was George Pearson, who handled giving for Charles Koch in Wichita. The rest were mostly friends Tibor had made in recent years. George sent us a letter asking a number of questions, which I answered, but they did not provide any funding. After follow-up calls to our other prospects, we ended up with a $400 gift and $1,250 in loans. That was way below expectations, so each of the partners chipped in $300 and that was our total starting capital.

Although we'd initially contemplated incorporating, we ended up deciding to form a general partnership, with Lanny to stay on, under contract, as editor for the first six months (a trial period) for nominal pay. To work out the details of the transition, we decided Lanny had to be in California for discussions and negotiation. Fortunately, Tibor (who was just getting his PhD in philosophy from UC Santa Barbara) had a grant to organize a Conference on Political Philosophy at USC in September. He included Lanny as a participant, so the grant provided travel money to fly him out, and Lynn and I agreed to house him for a week. The conference was quite an experience—half the participants were liberals (including Sidney Hook) and half were libertarians, including John Hospers. Among those I met there was Jack Wheeler, an Objectivist PhD philosophy student at USC, later to become famous as an author and adventure travel guide.

Lanny was a difficult house guest, and the negotiations were somewhat trying, but in the end we reached agreement. Our new Reason Enterprises would buy *Reason* from Lanny—meaning we relieved him of the subscription liability and acquired the assets: an addressing machine, some not-yet-published articles, and the mailing list. And we agreed on the six-month editorial contract for him, starting in January.

With Lanny doing the graphics and me writing most of the copy, we created a direct-mail subscription offer package, and we partners spent two weekends in October in Los Angeles, as Leon and his wife, Kathy, taught us typesetting and paste-up, and provided contacts with local printers, so that we could produce five thousand direct-mail packages. Our aim was to begin with a five-thousand-name subset of Nathaniel Branden's sixty-five-thousand-name Academic Associates (AA) mailing list, compiled during his years running NBI. Tibor knew Branden and managed to persuade him to let us rent that sample (though we had to sign a statement affirming that we were not anarchists).

On December 1, we "dropped" that promotion in the mail— and along with it our hopes for this start-up business. Had the mailing bombed, we would have been out of money and out of luck. Results trickled in at first, but by the end of the month had reached 150—a healthy 3 percent response. Reason Enterprises was in business! The next task was to produce our first issue. We met in a typesetting shop in Long Beach a week before Christmas and worked all night pasting up the January 1971 issue. It included a message from the new owners—and a promise that the magazine would henceforth appear reliably every month from then on. That meant from that time onward, we partners would be tied to a monthly publication schedule—in addition to our full-time jobs, of course.

Speaking of full-time jobs, PSSI's parent company, GRC, eventually came through with a job for Lynn—with a new division doing survey research. But its start-up got delayed for many months, awaiting an expected first contract, so she endured frustrating months without paid employment. But she pitched in as circulation manager for the now-growing *Reason* magazine. During 1971, Mark Frazier did yeoman work in Cambridge and Boston, conducting interviews with school reformer John Holt, novelist Robert Rimmer, and MIT urban-policy modeler Jay Forrester.

We desperately wanted to do more mailings to Branden's AA list; we'd heard that the Society for Individual Liberty (SIL)—which published *The Individualist*—was also planning to rent the list, and we wanted to get there first. We did two more small mailings with the money we had, and by the end of summer the circulation had passed one thousand. But the breakthrough came when Nathaniel Branden agreed to be interviewed by *Reason*. It took place at his house in Beverly Hills on August 8, 1971, and went pretty well. As amateur journalists, we did not object when Branden insisted on reviewing—and extensively revising—the transcript prior to publication.

We mailed to all fifty-two thousand remaining names on Branden's list and got over 3 percent again, giving another significant boost to the circulation. The Branden interview was big news to the libertarian/Objectivist community, since he had not talked openly about his break with Ayn Rand since a brief statement at the time, three years earlier.

Growing Pains and Strains

As 1972 dawned, we realized that we needed to move beyond Branden's list, and of the ones we learned were available, the most promising appeared to be that of Rampart College, compiled over the years by Robert LeFevre, whose Freedom School in Colorado had educated many libertarian notables during the 1960s before folding (with LeFevre relocating to Orange County, California). Our original idea was to test five thousand of the forty-eight thousand names, as we'd done with Branden's list. But for some reason we ended up throwing caution to the wind and mailing to the entire list, without testing it. What a disaster! We ended up with a net paid response of only 0.5 percent, so we lost a bundle on that mailing. Fortunately, we recovered later in the year by running an interview with popular investment author Harry Browne and mailing to several "hard-money" lists. With the growing workload and having higher cash flow than in 1971, we decided to hire libertarian friend Clarica Scott as part-time office manager, working from her home in Hollywood.

Meanwhile, my former MIT classmate from Students for

Goldwater, Dave Nolan, had founded the Libertarian Party (LP) in Denver in 1971. This took place around the time that Republican president Richard Nixon imposed wage and price controls and abolished the gold standard, among other big-government ploys. Those actions caused a number of libertarian-oriented Republicans to embrace the fledgling party as a needed alternative. My own response was skeptical, seeing a third party as unlikely to have much impact in our structurally two-party system, so I did not attend the founding convention, despite my ongoing friendship with Dave.

Manny Klausner was much more enthusiastic and persuaded the rest of us that *Reason* should do a special issue on the emergence of the LP. That issue, September 1972, won us a lot of friends and subscribers among our core audience at the time. We followed that up for several years with a regular column in the magazine, reporting on the LP's doings. John Hospers, whose book had come out in hardback in 1971, became the LP's 1972 presidential candidate, and he and VP candidate Tonie Nathan received one vote in the Electoral College, thanks to elector Roger MacBride (who later became the LP's 1976 standard-bearer). With Hospers being a big name among libertarians, we worked out a deal with his publisher for us to produce a paperback edition of his *Libertarianism* book. It came out as a production of "Reason Press, a division of Reason Enterprises." We sold thousands of them, and also used them as a premium in subscription promotion mailings.

In October 1972, we parted ways with Jim Weigl. We'd had ongoing problems with things he'd agreed to do by certain dates not getting done on time. His real job seemed to take more of his time than he'd expected, and we were all frustrated by the ongoing problems. It was hard parting with my old friend, but the friendship had worn pretty thin by that point as we struggled to keep our heads above water *and* keep the magazine coming out every month on schedule. Jim was the first to leave the partnership, and Marilyn was the second. She and Tibor had separated in January 1971, several months after they moved to Bakersfield where Tibor had his first post-PhD teaching position. She moved back to Santa Barbara and stayed in our guest room for several months. She continued as partner until the end of 1972, when she and her boyfriend relocated to rural Oregon. She continued doing copyediting long-distance until mid-1973.

In December 1972, Tibor and I exchanged letters over the direction of *Reason's* content. He'd expressed concern about some articles on libertarian political theory being turned down, and I responded by pointing out that we seemed to be running out of libertarian-type lists to market to and needed to expand the scope of our direct-mail marketing. A circulation of around three to four thousand was far too small, and we continued to lose money. "We have to find lists of people who seem likely to be predisposed to our views" who are not self-identified as libertarians, I wrote. "But then we have the problem of holding their interest" as we introduce them to more of the libertarian worldview. "This is how our marketing policy comes to influence our editorial policy," including article selection.

Early in 1973, SIL's magazine, *The Individualist*, folded and we worked out a deal with SIL for *Reason* to fulfill its unexpired subscriptions. That brought our circulation up to 4,500, at no real cost, which was a lucky break for us. In mid-1973, I discovered, only a few miles from our house in Santa Barbara, a relatively new company called Media Selection Corp. (MSC). Among its services was subscription fulfillment. Using computers, they would manage our mailing list, generating address labels and sending out the issues each month, as well as generating invoices and renewal notices. This also meant that we could selectively rent *Reason's* mailing list to customers we approved of, generating some additional income. Moreover, MSC's president Jim Lance was experienced in direct-mail work, and became our principal consultant on subscription promotional mailings. That summer, paid circulation reached six thousand.

In 1972, my cousin/honorary brother Tom Yorke married Lynn's younger sister Barbara (Babs) in Miami, and they soon thereafter moved to Santa Barbara, where Tom got a job at a local advertising agency. (His degree from the University of Florida was in advertising design.) Babs found a job, but did not find it very interesting. In mid-1973, MSC offered us the use of a spare office in its facility in Goleta (the suburb where Lynn and I lived), and we decided to hire Babs full-time as office manager and ad sales director, using that office. At about the same time, we hired Tom part-time to do inside artwork. Graphic artist James Garrison continued to do *Reason*'s covers, but that was all he had time for; now we had nicely designed opening pages of feature articles, too.

We had stayed in touch with George Pearson since 1970, and he had followed our progress with interest. That spring he let us know that he had found several people potentially interested in assisting *Reason*. In response to his request for more detailed information, I prepared a new business plan/proposal outlining how we would spend additional funds on *Reason*'s growth. As far as I can tell from documents in my files, the only definite result was a $2,500 loan from Charles Koch, which was renewed several times when we had difficulty paying more than the interest.

In the midst of the stresses and strains of keeping *Reason* afloat, an unexpected pleasure was learning that my hero Robert Heinlein was a subscriber. We started getting Christmas cards from him, which led me to correspond with Ginny Heinlein to ask about interviewing him. Though he really liked the magazine, Ginny said they had sworn off any more interviews after several bad experiences. But she also wrote that if we were ever in the Santa Cruz area, to let them know so we could come by for a visit. Lynn and I had already planned a "get to know California" vacation trip with Tom and Babs, so that summer we planned a route that included a day in Santa Cruz. We were invited to come for the afternoon, and got a tour of the house they'd designed themselves, with lots of built-ins and a pool heated by what Robert told us was one of the first solar heaters in California. Evidently, we passed their initial screening and were invited to stay for dinner.

I remember they put Chopin waltzes on the stereo at dinner, and we had a wide-ranging conversation, including his account of being a guest of NASA at Cape Canaveral for the Apollo 11 launch. And he told me that while he clipped articles from a number of magazines, *Reason* was one of the few that he saved, intact. Before we left, I asked if he might autograph a few books (from the box I'd brought along in the car, including some first editions), and he graciously agreed. When he found out that I could read German, he also gave me several German paperback editions of some of his novels.

Late in 1973, we published a special Ayn Rand issue, with all the feature articles being commentaries by various thinkers on the significance of her ideas and works. Manny had written to her in advance to tell her about the plan, inviting her to write an article or to suggest contributors to the issue, but we received no response. Several months after the issue appeared, however, her attorney, Eugene Winick, sent Manny a letter demanding that we publish some kind of retraction and cease selling any remaining back copies of that issue. Needless to say, they had no case, and after several exchanges with Manny, Winick gave up, but not before Manny had expressed willingness to engage in litigation, which he expected would be called "Rand vs. Reason."

In 1974, we continued testing mailing lists of taxpayer groups, conservatives, and hard-money investors, finding enough promising lists to continue building the circulation. Ed Crane and Bob Meier, both active in the Libertarian Party, had come to us in mid-1973 with the idea of putting together a special financial issue aimed at people interested in the state of the economy and protecting themselves from dire futures such as runaway inflation or a new depression. The idea was appealing, as a way both to broaden the base of subscribers and to attract new advertisers. Crane and Meier helped contact authors and provided leads to advertisers, and we did subscription mailings touting the forthcoming issue. At 140 pages, the resulting May Special Financial Issue was about three times the size of a regular issue, and set a new record for advertising pages. By the end of the year circulation had reached a new high of twelve thousand.

For Lynn and me personally, 1974 was a year of trouble. Our relationship had grown increasingly rocky, due partly to the stresses of keeping *Reason* going and Lynn's desire to become one of the editors (which the partners had agreed to 1973). In addition, GRC had shut down its survey research operation after only about eighteen months, leaving Lynn without a job. She started taking coursework in sociology at UCSB, and got a job as a night dispatcher with the local alarm company—hardly a fulfilling job. Conflicts over decisions at *Reason* easily morphed into personal conflicts between the two of us.

We decided to split in autumn 1974, and just about that time GRC decided to downsize PSSI dramatically, laying off most of the staff but holding out the possibility of consulting work to some of us. In very uncertain financial straits, I rented a small apartment and figured out the minimum amount of monthly consulting work I needed to do to keep the rent paid and food on the table. Fortunately, such consulting contracts materialized, some with GRC, several with former PSSI officers who'd gone to work for similar companies, and some others that are the subject of Chapter 4.

In 1974, Tom got a job with Disney in Burbank, so Tom and Babs relocated to Los Angeles. We hired my friend David Sutton's wife, Ruth, as the new office manager for the MSC office. Late that year Tom and Babs made a proposal to us to take over monthly paste-up of the issue, which we accepted. And in January 1975, Manny worked out an agreement with Lynn to withdraw from the partnership but to continue performing specified editorial duties at $200/month starting in February. Neither of those relationships worked smoothly. Both Lynn and Manny had ongoing problems meeting deadlines, which led to Tom and Babs quitting the paste-up work in frustration by mid-year, and me making some changes in who was responsible for doing what. We ended up contracting with unflappable Lou Rollins in LA to do paste-up, which he did for the next four years.

But conflicts with Lynn over the substance and tone of editorials and columns, as well as over late delivery of copy, continued until finally, in September 1975, Manny, Tibor, and I decided the time had come to end her contract. It was very traumatic and unpleasant, but Manny and I in particular (Tibor was teaching at SUNY-Fredonia, New York) felt like a huge burden had been lifted from our shoulders.

Overall, 1975 and 1976 were years of modest growth, with circulation fluctuating between twelve thousand and fifteen thousand throughout. We continued the annual financial issue for several more years, while it still seemed helpful in generating both advertisers and new subscribers. Over the previous several years we had done interviews with quite a few notables, including F. A. Hayek, Milton Friedman, science fiction author Poul Anderson, and former governor Ronald Reagan. One of the most-quoted lines in the 1975 Reagan interview was his comment that "Libertarianism is the heart and soul of conservatism." But based on some of the other things he'd said during the interview, I wrote in my journal, "It was interesting but somewhat disappointing—he's certainly no libertarian."

The 1970s was a period of real growth in the self-identified libertarian movement, sparked in part by the Libertarian Party getting organized in every state. An important phenomenon in California was the growth of monthly libertarian supper clubs, usually organized by LP activists. By 1975, there were active supper clubs in San Diego, Orange County, Los Angeles, Santa Barbara, and San Francisco. Supper clubs were eager for speakers, so they became my initial training ground for public speaking, with basically friendly and modest-size audiences. It was a great way to increase *Reason*'s visibility, as well as meeting new people who shared our libertarian values. And as state LP organizations grew, I started getting and accepting invitations to speak at their various annual conventions.

Upgrading the Magazine

In mid-1976, Mark Frazier moved to Santa Barbara. He'd graduated from Harvard in June 1974 and had done freelance journalism work in Washington—for *Human Events*, *Reader's Digest,* and columnist Jack Anderson. In autumn 1975, Mark moved to New Zealand for a year, working for several newspapers including the *Auckland Herald.* Arriving in Santa Barbara, Mark was brimming with ideas for improving *Reason.* I welcomed him back and made him managing editor, paid mostly in terms of free advertising space. He rented an apartment in the building where the *Reason* office and I were then located, so we were in daily contact. We brainstormed content, artwork, fundraising, publicity, etc.

One of Mark's biggest ideas was that *Reason* needed a real art director and a graphic redesign. He found a local graphic artist, Don Wood, and we worked out a contractual arrangement with him that led to a dramatic new look for the magazine in 1977. We also obtained several new columnists, including Edith Efron and National Taxpayers Union president Jim Davidson, and added contributing editors Eric Mack, Henry Manne, Karl Pflock, and Thomas Szasz. Our 1977 direct-mail marketing shifted from hard-money people to lists of people interested in economic and political issues. Mark also recommended that we "shift the feature articles from an explicit to an implicit libertarian content," in order to attract and keep a larger audience. The results of all these changes were impressive. Circulation increased to eighteen thousand, new advertisers came on board, and subscription renewal rates increased by one-third.

Tibor had remarried in the early 1970s, and in 1973 his wife, Marty Zupan, became copyeditor at $3 per hour. She was excellent at this, and the price was a bargain. At the end of 1976 she asked for a raise for the coming year, and we agreed, wishing it could be higher than the agreed $3.75. She also became book review editor.

Reason's tenth anniversary issue, a blockbuster for those days at seventy-six pages, showcased the magazine's improved design by Art Director Don Wood and included solicited articles from an array of libertarian luminaries—including Milton Friedman, Robert Nozick, John Hospers, Karl Hess, Robert LeFevre, Murray Rothbard, Dave Nolan, and Roger MacBride. My editorial in that issue summarized significant economic and personal liberty gains since *Reason's* founding year of 1968—including repeal of the military draft, transportation deregulation, marijuana decriminalization in ten states, equal rights for women, etc., as well as Nobel Prizes in economics for both F. A. Hayek and Milton Friedman.

Thoughts on Policy Change

In some of my *Reason* articles and editorials during the 1970s, as well as in conference presentations, I had taken a position on how libertarian policy ideas should be presented if we wanted to make change, as opposed to just making noise.[1] Since hardly anyone in government—the people who had the power to make policy changes—were even close to being libertarian, we should demonstrate that specific changes we advocate are objectively better than the status quo, and argue for them on that basis. Within libertarian circles, this approach was dubbed "gradualism," as opposed to its opposite (favored by many), "abolitionism."

The roots of my thinking came from reading, early in the 1970s, a history of the Fabian Society in England. *This Little Band of Prophets*, by Anne Freemantle (Mentor Books, 1960), explained the remarkable success of Sidney and Beatrice Webb, George Bernard Shaw, and other Fabian socialists in gradually bringing about major changes in British public policy over a number of decades, laying the basis for nationalization of industry and creation of the welfare state. They did this not only by writing numerous books, research papers, and articles but by getting their people into various organizations able to influence and shape future public policy. As an engineer trained to look for evidence of what works and what does not, this history made a powerful impact on my thinking.

A related influence was an evening course I took in 1971 at UCLA Extension on technological and social forecasting. An implicit message from this course was that forecasters with a point of view had an opportunity to "forecast" developments that they would like to see become reality. I could see a lot of ways that insight could be applied in *Reason* articles, and it was my inspiration for what became the long-running Trends feature in the front of the book, highlighting pro-liberty developments.

Needless to say, gradualism was far from a mainstream view among most libertarians in the heady days of the 1970s, and both *Reason* and I came in for repeated attacks as some kind of sell-out. When I started writing about local governments contracting out city services, many saw that as trivial, because the services were still being paid for by tax money (even if taxpayer savings were 15–25 percent). With some trepidation, I accepted

---

1   One example was my 1971 *Reason* article "Leverage Points for Social Change." (https://reason.com/archives/1971/06/01/leverage-points-for-social-cha)

an invitation from the Libertarian Supper Club in Los Angeles to debate "gradualism" with libertarian *wunderkind* George H. Smith. I felt well prepared after finishing the text of my twenty-five-minute presentation, and was pleasantly surprised at how well it went. My girlfriend at the time said she thought George's presentation was "superficial and glib," and I wrote in my journal that "everyone thought it was the best Supper Club program in years. A lot of people decided that gradualism can be a respectable position after all."

Nevertheless, gradualism was still a minority view of the movement's heavyweights. In the May 1978 tenth anniversary issue of *Reason*, we included a panel discussion, taped at the 1977 Libertarian Party National Convention in San Francisco. The panelists were Roy Childs, Joe Cobb, Ed Crane, Don Ernsberger, Mark Frazier, Manny Klausner, Charles Koch, Dave Nolan, Dave Walter, and me. Re-reading the transcript in 2016, I was amazed at how strongly the "abolitionist" position was defended, with Mark and me basically the only ones defending "gradualism." How things changed in subsequent decades, within Cato as well as the LP!

A late 1977 subscription pitch for the new *Libertarian Review* included this veiled attack on *Reason*, referring to existing libertarian-oriented magazines as follows: "Even when they do attempt to deal with ideas and issues, the approach is invariably gradualist and compromising—devoid of the truly *radical* thinking that is the hallmark of libertarianism."

A Major New Challenge

Despite *Reason's* healthy growth, our financial woes continued. In mid-1976 Tibor was in residence at the Institute for Humane Studies in Menlo Park, and discussed our situation with George Pearson, who was visiting at the time (since Charles Koch was a major supporter of IHS). George offered to help us find additional supporters but noted that this required production of a new business plan. Another topic they discussed was the possibility of changing *Reason's* organizational form to a nonprofit, tax-exempt organization like IHS.

Manny had a follow-up conversation with Charles Koch in August, which led to my sending him a proposal for a new Reason patrons program to attract thousand-dollar donors to support significant improvements in content and circulation. This led to a meeting of Manny, Tibor, and me with Charles at the 1976 LP National Convention in Washington, DC, that September. He agreed to provide a soft loan of $3,000 to help us launch that effort. At the end of October, Mark called from DC with news that Ed Crane was working with Koch on a start-up magazine aimed at left-intellectuals, to be edited by Ralph Raico. (This materialized in 1977 as *Inquiry*, edited by Bill Evers.) In my journal I wrote, "Damn! My dream of being saved [by Koch] is shot down in flames. Still stuck with *Reason* in its unviable form."

In January 1977, we learned that Charles Koch was planning to publish not one but two magazines; in addition to *Inquiry*, his group would take over Bob Kephart's *Libertarian Review* newsletter and convert it into a magazine aimed directly at libertarians. That same month I presented Manny and Tibor with my personal dilemma: since I was now fully responsible for producing each month's issue of *Reason* and developing and overseeing its marketing, being tied to a rigid monthly production schedule was seriously restricting the consulting assignments I could take on, especially ones involving travel. So I asked that I be given a part-time salary of $500/month—and they agreed.

By this point, the word was out that what Charles Koch and Ed Crane were planning was not just two magazines but a full-fledged libertarian think tank: the Cato Institute. It would be launched that year in San Francisco and would be the publisher of *Inquiry*. A separate entity would house *Libertarian Review*, next door, edited by Roy Childs. At a regional LP convention in Salt Lake City that April, Crane and Ralph Raico "kept ribbing me the whole time about how they (and Koch's money) were going to be such deadly competitors of *Reason*—only half in jest." But Ed also noted that Cato would commission and publish serious books, and invited me to submit a proposal I'd described to him for a book that would critique major federal regulatory agencies. I submitted a proposal, and they gave me a grant to research and write a sample chapter on the Federal Aviation Administration.

In early 1978, as pitches for the not-yet-published *Inquiry* appeared in people's mailboxes, our Viewpoint columnist Edith Efron penned a long critique of libertarians seeking to ally with the Left, which ended up taking both *Libertarian Review* and *Inquiry* to task for planning to publish material by such radical leftists as the head of the Institute for Policy Studies and the notorious Noam Chomsky. Needless to say, our erstwhile friends at Cato were not pleased.

Nonetheless, Reason Enterprises began *Reason's* tenth year of publication with its existence under threat. Our finances were still quite shaky, but the coming of two well-financed competing magazines presented an even bigger challenge. My conclusion was that we either had to come up with a far better business model—or call it quits. This part of the story picks up again in Chapter 6. The next two chapters deal with related activities I was engaged in during the Reason Enterprises years: libertarian new-country projects (Chapter 4) and researching privatization of local government services (Chapter 5). The former became a topic of a number of *Reason* articles, and the latter led to the first major public policy focus of the new Reason Foundation.

Chapter 4

Libertarian New Country Projects

A Desire to Start Over

In 2009, when Patri Friedman (Milton Friedman's grandson) unveiled his nonprofit organization, the Seasteading Institute, I felt a strong sense of déjà vu. The idea of creating self-sustaining libertarian communities outside the territory of any existing government was seen as new by most of those writing about Friedman's concept of developing floating sea cities. But it has libertarian roots dating back to the 1960s.

I first learned of libertarian interest in new countries from the first libertarian periodical that I discovered while working at Sikorsky in the late-1960s—*Liberal Innovator*, later called simply *Innovator*. It carried articles about a project seeking sites to develop new countries, whether on the ocean or elsewhere. That project was called Preform, and it produced a newsletter called *Preform-Inform Newsletter*, as recounted by economist John Snare in an article in *Reason*'s December 1972 special issue on new-country projects. Based in Los Angeles, the group researched possible locations and developed the basics of a "voluntary constitutional government," the Association of Free Isles. The project expired in the early 1970s, with some of the participants deciding their least-bad option was to live off the grid in the United States.

Another project, somewhat better known, was Operation Atlantis. It was the creation of Werner Stiefel, head of a family-owned multinational producer of soaps and pharmaceutical products called Stiefel Laboratories. A refugee from Nazi Germany, Stiefel was inspired, by reading Ayn Rand's *Atlas Shrugged*, to try creating a kind of Galt's Gulch (aka Atlantis), preferably on the ocean outside any existing state's jurisdiction. The project's initial headquarters was a motel that Stevens purchased in Saugerties,

New York. His newsletter about the project, *The Atlantis News*, began in 1968, and I subscribed.

To scout out prospective locations in the Caribbean, the Atlantis project built a thirty-eight-foot ferro-cement trawler, the Atlantis II. The boat arrived in the Caribbean in March 1972, and Stiefel leased a tract of land in the freeport area of Tortuga, Haiti, intending it to be a base of operations for the project's subsequent stages. But when the landowners learned of Stiefel's new-country plans, they cancelled the lease. He then built a small complex of buildings for Stiefel Laboratories (and the project) on Grand Bahama Island. According to a later account by Spencer MacCallum, Stiefel tried to develop several other Caribbean sites for a new country, but eventually gave up. Stiefel died in 2005, with his dream unrealized.

While there were many other (mostly on-paper) new-country concepts, the most prominent and best-financed projects were attempted by Mike Oliver, a land developer in Carson City, Nevada. Born in Lithuania, Oliver had spent four years in a Nazi concentration camp and grew up in Communist Lithuania, before immigrating to the United States in 1947. Like Stiefel, he was inspired by Rand's novel and sought to develop one or more new countries. He first came to the attention of the Objectivist/libertarian community via his book, *A New Constitution for a New Country*, self-published in 1968 (and with sales reported in the tens of thousands). The book created a sensation among libertarians—not just fringe types but serious professionals: engineers, doctors, lawyers, investment advisers, etc. He began publishing the *Capitalist Country Newsletter* (later renamed the *Mike Oliver Newsletter*) in 1968, to keep people posted on his New Country Project (NCP) activities, and I became one of its around four thousand subscribers. He raised enough money early on to pay several volunteers to make scouting trips to various parts of the world, such as the Turks and Caicos Islands in the Caribbean, Surinam, New Caledonia, and the New Hebrides islands in the South Pacific, among others. One of those scouts was philosopher/adventurer Jack Wheeler, whose book, *The Adventurer's Guide*, was published in 1976.

Mike Oliver's Projects

I first corresponded with Oliver in 1969, hoping to stop in to see him on the vacation trip Lynn Kinsky and I made to California, but he was not in town at the time we went through Reno. Correspondence resumed in 1971, after I learned that my new friend Tibor Machan had corresponded with him about the New Country Project's possibilities in the New Hebrides, long known as a tax haven. When Oliver learned that I was an engineer, he asked if I would review a concept paper on a proposed floating city structure. Since hydrodynamics is similar to aerodynamics, I asked PSSI colleague Terry Honikman, with an aeronautical engineering degree from Stanford, to review the concept, and I sent a summary of the plan's defects to Oliver.

Oliver's first (albeit fleeting) success was the proclamation of the Republic of Minerva in January 1972. The project filed a claim with the United Nations for the Minerva Reefs, two coral atolls in international waters on which it had built rudimentary concrete structures that would remain above water at high tide. The legal case was sound—the nearest sovereign state was Fiji, four hundred miles away—and a legal researcher for the project documented the case in an article in the *Columbia Law Review*. The plan was to bring in dredges to create land behind seawalls (as the Chinese are doing today in the South China Sea) and build a sea city. But the King of Tonga pre-empted this plan in June 1972 by sending patrol boats to occupy the undefended structures, plant the Tongan flag, and declare sovereignty. Investor support for the plan quickly dried up.

Lynn and I interviewed Mike Oliver in Santa Barbara in summer 1972 and included that interview in *Reason*'s December 1972 New Country Project special issue. Part of that interview discussed the failure of his 1971 project in the New Hebrides—a colony jointly administered by Britain and France, with a dual legal system. He'd leased land there and invited overseas settlers, but the British torpedoed that by restricting the term of visitor permits to four months. At the time of the interview, the Minerva project was still alive, and Oliver discussed a sea-city concept developed by the Pilkington Glass Company in London. The Pilkington Sea City was designed to accommodate thirty-two thousand people. But neither Minerva nor the Pilkington sea city came to be.

The next episode in Mike Oliver's quest represented a change of approach. Instead of seeking to create ocean-based communities, or to lease land in developing countries with as much freedom as could be negotiated, the new idea was to work with groups favoring independence in places that were being de-colonized and persuade them to adopt pro-freedom, limited-government constitutions. The first opportunity appeared in the Bahamas. Soon after the Bahamas got its independence from Britain, the Abaco Independence Movement (AIM) was launched, in August 1973, by locals Chuck Hall and Bert Williams.[2] AIM was a local political party, hoping to obtain self-determination for the Abaco Islands (Great Abaco and Little Abaco), comprising 766 square miles, 170 miles east of South Florida.

Some of those who founded AIM had previously appealed to the British government to leave Abaco out of Bahamian independence and retain its status as a colony, but their efforts were rebuffed in the British Parliament. Mike Oliver told me (in August 2016) that he first learned of AIM via a phone call from a Bahamas police official who was concerned about alleged Mafia ties of new Prime Minister Lynden Pindling. Mike then initiated contact with Chuck Hall, and they worked out an agreement under which the New Country Project would assist AIM, in exchange for obtaining a free trade zone on Great Abaco. One of Oliver's supporters, Hank Phillips in Fort Walton Beach, Florida, set up a nonprofit foundation called Friends of Abaco. One of its early activities was sending several hundred copies of John Hospers's *Libertarianism* book to AIM. Between AIM's first public meeting in October 1973 and mid-1974, its membership grew from zero to about one thousand (out of only 2,200 Abaco voters). AIM started publishing a modest local newspaper, *The Abaco Independent*, and it printed and distributed bumper stickers and T-shirts.

---

2 Rick Lowe, "Forgotten Dreams: A People's Desire to Chart Their Own Course on Abaco, Bahamas," Nassau Institute, 2010

In February 1974, AIM held its organizing convention. Speakers included John Hospers of the University of Southern California and Cleophas Adderly, an independent member of the new Bahamas Parliament. Hospers had been warned in advance by the government not to make a "political" speech, so he delivered an "economic" speech instead. Both his and Adderly's speeches made front-page news in *The Tribune*, the major newspaper in Nassau, the Bahamian capital. The convention adopted a party constitution, a statement of principles, and a plan of action for achieving self-government.

In May, AIM convened a development conference called "Prosperity 1974." The idea was to bring together economic experts to brainstorm how Abaco might become self-sufficient. About one hundred Bahamian business and community leaders attended. Speakers included adventure tourism expert Jack Wheeler, Los Angeles entrepreneur Alvin Lowi, and think-tank researcher Susan Love Brown (on improving the school system). Also attending were potential foreign investors as well as Lord Belhaven, a member of Britain's House of Lords who was supportive of Abaco independence. John Hospers was on the program, but was not allowed into the country and had to fly back to Los Angeles.

Lynn and I visited Abaco soon thereafter as tourists, with the primary aim of writing an article for *Reason* about the project and its potential, and a number of the points in the preceding paragraphs are based on that article in the October 1974 issue. In getting background information for that story, I interviewed Oliver again, and he provided materials on AIM in advance of the trip. The article also disclosed that AIM had developed the draft of a very limited-government constitution for a proposed Abaco Commonwealth, whose main points were summarized in the article.

Abaco and the New Hebrides

With all that as background, I was already fairly knowledgeable about Abaco when I received a call from Mike in late September 1974 asking if he could hire me for a consulting assignment in

Abaco. The timing was fortuitous: I had just received word that PSSI was going to lay off me and most of my colleagues, and my marriage was clearly coming to an end. I needed the money, I had some time, and I was supportive of the goals of the New Country Project, so I listened intently.

I was not surprised to learn that Mike had a representative on the ground in Abaco to work with AIM and edit its newspaper. He was a young British classical liberal, Adrian Day. For some reason, Mike was not sure if Adrian was fully on board with the project's goals, and he also wanted an independent reading on how AIM was doing. So my assignment was to go to Marsh Harbor (the largest town), where Adrian was based, and quietly ascertain the lay of the land. Mike put me in touch with NCP supporters Fred and Judy Miley in Miami, who'd made a number of trips back and forth, and I agreed to take on this several-week assignment in October.

Fred and Judy graciously put me up at their home, after my initial night in a motel near Miami International Airport, and explained to me that the pilots on Ft. Lauderdale-based Mackey Airlines were sympathetic to the project and could bring in documents that might arouse suspicion if brought in by me. They also briefed me on various AIM people I should probably seek to visit with while there. Armed with this useful local knowledge, I spent several weeks on Great Abaco. I met Adrian and learned of his extensive contacts with good people in the British free-market community. I met and talked with a number of AIM people and discovered nothing amiss. I also rented a car and drove to the south end of Great Abaco to see firsthand the huge tract of undeveloped land that was being discussed by AIM and the NCP as a major free-trade zone.

Mike was pleased with my report, and after I'd had a week or so to get my affairs in order in Santa Barbara (getting some overdue *Reason* work done, plus discussions with Lynn about sorting out our belongings prior to my moving out), Mike called me again for a second assignment, this time mostly in Nassau to meet with some key AIM allies there. For this trip, knowing that there would be large amounts of dead time waiting for appointments with people, I brought along piles of *Reason* work, in addition to books to read. I did the requested meetings, and made another brief visit to Marsh Harbor. I was a bit paranoid about being a "secret agent," so what I wrote in my journal about these two trips is very cryptic, not naming names, etc.—and it was so long ago that I really don't recall the details.

After this second Abaco trip, I assumed my "secret agent" days were finished, and things were starting to look promising for consulting work with PSSI and two companies that the two ex-PSSI vice presidents had moved to, so I was not desperate for more work from Mike. But he called to say he was expecting an important visitor from the New Hebrides and wanted me to join them in Carson City to discuss a big new opportunity. So I took two days and flew to Nevada (on Mike's dime) for this meeting. It included "two millionaire businessmen" (names forgotten) and the man from the New Hebrides, a Frenchman named Claude van Nerum. In my journal I wrote that the proposed project "looks a bit fantastic—almost too good to be true, and quite possibly capable of being pulled off." But I had no intention of going there. Back in Santa Barbara, I had just rented a one-bedroom apartment and was getting ready for the upcoming moving day over Thanksgiving weekend.

Mike called again a week later, with planning far more advanced. He told me they'd considered Jack Wheeler for the project, but needed someone more analytical to manage the whole operation for the next year or so. There was no way I could do that, with *Reason* struggling to survive and my need to keep consulting options open. After several further calls along those lines, they brought me back to Carson City for several days of planning and negotiating—the result of which was that I agreed to go to the New Hebrides for up to a month to do a detailed feasibility study, period.

On January 3, 1975, I flew Pan American to Nadi, Fiji, via a stop in Honolulu, and after a long wait in Nadi, flew Air Pacific to Port Vila, capital of the New Hebrides. It was an exciting, though grueling, month. My assignment was four-fold:

- Assess whether the proposed project was actually feasible;
- If so, estimate the time-frame and cost;
- Check out the validity of land titles claimed by Claude and others; and,
- Implicitly, assess the credibility of Claude and his claims about the overall situation there.

The New Hebrides at that time was a colony jointly governed by Britain and France, with two legal systems (plus native "custom") and a Condominium Court to resolve disputes among parties with different legal systems. It was also a well-known tax haven. Independence from Britain and France was on the horizon, and the leading political party was a left-wing socialist one not popular on most of the outer islands. The British favored the socialists, while the pro-development French generally favored the opposition. Claude had proposed creating an independence movement in the northern Banks and Torres (B&T) islands that would secede from the rest either before or at the time of decolonization. Claude owned significant land on one of those islands, Vanua Lava, with plans or dreams of developing a tourist resort.

I spent the first ten days in Vila, collecting data, reading everything I could find, and getting to know Claude. We worked out the plans for my week or more on Vanua Lava, to which I flew with Claude on January 15. I stayed mostly in the one completed "bungalow" of Claude's proposed tourist resort: one room with concrete floor, screens, electricity, a mini-fridge, and a tiny bathroom. The screens were very welcome, since the whole island was infested with flies and mosquitos, which I eventually got used to, sort of.

After Claude flew back to Vila, my fact-finding included a long trek through the jungle to a native village, where I was the overnight guest of the chief (my official role was as a tourism consultant). After dinner and a bit of entertainment, I slept under a mosquito net in an open-air thatched-roof hut. Other research included a boat trip to a nearby island to visit with an Australian archeologist and pick his brains on local culture and politics. The evening meal there included freshly killed flying fox, from which one had to pick out the buckshot particles. On another nearby island, I was able to board the monthly cargo boat—the lifeline for mail and supplies, as well as for sending copra (dried coconut) to market. On my return to Vila, I spent my last week researching land titles and reviewing various findings and observations with Claude, to make sure I was not misinterpreting things I'd observed.

My detailed twenty-page, single-spaced report was rather harsh. My overall conclusion was that the odds of success were poor, with great difficulty in finding and educating a critical mass of B&T natives to form a credible government, even if a political party could be created in what might well be a short span of time before elections came about. But for the sake of argument, I laid out a tentative plan, with a potential schedule and an assessment of the resources that would be required, including the need to withstand a highly likely economic boycott of the newly proclaimed country by the powers that be (which included a long-range supply plane and a cargo ship), and costed all this out. I concluded that "this plan has no more than a 20–30 percent chance of success," and that it "is significantly more-costly than I had expected initially." If it were my money, I wrote, "I would seek a project with a greater chance of success." The report concluded with a suggestion of possible alternative plans: either a longer-term, lower-risk effort to simply build a B&T political movement that would not take action until after the New Hebrides independence, or an all-New Hebrides project that would build on *already existing opposition movements*, such as the large Na-Griamel movement on the largest island, Espiritu Santo.

Mike was impressed with my report, and he and his colleagues decided to look into the alternative approaches. So I was at least temporarily off the hook for further New Hebrides assignments—I did not relish a repeat of the malaria shots, diarrhea, mosquito bites, and flies that had infected a burst blister on my foot after my overland trek. I ran into Mike at two conferences that spring, and was aware that work continued on both Abaco and the New Hebrides, but I was glad to be settling into several consulting projects in public safety and criminal justice with former employers.

To everyone's surprise, the Abaco project was the subject of a vicious attack in the February 1975 issue of *Esquire*. The article (by freelancer Andrew St. George, who had done firsthand reporting on Fidel Castro's guerilla movement prior to Castro taking power) claimed that AIM was being funded by an arms dealer and mercenary named Mitch WerBell, and that an armed insurrection was being planned. Mike was furious, and told me that the article was a fantasy. Whatever the truth, the negative publicity hurt AIM considerably. The next month it changed its name to the Abaco Home Rule Movement (AHRM), but continued work on its constitution. AIM leader Chuck Hall resigned, and there were no further media mentions of WerBell in connection with Abaco.

Decades later, in researching this chapter in 2016, I contacted several participants in the project—Adrian Day, Fred Miley, Grant LaPoint, and Frank Bond (subsequently a Reason Foundation board member) to ask what they knew about the WerBell connection. First, I was told that a retired military officer—Col. Colin Mitchell of the Argyll and Southerland Highlands—had visited Abaco in 1973 to do a defense assessment, presumably for AIM as it was forming. It was clear to AIM's founders that the newly independent Bahamas government might react to Abaco independence with force. I was told that AIM and the New Country Project had ascertained that the government had only two patrol boats—and no army or navy. So WerBell was contracted by Chuck Hall to prepare defense plans in case such were needed. Plans people recalled were to either disable the patrol boats in advance or to mine the harbor at Marsh Harbor to deter the boats, but not at a depth that would harm civilian sailing craft. Basically, everybody had known about the WerBell connection except naïve me!

In my August 2016 interview with Mike Oliver for this chapter, he confirmed that WerBell had been working with AIM prior to the New Country Project's involvement. He also told me that Andrew St. George had been given an exclusive on the story, to be published only after AIM declared autonomy or independence.

But at some point, St. George demanded to be paid by the NCP, and when Mike refused, he sold the story to *Esquire*. And he wrote it to look like WerBell had been in charge, with AIM and the NCP people serving merely as useful idiots.

The Phoenix Foundation

In any event, I spent the weekend of April 5–6, 1975, in Carson City for two days of meetings on the future of the New Country Project, which led to its being reorganized as the nonprofit Phoenix Foundation. In my journal I also noted that there was not much good news financially—most of the hoped-for large contributions hadn't come in. But several weeks later Mike called about a potential breakthrough. Well-known financial newsletter writer Harry D. Schultz had written in his internationally circulated newsletter that it was time to get a new country going. Mike had apparently been cultivating him for some time, so he proposed that we send a delegation to meet with Schultz in Amsterdam to sell him on the NCP and specifically the Phoenix Foundation—and he wanted me to be part of it.

So I ended up flying overnight to Amsterdam, for a day-long meeting with Schultz along with Mike and a wealthy American supporter named Dennis (plus a bit of sightseeing). The result was that Harry would join the Phoenix Foundation board, and endorse both the project and *Reason* magazine in his newsletter. (That initial board included Mike Oliver, John Hospers, Nathaniel Branden, Hank Phillips, and me, in addition to new member Schultz.) On Monday, Dennis and Mike flew on to Zürich to set up some bank accounts, while I flew back home.

At the end of May I made my last visit to Abaco, going with Fred and Judy Miley and meeting Adrian and Dennis there for a series of meetings with AHRM leaders. We learned that Chuck Hall "is thoroughly discredited among his former followers" and had left the island for good. AHRM had experienced a strong revival of activity after the reorganization, developing into a more-robust political movement and planning to run candidates of its own in the forthcoming election. It was continuing to publish *The Abaco Independent*, with Adrian remaining as editor.

However, we also noted that AHRM's gains had been achieved at the price of watering down its message, and that despite having some significant black support, the leadership was still 100 percent white, which was likely to limit AHRM's political effectiveness in a population split about 50/50 between blacks and whites. And when the election came, AHRM's candidates were out-polled by the major Bahamian parties.

AHRM pretty much faded away over the next two years. Adrian had returned to the United States in early 1976, but continued to edit the newspaper for some months thereafter. It ceased publication in 1977, and by 1978 there was little or no sign of AHRM. Adrian went on to become a financial newsletter editor and publisher, with the newsletter today called *Adrian Day's Global Analyst*. He and I reconnected at a Mark Skousen conference in Nassau in 2014, and we had a great time reminiscing about the Abaco project.

With the collapse of the Abaco project, Mike refocused his attention on the New Hebrides in 1975. He sent Bill White, a California libertarian whose wife was a Pan Am flight attendant (so he could fly on company passes) to the New Hebrides for four days in June for a firsthand assessment of the ongoing political situation. Bill's report suggested that the best way forward would be the longer-term, all-New Hebrides plan proposed in my January report. This would require finding and working with promising local political figures and developing a draft constitution and land trust. He'd met with Na-Griamel leader Jimmy Stevens and judged him to be someone we could work with. Mike sent his trusted lieutenant, Grant La Point, there on long-term assignment in July, and Mike himself visited in September, reporting "amazing progress" on his return. This included productive meetings with Jimmy Stevens, agreements on commemorative coins and "honorary citizenships" for overseas financial supporters of Na-Griamel. (When I later learned about the latter, I argued against it, but did not change Mike's mind.) He also brought news that on July 14 Jimmy Stevens had met with the French president and other high officials in Paris. Grant brought back a news article with photos, confirming the visit.

That August, Na-Griamel candidates won fifteen of sixteen seats in local Espiritu Santo elections. But in the first-ever national elections in November, over half the seats went to the socialist National Party (NP) with the rest going to a coalition of two French-oriented parties (UCNH and MANH), plus Na-Griamel. In response to reports of massive vote fraud (in favor of the NP), Na-Griamel mounted huge demonstrations, which led the British to pressure the French into sending in fifteen paratroopers for a one-day show of force. Stevens gave the government until December 27 to hold a census on which to base new elections—or else. Grant set up a make-shift radio broadcasting capability for Na-Griamel at its main village, Tanafo.

Mike believed that Jimmy Stevens planned a UDI—a unilateral declaration of independence—presumably for Espiritu Santo, where Na-Griamel was strongest. He concluded that this was make-or-break time for the project. He gave me the hard sell about going there to manage the next phase of the project, to work closely with Jimmy Stevens. I argued that I did not have the right skill set or experience for being effective in this situation, nor could I in good conscience leave *Reason* for an indefinite period. After the second or third such phone conversation, I had an inspiration: my libertarian ex-Marine friend David Sutton in Santa Barbara. A Vietnam veteran, he had jungle survival skills and self-defense expertise, plus strong libertarian convictions and knowledge. I called David to see if he'd be interested—and he was. It took some doing to persuade Mike, but he eventually saw the merits of the case.

With confirmation that Na-Griamel did indeed plan to declare the independence of Espiritu Santo over Radio Tanafo on December 27, and with investors ready to cover expenses, my immediate task was to get David outfitted for the trip and brief him as much as possible on everything I'd learned about the New Hebrides and Na-Griamel. With such short notice for planning the trip, the only flight with space available right away departed from San Francisco, not Los Angeles, so I drove David from Santa Barbara to SFO, with briefings continuing all the way.

I also alerted Mark Frazier in New Zealand about what was

going on and the New Country Project's involvement. He'd been interested in the NCP idea ever since Mike's book came out in 1968. My hope was that he could help bring about unbiased coverage of New Hebrides developments in the *Auckland Herald*.

On Sunday, December 28, Mike called to tell me that Na-Griamel had declared independence the day before and that he was in San Francisco with two delegates, en-route to the United Nations in New York, and that he needed me there to help. So on Wednesday, December 30, 1975, I found myself (along with Mike, Dennis, and the two Na-Griamel delegates) on the thirty-sixth floor of the New York Hilton, writing a news release and assembling mailing lists to send it to. The delegates made their presentations at the UN, and afterwards "we all went to see Bob Bleiberg at *Barron's*" to brief him in person. We also called Mark in Auckland, who told us that the story was on the front page two days in a row, and that he'd helped write the pieces. That evening we all drank a toast to independence and went out for "the biggest prime rib dinner I'd ever had." The next day I addressed envelopes to the heads of state of 155 countries and finished up and copied the news releases. The two delegates took them to the three wire services, and *Newsweek* and *Time*—then the most important news magazines in the United States.

Although Grant was expelled by the New Hebrides government in January 1976, David Sutton stayed on until April, as chronicled in a long article by Patrick Cox in the September 1980 issue of *Reason*. He engaged in many discussions with Stevens on individual liberty and government, and drafted a limited-government constitution, in English, as Stevens desired. David told me that Stevens readily embraced free-market ideas, and acknowledged that a written constitution would eventually replace "custom" law, but believed that a natural death was superior to execution by an overweening government. David then translated the constitution into the local Pidgin called *Bech le mer*, which is spoken widely in the islands in addition to dozens of native languages. The Pidgin version would facilitate local discussion. David was also running a tiny newspaper in *Bech le mer*. The constitution was subsequently adopted by a ten-tribe chiefs' conference, representing four or five of the most populous islands.

After learning of violence and threats of violence by National Party members against Na-Griamel members, Stevens had asked Sutton to provide self-defense training to those willing to participate. Rifles were largely prohibited to native peoples, so the training was in basic combat techniques, primitive weapons, as well as strength training and better nutrition. He trained officers not only for the Na-Griamel militia, but also for the police force that would be needed after independence. That force went into immediate deployment in Na-Griamel's main village of Tanafo.

Following up on the December 27, 1975, UDI, Stevens had given government officials until April 1 to vacate Espiritu Santo. Shortly before that date, an opposition group placed sacred *nagria* and *namele* leaves (used in Na-Griamel's symbol) on the flagpole outside the government building in Santo town. By custom, that meant the offices were protected, and Na-Griamel could not evict the officials. In response, a Na-Griamel member read a message over the organization's Radio Tanafo warning the officials to leave and using the words "fire and blood." The opposition demanded that military force be used, and French troops from New Caledonia landed on Santo. That basically made Stevens's April 1 deadline inoperative.

When Mike heard about the "fire and blood" broadcast, he was furious, assuming that David could have prevented it. He called me to contact David and order him to come home. I managed to reach David, via a pre-arranged radio-telephone method, and heard his case for staying put—which I thought was reasonable if he was willing to take the risk. I reported this to Mike, and he laid down the law: get him out now. So I called David back, and he agreed to depart. He arrived back in Santa Barbara on April 19, "filled with tales of the South Pacific." A month later Mark Frazier arrived in Santa Barbara, having stopped in the New Hebrides along the way, bringing me several souvenirs from Na-Griamel (including a wicked-looking four-foot long arrow that I still have).

The story doesn't end there, though the NCP's involvement

diminished thereafter. In May 1976, Mike sent a message to Stevens warning him not to alienate the French, who were their only hope against the British (who continued to back radical priest Walter Lini and his socialist National Party). John Hospers followed up with an eloquent letter to the French high commissioner in New Caledonia explaining the aims and role of the Phoenix Foundation. That led to Jimmy and a number of other native leaders being once again invited to France for Bastille Day in July 1976, where they met with all the top government officials. In the lead-up to New Hebrides elections planned for October, Mike sent a US political consultant (my old friend Dana Rohrabacher) to assist Na-Griamel with practical campaigning. Once again there was massive voter fraud, observed directly by Dana in Luganville (also known as Santo town).

By contrast, in the first elections for a real National Assembly, in autumn 1977, the non-socialist opposition won big—but Lini refused to accept the results. He and his party issued their own declaration of independence, declaring the "People's Provisional Government." The next year, Na-Griamel was being taken more seriously. A French delegation visited Na-Griamel's Tanafo headquarters, and after an extension of the runway at Big-Bay, Air Melanesia began offering air service. And in March 1979, Stevens came to the United States, meeting with officials at both the State Department and the United Nations. Na-Griamel had offered to take in three thousand Vietnamese boat people, but this offer failed to get US support. The June 1979 local elections were another defeat for the socialists, giving Na-Griamel and its allies hope for the November 1979 National Assembly election— the one just prior to official independence, in which the New Hebrides would become Vanuatu. This time, the official vote count proclaimed Lini and the socialists as the winners, albeit amidst new allegations of voter fraud. The British backed Lini, so Stevens and a large delegation of opposition chiefs went to Paris to press their case—but this time, the French offered no help.

Five of the chiefs went to Carson City on their way back home, talking with Oliver and his attorney, Tom Eck, about the socialist constitution Lini was promoting and seeking help to draft an alternative that would provide for a confederation rather than a centralized state. Eck agreed to go as an advisor to a planned constitutional convention, arriving in Santo on April 9, 1980. Twenty chiefs, representing every island, took part, and the document was completed on April 17—and signed by all twenty.

In response, Lini came to Santo, hoping to negotiate over the newly drafted document, but his intervention was rejected, and Lini appeared to have given up. However, back in Vila he managed to persuade the US ambassador to Fiji to tell an assemblage in Tanna that US foreign aid would be provided to Vanuatu only if Lini's government (and its constitution) prevailed. In response, Tannans (who had embraced the Eck constitution) revolted, seizing the government offices—an action quickly overturned by British police from Vila. The next day, May 28, Na-Griamel activists marched on Santo town, seizing the government building and declaring the northern federation of Vemarana (based on the constitution drafted with Eck's help) as a new country. Needless to say, Lini called on the British to put down this rebellion—and the French again failed to take any action on behalf of their ally, Jimmy Stevens. British police from Vila retook the buildings and the revolt was over.

With the official independence day less than a month away, I decided on a long-shot attempt to shift the new Thatcher government's policy toward Na-Griamel. The only person I could think of who might be sympathetic and have access was Ralph Harris, head of the classical liberal think tank Institute of Economic Affairs in London. He did not know me then, so I decided against a phone call out of the blue. Instead, I sent him a long Mailgram explaining what Na-Griamel was and what it was trying to do— and that a more-enlightened British approach could make a big difference. I did not get a reply.

As the official independence date of July 30 approached, Lini called for military aid from the socialist government of Papua New Guinea. Stevens called on the French for protection, and after conferring with the British, a joint force of one hundred French (from New Caledonia) and one hundred British police from Vila landed on Santo to "restore order." A number of disturbances took place, one of which led to the death of one of Stevens's sons. Troops from Papua New Guinea arrested Stevens in August. He was charged with many things by Lini's government and sentenced to fourteen years in jail, of which he served eleven. He was released in August 1991 and died of cancer in 1994.

That was the tragic ending of the New Country Project's largest attempt to create a haven of freedom. The Phoenix Foundation organization had undergone a major split in late 1976, with Harry Schultz and his assistant, Robert Doorn in Amsterdam, gaining control. Mike Oliver and the other American board members resigned. The foundation continued to exist for a number of years but without any serious attempts at founding new countries.

Aftermath

Since Na-Griamel was a genuine, grassroots political movement, it survived the loss of its long-time leader, Jimmy Stevens. It has continued as a political movement and party in the northern islands under the revised name "Nagriamel." In the 2008 Vanuatu general election, two Nagriamel members were elected to the national Parliament. And local candidates in the region still campaign under the Vemarana banner. A 2015 review article in the *Vanuatu Daily Post News* reported on the Ambae Nagriamel regional congress. Chief Moli Abel Nako's speech to the congress stated that "we have proved that Nagriamel has made great strides with numbers we have in the Provincial Councils, the Municipal Councils, and the three MPs in the National Parliament."

There is lingering impact from the project in Vanuatu. In 1994, the Prime Minister's Office contacted Claude Van Nerum about a possible Special Economic Zone—and Claude contacted Mike. Their idea was to create such a zone on Aore Island. Mike, Grant, and long-time project supporter Ralph Fair prepared and submitted a proposal, but nothing came of it. Interest in the idea resurfaced in 2006, when former prime minister Maxime Carlot Korman (then Minister of Lands) led a delegation to meet with Ralph Fair and two associates at Fair's ranch near San Antonio. The four-member Vanuatu delegation included Korman and his principal advisor plus two landowners representing Nagriamel. On June 27, 2006, they signed a Memorandum of Understanding to develop a free zone in the Big Bay area of Espiritu Santo. This was followed by a Vanuatu Free Trade Zone Conference in Honolulu in May 2007, with several of the same participants. It led to another signed agreement, but according to Grant, there was insufficient government support to proceed.

In my August 2016 visit with eighty-seven-year-old Mike Oliver, I asked what got him thinking about the idea of a New Country Project. He reflected on the urban riots of the late 1960s and early 1970s and told me he saw the need to create a lifeboat before the ship sinks. He's retired from new-country efforts, but remains very concerned about the future of the United States.

———

One impact of the New Country Project was the drafting of proposed constitutions. The NCP itself produced not only Mike Oliver's original 1968 book, but documents worked out in cooperation with grassroots groups in Abaco and the New Hebrides, as direct outputs of the project. In addition, sympathetic scholars who had no connection with the NCP were motivated to draft pro-freedom, limited-government constitutions aimed at avoiding the flaws in the US Constitution that have led to the creation of a highly centralized welfare state. One such document was crafted by University of San Diego law professor Bernard H. Siegan, *Drafting a Constitution for a Nation or Republic Emerging into Freedom* (George Mason University Press, 1992). And anthropologist and former Institute for Humane Studies scholar Spencer H. MacCallum drafted a constitution for a polity organized as a proprietary community—in this case conceived as a governing document for a space colony, "Drafting a Constitution for ORBIS" (Rampart Institute, 1965). I would imagine that today's Seasteading Institute will produce further works along these lines.

A more recent development—not directly springing from the various new-country efforts but motivated by many of the same concerns—is called Charter Cities. The most prominent advocate has been economist Paul Romer (now chief economist at the World Bank, but a professor at New York University when he promulgated the idea). As summarized by *The Economist* in 2011:

> The principle is simple: take a piece of uninhabited land big enough for a city of several million, governed by well-tried rules, and let those who like the idea move there. The aim is to replicate the success of such places as Hong Kong, not as colonial outposts but as models of development.

After searching the world for a receptive government, Romer in 2011 appeared to have won the support of the government of Honduras, which passed enabling legislation. Also that year, the free-market-oriented Universidad Francisco Marroquin in Guatemala created the Free Cities Institute to foster the concept. A US-based company called the Free Cities Group won permission from Honduras in 2012 to begin developing such a project. And *The Economist*, in a 2011 article on Free Cities called "Honduras Shrugged," linked the idea to various libertarian new-country efforts dating back to Minerva and Operation Atlantis. Should one or more of these charter/free cities be developed and succeed, that will be a legacy of five decades of new-country efforts.

Chapter 5

Discovering Privatization (1970–1980)

Developing the Concept

Privatization of government services via competitive contracting was the first major policy issue that Reason Foundation became known for. But the roots of my involvement with this concept date back to the late 1960s, a decade before the 1978 launch of the Reason Foundation.

In 1969, I read management guru Peter Drucker's new book, *The Age of Discontinuity*. In a chapter called "The Sickness of Government," Drucker drew a clear distinction between governing (i.e., making policy decisions) and its numerous "doing" tasks. The former was government's proper role, but it is often poorly suited to the latter, he wrote. Therefore, he called for "a systematic policy of using . . . the nongovernmental institutions of society, for the actual *doing*." He added that "such a policy might be called *reprivatization*. The tasks which flowed to government in the last [nineteenth] century because the original private institution of society, the family, could not discharge them, would be turned over to the new, nongovernmental institutions that have sprung up and grown over the last 60 to 70 years."

For me, this was a revolutionary insight, opening the door for creative libertarian thinking on the potential for private-sector institutions (both nonprofit and for-profit) to take on many of the "doing" activities of government. But I thought the word "reprivatize" sounded clunky. Moreover, some of the activities that government might farm out, it seemed to me, might be ones that had not previously been done privately. So I was more comfortable with calling it "privatization," which is the term I began using.

My next discovery was a little-noticed book that I bought from the Conservative Book Club: *Uncle Sam, The Monopoly Man* by William C. Wooldridge (Arlington House, 1970). The whole book was a catalog of colorful examples of private provision of public services, from postal service (e.g., the Pony Express) to private schools, arbitration, and even fire protection. In Chapter 6 I learned that the rapidly growing private security industry already accounted for 56 percent as much as was being spent on local police services. Even more amazing to me was learning that Scottsdale and a number of other cities in Arizona received their fire protection from a for-profit company called Rural/Metro. If even fire protection could be privatized, I concluded, then nearly every service provided by state and local governments was a candidate for some form of privatization.

My job at PSSI, starting in February 1970, involved numerous projects with city and county governments in Western states. In the first several years, most of these concerned coming up with preliminary designs for the new 9-1-1 dispatch centers and/or emergency operations centers for cities and counties. Early sites for projects that I worked on included El Segundo and Huntington Beach, California; Las Vegas/Clark County, Nevada; and Phoenix, Arizona. Typically, a PSSI project team would spend from several days to a week on-site, visiting existing public safety facilities, learning how each separate agency dispatched people and vehicles to emergencies, and often doing ride-alongs in patrol cars. Working on these projects was my first real introduction to how local governments are organized, what they do and how they do it.

One thing I discovered via these projects and site visits was that some of the newer cities and counties in Western states (like Scottsdale) were already making use of contracts to obtain various services, whereas the phenomenon was virtually unknown in the large urban areas of the Northeast and the Midwest. Some of these contracts were intergovernmental, such as when a newly incorporated city contracted with the county sheriff's office for police services or with a larger neighboring city for fire services. But many other contracts were with for-profit companies, especially for garbage collection and various maintenance functions. At that time nobody called this "privatization," and there was hardly any media coverage or academic research into this phenomenon as of the early 1970s.

One notable exception was an article I came across late in 1971 called "Municipal Monopoly" in the December issue of *Harper's Magazine*. It was written by a Columbia University professor named E. S. Savas. His article explained how lack of competition in municipal services like garbage collection, street sweeping, operating parks, etc., leads to low productivity and high costs—and that putting such services out to competitive bids would be a good thing for taxpayers. I was excited to learn that a scholar at a major university had embraced the idea and gained a national platform to write about it.

My own first article on the subject, which cited the Savas article from *Harper's*, was "Contracts: Key to Urban Rebirth," published in a special urban policy issue of *Reason* that I put together (the April 1972 issue). The issue included an article by my MIT friend Adam Powell on block associations in New York City and another by Harvard University's James Q. Wilson, called "Market Control of Public Services." It was based on a 1970 presentation he'd given at a UCLA conference. Wilson cited the "Lakewood Plan," under which the Los Angeles suburb of Lakewood had incorporated as a city in 1954, but obtained most of its public services via contracts with the county government or with older cities. Wilson asked the provocative question: Why shouldn't cities such as Lakewood be able to purchase most or all of their public services from *private* suppliers? In fact, this was already happening by that time. The California Contract Cities Association (CCCA) was created by Lakewood and seven other new cities in 1957 to share information and provide technical assistance to newly incorporated cities. Like Scottsdale, these cities were already contracting services from private-sector companies in the 1960s. (As of 2016, CCCA had grown to sixty-two members and held its fifty-seventh annual conference.)

Private Fire Service
One of my PSSI assignments was in 1972 for an emergency operations center in Phoenix. Since Scottsdale, with its privatized fire service was right next door, I decided on a firsthand investigation. I called Rural/Metro's headquarters office in Scottsdale

and managed to speak with its founder and president, Louis A. Witzeman. Although he was cautious, I talked him into letting me visit, and I spent an hour or more getting a tour and asking many questions.

Having by then had about eighteen months of direct interaction with city fire departments, I was amazed at how different Rural/Metro was. It was not just little things like painting their fire trucks lime yellow instead of red (for much better night-time visibility). Witzeman explained to me their paid-reservist system, under which they had a core staff of full-time paid firefighters but also a large corps of on-call "Fire Wranglers" who had regular jobs with the city but got periodic fire training from Rural/Metro and had permission to respond to emergency calls whenever their beeper called them. Rural/Metro paid them only for hours spent in training and in responding to calls. This dramatically reduced the cost of fire protection (which is largely labor cost); in the early 1970s, the per-capita cost of fire service in Scottsdale was *one-fourth* that of comparable cities in the West.

Witzeman also showed me some of their technology innovations, such as larger-diameter hoses (which meant the city did not have to install fire hydrants as close together as in other cities), an economical "attack truck" well suited to brush fires, and even a tractor-treaded remote control fire buggy (called the "Snail") that could be sent into very hazardous situations dragging a fire hose. And despite the Rural/Metro model being anathema to the fire unions, it was meeting a market test. The Insurance Services Office (ISO) gave Scottsdale a very good rating for fire service, which meant the taxpayers there got affordable rates on their homeowners' insurance. Rural/Metro served its city customers via contracts with their city governments. But in Arizona's rural desert communities, where there was no government fire service, the company operated by annual subscription. The property owner's incentive to subscribe was that fire insurance cost significantly less if the property had fire service, with the difference in premium costs being less than the cost of the subscription. Rural/Metro would put out non-subscribers' fires, but had legal permission to send the owner a hefty bill.

I was very impressed by this example of privatization. It was a powerful example of innovation and taxpayer cost savings, thanks to the incentives provided by competition for the market, as opposed to municipal monopoly. So I decided to make it a kind of poster child for introducing people to municipal privatization in a dramatic way. I was always on the lookout for examples of municipal privatization and for academic research on the subject, while editing *Reason* magazine and writing its regular "Trends" feature each month.

In 1975, when I still had a consulting relationship with the former PSSI (by then folded into GRC as the Public Safety Systems Operation division [PSSO]), my libertarian dentist, Garvan Kuskey, came up with a project idea. He lived in the affluent, unincorporated Santa Barbara suburb of Hope Ranch, which had its own fire district that contracted with the county fire department for its fire service, and Garvan was on the district's board. The cost of the county fire services contract had *tripled* in recent years, and Hope Ranch taxpayers were upset about this. The board did a small in-house study about setting up their own semi-volunteer department. Based on what I'd told Garvan about Rural/Metro, he persuaded the board to authorize a feasibility study of the alternatives, including private contract service (which the rest of the board had never heard of before that time). I took the idea to PSSO, and they authorized me to write a proposal to do the study. The reason for PSSO's involvement (and their overhead cost) was to have the clout of a respected local institution standing behind the study's findings, but the study was done entirely by me.

The proposal was accepted, and I spent about five months on the study, including three or four days in Scottsdale collecting data, which included going with Witzeman as Rural/Metro responded to a gas station fire in Scottsdale. I took numerous color slide photos, so that I'd be able to make a presentation to show the Hope Ranch board that this was a real, highly effective professional organization. I also researched the other small fire departments in Santa Barbara County to find out how they were organized and what they cost, and I got details on the county fire department itself.

My 113-page report, edited and produced by GRC, analyzed three alternatives to the costly county fire department contract: a volunteer department with a full-time fire chief (as had been proposed by their board), a part-paid department (mix of full-time and volunteers, as in some smaller cities in Santa Barbara County), and contract service from a private firm (with costs based on Rural/Metro's operational model). All three were feasible alternatives to the status quo, and all three were less costly. Rural/Metro and the local Santa Barbara Ambulance Company submitted a joint letter expressing their interest in providing contract service, which the study estimated would cost slightly more than the part-paid department but would still be a 28 percent savings compared with the status quo.

My presentation to the Hope Ranch Fire District Board on July 29 was well received. After a similar presentation to County Supervisor Bob Kallman, a friend, he and the county administrative officer arranged for a public meeting at which I would present the study's findings. Before that took place, Lou Witzeman flew in to discuss a possible joint venture with the Santa Barbara Ambulance Company, to go after the contract if it were to be offered. He warned me in advance that fire union people would likely turn out in force at the meeting—and he was right. With that warning, I asked my ex-Marine friend David Sutton to serve as my slide show "projectionist" for the evening. Several hundred people (many of them local firefighters) attended, including the national president of the International Association of Fire Fighters, who'd come all the way from union headquarters in Kansas City. In my journal I wrote that this official "made a fool of himself by standing up and announcing that it was all a bunch of lies."

Despite the positive findings of the study, the Hope Ranch board ended up not proceeding to implement any of the recommendations. But the furor over the study led to pressure from the board of supervisors to crack down on the county fire department's budget escalation, which led to the fire chief resigning and at least some budget reductions. So the pressure that had led to the Hope Ranch district's interest in alternatives abated.

Nevertheless, I got several things out of this experience (in addition to a firsthand introduction to public-sector union opposition to privatization). First, I used my research and photos of Rural/Metro in Scottsdale for a *Reason* cover story in the May 1976 issue. Second, I developed a presentation about privatizing municipal services, including the Scottsdale Fire Department as a prime example of improved service and taxpayer savings. It was one of the first presentations libertarian groups had ever heard on practical applications of libertarian ideas—but of course it was denounced as trivial or counterproductive by abolitionist libertarians (because, despite the taxpayer savings, this was still *tax money* being spent!). And third, my *Reason* cover story was picked up by major media.

One day in 1977, I got a call from Norm Gorin, a producer at CBS's *60 Minutes*. He'd read the article and quizzed me for about half an hour about Rural/Metro, Scottsdale, union opposition, etc. He asked for Lou Witzeman's phone number, which I gave him. Lou was very nervous about taking with *60 Minutes*, given their known practice of ambush interviews, and he worried that a big New York media company would be inclined to take the union's anti-privatization line. In the end, after Gorin and colleagues had done more research, they persuaded Lou that it would not be a hit piece, and he opened Rural/Metro's doors to their production crew. The presenter for the resulting segment was Mike Wallace—and to my pleasant surprise, the story portrayed a heroic innovator struggling against a status-quo, traditionalist union. It aired in November 1978, just after California voters had approved Proposition 13 limiting property taxes, and a "tax revolt" was underway in various parts of the country. Tapes of the program became part of Rural/Metro's marketing efforts from then on. This was *Reason*'s first national media coverage.

Outreach on Local Government Privatization

Mark Frazier's arrival in Santa Barbara in 1976 had been a catalyst for improving *Reason* magazine, as noted in Chapter 3. But Mark also provided the spur for me to get more serious about marketing the idea of privatizing public services via competitive contracting. We talked a lot about this subject, and one day Mark asked me, "If you put your mind to it, could you show a city how to cut its budget by 25 or 30 percent—without crippling public services?" I thought about it for a while and replied that I probably could. He suggested that I write a booklet explaining how and why privatization was better than municipal monopolies, and walk the reader through examples in a number of public service areas. Together we worked up an outline, and I began research and writing. (Looking back on it from forty years later, I have no idea how I came up with so much material without the Internet as a research tool.)

Mark had gotten to know Jim Davidson, founder and president of the National Taxpayers Union in Washington, DC, during a 1972 internship at the organization. The next year Mark and Harvard classmate Larry Siskind did a study for NTU adding up the cost of all bills each senator proposed or voted for in 1973. As a result, Mark was invited to join NTU's board that year. Thus, when he approached Jim and NTU about our privatization booklet, they agreed to pay me a modest stipend to research and write it, and they committed to printing and distributing it nationwide.

The 46-page booklet, *Cut Local Taxes—Without Reducing Essential Services*, was released in 1976 (as the second publication of Reason Press, after the John Hospers book in 1972). Its seven chapters covered fire protection, policing, schools, garbage collection, public works and parks, and administration, plus a chapter suggesting how taxpayer activists could work for such changes. The chapter on garbage collection cited new empirical work by Prof. Savas at Columbia that had been published in October 1975 (which was followed by a more detailed book-length version published in 1977). Via his NTU contacts, Mark rounded up meaty endorsement quotes from Sen. William Proxmire and Rep. Ron Paul, which graced the inside of the front cover of the booklet.

The Local Government Center

NTU liked the booklet enough to contract with me to produce a monthly newspaper column, which they distributed to hundreds of weekly newspapers around the country. Called "Fiscal

Watchdog," each month's column covered a specific public service or privatization technique. Mark was very big on creating new organizations and came up with the idea of a nonprofit Local Government Center (LGC) to advise public officials on municipal privatization. I commissioned cousin Tom to design its logo, and Mark took care of getting it incorporated and applying for tax-exempt status.

My friend John Blundell, whom I knew from the Institute for Humane Studies, had moved back to England after *Cut Local Taxes* came out. He bought copies and distributed them to colleagues in the Conservative Party. One of them—Michael Forsyth, a Westminster city councilman (and later a Member of Parliament)—liked it a great deal. Adapting my US examples to British circumstances, Forsyth wrote three monographs on contracting out municipal services, two for the Conservative Political Centre and one for the newly formed Adam Smith Institute. The latter, released in 1980, was called "Reservicing Britain." The Institute much later told Blundell that it was their all-time best-selling publication, with over twenty thousand copies sold. It sparked a contracting-out movement that began in Wandsworth and "spread like a contagious disease throughout the country," Blundell wrote in his book, *Margaret Thatcher: A Portrait of the Iron Lady* (2008). Though now out of print, "Reservicing Britain" is still described on ASI's website.

The booklet and the column were the only marketing we did, but gradually the word got around that LGC existed. I started to get speaking invitations, and we began to get feelers from public officials about advisory work. My archives contain only four LGC studies, and that is probably all that we did, since we were in de-facto competition with for-profit consulting companies— and that was not permitted by our tax-exempt status. We were simply too naïve to realize that, but once the Internal Revenue Service notified us (fortunately without either fining us or yanking our tax exemption), we stopped competing for studies. Two were for public-sector clients, one was for a taxpayer group, and the fourth was commissioned by a private foundation. Only the first two were problematic for the IRS.

Our initial project was an "efficiency study" of the Whatcom County (Bellingham area), Washington Sheriff's Department. The county commissioners hired LGC to resolve a controversy over whether the agency needed more officers. My former PSSI colleague Gordon Zenk and I spent months on the study, including two on-site visits. Our 150-page report documented poor staffing allocation and proposed a revised plan that would match on-duty staffing to variations in the volume of calls for service over the 24-hour cycle (i.e., no budget increase was needed). The second study, for California's Office of Criminal Justice Planning, estimated what new costs had—and had not—been imposed on local governments by a significant change in the state's juvenile justice law. Again, there was no opportunity to propose privatization, but it was an opportunity for honest analysis with taxpayers' best interests at heart. For this study, Mark had found a young researcher, Jim Lewis, willing to do contract work, and Jim assisted me on this project.

The third study was done by Mark and Jim. The Charles Koch Foundation gave LGC a grant to research prospects for privatization in K–12 public schooling. This very provocative report, which was never publicly released, came up with quite an array of strategies and tactics to create a favorable climate for privatization, as well as alternative political approaches. In some respects, it foreshadowed many of the developments we've seen in the arena of school choice and charter schools over the last several decades.

The last study, in 1979, took place in the wake of the November 1978 enactment of California's tax-cutting Proposition 13. To cope with limitations on its future local property tax revenue, the City of Santa Barbara Fire Department had produced a draft master plan that included a number of organizational changes, including getting into the paramedic business, as well as the imposition of a new fire service fee to increase its revenues. Local taxpayer organization Taxwatch 13, whose vice president was dentist Garvan Kuskey, commissioned LGC to review the plan and make recommendations. With my public safety background, the task fell to me. The report supported several of the changes, but rejected the takeover of paramedic service on the grounds that this need was already being well served by private companies at no taxpayer expense. And while it supported a fire service fee in principle, the report called for its cost to be offset by a reduction in property tax support for the department. Needless to say, the fire department went ballistic—but they did not get their proposed fire service fee.

Cutting Back City Hall

Mark and I talked a number of times about my possibly expanding the *Cut Local Taxes* booklet into a full-length book. I'd continued to research municipal privatization for my "Fiscal Watchdog" column, and by that time I was aware of many more examples of services being contracted out by city and county governments. There was also more academic research, including a 1977 book by Savas called *Alternatives for Delivering Public Services: Toward Improved Performance*. I also learned that a UCLA economist named Werner Hirsch had begun studying the phenomenon, though we never met. Despite speaking about the idea at conferences and writing papers, the first book on the subject by Hirsch that I could find was not published until 1991 (*Privatizing Government Services: An Economic Analysis of Contracting Out by Local Governments*). Long before that, Prof. Savas had published *Privatizing the Public Sector* (Chatham House, 1982).

Even though I knew it would be a lot of work (in addition to consulting projects and getting *Reason* out every month), I could see the value of a practical book on municipal privatization that could be understood by elected officials, city managers, newspaper editors, and others who influence which public policies do and don't get implemented. So I was happy when Mark introduced me by phone and letter to Chuck Hamilton in New York. A libertarian, Chuck ran a small publishing operation, Free Life Editions. He was impressed with *Cut Local Taxes*, and agreed that a book-length treatment of municipal privatization was worth doing, though it should include a theoretical framework as well as examples from a wide array of public service sectors.

We signed an agreement and I then engaged in nearly two

years of research and writing to produce *Cutting Back City Hall*, somehow squeezing this in while doing consulting projects, overseeing *Reason*, and making arrangements to start up Reason Foundation (see Chapter 6). Chuck came through with a publisher, Universe Books in New York. It was perhaps best known for the 1972 book *The Limits to Growth*, produced by the Club of Rome. That book was hardly to my taste, but at least Universe was a credible publishing house. After finishing the manuscript, I worked with their copy editor and then proofed the galleys (and was surprised to find that I also had to produce the index, on short notice).

Mark had been a freelance speechwriter for former Treasury secretary William E. Simon, thanks to an introduction from *Reader's Digest* editor William Schulz. Mark persuaded Simon to write a forward for the book. I was pleased when the book appeared in hardcover in 1980. It sold well enough to justify a paperback edition several years later. It was very gratifying during the 1980s and into the 1990s, as I did speaking engagements and was invited to meet with mayors and city managers, to learn how many of them had been introduced to privatization by that 224-page book. *Cutting Back City Hall* also has the distinction of being the first book to use the word "privatization" to describe competitive contracting for municipal public services.

Lou Witzeman sold Rural/Metro to its employees via an Employee Stock Ownership Plan (ESOP) in 1978 and retired in 1981 (though remaining on the company's board). The new CEO, recruited from outside, had plans for nationwide expansion, primarily in the paramedic business (since expanding private fire service was very difficult, politically). To raise capital for expansion, Rural/Metro had an initial public offering of shares, and was actively traded on the NASDAQ for a number of years. Unfortunately, while R/M succeeded in its paramedic expansion, it ended up losing money and filing for Chapter 11 bankruptcy reorganization. Long before that, Lou and I had become good friends, and he even got briefly involved with the Libertarian Party in Arizona. Several years after surviving a bout with lung cancer, Lou died in 2004. His archive of material on Rural/Metro is preserved as the Louis A. Witzeman Collection of Rural/Metro Corporation at the University of Arizona in Tucson.

Chapter 6

Launching Reason Foundation (1978–1986)

Creating the Foundation

As 1978 began, my Reason Enterprises colleagues and I knew we were in an untenable position. With Charles Koch putting sizeable funding into start-up magazines *Inquiry* and *Libertarian Review*, we could not hope to succeed with *Reason* being run as a hand-to-mouth, part-time hobby business. We had to devise and implement a way to put the magazine on a more sustainable course, with serious funding and full-time staff.

In 1977, at a conference in Houston, I met a *Reason* subscriber named John Hilberg. He'd founded a Boston company called StockCross, the first discount stock brokerage firm, and later founded a California cogeneration company, Calcogen. We had a discussion in Houston about *Reason*'s situation, and he visited me in Santa Barbara later that year for more serious discussions. Starting a for-profit company via an IPO (his idea in Houston) seemed wildly impractical, so John suggested we poll subscribers about their likelihood of supporting a nonprofit tax-exempt foundation.

I discussed the nonprofit tax-exempt idea with Manny and Tibor, and based on what we'd learned about the inherent unprofitability of magazines of ideas (*American Spectator*, *National Review*, *The New Republic*, *The Nation*, etc.), the idea of a nonprofit entity seemed like a good fit—especially since those who contributed to it could get a tax deduction for their contributions. We also learned that nonprofits were eligible for lower postal rates, which would be an additional advantage, considering how dependent the magazine was on using the mail. Moreover, since *Inquiry* was part of the nonprofit Cato Institute, it was already benefitting in those ways. We also learned that *Mother Jones* was published by a nonprofit called the Foundation for National Progress.

So while Manny, the attorney among the partners, was researching the details of incorporating and gaining both federal and state tax-exempt status, Tibor and I had the task of trying to find an angel investor to provide start-up capital for the new venture. Given Charles Koch's ongoing investments in *Inquiry* and *Libertarian Review*, he was not a good prospect. But we did not know any other multi-millionaires, let alone billionaires.

Charles was, of course, well aware of our predicament. I think he and Cato President Ed Crane would have been just as happy for *Reason* to close up shop as for us to find serious financial support. So I was not totally surprised in September 1977 by a call from Charles, offering me a job. They were about to create a Washington-based lobbying group tentatively called Business Leaders Against Subsidies and Tariffs (BLAST), and he asked if I'd like to be its director. I politely declined. The group subsequently materialized with a better name, the Council for a Competitive Economy.

In December, I wrote in my journal: "It's really getting interesting—the whole situation of *Reason* and the two Koch-backed magazines. They're having a lot of problems with [*Libertarian Review*] and are worried that *Reason* isn't going to roll over and die. So now we are getting all kinds of overtures about some kind of merger." But I had no intention of becoming dependent on one overwhelming source of funding who would likely want to call the shots, nor did I want to be under the supervision of Ed Crane, who'd already made numerous snide public comments about *Reason* and my "gradualist" approaches to policy change.

Fortunately, by that point we had identified a potential angel investor. *Reason*'s "Money" columnist, investment newsletter writer Mark Tier, had introduced us by mail to a man named Clyde Packer. Though Mark was based in Hong Kong, he was Australian, and had gotten to know Clyde as a member of a wealthy Australian family. Clyde's brother, Kerry Packer, was a multi-millionaire publisher and media mogul in Australia. Clyde, somewhat less well-heeled, lived in Los Angeles and published sports magazines. Mark assured us that Clyde's views were libertarian, so we asked him for a meeting to discuss *Reason*. Manny and I had our first meeting with Clyde in December 1977, at his LA home. He'd apparently read enough *Reason* issues to see the magazine's potential, and Manny and I made a positive impression. We therefore decided to explore the scope of a business relationship. He could see the logic of a nonprofit, tax-exempt entity, given the very modest advertising revenues of a think magazine compared with those of sports, car, and lifestyle magazines.

My post-meeting assignment was to write up a concept paper on the start-up nonprofit entity for Clyde to review. I got it to him a week later, and on December 24, 1977, he called me to say he liked it a lot and wanted to get going on further decisions. My next assignment was to develop financial projections for him to review. Tibor and Marty (then living in Fredonia, New York) arrived in Santa Barbara for a visit in mid-January, and we spent a whole day brainstorming the nonprofit transition. Marty, who'd been book review editor and copy editor for an hourly pittance, expressed great interest in becoming one of the new hires as managing editor. Tibor was willing to take a two-year leave of absence from his tenured philosophy teaching position at SUNY-Fredonia if this came about, so they could be in California.

The next week was our long-planned tenth anniversary of *Reason* banquet in Los Angeles. Nathaniel Branden was our dinner speaker, and attendees included John Hospers, Davis Keeler of the Institute for Humane Studies, and Clyde Packer and his wife, Kate. Photos of the banquet, including our only photo of Clyde, appeared in Reason's tenth anniversary issue (May 1978). I read congratulatory messages from luminaries including Robert Heinlein, Thomas Szasz, Murray Rothbard, Henry Manne, and even Ed Crane. Branden gave a warm speech, emphasizing how far *Reason* had come from its early days.

The next day, Tibor, Manny, and I spent many hours with Clyde, drawing up an association to form a nonprofit corporation, so that Manny could get working on all the legal paperwork needed to incorporate and apply for federal and state tax-exempt status. Over the next few months there were still many details to be thought through and negotiated. In the end, Clyde agreed to contribute $25,000 per year for two years and to give us a suite of office furniture. He would get a seat on the five-member board of Trustees—and of course, had the option of walking away if he fundamentally disagreed with something we were doing. Before we made the deal final, Manny developed some concerns about Clyde's libertarian bona-fides, but these were extinguished via a phone call to Mark Tier in Hong Kong. So the deal was closed.

Interestingly, up until the last minute the name was not going to be Reason Foundation. For some reason, we were worried that explicitly creating the nonprofit to run a magazine might not look legitimate to the IRS, so we (a) wanted a more innocuous name, and (b) wanted a description that included broader educational aims than just the magazine. So what became Reason Foundation nearly began life as the Pacific Cultural & Research Foundation! Only a last-minute coming to our senses about the name-recognition value of "Reason" led to it being launched as Reason Foundation.

Once we'd gotten past that hurdle, each of us partners began to think about what else the Foundation might do besides publishing *Reason*. Tibor was interested in philosophical papers and monographs, Manny aspired to *amicus* briefs in Supreme Court cases, and I thought about policy research like what my original idol RAND Corporation does and which the recently launched Cato Institute was starting to do. Those differing views would eventually lead to conflicts, but in spring 1978 we were mostly focused on getting launched.

The original plan was to set up Reason Foundation in Los Angeles, because it is a major media and corporate headquarters city—even though I was not that keen on moving to smog-land from idyllic Santa Barbara. So in between finishing up several consulting projects I'd committed to the previous year, keeping *Reason* coming out every month, and attending the Publishing Expo in Los Angeles to get better educated on the business of publishing, I also had to look for office space. As of mid-May, I wrote in my journal, "Two days of driving around in 90-degree heat didn't turn up much—but I found one place that would be OK if we can get it." It was a second-floor space above a karate studio at the corner of Pico and Sepulveda in West LA.

We had not yet signed a lease when a momentous election day occurred. On June 6, 1978, California voters passed Proposition 13, a major tax-cutting initiative measure that nearly all California libertarians had worked on. This was the biggest development in an ongoing "tax revolt" then taking place mostly in Western states. Within the next few days, Mark Frazier told me that NTU had decided to open a full-time West Coast office in California, to be staffed by young attorney Tim Condon (author of NTU's *1978 Income Tax Guide*). Mark had pitched Santa Barbara as a good central location for the office. He and I realized that our Local Government Center, with my "Cut Local Taxes" booklet in wide circulation and my *Cutting Back City Hall* book due out within a year or so, was likely to be in great demand. So the idea emerged of renting a suite of offices in Santa Barbara to be divided up among Reason Foundation, NTU, LGC, and Mark's newest venture, the Earthport project (see text box). I ran this idea past Clyde, Manny, and Tibor—and everyone was happy with it. (Clyde, who I hadn't known was thinking of moving to Santa Barbara himself, had originally assumed we'd start up Reason Foundation there.)

The Earthport Project

Mark Frazier got the idea for Earthport after visiting with Mike Oliver in 1976 about the New Country Project's unsuccessful efforts. He told me (in 2016) that his visit "left me admiring the audacity of the New Country venture—yet deeply skeptical that any such venture could succeed against the opposition of incumbent political forces." But what if the creation of a free society could be turned into a global prize that nations would compete to win?

Mark recalled previous discussions with Harvard classmate Paul Siegler about the potential of private space launch companies, and his noting that the ideal launch site for commercial space ventures would be on or near the equator, where the spin of the earth adds the most velocity in gaining orbit. So the prize opportunity would be to host the world's first commercial spaceport. It would have to be a tax-free zone of the scale of Hong Kong or Singapore, with lease revenues paying for infrastructure and services.

As a veteran of unsuccessful New Country attempts (Chapter 4), as well as a space commercialization fan, I was intrigued by Mark's idea, and signed on as the first member of the Earthport advisory board. I recommended that he get in touch with Alvin Rabushka at the Hoover Institution, who'd done excellent work on free-trade zones, and he became the second adviser. Mark then rounded up many other noted advisors and backers, including science fiction authors Robert Heinlein (via me) and Arthur C. Clarke, Larry Smarr of the Harvard Astrophysics Center, rocket scientist Krafft Ehricke, former NASA deputy administrator Ray Bisplinghoff, and others.

Mark's former Harvard tutor, Josiah Lee Auspitz, helped secure seed funding from the Sabre Foundation to enable production of an Earthport Project brochure, which Mark mailed out to the heads of state of forty countries on or near the equator. That generated a flurry of letters, telegrams, and phone calls, and the ambassadors of Liberia and Rwanda called about coming to visit the Earthport office. That occurred prior to the shared office-space arrangement with Reason Foundation; the only office then was in Mark's bedroom in Santa Barbara. Fortunately, thanks to doing some writing for *Reader's Digest* during 1976–79, Mark had travel money to fly to Washington to meet these people. Sabre board member Peter Wallison and Larry Smarr accompanied Mark on these meetings.

The country expressing the strongest interest was Liberia. Its government committed to creating a 200 sq. km. free zone near Port Harcourt, and introduced a

UN resolution blessing the creation of an international space freeport. But the US State Department had objections. In early 1979, its Dr. Irwin Pikus met with Mark in Washington to explain that State would not permit US aerospace firms to launch from an overseas spaceport, and would be prepared to use technology export controls to prevent such activities. The Liberian government was prepared to go ahead, regardless, but it was overthrown in a coup in 1980, in which the entire cabinet was murdered.

The idea was a sound one, but it was way ahead of its time. Mark shifted gears in 1980 and started a free-zone consulting firm, initially named Free Zone Authority Ltd., then Free Zone Authority Services, and later The Services Group that grew to $2 million in annual revenues between 1980 and 1995. Mark advised on over a hundred free-zone and teleport projects, including the first free zones exempted from national telecommunications monopolies. Among these were the Montego Bay Free Zone in Jamaica (1986), the San Isidro Free Zone in the Dominican Republic (1988), and the Montevideo Free Zone in Uruguay (1990).

In 2018, with US space launch policy now favoring commercialization, there are half a dozen commercial US spaceports, as well as several international ones, the best known of which is France's Guiana Space Center at Kourou, French Guiana, close to the equator.

So in a great flurry of activity, I cancelled the impending lease in Los Angeles and located second-floor office space in downtown Santa Barbara at 1129 State Street—with a nice restaurant on the ground floor, which was handy when we had out-of-town visitors. Given Clyde's initial two-year funding commitment, we signed a two-year lease. We got everything moved in and set up by July 4, my thirty-fourth birthday. What a great birthday gift! Starting out, the staff was three full-time (me as president, publisher, and editor-in-chief; Marty as managing editor; and an office manager) plus Tibor on an undefined part-time basis. Mark Frazier and Jim Bennett staffed the Earthport office; Mark also was the (unpaid) Local Government Center office person; and Tim Condon staffed the NTU desk (subsequently replaced by Bill Burt).

Tibor played a key role in early Reason Foundation funding prospects, because he had contacts with several grant-making foundations—Liberty Fund in particular. He began working on proposals for two-day academic seminars as well as summer research seminars in which a group of scholars would spend a summer in Santa Barbara pursuing individual research projects, with guest lectures every so often from a visiting scholar. Things like this have a long lead time, so nothing like that could take place during the Foundation's first six months, July–December 1978.

With promising future prospects but no immediate income, Tibor grew increasingly anxious. Marty was pregnant (I learned soon after the office opened), so they would soon have three mouths to feed on Marty's modest salary. His anxiety led him—without asking or telling me beforehand—to meet with Clyde to ask for money. Neither Clyde nor Tibor ever told me the specifics, but this unexpected behavior infuriated Clyde and he decided to walk, resigning from the board and reneging on his two-year financial pledge. Since he'd agreed to make it in four installments, all we had to show for it was the first $12,500.

Needless to say, recovering from that loss became my top priority. I signed up and took a two-day fundraising course at the University of Southern California, and while in LA I visited economist Tim Ozenne, whom I'd hired at PSSI some years before, and who was now chief economist at Getty Oil. He told me that Getty had a modest contributions budget, and arranged for what became our very first corporate contribution (I think it was $2,500, which seemed like big money at the time). I also heard out of the blue from Frank O'Connell at the John M. Olin Foundation in New York. He was a *Reason* reader and had read about the Reason Foundation's start-up, and asked if we might need a start-up grant. Yes, we did, and Frank became one of my early friends and mentors in the grant-making foundation world. We also sent out a year-end fundraiser to *Reason* subscribers, and that did pretty well, too. So we survived our first six months, despite being abandoned by our angel.

Revamping *Reason* Magazine

To be credible to our subscribers, whom we hoped to turn into donors, it was important to produce tangible improvements in *Reason* magazine. Part-time art director Don Wood had already made a noticeable improvement in the magazine's design and appearance starting in 1976. But the first change we made as Reason Foundation was to add color to the magazine's covers, beginning with the July 1978 issue. That was mostly one- or two-color, for budgetary reasons, but full four-color covers became standard a year later. This change alone made a tangible difference in *Reason*'s credibility, and helped position it for future bookstore and newsstand sales.

One of the magazine's biggest shortcomings—especially now that we had serious competition—was the pittance we paid to authors. For the most part, all through the Reason Enterprises years and the first year or so of the Reason Foundation era, we did not commission articles from authors. Instead, we editors mostly reviewed the fairly large number of articles that arrived "over the transom," weeded out the obvious rejects, and then circulated the remainder with a comment sheet attached. Once a month we'd have an article review meeting to select the ones that were good enough to be edited into publishable shape, and then the managing editor (formerly me, de-facto; Marty as of 1978) would plan which articles would go into which issue, on a schedule worked out several months in advance.

While we couldn't abandon that old system right away, a clear priority was to become more pro-active—by cultivating promising writers like John Blundell, Glenn Garvin, Tom Hazlett, Alan Reynolds, Peter Samuel, and a number of others; paying them more; and working with them to select worthwhile topics for articles and interesting people to interview. That gradually improved the quality of the magazine's content.

I had made it a practice to subscribe to and read many of the competing magazines, including *The Nation* and *Mother Jones* on the left as well as *The New Republic, Harper's, National Review,* and *American Spectator. Mother Jones* specialized in investigative journalism, which in those days appeared to be something done mostly by leftist media. When I read an alleged exposé by left-wing journalist Tad Szulc, published (of all places) in *Penthouse* (December 1977), I was intrigued—because he was writing about a topic I was already familiar with. An entrepreneurial German company, OTRAG, was developing a family of modular, low-cost space launch vehicles and using a large tract of leased land in Zaire for initial testing. Szulc sensationally claimed that these were really cruise missiles (i.e., weapons) and that this dangerous, secretive project needed to be exposed—and stopped.

As a long-time reader of *Aviation Week* and other aerospace media, I was already quite familiar with the company and its plans. That magazine, as well as *Popular Science*, had published detailed articles, as had several other publications, with no hint of OTRAG being anything but a fledgling space-launch company. So that winter, in the midst of the planning for Reason Foundation, I researched and wrote a detailed seven-page *Reason* article exposing Szulc's exposé for the disinformation that it was. I discovered that his basic thesis had been lifted from a Paris-based magazine that was a known source of propaganda from East Germany. I also discovered that there were already pressures coming from the French and German governments to push Zaire into cancelling the lease of OTRAG's test range. Why? Their real reason was to protect the launch-vehicle monopoly of the European Space Agency's forthcoming Ariane rocket. If OTRAG succeeded, its far lower launch costs would make Ariane uncompetitive.

My "Rockets in Africa" was the cover story of the July 1978 *Reason*, the first with color on the cover. It was the first example of investigative journalism that became a key feature in the magazine's growth and financial health in Reason Foundation's first decade. The article itself did not receive any media coverage that I can recall. But I like to think that it helped OTRAG survive, despite losing its lease in Zaire. Interestingly enough, in August 2016, as I was writing the first draft of this chapter, I received an email from a German documentary producer working on a film about OTRAG. He'd read my 1978 article and had a number of questions about how I'd debunked Szulc's piece. I was told the documentary would recognize OTRAG as a pioneer of what we today call the New Space industry—companies like Blue Origin and SpaceX that are using techniques such as modularity and re-usability to dramatically reduce launch costs.

Reason's first investigative piece that *did* make national news came to us out of the blue. A researcher named Patty Newman, who worked at World Research, Inc. (WRI, a free-market outfit near San Diego where Susan Love Brown also worked), came to us with a mountain of research on Cesar Chavez and his United Farm Workers union—a cause celeb for the Left in those days. She said she had the documentation to prove that the UFW was illegally using federal grants to build up the telecommunications infrastructure of the union. Her story sounded very credible, so we gave her the go-ahead to write it and agreed on a price (far beyond our usual pittance!). And when the story came in, Marty and I decided that we needed to fact-check everything in it, to make sure it was bulletproof. We had no desire to be sued and put out of business! So we arranged to spend a day at Patty's house, going through all her documentation in detail, and as I wrote in my journal, "nearly everything checked out."

We also decided that we needed professional assistance to make sure the article got noticed when it came out as the cover story of *Reason*'s November 1979 issue. One of my contacts in Washington recommended Donna Dudek, who ran her own small PR company, and she worked closely with us. The original plan for a DC press conference with Sen. William Proxmire—a fierce critic of waste and fraud in federal spending—was cancelled when Proxmire backed out at the eleventh hour. But our news release did get noticed. Syndicated columnist Nick Thimmesch featured the story, and Patty did a number of radio interviews. The biggest exposure was on NBC's weekly magazine show, *Prime Time Saturday*, which did a feature based on the article.

Thanks to her work at WRI, Patty knew the grant-making foundation community far better than we did. She suggested that I contact Dick Larry at the Scaife Foundation in Pittsburgh, to whom she had already sent the *Reason* issue with her article. I did so, and that led to me writing a proposal for them to fund a new *Reason* Investigative Journalism Fund. That effort paid off in May 1980 with a $46,000 grant, our biggest one ever at that point. Scaife became a reliable annual supporter, and I looked forward to my annual lunches with Dick Larry. Thanks to the IJF, we were able to commission articles on promising topics, as well as review proposals that came in from authors with an exposé in mind.

While we published several dozen IJF articles during those Santa Barbara years, some of which also made network television, the biggest blockbuster was "Love Canal: The Truth Seeps Out," the February 1981 cover story. Freelance writer Eric Zeusse came to us with the claim that the mainstream media story of what happened at the infamous canal was all wrong. It was not a story of a careless, irresponsible chemical company poisoning the neighborhood near its plant. Rather, it was a story of a school board that condemned land where toxic wastes had been buried in accord disposal practices that were current at the time. Despite Hooker Chemical having insisted on a deed restriction noting that hazardous wastes were buried there and stating that no structures for human occupancy should ever be built there, the school board excavated the land and built a school on it. The excavations inadvertently created channels by which the wastes leaked out into the neighborhood.

Like Patty Newman, Zeusse had done his homework, and his documentation passed our meticulous fact-checking. Donna Dudek again did the PR, and this time the author did numerous radio interviews (including Larry King), syndicated columnists wrote about the story, and *ABC Nightline* did a feature on the story, interviewing "Eric Zeusse, *Reason Magazine*" standing in front of Love Canal houses. More than any other single thing, the Investigative Journalism Fund put *Reason* on the map as a serious magazine, and led to a much-needed increase in both foundation and corporate contributions.

Another sensational IJF project was a six-part series by Jack Wheeler, the noted adventurer. He came to us with a proposal to do firsthand reporting on anti-Soviet guerilla movements in five countries (Afghanistan, Angola, Cambodia, Mozambique, and Nicaragua), plus an overview article on the significance of these movements. The travel costs alone would have been far above our normal IJF articles budget, but we did special fundraising to amass the money, and Jack made all five trips. One inspiration for the series was the book *Power Through Subversion*, by Laurence Beilenson, a friend of President Reagan from their days in the Screen Actors' Guild (Reagan as president, Beilenson as its attorney). I had met Beilenson at a Liberty Fund seminar, and liked this and his other books. My friend Dana Rohrabacher by this point was a White House speechwriter, and was very supportive of the project. The series got considerable publicity and led to Reason Foundation receiving a George Washington Medal from the Freedoms Foundation at Valley Forge in 1985. Jack Wheeler was the featured speaker at the awards dinner in Los Angeles.

During the years when I served as editor-in-chief, major articles reflected my emphasis on policy change. Among the topics featured in cover stories were the following:

- The FAA and its poor air-safety record (1979)
- FDA opposition to surgical uses of "human-body glue," as used successfully by the military during the Vietnam war (1980)
- Affordable encryption for everyone (1981)
- NASA versus space-launch entrepreneurs (1981 and 1985)
- The coming competition in cable TV (1982)
- Telephone deregulation and competition (1983)
- Competing fire departments (1983)
- Houston thriving without zoning (1983)
- Margaret Thatcher's privatization (1983 and 1986)
- School vouchers in Vermont (1984)
- The future of telecommuting (1984).

These articles all highlighted developments most readers were unaware of, and most were far ahead of their time.

Another cover story led to *Reason's* first-ever journalism award. "Two Utilities Are Better than One," by Jan Bellamy (October 1981) told the story of competing electric companies (typically one investor-owned, the other a municipal utility) in a number of localities, especially Lubbock, Texas. I'd discovered this phenomenon based on the work of economist Walter Primeaux, who'd done several journal articles on the subject, but it was virtually unknown outside of academia. Jan was doing some part-time work for us, and being from Texas, she was very interested in doing the story. We used IJF money to pay for her trip, but the article took some heavy editing to strike the right balance between theory and consumer interest. We entered it in the competition for the annual John Hancock Award for Excellence in Business and Financial Journalism—and it was declared the 1982 winner. In winning, we beat out articles submitted by *Atlantic Monthly*, *Harper's*, *Mother Jones*, and *Washington Monthly*, among others.

As part of relaunching *Reason* under the Foundation's auspices, we strove deliberately to "de-movementize" its content. In addition to interviews with market-friendly notables such as Henry Hazlitt, Charles Murray, William Simon, and Thomas Sowell, we broadened the scope of interview subjects to include interesting people who were not libertarians—William Buckley, Irving Kristol, former CIA veteran Victor Marchetti, a reformed Eldridge Cleaver, and others.

The most controversial change we made to the magazine was removing the monthly "Frontlines" column. Written by various people during the Reason Enterprises years, the column was where the magazine had reported on interesting people and events within the self-defined libertarian community, including the Libertarian Party. Instead of just dropping the column, we decided to spin off a newsletter available to those subscribers really interested in that kind of information, as a separate subscription. This would enable us to keep our core libertarian readership happy while not turning off newcomers who were the key to large growth in *Reason* circulation.

In hindsight, starting the newsletter was a mistake. Though we kept the costs low by not typesetting *Frontlines* and by using an inexpensive printer, the market was a lot smaller than we'd expected. Of course, producing what became an eight-page newsletter every month took staff time away from the magazine itself, which was already seriously understaffed. And the publication was controversial by design.

We sought to cover the ins and outs of the growing libertarian movement, warts and all, rather than producing a bland house organ. The very first issue, September 1978, set the mold. The cover story reported on controversial resolutions approved by the Libertarian Party's National Committee earlier that year. Both resolutions were drafted by Murray Rothbard and expressed his hard-core, abolitionist perspective (as a kind of libertarian Leninist). Very little debate on them had been published in the *LP News*, so we thought a wider discussion was warranted.

But the biggest reaction to the initial *Frontlines* issue was about an opinion column by Tim Condon, our NTU office mate. Tim had attended a Cato Institute event that summer—and had come away appalled. His opening line was "to step into the Cato Institute's recently completed Summer Seminar in Political Economy is to immerse oneself in the most authoritarian libertarian atmosphere imaginable." It was not only little things like the outside dorm doors being kept locked and photo ID badges being required at all times. It was also the content being provided. Condon wrote that the event was "suffused throughout with constant, harping attacks on any and all libertarians who might dare to differ from the Rothbard/Koch monolith in policy, tactics, or strategy." Not to mention cheap shots like this quote from Rothbard: "The Jeffersonians were against slavery in theory, but kind of like *Reason* magazine—they believed that slavery could only be eliminated gradually. . . . So what you get is abolition in theory and no change in reality." I knew the piece would be controversial, but it represented an honest reaction to what Tim experienced. Not being happy about what sounded more like indoctrination than discussion, and annoyed by the cheap shots at *Reason*, I went ahead and included it.

Needless to say, there were repercussions. At the LP national convention in Boston that fall, I was raked over the coals by Ed Crane and Roy Childs. In addition, Manny and I were summoned to a private meeting with Charles Koch in his hotel room in which he expressed his great displeasure—and we kind of apologized, given that we still hoped Charles would back our struggling start-up.

We were somewhat more cautious about *Frontlines'* content in subsequent issues. But as factions and alliances changed (e.g., Rothbard was fired from Cato in March 1981), *Frontlines* was looked to by former opponents as their only outlet for dissent from what became known as the "Crane Machine" within the Libertarian Party. We kept the newsletter going until May 1983, when we finally concluded that both the direct costs and the opportunity costs could not really be justified.

In further revamping of *Reason*, we made periodic changes to the roster of regular columnists in the back of the book. One fairly longstanding columnist was Murray Rothbard, who became, after his ouster from Cato, a new fan of *Reason* (at least for a few years). While always entertaining, some columns were quite controversial, such as his "The Death of a State" in June 1979, celebrating the ouster of the Shah of Iran and thereby foolishly welcoming the even-worse Khomeini regime. But the last straw for me was a column he submitted toward the end of 1983. It lauded the murder of an IRS agent by a tax protester somewhere in the rural West. I told Murray it was unacceptable, and in response, he quit.

Another well-liked but controversial column was called "Health & Welfare," written by libertarian scientists Durk Pearson and Sandy Shaw, authors of the bestselling book, *Life Extension: A Practical Scientific Approach.* They offered health and longevity ideas based on current research findings every month from March 1981 through August 1983. We got letters from several physicians attacking their writings as pseudo-science, but my reading was that they were well grounded in research, so I stood my ground. And I still take "One-Per-Meal Radical Shield" vitamin and mineral supplements formulated decades ago by Durk and Sandy (along with many other supplements).

Building *Reason's* circulation was my number one goal during those years, aside from raising enough money to keep the doors open and the Foundation growing. With a larger budget each year, thanks to increasing support from individuals, foundations, and corporations, we were able to do larger mailings to rented lists of potential subscribers. The numbers climbed pretty steadily. In our quarterly donor newsletter, *Reason Report*, we noted that *Reason* had reached 17,000 by mid-1979, and 22,500 by mid-1981; the new high by 1985 was 38,000. Most of that was due to successful direct mail. But some of it was due to the demise of other libertarian magazines.

Both of the Koch-supported magazines, *Inquiry* and *Libertarian Review*, ceased publishing during the early 1980s, and they made deals with us to take on their subscription liability. In other words, instead of spending a small fortune to rent lists and net five hundred or a thousand new subscribers, we agreed to take on all the subscribers of the defunct magazine and send them *Reason* for the remaining issues that they had paid for (as we'd done when *The Individualist* had folded several years earlier). The net acquisition cost to us was zero, and we had only the same subscription fulfillment costs as if we'd spent a lot of money to acquire all those people via direct mail. I must admit it was satisfying that we amateurs with scraped-together funding learned how to succeed at publishing a think magazine while our much better-funded competitors failed.

The larger circulation also made *Reason* a somewhat better market for advertisers, and the subscription list a better proposition for those who rent mailing lists. By 1981, we were able to go from a part-time to a full-time advertising manager. And being able to include four-color printing on selected inside pages opened the door to more four-color expensive ads. Both ad revenue and list rental revenue grew to non-trivial portions of the magazine's budget by the mid-1980s.

Building the Foundation's Infrastructure

A real challenge during those early years was figuring out which missing capabilities we could afford to add when. Our first full-time addition, in 1979, was a journalism intern, Christine Dorffi. We'd applied to a New York-based grant-making foundation called the Institute for Economic Affairs, which was receptive to proposals for such interns. The $10,500 grant made it possible to hire Christine (who had written previously for *Reason*), which was a big boost for the magazine's content production. By the end of our second fiscal year (1980), we'd also added a bookkeeper, a part-time advertising director, and part-time art director, Nannette Boyer (since Don Wood had moved on to other things). So our staff had increased to five full-time and two part-time.

What we really needed instead of a part-time bookkeeper was a full-time business manager, and by the end of 1980, our budget looked as if it could sustain that. We recruited Madelyn Romaszewski from Save the Children Federation headquarters in Connecticut, and she came on board early in 1981. Though her primary function had been direct-mail fundraising, she also understood accounting and business management basics, and was an excellent addition. In early 1981, we moved to larger quarters several blocks from State Street, at 1018 Garden Street. That year also saw the advertising director position increased to full time, and full-time art director Matt Burbott replaced part-time Nannette. That gave us a staff of seven. By 1985, we were up to thirteen full-time and two part-time staff.

"Business manager" proved to be a high-stress position for all who held it during those years. After successfully implementing Reason Foundation's first desktop computer (a VectorGraphics 3005, with a five-megabyte hard drive) in 1982, Madelyn returned from a spring 1983 vacation in Connecticut to announce that she had gotten engaged to her boyfriend, and would be moving back later that year to get married. So my immediate priority was to recruit a new business manager, hopefully someone with greater staying power.

We advertised the position, and the most promising resume came from John Northrup, a libertarian accountant and tax advisor in Syracuse, New York. I interviewed him at my hotel in New York City in May, and he seemed like an excellent fit. After dinner, he asked me if I'd like to accompany him to an event being held at Laissez-Faire Books down in the Village. I agreed, and there I was in for a surprise. As we walked into a crowded room, someone John knew walked up to us and asked, "Is this your new lover?" Turns out John was gay. That was fine with me, but as far as I could recall, he was the first gay person I'd ever met (naïve, sheltered me!). He started work July 1, 1983, and was an excellent business manager.

By the end of his first year, John had been promoted to controller and vice president for development. But a month later, in August 1984, he was recruited away by Northeastern University's Graduate School of Professional Accounting. Our next business manager lasted barely a year, and left under something of a cloud, with the audit just getting underway that found a number of problems. After getting through the audit with the help of a retired accountant, we finally hired a new business manager late in 1985—a computer and business guy named P. K. Lowrey from eastern Tennessee. He got things under control and made a positive impression with our board at the January 1986 meeting.

One very important development in my life took place during these years. Early in 1981, at a meeting of Santa Barbara's Libertarian Supper Club, my friend "Jungle David" Sutton introduced me to Lou Villadsen, whom he'd been dating casually. She was a *Reason* reader, recently divorced (amicably), and a graduate of UC Santa Barbara. Since my own divorce in 1974, I'd been dating various libertarian women, learning a lot about myself, women, and relationships—things most people probably learn via dating in high school and college. She was pretty, obviously bright, shared my somewhat weird sense of humor, and for some reason was interested in me. At a subsequent libertarian meeting, she passed me a note asking how to get in touch with some libertarian group, which led to a phone call in which we agreed to a first date. That event had to wait for my February rail-fan trip to Cuba (which led to my October 1981 *Reason* article, "Inside Cuba Today"). Our first date began an increasingly serious relationship. After a year and a half of dating, in December 1982 we decided to get married the following spring.

Lou had earned an MBA with a dual concentration in accounting and nonprofit administration, and during those years she was director of administration at Planned Parenthood of Santa Barbara. As such, she knew a lot more than I did about nonprofit management. She was shocked to learn that we were not yet (in early 1981) using double-entry bookkeeping. She was also dismayed to learn that our board consisted mostly of friends and academics, not heavy-hitter business leaders and other wealthy people, like most non-profit boards, including hers at Planned Parenthood. So in addition to becoming the love of my life, Lou became an advisor and coach on improving Reason Foundation's infrastructure.

The evolution of the Foundation's board of trustees is a good example. During our first two years, the five-member board (after Clyde Packer's early departure) consisted of founders Bob, Manny, and Tibor plus local (Santa Barbara City College) philosophy teacher Jim Chesher and UC Santa Barbara economics professor M. Bruce Johnson. In 1981, we added three new members: Joe Coberly (a prosperous automobile dealer in Southern California who was on the board of the Council for a Competitive Economy), Norm Karlin (law professor at Southwestern University), and Bill Niskanen (former chief economist at Ford Motor Company—who soon went on leave to serve as a member of President Reagan's Council of Economic Advisers).

In 1983, Bruce Johnson left the board and David Koch joined it. How the latter came about is worth recounting. In 1979, the campaign led by Ed Crane to run Ed Clark as the LP's 1980 presidential candidate was hard-fought, with the anti-Crane faction backing a New Hampshire businessman, Bill Hunscher. But Crane came up with a brilliant plan to ensure that a Clark campaign would have unprecedented funding. He and Charles Koch persuaded Charles's younger brother, David, also a libertarian, to take the vice presidential slot on the ticket. Candidates themselves can legally spend unlimited money on their campaigns—and this factor very likely pushed the Clark/Koch ticket to victory at the September 1979 nominating convention.

Despite my having sympathized with the anti-Crane faction, I agreed to be part of a "program review committee" of respected libertarians, whose purpose was to vet campaign materials and assure that they did not soft-pedal libertarian ideas. After the convention I started thinking about how challenging it would be for David Koch to face tough questions from reporters about the vast array of policy issues that might be thrown at him. Despite his general libertarian views, I surmised that as a senior executive of Koch Industries, many of these would be topics he'd neither researched nor thought through. So I sent him a letter introducing myself and Reason Foundation, offering to be an informal advisor on any and all issues where he might need getting up to speed on libertarian arguments and supporting information.

He sent me an invitation to meet with him at his apartment on Central Park South in New York, late in November 1979. I'd expected to spend an hour, but we ended up talking for three and a half hours. And subsequently he did make occasional requests for background information on issues during the nearly year-long campaign in 1980. The Clark/Koch ticket set a new record for LP presidential campaigns, getting about 1 percent of the vote, which probably would have been much higher had it not been for John Anderson running as an independent and siphoning off 6.6 percent of the non-Reagan/non-Carter vote.

David stayed somewhat involved with the LP for several years. The first time he heard me give a presentation was at a California LP convention in early 1981. I gave a talk on municipal privatization, based on my recently published *Cutting Back City Hall*, and it made a positive impression on him. We kept in touch, and in April 1982 he gave us a grant of $50,000, plus the services of a Koch Industries accountant to get a proper accounting system set up. The next year we invited him to join the board of trustees. Not only did he accept, but he regularly flew out to California for board meetings, playing an active role.

The following year we further beefed up the board. We bade goodbye to Jim Chesher, leaving us with just one academic slot (Karlin) and added Burton Gray and Bob Smiley. Burton was part of a wealthy North Carolina family who basically invested in start-up companies. He was friends with Tibor and Marty, and I'd gotten to know him over the previous four years or so.

Having nurtured start-up companies, he became something of a mentor to me as problems and setbacks occurred during our Santa Barbara years. Bob Smiley was a libertarian whom Jim Weigl had known in graduate school at Stanford University in the late 1960s. He was one of the pioneers in employee stock ownership plans (ESOPs) via his firm, Benefit Capital, and had many contacts in entrepreneurial companies. Finally, we were getting a board whose members could make significant gifts and who knew other people who might be persuaded to do likewise.

The more business-oriented board was increasingly helpful in the mid-1980s, but prior to that nearly all the fundraising was my responsibility. I wrote the annual (and later several times a year) fundraising letters to *Reason* subscribers, and I made numerous trips to cities where there were concentrations of current and potential donors—especially New York, Pittsburgh, and Los Angeles in the early years, and later Chicago, Detroit, Houston, San Francisco, and Washington, DC. Many of these trips were all-week affairs, and at least one, in 1981, spanned ten days and multiple cities. In addition, we drew on libertarian contacts in Santa Barbara, Orange County, San Diego, and the San Francisco Bay Area for leads and introductions to potential California donors.

Our first annual report listed four foundation donors: the Earhart Foundation, the Fred C. Koch Foundation, Liberty Fund, and the John M. Olin Foundation. There were just three corporate contributors: Allegheny-Ludlum, Getty Oil, and Pfizer. Individual contributions totaled a bit over $23,000, and included first gifts from very long-time donors Paul F. Glenn in Santa Barbara and Carol Sanders in San Diego. The second year was much better, with seven foundation gifts (including Scaife) and eleven corporate contributions including the Ford Motor Company Fund (thanks to Bill Niskanen). Those numbers kept growing year by year, reaching twenty-three foundations and twenty-eight corporations in 1985. Total revenue in 1985 was $1.5 million, compared with just $193,000 in our start-up year. It was gratifying to me that for our first three years, despite some differences with Charles Koch (e.g., over *Frontlines*), the Fred C. Koch Foundation provided modest grants each year. When David started giving larger sums, he became our primary Koch contact.

In 1983, I came up with the idea of a giving club for large individual donors—the National Advisory Council. The minimum for membership would be $10,000 a year. We decided to hold an annual event for the NAC members, with a program showcasing our best work for the current year and one or two outside speakers. It was successful enough that we decided on a junior-level group called Regional Advisory Councils, to be launched in any city where we had at least one enthusiastic $2,500 a year (or more) donor willing to try recruiting others giving at least $1,000 a year. We promised each group at least one visit per year from me, to keynote an event to which they could invite current and prospective members. Once the RAC program was up and running, the leader of each group would also be invited to the annual NAC meeting.

The first combined meeting of NAC members and RAC chairs took place in Santa Barbara in October 1984. Council of Economic Advisers member Bill Niskanen presented a behind-the-scenes look at the battle of ideas within the Reagan administration. And the closing dinner heard a presentation from Bob Chitester, producer of the 1980 PBS series "Free to Choose," hosted by Milton and Rose Friedman. For many, the highlight of the weekend was a visit to an oil platform in the Santa Barbara Channel. I'd arranged this via former LP presidential candidate Ed Clark, who was a senior attorney at ARCO in Los Angeles. They provided helicopter transport for those of us who opted for this excursion, instead of a local winery tour. David Koch, of course, chose the oil platform trip. Those giving us the guided tour of the platform had no idea who he was, but were amazed at all the technical questions he asked.

In May 1983, we celebrated *Reason*'s fifteenth anniversary with a special anniversary issue of the magazine and a gala banquet in Los Angeles. We did not have an event planner on our staff, needless to say, so Lou (with her Planned Parenthood experience) volunteered as banquet coordinator and put in countless hours coordinating with the Beverly Hilton Hotel and various suppliers (flowers, wine, etc.,), with some input from Manny, especially on the wines. She did all this during the same time period when she and I were planning our May 28 wedding party and subsequent honeymoon in Jamaica, so this was a very hectic time for both of us. In my journal I noted that the night before the banquet, we were at the office until 12:15 a.m. finalizing the seating chart.

The event was a big success, with 220 people (compared with twenty-four at the tenth anniversary five years before). The emcee was John McCarty, a libertarian VP of Adolph Coors Co., and the featured speakers were Rep. Ron Paul (R-Texas) and economist Walter Williams, both of whom were real crowd-pleasers. A head table of other notables offered their congratulations on Reason Foundation's accomplishments, including authors Bob LeFevre and Robert Ringer, board member Bill Niskanen, and economist Art Laffer. Tibor, Manny, and I each made brief remarks, and Marty wrapped up the evening by presenting me with a framed cover of *Reason* with my photo on it and a banner declaring me "Man of the Year."

That fall we presented the board with an ambitious five-year plan for Reason Foundation's second five years. The plan had five specific goals:

1. Build *Reason's* circulation into the same range as *National Review* and *The New Republic* (which we put at one hundred thousand);
2. Put the Local Government Center on a full-time basis as a national center of expertise on privatization;
3. Develop an extensive public policy program with a full-time director, doing books, conferences, and weekend seminars;
4. Strengthen the academic program, with a full-time director and several conferences per year; and,
5. Put the Foundation on a stronger financial footing by expanding the donor base and developing an operating reserve fund.

How most of this turned out is the topic of subsequent chapters.

Meanwhile, at the October 21 board meeting, a long discussion of an impending budget shortfall led to David Koch proposing—seemingly out of the blue—that the Foundation merge with the Kochs' new Citizens for a Sound Economy (successor to the Council for a Competitive Economy) and move to Washington, DC. He wanted me to drop everything and fly to DC the next week to meet with Richie Fink (CSE's incoming executive director) to talk over this proposal. After the meeting and David's departure, Tibor, Marty, Lou, Burton Gray, and I had dinner to discuss what to do. Since CSE would be doing lobbying, it seemed very inconsistent with the idea of *Reason* as an independent think magazine; it would come across as a house organ of CSE instead. So we brainstormed ideas on how to derail the proposal.

My meeting with Richie was delayed by the sudden heart-attack death of my father back east. After my return, Richie agreed to come out to Santa Barbara to discuss what to do. We had a very candid discussion, and agreed that the magazine and CSE were so different in purpose and modus operandi that merging them into one organization did not really make sense. He also visited with Manny in Los Angeles. Richie and I agreed on a joint visit to David to explain our case against the merger and the move, while also being open to ways in which our two organizations could cooperate, on a case-by-case basis. I have no recollection of that meeting ever taking place, so Richie probably had a long talk with David and persuaded him that it was not a good idea. Still, I was very worried that David might resign from the board because we'd rejected his idea (but he did not).

Fortunately, we ended 1984 in the black, thanks to several higher-than expected year-end grants. We presented a conservative and well-supported 1985 budget to the board at the January 1985 meeting. We'd spent weeks on the budget and on planning the meeting agenda, and Burton had visited with us the day before, suggesting a somewhat revised agenda. To my great relief, the meeting went very smoothly, and David was pleased. And to top it off, as I wrote in my journal: "After it was over, Koch turned to me and said, 'If you ever get tired of doing this, we'd have a place for you in Koch Industries.'" I walked out of that meeting on a cloud.

But the discussion about a possible move to Washington triggered some serious board and staff thinking and discussion over the subsequent year: Was Santa Barbara really the best place to grow a national think tank that we hoped would be increasingly effective in changing minds and changing policy?

Actually, my first thought we might need to move had occurred earlier. In mid-1982 Lou got a job offer from the Exploratorium, a very interesting museum in San Francisco. She agonized over whether or not to accept it, which would mean trying to keep our relationship going long-distance. She pointed out that her future job options were very limited in Santa Barbara, and asked if I would ever consider moving Reason to a larger city. That made me think seriously about the limitations of Santa Barbara as a place to build a real national think tank. She and I agreed that she would turn down the job offer and that we would start researching possible future locations for the Foundation.

I raised the possibility at a management meeting that October (1984), with neither Marty nor Madelyn being keen on the idea. I also put the topic on the November board meeting agenda, and the board agreed that for the longer term, we should probably be in a major metro area. Several places Lou and I had talked about that seemed to offer a nice quality of life—Phoenix and San Diego—were dismissed as not being large enough. Since we all saw benefits in remaining a think tank based in California (which still had a reputation in the 1980s as a place where new ideas came from), that basically left us with Los Angeles or San Francisco.

With several of our board members living in Southern California, the focus pretty much shifted to Los Angeles. Lou and I spent several weekends scouting out possible residential areas in LA, and I studied smog maps, concluding that we would want both homes and the office to be relatively near the coast rather than inland where the smog was far worse. By June 1985, Marty was convinced that LA made the most sense as our future location and began researching private school possibilities for her young daughter, Kate. The initial idea was that we would seek to buy a small office building, but the board considered that too risky, given our still-modest size. I noted in my journal that at the May 1985 board meeting, the board was now happy with the planned 1986 move, to leased office space probably in West Los Angeles.

There was still some staff anxiety, so Trustee Norm Karlin conducted an LA orientation tour for senior staff. We also arranged a summer outing to the Hollywood Bowl for a picnic and concert, hoping that would get people more familiar with the amenities that LA had to offer. That fall Lou began LA job-hunting, and soon had an excellent offer from the Chancellor's Office at UCLA. Unfortunately, they wanted her to begin in January, and the Reason Foundation move was not scheduled until late June. But it was too good an offer to turn down, so we agreed to six months of a commuter marriage, seeing each other only on weekends.

We'll return to the move to Los Angeles and its consequences in Chapter 8. Chapter 7 explains how the young Reason Foundation developed its original research program during the Santa Barbara years.

Chapter 7

Developing an Initial Research Program
(1978–1986)

What Kind of Research?

As described in Chapter 6, we launched Reason Foundation primarily to create a more viable framework to build *Reason* magazine into a serious national publication. But from the outset, we realized that as a nonprofit think tank, we had opportunities to carry out (and seek grant funding for) a large array of possible research efforts to advance the cause of liberty and limited government.

Initially, there was no overall plan for a research program. Tibor, as a newly minted PhD philosopher, wanted to promote scholarly research on the underlying principles of a free society. In my case, writing a book on privatization of municipal services led me to see books on public policy as a sensible research agenda. The idea of producing stand-alone policy studies did not occur to me until some years later, after being commissioned by other organizations to write studies for them.

An adjunct to what became the research program was expanded outreach efforts on policy issues: conferences and seminars, radio commentaries, and a television documentary. This chapter describes the evolution of these efforts during the Santa Barbara years.

Academic Conferences and Seminars

When we began, Tibor had the best knowledge of and contacts with grant-making foundations that were supportive of center/right nonprofit organizations. One of these is Liberty Fund, which does not make grants, per se, but carries out programs proposed and organized by academics and research institutes.

In our first several years, Tibor was very successful in proposing events that appealed to Liberty Fund.

The largest of these were Summer Research Seminars in Political Philosophy held in Santa Barbara, in the summers of 1979, 1980, and 1981. The format was similar in each of the three years. Fifteen or more academics were selected to spend their summer in residence in Santa Barbara, giving them each concentrated time to work on a research/writing project. In addition, each week a distinguished visiting scholar would give a seminar on a relevant topic in political philosophy. Among the first year's visiting scholars were John Hospers, Nicolas Capaldi, Charles King, and Murray Rothbard.

Here are a few of the projects worked on by the seventeen participants in the 1979 summer seminar.

- Douglas Den Uyl and Douglas Rasmussen completed work on their edited volume *Freedom and Reason: Essays on the Thought of Ayn Rand.*
- Allan Buchanan finished the draft of a ninety-five-page monograph on Marx and Rawls.
- Randall Dipert produced a draft paper on immigration policy, "The Ethical Basis of Immigration Restriction," for submission to a journal.
- Bruce Bell wrote a paper on the burden of proof as applied to FDA drug regulation.

In addition to selecting the participants and the visiting scholars, it was up to Tibor to lease office space for the seminar and make rental housing arrangements for the participants. He also came up with the idea for an all-day, mid-summer excursion each year—a trip to one of the islands in the Santa Barbara Channel on a motorized sailing ship, the *Swift of Ipswich* (owned by the Sierra Club). As president, I got to go along, and these were wonderful, relaxed events allowing for lots of personal interactions.

Between 1979 and 1983, we also hosted six Liberty Fund colloquia or symposiums. In each case, Tibor (sometimes along with another scholar) came up with a theme, identified a set of knowledgeable participants (presenters and discussants), developed a budget, and submitted the proposal to Liberty Fund. The ones that were funded and carried out included an interesting and diverse set of scholars (see the below text box).

Tibor's Liberty Fund Seminars

<u>Government Regulation, Individual Liberty, and Justice</u> (co-sponsored by the UC Santa Barbara Economics Department), November 1979

- Steven Kelman, Kennedy School of Government, Harvard University
- Yale Brozen, School of Business, University of Chicago
- Leland Yeager, Department of Economics, University of Virginia
- Karl Brunner, Graduate School of Management, University of Rochester
- Nicholas Rescher, Editor, *American Philosophical Quarterly*
- M. Bruce Johnson, Department of Economics, UC Santa Barbara
- And others

<u>Virtue and Political Liberty</u>, April 1980
- Gilbert Harman, Princeton University
- George Mavrodes, University of Michigan
- Paul Kurtz, SUNY Buffalo
- David L. Norton, University of Delaware
- Douglas Den Uyl, Marquette University
- And others

(continued)

<u>Extension of Property Rights to Uncharted Areas</u>, November 1980
- Eric Mack, Tulane University
- Norman Karlin, Southwestern University
- Ross Eckert, Claremont Men's College
- Robert Bish, University of Victoria
- Richard Stroup, Montana State University
- Joseph Martino, University of Dayton
- Robert Poole, Reason Foundation
- And others

<u>The Justification of Property Rights</u>, May 1981
- David Friedman, UCLA
- John Goodman, University of Dallas
- Israel Kirzner, New York University
- Robert Nozick, Harvard University
- Loren Lomasky, University of Minnesota
- Manuel S. Klausner, Reason Foundation
- Paul Heyne, University of Washington
- And others

<u>Natural Law vs. Positive Law</u>, April 1982
- Herbert Morris, UCLA
- J. Roger Lee, Virginia Polytechnic Institute
- Kent Greenawalt, Columbia University
- Henry Veatch, Georgetown University
- Ernest van den Haag, Fordham University
- Joseph Cropsey, University of Chicago
- Wallace Matson, UC Berkeley
- And others

The Welfare State and Individual Responsibility, March 1983
- William Allen, Harvey Mudd College
- J. Roger Lee, California State University, Los Angeles
- Robert Bish, University of Victoria
- Thomas Morawetz, University of Connecticut
- Jack D. Douglas, UC San Diego
- Robert Poole, Reason Foundation
- And others

The March 1983 seminar was the last of Tibor's Reason Foundation/Liberty Fund events. Nothing was ever said to me, either by Tibor or by Liberty Fund, about why they ceased, but I recall with some dismay that at the closing session of the 1983 event, Tibor and one of the other participants got into a shouting match, which embarrassed everyone else, so that might have been a factor. The Winter 1983/84 *Reason Report* announced plans for a follow-up to the 1982 Liberty Fund seminar on natural law vs. positive law, but there is no report of that taking place the following spring. Over the next decade or so, I was invited to a number of Liberty Fund seminars or colloquia hosted by other organizations, and later on Lynn Scarlett was invited to others, so the end of Tibor's events does not seem to have been due to a philosophical or policy difference with Reason Foundation.

I got a lot out of the Liberty Fund seminars I took part in, including one that included free-market economist Vaclav Klaus from then communist Czechoslovakia. We had no idea that within a decade, communism in Eastern Europe would be overthrown, and that Klaus would eventually become president of the Czech Republic and preside over a Mont Pelerin Society meeting in Prague in 2012.

But my favorite Liberty Fund story involves a seminar held at its Indianapolis headquarters in around 1983. Liberty Fund has strict rules about decorum and being present and involved in all sessions. So everyone was surprised that in the middle of a morning session, a secretary interrupted to say that Mr. Poole had a call from the White House. I was excused to leave the room to take the call. It was from White House speechwriter Dana Rohrabacher. He'd just received our 1983 annual report and was calling me to find out more about the pretty new art director whose photo was included in the report. Needless to say, I said nothing to anyone about the nature of the call.

For a number of years we also published the small academic journal Tibor had launched several years prior to Reason Foundation. *Reason Papers* was an annual interdisciplinary journal focused on normative issues. Issues 1 through 4 were published by the department of Philosophy at SUNY Fredonia, from which Tibor took a leave of absence when the Foundation started up. It continued to receive support from the Koch Foundation and Burton Gray when it became a publication of Reason Foundation. (*Reason Papers* continues to exist, as an online journal, based at Marymount Manhattan College, with no connection to Reason Foundation.)

Over the years, both during and after his affiliation with Reason, Tibor wrote and edited numerous books and hundreds of articles. One of these books, *Rights and Regulation: Ethical, Political, and Economic Issues*, based on the presentations at the 1979 Liberty Fund seminar, was edited by Tibor and Bruce Johnson and was published by Ballinger in 1984.

Books on Public Policy

From the outset, I wanted the main focus of our research program to be public policy, and at that time, I saw quasi-academic books as the primary vehicle. By quasi-academic I mean well-researched and well-written books with necessary citations, but written in a manner that non-specialists, such as legislative staffers and journalists, could readily understand.

Before we began planning to launch Reason Foundation, I had come up with the idea for such a book: solid critiques of perhaps a dozen federal regulatory agencies, in each case setting forth a plausible alternative way of addressing the problem(s) the agency was intended to deal with. I wrote up a proposal in 1977 and sent it to the new Cato Institute requesting grant support. Rather than funding the whole project, the folks at Cato gave me a modest grant to research and write a sample chapter, so they could make a better assessment of the overall project idea.

I chose the Federal Aviation Administration (FAA), since I had some prior knowledge of that agency dating back to the research for my 1969 *Reason* article, "Fly the Frenzied Skies." During my years working at PSSI, I learned that two of my colleagues there had previously worked for a nonprofit company called Aeronautical Radio, Inc. (ARINC). They told me that it was ARINC, back in the late 1920s or early 1930s that had started the air traffic control (ATC) system in this country, later taken over by the Department of Commerce and subsequently to become the largest part of the FAA. Mike Levine, then teaching at Cal Tech, had written a *Reason* article on airport runway pricing in 1973, so I asked him what he knew about this. In a visit with him in May 1977, he confirmed the ARINC story and told me that the company had remained in business developing airborne electronic and communications equipment for airlines—and had also set up nonprofit ATC corporations for Cuba and Mexico after World War II. (Mike had a private pilot's license and had flown back and forth between Los Angeles and Mexico.)

That fall I made a week-long research trip to Washington, DC, including a day at the library of the Smithsonian Air and Space Museum, getting deeper into the history of what became the FAA. I also arranged to visit ARINC, in Annapolis, Maryland, where they gave me access to their archives and let me copy various documents confirming the private-sector origins of US air traffic control. The idea of reviving the nonprofit corporation idea seemed obvious to me, and that became a major focus of the chapter. I also researched aviation insurance as a possible alternative to direct FAA air-safety regulation, drawing on what I had learned about the role played by the fire insurance industry in developing rating standards for residential, commercial, and industrial properties.

I had several people review the chapter before sending it to Cato, so I was satisfied that it made a credible case. But Cato decided not to proceed with the proposed book, relinquishing to me the rights to the FAA paper. Once Reason Foundation was up and running, I realized that I could not possibly find the time to research and write another ten chapters. Instead, I decided to look for market-friendly academics familiar with various economic and safety regulatory agencies, and sounded each of them out about writing not merely a critique of said agency but also a thoughtful proposal for an alternative way of dealing with its area of focus. Once I had a critical mass of chapter authors, I wrote a grant proposal to the Earhart Foundation, which responded positively, and we also raised modest corporate support. All but one of the committed authors came through with their chapters, which were submitted to outside review prior to final editing by Marty Zupan and Lynn Scarlett.

The final composition of the chapters was diverse.

1. How Airline Deregulation (CAB) Happened, Stephen G. Breyer and Leonard R. Stein
2. Interstate Commerce Commission, George W. Hilton
3. Department of Energy, Alan Reynolds
4. Federal Communications Commission, Ida Walters
5. Federal Trade Commission, Kenneth Clarkson and Timothy Muris
6. Securities and Exchange Commission, George J. Benston
7. Federal Aviation Administration, Robert W. Poole, Jr.
8. Food and Drug Administration, David Leo Weimer
9. Consumer Product Safety Commission, Roger E. Meiners
10. Occupational Safety and Health Administration, Robert W. Smith
11. Environmental Protection Agency, Peter H. Aranson

Lexington Books agreed to publish *Instead of Regulation: Alternatives to Federal Regulatory Agencies,* and it came out in fall 1981. We managed to get strong endorsement quotes from an array of notables, including Milton Friedman, Art Laffer, former Treasury secretary William Simon, and Reagan White House policy advisor Martin Anderson. On October 21, three of the chapter authors and I gave a congressional staff briefing on the book in the Russell Senate Office Building. Chris DeMuth, then the deregulation czar at the Office of Management and Budget, hosted a reception in the Old Executive Office Building, which various Reagan administration notables attended. I did several radio and TV talk shows while in town and also spoke at the Council for a Competitive Economy's National Conference on Economic Freedom. The following week I gave a presentation on the book at the Lehrman Institute in New York, garnering extensive media attention, including a column in the *Wall Street Journal* by editorial writer Susan Lee. This serious attention was very gratifying and reinforced my view that this kind of research could make a difference (and put Reason Foundation on the map).

The American Political Science Association (APSA) published a generally favorable review of the book in 1982, and Lexington Books brought out a paperback edition that autumn. That September I spoke on federal agency deregulation at an APSA conference in Denver, and I wrote in my journal of being pleased that the political scientists in attendance took my presentation pretty seriously.

This was far more immediate attention than my book *Cutting Back City Hall* (described in Chapter 5 and published in 1980) had received. I had written that book on my own time, during late 1977 and 1978, and saw it as a Local Government Center project, not Reason Foundation's. We did announce its publication in *Reason Report,* but there was no publicity campaign (because there was no time or money). However, knowledge of the book spread by word of mouth, and I accepted speaking engagements all over the country for three or four years, championing competitive contracting of city and county public services. Speaking trips were arranged by donors, including Regional Advisory Council chairs like Cliff Slater in Honolulu and Dennis McCuistion in Dallas, by state Libertarian Party groups for their annual conventions, by civic groups, and later by government organizations. The book sold well enough that Universe Books brought out a paperback edition in 1982.

With the big success of *Instead of Regulation*, I decided to try a similar approach for a book on national defense policy. The Cold War was still raging, and while conservatives were pushing for huge increases in the defense budget, the liberal Left was naively promoting various disarmament ideas. Most libertarians were staunchly anti-communist, but most of the libertarian advocacy on this issue was coming from people like Murray Rothbard, who seemed to blame most of the Cold War on the United States. And the Libertarian Party platform, in my view, was hopelessly naïve in calling for bringing all our troops home from Europe, slashing defense budgets, and abolishing intelligence agencies. I saw the need for a defense policy consistent with our limited-government principles but also realistic about the threat we faced then from the Soviet Union.

I wanted to find a group of knowledgeable and tough-minded but limited-government-friendly thinkers on defense policy, so I eagerly accepted an invitation to a Liberty Fund conference on the subject in October 1981. I don't have a list of those taking part, and the only one I mentioned in my journal was eighty-two-year-old Larry Beilenson, a legal scholar and author of several tough-minded books on defense and foreign policy—but definitely not a war-hawk. After the conference, I roughed out an outline and recruited Larry and several others from the conference, and they helped me find still others, each to do a chapter of the proposed volume.

With initial funding (again) from the Earhart Foundation, each author produced a draft chapter. There were some significant points of disagreement, so I came up with the idea of bringing them all together to discuss and debate the issues, aiming to produce a more coherent overall approach. Liberty Fund agreed to support this follow-up to their conference that had inspired the volume, so we convened at the El Encanto Hotel in Santa Barbara in December 1982. As I wrote in *Reason Report*, "After three days of working sessions, cocktail hours, and shared meals, we were able to iron out [most of] the differences."

Defending a Free Society challenged the doctrine of Mutual Assured Destruction, called for a tougher approach to alliances, more effective land and naval forces, a strong role for intelligence, aiding anti-Soviet freedom fighters, and embracing a grand moral strategy in defense of free societies, in eleven chapters:

1. The Moral Basis of National Defense, by Eric Mack
2. Empirical Basis of Defense Policy, by R. J. Rummel
3. Current Strategic Realities, by R. J. Rummel
4. Rethinking Strategic Defense, by Sam Cohen
5. Military Alliances and Far-Flung Forces, by Lawrence W. Beilenson
6. Naval Forces and Freedom of the Seas, by Michael J. Dunn
7. Effective Land and Tactical Air Forces, by Michael Burns
8. Military Personnel without Conscription, by Roger Nils Folsom
9. Intelligence in Defense of a Free Society, by Joseph B. Ford
10. Aid to Freedom Fighters, by Lawrence W. Beilenson
11. A Grand Moral Strategy, by Jack D. Douglas

Lexington Books agreed to publish this new Reason Foundation book. It came out in spring 1984 and won praise from an array of people, including Gen. Daniel Graham (of the High Frontier project), former White House strategist Martin Anderson, Congressman Ron Paul, and columnist John Chamberlain. Contributor Sam Cohen and I did a series of Washington, DC, briefings and media interviews, as well as addressing a luncheon audience at the Lehrman Institute in New York attended by such notables as Robert Bartley of the *Wall Street Journal*, Irving Kristol of *The Public Interest*, Robert Silvers of the *New York Review of Books*, economist (and *Reason* author) Melvyn Krauss of New York University, and Ernest van den Haag of Fordham. While the book was not as big a success as *Instead of Regulation*, I was pleased that we had brought into being a realistic libertarian approach to defense and foreign policy (which was also reflected in articles and editorials in *Reason* magazine during the 1980s).

Still focused largely on books as the vehicle to advance new policy ideas, I developed the concept for another volume. The journalism award for *Reason*'s cover story on competing electric utilities led me to think seriously about whether traditional public utility monopolies, enforced by regulatory commissions, were obsolete. The huge Bell Telephone system had just been broken up, thanks to the emergence of competitors like MCI in long-distance service. So I conferred with a number of free-market economists and generated the concept for *Unnatural Monopolies*. We had already published *Reason* magazine articles on telephone competition (Peter Samuel) and cable TV competition (Tom Hazlett), so it was not hard to recruit a set of chapter authors. A grant from the Alex C. Walker Foundation made the project possible, and Lexington Books once again was happy to be the publisher.

The contents of *Unnatural Monopolies: The Case for Deregulating Public Utilities* ended up as follows:

1. The Curious Evolution of Natural Monopoly Theory, by Thomas Hazlett
2. Public Utility Rate Regulation: Can It Ever Protect Consumers? By Nina W. Cornell and Douglas W. Webbink
3. Public Utilities: Antitrust Law and Deregulation, by William H. Mellor III and Malcolm B. Allen, Jr.
4. Private Contracting versus Public Regulation as a Solution to the Natural Monopoly Problem, by Thomas Hazlett
5. Total Deregulation of Electric Utilities: A Viable Policy Choice, by Walter J. Primeaux, Jr.
6. Cable and Public Utility Regulation, by Charles L. Jackson
7. Telecommunications: After the Bell Breakup, by Peter Samuel.

The book was released in spring 1985. We got an excellent array of endorsements for the book, including one from FCC Chairman Mark Fowler, others from law-and-economics scholars

Harold Demsetz and Sam Peltzman, and from Thomas Gale Moore (just then joining the Council of Economic Advisers) and Bill Niskanen (who had recently stepped down from the CEA). Despite these endorsements, the book was the least successful of the three, and by the time it appeared I had a developed serious interest in policy studies as offering more bang for the buck in terms of policy impact.

Discovering Policy Studies

During a Washington, DC, trip in December 1979, I visited the Heritage Foundation, then a relatively small and new conservative think tank based in several row houses just east of the Library of Congress. My contact there was economist Stuart Butler, brother of Eamonn Butler of the Adam Smith Institute in London. I stopped in at Heritage again in March 1980 and was allowed to use a vacant office to get some typing done. Stuart and his colleagues were already anticipating a possible Reagan victory in the November 1980 election, and were making plans for two books to lay out an agenda for the new administration: *Mandate for Leadership* and *Agenda for Progress*. Stuart asked if I would be interested in writing a chapter for one of these, and given my work on municipal privatization, we settled on a critique of various federal urban grant programs.

That was how I came to write what was, in effect, my first policy study (although it was actually a book chapter). Federal "community and regional development" programs were spending around $9 billion a year (in 1980 dollars): Community Development Block Grants, Urban Development Action Grants, and Economic Development Administration grants and "loans." Not only were these unconstitutional as federal government activities, but as Public Choice Theory would predict, they were awful boondoggles. In researching them that summer and fall, I discovered the gold mine of data produced by the General Accounting Office (later renamed the Government Accountability Office). Heritage's bet paid off when Reagan was elected, so I trooped back to DC in January 1981 for the news conference unveiling *Agenda for Progress*, including my chapter.

In working with Stuart on this project, I was also introduced to Heritage's president and co-founder, Ed Feulner, and several others in its management. Feulner explained that Heritage differentiated itself from older conservative/free-market think tanks by stressing direct engagement in the policy process—as opposed to academic detachment. That was one reason why Heritage was putting major emphasis on policy studies they called Backgrounders—typically fifteen to twenty pages—that could be produced in a few months and released while a policy issue was being debated, instead of the two or three years to do a typical policy book. This approach struck me as making sense, but it took a few years for it to lead to changes in Reason Foundation's approach to policy research.

Another key event for me was my first participation in the Mont Pelerin Society, in 1980. MPS was founded in 1947 by a small group of classical liberal thinkers including F. A. Hayek, Ludwig von Mises, and Milton Friedman. In those days, long before the Internet and email, they saw the need to create an international network of classical liberals—academics, policy researchers, and business leaders—to exchange ideas, nurture next generations of such people, and eventually change the climate of opinion and hence government policies to be more consistent with individual liberty, free markets, and limited government.

Either Tibor or Manny nominated me as his guest, which allowed me to attend the September 1980 meeting, hosted by the Hoover Institution at Stanford University. It was my first time at Hoover, and my first contact with numerous thinkers and scholars, many of whose names I'd heard but had never met. Among those whose names I noted in my journal were Milton Friedman and his son David, William Simon, Thomas Sowell, Murray Rothbard, Alan Reynolds, and Alvin Rabushka. I also noted that "it was a nonstop round of meeting people, making contacts for Reason Foundation, etc. It cost me a pile but was well worth it." I was also struck by Sowell's statement, in an address to the group, to the effect that "you will never beat a moral vision with a cost/benefit analysis."

Like the Heritage people, most of the Americans at the MPS

meeting were optimistic that Reagan would win the election, and that this would be a great opportunity for rethinking the size and scope of the federal government, deregulation, privatization, etc. I was more skeptical than most of them, but could see that if Reagan did win, there would certainly be opportunities to promote such policy changes.

On Election Day, most of us libertarians were hoping for a big showing by the Clark/Koch Libertarian Party campaign. A group of Santa Barbara libertarians, including about half the small Reason Foundation staff, planned to attend the Clark campaign "victory party" in Los Angeles on election night, so I rented a van and drove the whole group to LA. On the way that evening, with the polls back east having closed several hours before, we listened to the election results. One after another, big-government liberal icons in the Senate and House were going down to defeat, and it looked likely that Reagan would win big. I was more elated by this news than by whatever the LP result would be, seeing opportunities for the policy ideas of Reason Foundation and other like-minded think tanks and academics.

The first few months of the Reagan administration did not disappoint. A whole raft of free-market writers and economists were recruited to the White House staff, the Council of Economic Advisers, and to positions in some cabinet agencies. My friends John McClaughry and Dana Rohrabacher became, respectively, a White House domestic policy advisor and a White House speechwriter. Reason Foundation Board Member Bill Niskanen joined the Council of Economic Advisers, and our friend David Henderson became a CEA staff economist. Privatization guru Steve Savas was recruited to a senior policy position at HUD, and Reason contributors Bruce Bartlett and Steve Hanke also got White House jobs, as did libertarian columnist Doug Bandow. On an April 1981 trip to Washington, McClaughry convened a dinner with me as guest of honor, and I had lunch with Dana in the White House Mess. This was very exciting for me, as the founder of a still-tiny and little-known Santa Barbara think tank.

Those contacts paid off for Reason Foundation that August. The air traffic controllers' union, PATCO, launched an illegal strike on August 3, and President Reagan ordered them back to work within forty-eight hours, on penalty of being fired if they did not return. When only about 10 percent of them returned to work, Reagan fired the rest and de-certified their union. That led to a major scramble within US DOT and the FAA to implement contingency plans to restore as much ATC service as possible, quickly.

On August 16, the *New York Times* published my op-ed, "Maybe It's Time to Dismiss the FAA," suggesting a nonprofit corporation along the lines of the original ARINC (per my chapter in the forthcoming *Instead of Regulation*). John McClaughry circulated that piece within the administration (and possibly also my January 1979 *Reason* cover story on the FAA's problems). And in early September, he called and asked me to fly to Washington to give a briefing on privatizing the ATC system. I was able to get plane reservations (only about 50 percent of normal flights were operating), and I spent the next day in a vacant office in the Old Executive Office Building preparing a briefing. I presented it the next day to DOT Secretary Drew Lewis and FAA Administrator Lynn Helms, along with several White House staffers. Though Lewis seemed intrigued, Helms was absolutely opposed, and that was that. I did get interviewed on NPR's "All Things Considered," though.

But that was not the end of the story. I presented the ATC reform idea in October 1981 at a user-charge conference organized by the Council for a Competitive Economy, where DOT Assistant Secretary Judith Connors praised the idea, and Susan Lee of the *Wall Street Journal* discussed it with me at lunch. I also did another round of radio talk shows and other media interviews. The next month Heritage asked me to write up the idea as a Backgrounder—my first freestanding policy study. Heritage released it, with appropriate fanfare, in October 1982. On my DC trip in connection with the release, I had meetings with House and Senate staffers, breakfast with OMB's Chris DeMuth, another breakfast with various aviation people, and did a lunch presentation for the Council for a Competitive Economy's Manchester Forum.

The Heritage paper led to an invitation to submit a more-academic version to the Transportation Research Board and present it during a session at TRB's January 1983 Annual Meeting. It was well received, and was published in TRB's journal, *Transportation Research Record*. This was my first exposure to TRB, and at the time I had no idea how few of the thousands of papers submitted for each year's annual meeting (a) lead to presentations, and (b) actually get published in *TRR*. I wasn't as elated by this first-timer success as I should have been.

The ATC experience really impressed on me the value of policy papers, coupled with serious public relations efforts. A year or two later, Heritage asked me to do another Backgrounder, this time an overview of municipal privatization, drawing on *Cutting Back City Hall* and the ongoing work of the Local Government Center. That made a far larger community of conservatives aware of the topic, and also of Reason Foundation and LGC.

Two *Reason* magazine articles during the 1980s served as de-facto policy papers, also in the aviation area. The May 1983 issue featured "Towering Entrepreneurs" by airline pilot John Doherty. It was a detailed look at the Reagan administration's new policy of hiring private companies to operate small-airport control towers—at far less than half the cost of comparable towers operated directly by the FAA. It led to an interview with Doherty on the *Today* show and a follow-up article by him in *Airline Pilot*. These articles strengthened the hand of those in the Reagan administration pushing to expand the new FAA contract tower program. In April 1984, I received a letter from Spencer Dickerson of the American Association of Airport Executives stating that "John Doherty's article on this program has been extremely beneficial in getting the FAA to expand this private-sector program." Contract towers were subsequently expanded by the Bush and Clinton administrations, and as of 2016 there are 253 small-airport contract control towers. (Periodic studies by the DOT Office of the Inspector General find that contract towers continue to cost less than half as much to operate as comparable FAA-run towers.)

Reason's September 1983 issue included Paul Feldman's article, "Free the DC 2," arguing that Washington's Dulles and National

Airports—then owned and operated by the FAA—should be privatized. Based on a paper Feldman had prepared for the Transportation Research Board, it was the first time a magazine had made a serious case for privatizing a US airport. The next year, the Grace Commission (appointed by the Reagan administration to look for opportunities to reduce the federal budget) recommended divesting those two airports to a newly created local airport authority (but rejected privatization out of hand).

DOT Secretary Elizabeth Dole in mid-1984 announced that her agency would ask Congress to lease or sell the airport to either a state or private entity. Late that year Citizens for a Sound Economy asked me to write a policy study making the case for privatizing those airports. They released my "Privatizing Washington's Airports" on May 28, 1985—and it stirred up a hornet's nest. Years later I learned that Dole's DOT had been fighting serious congressional opposition to the less-radical idea of divesting the DC airports to a newly created airport authority, and they saw promotion of the idea of privatizing them as a needless distraction. They eventually succeeded with the divestiture in 1987, which led to major improvements to both airports in the following decade.

I did another policy paper in 1983 for another outside organization, the Eno Foundation for Transportation. On June 28, 1983, the northbound span of the bridge on I-95 in Greenwich, Connecticut, collapsed, killing three people. On July 9, the *New York Times* published my op-ed piece, "How Should We Fix I-95's Ailing Bridges? By Selling Them Off." I drew on examples of privately financed toll bridges in *Cutting Back City Hall* to argue that the incentives for good stewardship of an investor-owned bridge company were stronger than those of a politicized state transportation department. Eno was then based in Westport, Connecticut, so the bridge collapse had occurred nearby. Eno staff asked me to write a paper fleshing out this case and invited me to a conference there in October 1983 to present it. It was published in the first-quarter 1984 issue of Eno's journal, *Transportation Quarterly*. In March 1984, I presented another version of this paper at a TRB conference in Dallas. Why I did not think to publish a version as a Reason Foundation policy study I don't know, but after having written the CSE airports paper and the Eno toll bridge paper in 1983, I vowed that Reason Foundation would soon begin doing policy papers, a la Heritage Foundation.

Our first bona-fide Reason Foundation policy paper was done under contract by Alvin Rabushka of Hoover, an expert on tax policy. We commissioned him to do a study of whether California's landmark property tax limitation amendment, Proposition 13, had actually curtailed government growth. Released in early 1984, it found that despite having saved property taxpayers some $50 billion from 1978 to 1982, per-capita state and local government spending had increased to an all-time high, as governments found workarounds. The study had the innocuous title of "Report on State and Local Government Finances in California." We obviously still had a lot to learn about marketing!

Our big move into policy studies came when we launched our Federal Privatization Project in late 1985. That project was the outgrowth of a series of discussions I'd had earlier that year with Chuck Hobbs, deputy director of the White House Office of Policy Development. At Chuck's request, I had several visits with him to discuss specific ideas the Reagan administration was considering, such as devolving federal functions to state and local government and privatizing the Postal Service. I'd been reading and writing about the massive privatization effort underway, with considerable success, in Britain under Margaret Thatcher. Instead of making piece-meal proposals, I suggested, why not develop a comprehensive privatization agenda and educate Congress and opinion leaders that we could do something comparable in this country?

Chuck liked the idea in principle, and asked me to develop it into a specific proposal, which I did. I proposed a two-day seminar bringing experts from the private sector (discussion leaders and discussants) together with senior administration policy people, to be held off-site to avoid distractions and without media. It would "explore the full scope of a possible privatization/divestiture program and seek to devise a medium- to long-term strategy for implementing it by the Reagan administration and its successor." Chuck got it approved, and made arrangements to use the Aspen Institute's Wye Plantation conference facility in Queenstown, Maryland, on July 29–31, 1985.

The overall agenda was as follows:

1. Political philosophy of privatization, Gordon Tullock (Public Choice Center)
2. Successful privatization in Britain, Stuart Butler (Heritage Foundation)
3. Review of Reagan first-term initiatives, Fred Smith (Competitive Enterprise Institute)
4. Decentralization and divestiture, Larry Hunter (Advisory Commission on Intergovernmental Relations)
5. Privatization approaches, by type of program, Stuart Butler
6. Case study exercises, Robert Poole (Reason Foundation)
7. Institutionalizing the process, Fred Smith (CEI).

Overall, the event went well. The main action item turned out to be creating a President's Commission on Privatization. Given how slowly the wheels of government turn, it took until 1987 before President Reagan issued an executive order creating the commission, and it delivered its report in March 1988. Perhaps anticipating that the administration would be slow to take action, in my thank-you letter to Chuck, August 2, 1985, I told him that Reason Foundation would begin work immediately on a Federal Privatization Project, commissioning as many as twelve policy papers making the case for privatizing individual federal enterprises.

Getting seriously into policy studies required an increase in staffing, so in late 1985 we hired (very part-time) *Reason* book review editor Lynn Scarlett on a half-time basis as research director. Her first priority was to coordinate and manage the Federal Privatization Project (while also continuing work on her PhD dissertation in political economy at UC Santa Barbara). We decided that as each policy study was completed, it would be published and publicized as a Reason Foundation policy study, albeit part of an ongoing series.

Adding the Local Government Center

Every month, beginning in December 1976, I researched and wrote a five-hundred-word *Fiscal Watchdog* column, modestly compensated by the Taxpayers' Foundation (an affiliate of the National Taxpayers' Union) and distributed by them to hundreds of local newspapers. Coming up with new subjects on private-sector delivery of public services and infrastructure required me to do ongoing research. This also put me in touch with established institutions that were starting to look into this emerging field, such as the Institute for Local Self-Government, the Council on Municipal Performance, and the International City Management Association. This led to new researcher contacts and sometimes to speaking invitations. The column also helped considerably in publicizing *Cutting Back City Hall* when it was released in 1980.

The masthead on the column identified the source as the Local Government Center, which was basically Mark Frazier and me; putting out *Fiscal Watchdog* every month from 1979 onward was LGC's only activity. Mark Frazier moved to Washington, DC, in June 1979, and it would have made sense to merge LGC into Reason Foundation at that point, but Mark wanted to keep its separate identity, and the Foundation had no money to do anything else with it at that point in time.

By spring 1982, however, the Foundation had grown large enough—and municipal privatization had become a big enough phenomenon—that I decided the time was right to absorb LGC and start doing more with it. Mark agreed, and at the June board meeting, our trustees approved my proposal to do this. We decided that LGC would begin to serve as an information clearinghouse on privatization. Many queries that came in from concerned citizens or local officials could be answered by sending the person one or more previous *Fiscal Watchdog* issues that dealt with the topic in question. Examples of such queries in spring 1983 included a Colorado state senator interested in deregulating taxis, intercity buses, movers, and freight haulers; the Oklahoma State Auditor's Office seeking an overview on state/local public service contracting; and the Denver Regional Council of Governments seeking knowledgeable speakers for a workshop on free-enterprise transit.

We began doing fundraising to expand the work of the Local Government Center, and by mid-1983 were in a position to pay *Reason*'s half-time editorial intern, Eric Marti, to spend part of his time expanding LGC's Directory of Private Service Providers, which we sent out on request to public officials or citizens interested in finding out what firms were available to provide various public services under contract. Eric also began a new project: creation of a computerized Privatization Database. A national research organization had shared with us a data tape from its national survey on city and county contracting for specific public services, and this became the starting point for this database (which we then expanded every month as new examples came to our attention).

Now that *Fiscal Watchdog* was "ours," I was no longer getting paid to write it by NTU's foundation (but since I was now full-time president of the Reason Foundation, I absorbed it into my workload). Starting with the July 1982 issue, *Fiscal Watchdog* appeared with a new masthead, identifying LGC as part of Reason Foundation and including an advisory board of Mark Frazier, Patrick Gallagher, M. Bruce Johnson, John McClaughry (no longer on the White House staff), Richard Muth, and Bill Niskanen. We also began marketing it to public officials and interested citizens, as a free information service of LGC.

With an increasingly higher profile, and LGC/Reason work being used by officials such as Mike Antonovich (chairman of the Los Angeles County Board of Supervisors) and Mayor Pat Pappas of Parkesburg, West Virginia (who'd won his election with a campaign based on *Cutting Back City Hall*), Reason began to get grants to expand LGC's work. In February 1984, we hired a full-time director for LGC. Phil Fixler, a libertarian with a PhD in political science from the University of Southern California, came to us from the City of Los Angeles, where he'd been a policy and budget analyst. In addition to taking over responsibility for researching and writing *Fiscal Watchdog*, he was charged with continuing the expansion and improvement of the Privatization Database and becoming our primary point of contact in responding to queries from citizens and public officials on privatization.

Soon Phil was accepting speaking invitations from taxpayer groups, local governments, and public-sector research organizations. One of those visits, from the League of Placer County Taxpayers, led to us doing a brief study of the potential for savings in the county's $73 million budget; Phil's study found privatization opportunities that could save $5.1 million per year. He was also able to expand the Privatization Database, thanks to the results of a new survey of city/county service contracting funded by the federal Department of Housing and Urban Development and carried out by the International City Management Association.

In June 1984, LGC got its own computer, no longer having to share the office's lone Vector Graphics machine. Kaypro Corporation donated one of its new Kaypro 10 portable microcomputers (which Lou and I successfully assembled). Phil put summer interns Scott Hodge and Jeffrey Smith to work tailoring the software and entering data to expand the Privatization Database. Phil also worked closely with reporter Kevin Farrell of *Venture* magazine for a cover story, "When Entrepreneurs Take Over the Government." The excellent publicity for LGC and the database led to other media queries and further raised the Reason/LGC profile as the go-to place on municipal privatization.

In 1985, Phil helped organize a study tour on European privatization, co-sponsored with the International City Management Association, the Council for International Urban Liaison, and London-based Adam Smith Institute. The tour included visits with governments engaging in public service contracting in Denmark, England, and West Germany. And in April 1986, thanks to some diligent networking by Phil, we reached agreement with the Law and Economics Center of the University of Miami to accept a $70,000 grant from the Florida Chamber Foundation for a six-month study of the prospects for privatization of state and local services in Florida.

Outreach Activities

Once we had moved into larger quarters on Garden Street in 1982, we decided to try to raise the Foundation's profile somewhat higher in Santa Barbara—partly to gain media attention but primarily to flush out prospective donors from this very wealthy community. So we began a Public Policy Seminar Series.

The idea was to invite a somewhat notable person to give a public-invited talk in a meeting room in a nice hotel, such as the Santa Barbara Biltmore. Our first seminar, in October 1982, featured Steve Hanke—who until a few months before had been a senior staff economist on the White House Council of Economic Advisers. Steve was one of a group of early free-market Reagan appointees who began departing after two years—including Martin Anderson, John McClaughry, Norm Ture, and Murray Weidenbaum. He gave a rather scathing talk about the administration having talked a good line about markets and deregulation, but not having taken substantive actions: "The level of taxes and of government expenditures as a percentage of GDP have gone up, not down. . . . There's a massive gap between rhetoric and reality." And he added, "What you have now in the White House is the Nixon-Ford administration without Nixon or Ford." While his talk was eye-opening and hard-hitting, I don't think it was what our mostly Republican audience had wanted to hear.

We followed up with Steve Savas, the privatization expert who was then assistant secretary for policy development and research at HUD, on leave from his teaching position at Columbia University. He gave a talk outlining the rationale for government to distinguish between making policy (inherently governmental) and delivering services (which might be done more efficiently via competitive contracting). This talk was well received by an audience that included representatives from Santa Barbara County government. At dinner with Steve that night, he and I finally had an opportunity to get personally acquainted, rather than merely being long-distance correspondents.

Our third (and final) seminar, in 1983, featured Jim Davidson, founder and president of the National Taxpayers Union. My recollection is that Jim's talk came across to our audience as rather too cynical about government. After this three-speaker trial run, we decided that the seminar series was not a very good use of the time and money, given the small size of Santa Barbara and the minimal results in terms of developing new donors. (We would revisit the concept when we relocated the Foundation to Los Angeles.)

Accordingly, our outreach efforts shifted to the national level and the use of broadcast media. For several years I had been a commentator on a national radio series called "Perspective on the Economy." It had been started and operated by the Manhattan Institute, with five regular commentators; as of 1984, besides me they included Tom Hazlett, John McClaughry, Jennifer Roback, and Rich Wilcke. The program was offered at no charge to any radio station that agreed to air it at a regularly scheduled time each weekday. Radio stations liked the idea, because in those days before radio deregulation, stations had to periodically document to the Federal Communications Commission that they were devoting a certain amount of airtime to serious commentary—and they were getting the material at no charge.

These micro-essays were only sixty seconds long—and they were the most difficult writing I've ever done. Making the case for a free-market concept in just one minute is a lot harder than it may sound. So doing these commentaries really forced me to pay attention to constructing a concise message, and doing so in lay-person language. Once a month I would go to a local radio station and record four or five commentaries, and the tape would be sent to a tiny production house that put a whole month's worth, from the five contributors, onto a master tape that was sent to the radio stations.

At the end of 1983, Manhattan Institute decided to pull the plug on "Perspective" for budgetary reasons. As a think tank, its primary focus was New York, yet the broadcasts were nationwide. I reviewed the numbers and decided that this might be a good way to increase Reason Foundation's national visibility. The board agreed to give it a try, and the Olin Foundation provided a special start-up grant for the takeover. During our first year, we increased the number of participating radio stations from 155 to 185, of which forty were in top-100 markets. In 1985, the number of stations declined to 170, but the audience size increased. We also launched a Spanish-language version, "La Economia en Perspectiva." Not as successful as the English edition, it peaked at 27 stations in 1986. Unfortunately, funding never covered all the costs, so we terminated the radio efforts in 1987.

A much bigger prospect came along in 1984—a potential television documentary along the lines of the highly successful 1980 PBS documentary series "Free to Choose" with Milton and Rose Friedman. In September 1984, Lou and I attended a conference near London organized by Libertarian International, with speakers (including me) and participants from a number of countries. Britain's independent Channel 4 covered portions of the conference, and Eben Wilson (who'd worked on the Friedman series) introduced us to producer David Graham of Diverse Productions. He and his wife took us out to dinner to discuss his planned documentary series, to be called "The New Enlightenment." It would cover the emergence of a serious classical liberal/libertarian movement in Europe and the United States, and he already had interest from Channel 4 to broadcast the series in Britain. Might Reason Foundation be interested in working with him on the project, and obtaining US marketing rights?

I was excited by the idea, and in subsequent months David and I exchanged ideas and further developed the concept so that it would appeal to US audiences. We worked out an arrangement to co-produce the series, and I got our board's approval to proceed with fundraising for it. It became a six-part series:

- The Road from Serfdom
- Flashpoint of the Welfare State
- Looking After Yourself
- The Return of the Entrepreneur
- A Constitution for Liberty
- North, South, East, and West

Filming was completed by mid-1986 and the series aired on six consecutive weeks on Britain's Channel 4, getting good reviews during these years of Margaret Thatcher's triumphs. We spent much of 1987 marketing the series to the Public Broadcasting System, which judged it to be "too British," but expressed interest in an Americanized version—if we could find a lead PBS station. We pitched it successfully to KQED in San Francisco, which led to a three-way agreement among KQED, Reason, and Diverse to produce the Americanized version. Economist Walter Williams was signed on as the host/presenter. Unfortunately, we were unable to raise the large sums of money required for the agreed-upon budget. Reason Foundation and Laissez-Faire Books both sold videocassettes of the British version, but that was as far as the project went.

We did score a television success in early 1986, albeit based on a tragedy. On January 28, the Space Shuttle Challenger blew up during its launch, killing all the astronauts aboard. Because I had written about space policy, someone at CNN's "Crossfire" called me that morning and asked if I could be on that evening's program. They could arrange for me to do this from a studio in Los Angeles, while the other participants were on their regular set in Washington, DC. I agreed, knowing this would be difficult to do. I pulled together my arguments, drawn from extensive reading (*Aviation Week* and elsewhere), that the Shuttle was the product of many political compromises, optimized for none of its diverse functions, and with political decisions about things such as launch dates. And unlike the previous Apollo program, the Shuttle was irresponsibly designed without any emergency escape system (which could have saved the doomed crew).

I drove down to Los Angeles that afternoon, with an outline of talking points beside me on the passenger seat. It was weird sitting by myself in a darkened studio, listening to hosts Tom Braden and Robert Novak, and fellow guest Norman Baker of *Defense Daily*. My assessment was a minority view that day, but would ultimately be vindicated by the NASA inquiry that found political factors had overruled engineers' judgement that the launch should not have taken place that cold January morning. I did several subsequent radio interviews on the subject, as well.

Local Political Action

This account of the Santa Barbara years would not be complete without a brief discussion of Reason Foundation's people taking part in local politics. The demographics of Santa Barbara were skewed, already by the 1980s, in the same way that happened to much of coastal California in subsequent decades. Local policies were strongly anti-growth, with a de-facto moratorium on housing development in the unincorporated suburbs due to politicians' refusal to connect Santa Barbara to the state water project—and without water, housing could not be built. The result, already, was a community divided into haves and have-nots—especially very wealthy people in the close-in suburbs of Hope Ranch and Montecito, many low-income people performing service jobs, and a large student population at UC Santa Barbara. A demographer colleague at General Research Corp. in the late 1970s had confirmed the everyday observation that Santa Barbara had a much smaller than average middle class of families raising children.

Limited housing supply but strong demand (from students, service people, etc.,) led to high and rising rents and ever-increasing housing prices by the late 1970s and early 1980s. Thanks to a former girlfriend who invested in real estate, I had bought a few rental properties in the mid-1970s, so I was very concerned when the local left-wing groups started serious agitation for rent control in Santa Barbara. Our local libertarians formed Tenants Against Rent Control, and when I was part of those working for passage of the tax-cutting measure Proposition 13 in 1978, I promised my tenants that their rents would not go up if my property taxes were cut. These kinds of efforts by many small landlords and libertarian tenants helped to defeat Santa Barbara rent control on the same 1978 ballot on which Prop. 13 passed.

But the lefties were not about to give up. They created an umbrella group called Network and had increasing influence on the editorial policies of the local alternative weekly newspaper.

People in the business community grew increasingly worried over where this might lead, and some of them formed the Santa Barbara Futures Foundation (SBFF) to advocate city and county policies friendly to property owners and businesses. Because I'd had some success getting market-friendly ideas into the local newspaper, I was invited to join, and by March 1980 had been elected to their board.

The Network folks began a new push for rent control that year, but for some reason, SBFF was reluctant to take them on directly. So working with Marty and my former PSSI colleague John Caldwell, we produced (in our "spare time") a twenty-two-page report, "Rent Control in Santa Barbara: a Disaster for Tenants." It documented the dire effects of rent control on new construction in other US cities and directly countered the arguments being made by supporters of the new Santa Barbara ballot measure. Since such a report would be more credible if released by an organization, we invented the "Community Research Council" for this purpose. This report led to my making a presentation before the city council, and probably helped lead to the second defeat for rent control in June 1980.

Later that year, our CRC produced two additional reports, criticizing proposed efforts by the city's housing and land-use bureaucracies to "downzone" certain areas currently zoned commercial, so that more housing could be built there. This would reduce property values in the target areas, we pointed out, enabling leftie groups that wanted to build "limited-equity co-ops" to buy up these properties at below-market prices. We also did a detailed critique of the city's proposed revision of the "Housing Element" of its general plan.

CRC's final project was done for the Santa Barbara Futures Foundation in 1980. It presented—to the Chamber of Commerce's Business Improvement Forum—a market-friendly vision of what Santa Barbara could be by the year 2000 if its public policies were rethought. It identified water supply as the key constraint and laid out a possible scenario in which market-priced water led to conversion of the remaining citrus groves to residential and commercial uses, housing therefore was allowed to expand, and medical and high-tech industries attracted by UC Santa Barbara would flourish. While that scenario was radical for its time, the dire water situation eventually led to Santa Barbara getting connected to the state water project, and technology industries did expand in the suburbs near UCSB.

The final story involves my wife, Lou, primarily. In those years, there was a lot of encouragement for libertarians to seek to be elected to local boards and commissions. In 1984, Lou noticed that all three seats on our local fire district board in Mission Canyon had become vacant and would have to be filled on the next election day. So she took out papers as a candidate. As it happens, only two other people did likewise, so all three were automatically elected with no opposition. At their first meeting, they discovered that all three were *Reason* subscribers and at least somewhat skeptical of government.

The county fire department had built a one-engine fire station in Mission Canyon several years before, and all of us had a special assessment on our property tax bills to pay for it. Based on my prior experience with fire departments and paramedics, I suggested to Lou that the new board obtain detailed statistics on fire and paramedic calls made from "our" station—and find out how many of them actually were responding to Mission Canyon incidents. All three board members thought this made a lot of sense, so they assembled the data over several months, and I gave them pointers here and there. It turned out that the large majority of activity from "our" fire station was mutual-aid calls to other parts of the city and county. And looking at maps showing the locations of fire stations and the pattern of activities, it seemed likely that the county fire department would locate a station there regardless of whether there was a Mission Canyon Fire District paying for it.

The result was a decision by the three-member board to put a measure on the next (1986) ballot calling for the Mission Canyon Fire District to be abolished. It had been created by such a vote, and could be terminated by such a vote, along with the special assessment. The board prepared a mailing piece summarizing their findings and recommending abolition, and the measure was duly put on the June ballot. The mailing went out a week before the election, too late for the fire department to mobilize in opposition. And it passed. Lou became, as far as we know, the first elected libertarian to abolish the agency she was elected to govern.

Chapter 8

Putting Reason Foundation on the Map
(1986–1991)

Getting Known in Los Angeles

By April 1986, I had located and negotiated the lease for our new office space, in a business park located on property that is part of the Santa Monica Airport, on Ocean Park Blvd. in Santa Monica. To me as an aviation buff, a nice bonus was that this was the former site of the original Douglas Aircraft production plant, which had built many thousands of military planes for World War II as well as the post-war DC-3, DC-4, DC-6, and DC-7 airliners that I had grown up flying on Eastern Air Lines passes. But the runway at that airport was too short for jetliners, so Douglas shifted aircraft production to a larger facility at Long Beach Airport when its DC-8 jetliner was developed, and it closed the Santa Monica plant. During our years in the Ocean Park building, a private group built an aviation museum on the property, a very short walk from our offices, which included a nice restaurant with a view of the runway, where we sometimes entertained visitors.

Moving is always somewhat traumatic, and the Foundation's relocation from Santa Barbara to the big city was certainly that. Our new quarters were finished to our specifications, but inevitably last-minute work was still going on the day before the movers were to arrive. I spent all that day babysitting the phone installers and running various errands. And when the moving truck arrived Saturday morning with only the driver (the crew were no-shows), I spent most of that day helping the driver unload and get all the desks, file cabinets, tables, and boxes into the correct offices.

Despite most of the staff assuring me they would make the move, when push came to shove, only eight of the fourteen actually relocated, including five of the six senior staff but only three of the eight support staff. So in addition to all the normal hassles of moving into new space, we had to recruit and train a number of new people. Fortunately, the art director made the move, so there was only minimal interruption of the magazine's publishing schedule.

Starting out with only a skeleton staff (Marty, Virginia Postrel, Phil Fixler, Lynn Scarlett, Business Manager P. K. Lowrey, and Art Director Laura Main) meant that recruiting was a top priority for me during the first few months. We needed a new office manager, advertising director, circulation director, bookkeeper, and public affairs director. That made the first few months very hectic, but we kept *Reason* magazine and *Fiscal Watchdog* coming out on schedule.

The rationale for the move was to increase Reason Foundation's visibility and accessibility—to the media, to donors and prospects, and to the world at large. We had the good fortune of getting a long article in the June 25, 1986, *Los Angeles Times*, "The Coming of Age for the Reason Foundation." During all our years in Santa Barbara, we'd been virtually invisible to the West Coast's leading newspaper, so this was a real coup. The piece included a photo of me holding blueprints for the new offices and a photo of a recent *Reason* cover. Reporter Garry Abrams obtained some positive quotes about Reason Foundation from the editor of *The New Republic*, Michael Kinsley, and Heritage Foundation's Robert Huberty about our influence with the Reagan administration. So that was a great start.

But a one-shot media hit was only the beginning. Lynn Scarlett was in charge of developing increased visibility on an ongoing basis by creating a monthly lunch event in downtown Los Angeles called Reason Forum. Each month we brought in a speaker on a topic of current interest, inviting local donors, prospects, business and government leaders, and reporters to attend. Thanks to Ed Clark of ARCO, we were able to use a suitably large room in the ARCO Towers as our venue. The first two events, in fall 1986, focused on hot-button issues. UC Berkeley biochemist Bruce Ames discussed facts and fallacies about carcinogenic chemicals—highly relevant given a pending ballot measure on that topic. And at the second event economist, Tom Hazlett previewed a First Amendment challenge to local cable TV franchising laws.

Over the next several years, Reason Forums developed a nice following. Some of these events provided a platform for us to discuss some of our new policy studies, on topics such as freeway congestion, Los Angeles air quality, and mass transit. Others showcased visitors to Los Angeles such as Charles Murray, Hernando de Soto, White House staffer Jim Pinkerton, and South African free-marketers Leon Louw and Frances Kendall. Thinkers such as these had never had a platform like this in Los Angeles, and these events definitely increased our visibility with all the intended audiences. We eventually phased out the monthly forums in favor of single-issue conferences and seminars.

The second element of our visibility campaign was to hold an annual banquet in downtown Los Angeles. A fundraising consultant had explained to me several years before how such events often work. You select an honoree who has a large following and give him or her some kind of award, she advised. And you need a well-known keynote speaker who will draw a large crowd. Together, these features should bring in enough ticket-buyers and table-buyers to get the event well beyond the break-even point and hopefully produce significant net revenue, in addition to the visibility and networking opportunities.

This model worked pretty well, though we had a tendency to overdo the program, creating too many speaking slots (which made some of the events go on too long). For our first banquet, in October 1986, we selected Clay La Force as our honoree and Milton Friedman as our keynote speaker. La Force, a strong free-market thinker, was dean of the UCLA Graduate School of Management and a legendary fundraiser, as well as being a friend of Reason Foundation. Friedman had long been a friend and occasional *Reason* author. His popular 1980 PBS series *Free to Choose* was still fresh in people's memories. As emcee for the evening we chose Bob Chitester, the producer of the PBS series, also a friend.

About three hundred people attended—pretty good for our first such event—and guests included economist Thomas Sowell, federal judge Alex Kozinski, authors Barbara Branden, Jerry Pournelle, and Durk Pearson and Sandy Shaw, as well as a number of local business leaders. The *Los Angeles Times Magazine* did a feature story on the event, including a large photo of Friedman talking with a group of Reason Foundation Trustees.

Given this initial success, the annual banquet became a regular feature of our fundraising program. In addition to broadening our donor base and raising money, it provided a good occasion (on the day before or after the event) to provide presentations for and discussions with our Regional Advisory Council chairs and National Advisory Council members, many of whom came to LA for these events.

One of the largest banquets (four hundred attendees) took place in 1988, celebrating the Foundation's tenth anniversary and *Reason* magazine's twentieth. Since Reason Foundation was essentially the honoree, we had just a keynote speaker this time. I chose Steve Forbes, who had taken a shine to *Reason* and our policy ideas several years before. He gave a very upbeat speech, and I presented him with a leather-bound, autographed copy of F. A. Hayek's classic book *The Road to Serfdom*. Judge Kozinski served as emcee and at some point during the program referred to me as "the Rambo of the privatization movement." Other nice comments about our work came from University of San Diego law professor Bernard Siegan, Ron Utt of the new White House Office of Privatization, and former Council of Economic Advisers member Jerry Jordan.

Another benefit of being in Los Angeles rather than Santa Barbara was accessibility to visitors. We often had visits from university scholars and think-tank researchers, for most of whom Santa Barbara would have been too far off the beaten path. We were also discovered by organizations promoting idea exchange with people from overseas. The Eisenhower Fellows program would send a delegation of foreign visitors our way about once a year. In 1987, such visitors included a sociology professor from Hungary (still behind the Iron Curtain in that year) and a senior official from New Zealand's state-owned PetroCorp (which had recently been converted from a government agency to a self-supporting company). In 1988, we hosted an official from Amoco Egypt Oil Co. and another from the Economic League of Vienna, both interested in discussing privatization.

One visiting delegation was referred to us by our friends at the Free Market Foundation in South Africa. Eleven black transit entrepreneurs visited us in November 1987, knowing of our support for market-based transit. Phil Fixler and I gave them a seminar on privatization and deregulation of transit, but it turned out what they actually wanted was friendly regulation to protect their companies from being put out of business by the government.

Building *Reason* Magazine

As publisher of *Reason* during these years, I had four goals for the magazine as a business. They were:

- Get *Reason* indexed in *Reader's Guide to Periodical Literature*, in those days the primary index to the content of serious magazines;
- Obtain meaningful newsstand and bookstore distribution;
- Start obtaining mainstream national advertising; and,
- Double the paid circulation, to put *Reason* closer in size to *National Review* and *The New Republic*.

Those were ambitious goals, but we achieved three of the four by 1991.

I'd discovered *Reader's Guide* in high school, during the one year when I participated in high school debate. And since the late 1980s/early 1990s were pre-Internet, *Reader's Guide* was vitally important if material in *Reason* was going to be as accessible to students, reporters, and researchers as was the content of the other think magazines. We knew that larger circulation and greater media coverage would help, but with advice from MTA Publishing Consultants, in 1990, we mounted a serious marketing campaign. Part of this involved ongoing efforts to have current subscribers donate gift subscriptions to their favorite university and local public library, so that more librarians would be aware of *Reason*. Our circulation director sent press clippings to librarians around the country to demonstrate *Reason's* wide impact. We arranged exchange ads with *Harper's* and *The New Republic* (both indexed in *Reader's Guide*) so that our ads would appear in their pages. Most important, we organized a nationwide letter-writing campaign recommending to the *Guide's* publisher, H. W. Wilson Co., that *Reason* be included. Among those who sent such letters were economists Milton Friedman and Murray Weidenbaum, Congressmen Dana Rohrabacher and Chris Cox, and many others. We were very pleased to hear from H. W. Wilson early in 1991 that they would begin indexing *Reason* starting with the February 1991 issue. Possibly as a result, the number of library subscriptions increased from 389 at the start of 1991 to 470 by the end of the year.

Newsstand and bookstore distribution was a harder nut to crack. *Reason* had long been carried in a handful of independent bookstores, and a few small distributors had tried *Reason* on newsstands in several cities. But national distribution had eluded us. Finally, by 1988, we persuaded Eastern News to distribute *Reason* in a number of major cities. But bookstore chains were mostly not requesting the magazine from Eastern. In fall 1988, we sent a promotional mailing to over three thousand stores in prominent bookstore chains B. Dalton, Crown, Encore, and Waldenbooks, which led to a significant increase in those carrying *Reason*. We never made much money from newsstand and bookstore sales, but figured that the exposure was worth it to put *Reason* on an equal footing with other think magazines.

New Advertising Director Art Markos was the first ad-sales professional on *Reason's* staff, and he was diligent about pitching the magazine to mainstream advertisers. He achieved some degree of early success; compared with twenty pages of ads in *Reason's* fifteenth anniversary issue in 1983, there were twenty-nine pages in the twentieth anniversary issue in 1988. I helped also, pitching donors such as ARCO, General Motors, Steve Forbes, Loews hotels, and Philip Morris to make full-page ads part of their support, which they did to some extent. And exchange ads with other think magazines helped as well. Between increased ad pages and increased paid circulation, we decided it was time to approach the Audit Bureau of Circulation (ABC) so that our circulation numbers would be audited by the entity that advertisers relied on. We were accepted into ABC in fall 1990.

Circulation doubling was the one goal we did not achieve by 1991. Although circulation had reached a high of thirty-eight thousand at one point in 1986, our circulation-doubling goal was based on paid *subscription* numbers, and that number had been closer to thirty thousand in 1986–87. So when we launched the doubling effort in spring 1988—our twentieth anniversary year—the goal was to reach sixty thousand paid subscribers. One of our board members offered a challenge grant of $50,000 if we could raise $100,000 in new money for this project, so that was my goal for the next year. The money would be spent on increased direct-mail marketing, the primary source of most of our paid subscriptions. Our model said that to achieve doubling within two years we needed to raise and spend $300K, but I figured that $150K would be a good start.

By fall 1990, I was able to tell readers of *Reason Report* (our quarterly donor newsletter) that circulation had reached a new high of forty thousand, thanks to two new direct-mail packages that were working well, paid for by increased donor contributions. Unfortunately, several of our large foundation donors told me frankly that they were not going to make grants earmarked specifically for the magazine (as opposed to general support or policy research). This was because they were uncomfortable with some of the more libertarian personal-freedom issues featured in the magazine. At that point in Reason Foundation's history, we simply did not have enough major individual donors to generate the $300K needed for circulation doubling.

Meanwhile, Marty and her editorial staff had been breaking new ground in producing the magazine. *Reason* was one of the first magazines to adopt computerized page layout, shortly after we moved into the Santa Monica offices. We bought the new software Superpage from Bestinfo, and hired as production manager Nanette Campbell, formerly art director for a Denver publisher. She mastered the software in her first month on the job, and the October 1986 issue was the first one in which the pages were "poured" from edited text to completely laid-out pages. That issue came out "very nearly" on schedule, and it was relatively smooth sailing from then on. Business manager P. K. Lowrey estimated that by eliminating old-fashioned, labor-intensive paste-up of the individual pages, the software would pay for itself in staff cost savings within seven months.

With 1988 being the twentieth anniversary of *Reason* magazine, it was clearly a year to celebrate. Marty planned well ahead for a gala twentieth-anniversary issue, which appeared as Vol. 20, No. 1 in May 1988. At eighty-four pages, it was larger than usual and included an array of special content. That included reflections on sections of the preamble to the US Constitution by Richard Epstein, Karl Hess, Loren Lomasky, Tibor Machan, Charles Murray, Robert Nisbet, and Walter Williams. It also included my article looking at how America had changed between 1968 and 1988, "Things Are a Lot Groovier Now." In addition to being reprinted as an op-ed in a number of newspapers, that piece led to my first contact with ABC-TV's John Stossel. It turns out he'd been reading *Reason*, and was very impressed by my article. After calling me to talk about the article, he did a *20/20* segment on that theme, which was the start of a long and continuing relationship with Reason Foundation. In addition, reporter John Gabree wrote a long, complimentary *Los Angeles Times* article about the magazine's anniversary and the Foundation's growing influence.

We also decided to throw a twentieth-anniversary party for friends and supporters. Trustee Manny Klausner, known as a foodie and investor in restaurants, arranged to have four noted chefs collaborate on a four-course dinner, for which we took over the trendy City Restaurant for the evening. First were Laissez-Faire Appetizers from Ken Frank, Susan Feniger, and Mary Sue Milliken. Next came Subversive Salad by Ken Frank. This was followed by Revolutionary Rigatoni (Susan and Mary Sue) and then Roy Yamaguchi's Capitalist Pork. Dessert was an array of delicacies by all four chefs, accompanied by Essensia dessert wine from libertarian winemaker Andrew Quady (Quady Winery).

Some 150 people attended, and special guests included Alan Reynolds, Nathaniel Branden, John Hospers, David Bergland, and Jack Wheeler. Manny served as emcee for the program which featured no speeches (it was a party!). Marty and I gave a few reminiscences of *Reason*'s early years, followed by table-side magic tricks by Judge Alex Kozinski, libertarian folk-songs by former White House speechwriter Dana Rohrabacher (soon to be elected to Congress), and humorous recordings presented by radio personality Dr. Demento (musicologist Barry Hansen). It was definitely a night to remember.

But summer 1988 was not as happy. Spending was outpacing revenue, in part because I'd been so committed to spending money on the circulation doubling project. Business manager John Runde (who'd replaced P. K. Lowrey in 1987) and I had a visit from two loan officers at our bank, concerned about the increased draw against our line of credit that year (compared with the previous year). In response, we implemented some cost reductions, and those, of course, affected staff morale. At a late-September lunch with Marty, she expressed discouragement over our chronic money woes—and by that point, despite the cost-cutting, things were still looking bleak.

The next month, when Marty and I were both at a conference in Washington, trustee (and mentor) Burton Gray had a long talk with us about Reason Foundation's financial viability. The upshot of this was that since the magazine was costing far more than we were bringing in, shouldn't we at least evaluate the pros and cons of shutting down the magazine and just doing policy research? That hit me very hard, but I could not deny the logic of the question. And the next day, Marty confided that she was nearing forty as a single mother and really needed to decide what her career path should be.

My approach was to make a new effort to raise money from individual donors, in a do-or-die effort that I (privately) called the *Reason* bail-out project. Meaning: either I raise enough to bail *Reason* out of its financial predicament or we would have to bail out of being in the magazine business. At the November board meeting, the trustees pledged to provide at least $45K in new money before the mid-January meeting so that we could provide modest raises to improve morale—but basically left it up to me to find the rest of the "bail-out" money. I spent much of November/December/January on the road, and got some new individual commitments, but also decided that we had to make additional expense reductions, including less spending on new-subscriber direct mail.

Just before Christmas, Marty came into my office to tell me she would be leaving. She would take a new position at the Institute for Humane Studies, by then located in a DC suburb. Fortunately, she was giving six months' notice, partly so as not to interrupt daughter Kate's school year and to give us ample time to find her replacement as editor. Business manager John Runde had resigned in October, unable to take the stress of another year. Since we had no immediate candidate to replace him, that meant short-term payroll savings. And by that point our professional advertising director was no longer producing effectively, so I had to lay him off—another short-term payroll saving. The year 1989 would turn out to be a better year for grants and contributions, but I had no way to know that during those dark days at the end of 1988.

Early in 1989, the effort to find Marty's replacement got underway. We put out the word through various (pre-Internet) networks and a number of excellent people turned out to be interested—including Virginia. As part of the screening process, Lou and I invited several long-time *Reason* authors who were not candidates for the job to a half-day session at our house to brainstorm what the ideal *Reason* editor would be like. That generated some useful criteria that I used in the candidate screening process. It boiled down to three finalists—Virginia and two libertarian journalists at non-libertarian publications. I asked each one to complete a set of written assignments and reviewed the results comparatively. I also did in-person interviews with each, and Virginia was the best all-round candidate.

And it turned out to be an inspired choice. Although Marty's last day was not until the end of June (with a very nice farewell lunch), Virginia moved smoothly into the editor's chair and soon made a number of changes. She contracted with Martin Morse Wooster to be Washington editor and brought on Rick Henderson, Charles Oliver, and Jacob Sullum as editors who would be responsible for writing a larger share of each month's content. A major change was that as a professional journalist, Virginia was interested in being a public intellectual. That meant going on talk shows, re-packaging *Reason* editorials and columns as op-eds sent to newspapers, and writing and placing original op-eds in major national newspapers.

The results showed up fairly quickly in figures on media impact. As we recounted in the spring 1990 issue of *Reason Report*, "In 1989, the media turned to experts at Reason Foundation and the editors of *Reason* magazine more than four times as often as in any previous year." This included articles in the *Washington Post* and *New York Times*, as well as increased coverage in the *Los Angeles Times* and *Wall Street Journal*. And in 1991, we were proud to report that as measured by total paid circulation in 1990, *Reason* had become the fourth largest US think magazine, at fifty thousand, behind *National Review*, *The New Republic*, and *The Nation*. From that point on, there was no further question about *Reason*'s survival.

Policy Research with Impact

The other side of Reason Foundation, the policy research program, really hit its stride following the move to Los Angeles. Between our Federal Privatization Project, new initiatives on airports and toll roads, and expansion of the Local Government Center, we demonstrated that Reason Foundation was a think tank putting new policy ideas into circulation.

Federal Privatization Project

As noted in Chapter 7, our work with the Reagan White House led to the creation of the President's Commission on Privatization. Though I was disappointed at not being named a member, we decided to be a resource to the commission as it carried out its work—and I was invited to testify before it on several issues. However, it soon became apparent that the commission was not really looking into Margaret Thatcher-type sales of state-owned enterprises, which was what our White House conference discussions had intended.

So we made a decision to create the kind of federal privatization agenda that the commission should have done. Inspired by the Shadow Open Market Committee, created by a group of free-market economists to ride herd on the Federal Reserve, we created a Shadow Privatization Commission, made up of leading privatization researchers. Its agenda was to develop a set of position papers on up to a dozen federal assets that were plausible candidates for privatization. One of our early successes was to persuade the President's Commission to add postal privatization to its agenda.

But commission chairman David Linowes, while appreciating our expertise, was offended by the name "Shadow Privatization Commission." In order to maintain good relations, we discontinued use of that name and returned to the original Federal Privatization Project name. We commissioned policy papers, each by a recognized expert and each detailing how and why a specific federal asset or enterprise should be privatized. A preliminary version of the whole set was released in summer 1988 (shortly after the release of the President's Commission report), titled *Federal Privatization: Toward Resolving the Deficit Crisis*. At 136 pages, it identified more than $300 billion in assets and enterprises that could be sold or otherwise privatized. Among these were federal commercial lands, federal loan assets, Amtrak, the Postal Service, the Tennessee Valley Authority, the air traffic control system, and many others. The report was presented to the White House National Economic Commission, charged with proposing a solution to federal deficits by the end of 1988. The more-detailed individual policy papers were rolled out one by one over the several-year period ending in 1991, each with its own media campaign.

Trustee Bob Smiley and several of our donors were deeply interested in employee stock ownership plans (ESOPs) and saw this idea as a potential way of making it possible for federal employees to benefit directly from having their agency privatized. We raised financial support from several companies to hold a two-day conference in Washington, DC, in September 1989. Ambassador William Middendorf and President's Commission Chair David Linowes were the keynote speakers at the "ESOPs and Privatization" conference. Also speaking was my old friend, and now congressman, Dana Rohrabacher (R-CA).

The Federal Privatization Project was also the occasion for my first Reason Foundation policy paper on an air traffic control corporation. "Privatizing the Air Traffic Control System" was released in November 1986. It called for converting the FAA's ATC system into a federally chartered nonprofit corporation, structured as a user cooperative. It also called for divesting all airport control towers to the airports—the system that prevails in the United Kingdom. In a February 1988 speech at the National Press Club, DOT Secretary Jim Burnley said that DOT was looking seriously at a proposal to divest ATC to a nonprofit, user-owned corporation—essentially the Reason plan. Little did I realize that I would still be working on this effort in 2017, as recounted in Chapter 13.

Toll Roads and Road Pricing

One of the biggest adjustments we all had to make in living in Los Angeles (as opposed to small-town Santa Barbara) was commuting in terribly congested traffic, especially on the LA freeways. For a number of years, I'd been reading about road pricing as a way of using market signals to give people incentives to adjust their commuting times away from the most-congested hours. Economists loved the idea, but it seemed politically impossible to ever be implemented.

Thanks to my having gotten to know libertarian-oriented Caltrans engineer Joe Gilly (whom I'd met in the 1970s at one of the USC libertarian conferences), I'd learned that in France and Italy private companies had developed those countries' major highways as toll roads. Thinking about LA freeways, I reasoned that if it was not politically possible to use pricing on the existing lanes, maybe it would be feasible to price brand-new lanes that would be financed, developed, and operated by private toll-road companies. So in early 1988, I set about researching this idea in some detail.

The previous year we'd received a small grant from the Irvine Company (the largest landowner in nearby Orange County) to write a paper on the current state of the art of toll roads in America. The company subsequently led the effort that created two local toll agencies that developed three new toll roads which helped to open up southern Orange County for housing and commercial development. That research effort had put me in touch with a small group of companies that had begun looking into the idea of private-sector toll roads, and the emergence of prototype technology to do tolling electronically. In summer 1987, I gave a Reason Forum presentation on the basic idea of privately financed express toll lanes being added to congested freeways—and ended up doing four news-radio interviews and three talk-show appearances on the subject.

Inspired by that interest, I set about writing a detailed policy study on this idea. During that research, I discovered that a company called Amtech had produced and was starting to market the first windshield-mounted transponder for electronic toll collection. I contacted them for further information, and was invited to Dallas where they were in the process of installing the system on the Dallas North Tollway. I was very impressed seeing the system in operation, and even though their initial use was simply to enable cars to roll through toll-booth lanes at 5 mph instead of stopping to throw coins in the basket, I learned that Amtech had tested the transponders at highway speeds and found that they worked reliably. I also realized that the toll rate could be changed in real time via software. Thus, this system would make it possible to do real-time market pricing on express toll lanes, to keep them moving during peak periods without congestion, and without any toll booths or toll plazas.

The resulting policy paper, "Private Tollways: Resolving Gridlock in Southern California," was released in May 1988, with appropriate PR. But it got no attention at the time. Everyone in

California transportation was focused on a large transportation bond measure on the June ballot. When polls made it look doubtful that the measure would pass, I took a chance and wrote an op-ed piece for the *Los Angeles Times*, to be published if the bond measure failed. It did fail, and they ran the piece—and the next day we got calls from both the Caltrans Director's Office and the Governor's Office, requesting copies of the paper.

Further discussions with Caltrans led to Reason Foundation helping Caltrans put together an August 1988 workshop on the idea, to which I invited the people I'd gotten to know from several engineering companies while working on the Orange County study the year before. The consensus of the workshop was that the idea was, in fact, feasible. Caltrans headquarters then drafted legislation to create a four-project pilot program to test out the idea. And to my surprise, that legislation passed in June 1989—just twelve months after my op-ed had appeared in the *Los Angeles Times*.

Shortly after the legislation passed, Caltrans Assistant Director Carl Williams invited me to become a member of the newly formed Caltrans Privatization Advisory Steering Committee. Our job was to develop the framework under which the agency would seek proposals from private consortia to design, finance, build, operate, and maintain new toll roads and toll lanes, wherever in California they saw a market opportunity. The idea had attracted so much attention that the *Los Angeles Times* assigned reporter Paul Ciotti to interview me and, with Caltrans's permission, to accompany me to the initial Steering Committee meeting in Sacramento. This led to a major story in the *Los Angeles Times Magazine*, September 10, 1989, captioned "Toll Road Warrior." I served on the committee for several years, helping devise the process and selection criteria for the nine proposals the agency received in 1990, from which the highest-scoring four were selected, and long-term franchises negotiated.

Only two of the four ended up getting financed and built—the other two fell victim to environmental and NIMBY opposition. But I was very pleased that the first one financed and built was for my idea of express toll lanes, added in the wide median of the highly congested Orange County freeway, SR 91. It was gratifying to be present at the groundbreaking, wearing the required hard hat (which I still have), and even better to be present on opening day in December 1995. The 91 Express Lanes were the first of what we now call "long-term toll concession projects" in the United States. They were also the world's first express toll lanes, with similar projects now in operation in more than a dozen major metro areas, with plans in place for entire congestion-relief networks of such lanes. In the next several years, I wrote several other Reason policy papers, to explain electronic toll collection, to elaborate on the long-term concession concept, etc. I presented these ideas at numerous transportation conferences around the country. And I'm still doing so.

Airport Privatization

In 1987, Margaret Thatcher ignited what became a worldwide trend of governments privatizing commercial airports. Having been frustrated by the Reagan administration divesting National and Dulles Airports to a government airport authority rather than privatizing them, in 1989 I wrote a "working paper" to explain the case for airport privatization to federal, state, and local policymakers. Our public affairs director, Kevin Teasley, was able to hand a copy to White House Chief of Staff John Sununu during a conference in Washington, DC, that summer.

The working paper generated interest and feedback, so I followed it with a policy study in January 1990. It made several arguments for why privatizing airports would be beneficial (more capacity, increased competition, better facilities). And it included an analysis of the fifty largest US airports, showing how they are systematically short-changed by the federal ticket tax system, getting back only cents in airport grants for each dollar of tax collected from their passengers. We sent tailored news releases to media in each of the fifty metro areas—and got a good deal of publicity.

After learning that the long-time director of Los Angeles International (LAX), Clifton Moore, was interested in the idea, we organized the first US conference on airport privatization, convened in March 1990 in a hotel overlooking LAX. Moore was one of the featured speakers, along with Viggo Butler from Lockheed Air Terminal and Roger Kitley from BAA (the privatized company that was formerly British Airports Authority) in London. The following spring, Councilwoman Joy Picus, of the Budget and Finance Committee, proposed the sale of LAX as a way to address the city's budget crisis, and the City Administrator's Office looked into the idea. But the political will to do this was not there.

By this time, Reason Foundation had become *the* think tank on airport privatization, and one of those who contacted us was Ronald Lauder (of the New York-based cosmetics family). He was interested in running for mayor of New York and was intrigued by the idea of selling city-owned Kennedy and LaGuardia and using the proceeds to reduce the city's debt. Could his foundation commission us to do a study? Yes, it could, and the study was released in May 1990. It estimated that the airports were worth $2.2 billion, but the proceeds would have to be shared with the Port Authority, which had made significant capital investments in the airports. Our estimate was that the city would net $1.29 billion. The study was released at a well-attended news conference and was covered by the *New York Times* and *New York Daily News*, among others. Immediately thereafter, I spoke at a Lauder-sponsored conference on privatization at New York University whose other speakers included Steve Savas (now at Baruch College), Madsen Pirie of the Adam Smith Institute, and several experts from Eastern Europe.

I was not that surprised that when Albany County, New York, decided to privatize its airport, I was invited to weigh in. Given the complex relationships between airports that get federal grants (all commercial airports) and the Federal Aviation Administration, I was soon getting calls for information and advice from both the Albany Airport's management and FAA staffers who were trying to figure out if privatization was legal. This controversy went on for many months, before the agency finally decided that federal grant agreements (which airports must sign each time they accept an FAA grant) precluded selling or leasing an airport.

Before that was decided, however, Albany Airport Director Jim Coyne and I got invited to appear on ABC's "Good Morning America" on May 29, 1990, to discuss the subject. ABC flew me to New York, put me up in a hotel, and conveyed me by limousine to the studio at an extremely early hour (especially given the three-hour time difference between New York and LA). But I did fine, and in the course of further discussions with Albany, I got to know Viggo Butler, the CEO of Lockheed Air Terminal, the company seeking to acquire the airport. Following the FAA's negative decision, Lockheed was able to negotiate a management contract for the Albany Airport, which was permitted under FAA regulations. Viggo and I became friends and fellow advocates of airport privatization.

Over the next several years, mayors or would-be mayors in a number of other cities proposed privatizing their airports, hoping to find a work-around to the federal obstacles. We commissioned attorney John Giraudo to write a paper taking issue with FAA's interpretation of federal grant restrictions (February 1991), while doing several other studies of specific airports that people were interested in privatizing, including Boston Logan Airport and (again) Los Angeles International (LAX). Once again, however, the prospect of having to do legal battles with the FAA dampened the political enthusiasm for actually privatizing those airports.

The Local Government Center Comes of Age.

Board member David Koch was already impressed with Reason Foundation's work on privatization in 1986. During my visit with him in New York that year, he suggested that we might try producing an annual report on privatization, tracking new developments in this country and contrasting US efforts with developments overseas. I brought the idea back to Los Angeles and Phil Fixler took it and ran with it. In March 1987, we released *Privatization 1986*, and it garnered immediate media attention. We decided this was a useful tool, and subsequent annual volumes got larger and more ambitious. By the early 1990s, the *Annual Privatization Report* (the *APR* as we called it) was garnering serious media coverage, especially in contrasting more-dramatic privatization overseas with generally modest activity here at home. The second edition, *Privatization 1987*, dubbed 1987 "the year of privatization," due to a record $92 billion worth of state-owned enterprises having been privatized worldwide that year.

Our major Florida privatization study, commissioned in 1986, was completed in early 1987, consisting of a 450-page report plus three diskettes containing Privatization Candidate and Budget Analysis programs. It made quite a splash, and led to queries about similar studies from other states and to numerous speaking requests for Phil and me. Later that year Phil was flown to Fiji to give a speech and conduct several workshops on privatization, co-sponsored by the US Agency for International Development (USAID) and the Department of the Interior. That summer, I delivered a paper Phil and I had written on privatization of policing services at the Western Regional Science Association's annual conference. In 1988, LGC did a privatization study for Anchorage, Alaska, identifying services that could be contracted out and enterprises that could be sold off. And LGC also carried out a study funded by the Los Angeles Taxpayers Association of privatization opportunities for the City and County of Los Angeles.

Also in 1988, we took a step that should have happened years earlier: renaming LGC's newsletter *Privatization Watch*, instead of the bland *Fiscal Watchdog*. Basically, since privatization was no longer a radical idea, we wanted to be more up-front about this being a must-read source of information on the subject. And that winter we released the Los Angeles privatization study, finding that the city and county governments could save $740 million a year by contracting out services such as garbage collection that cost considerably more than service available from commercial contractors. Other proposed contracts included asphalt resurfacing, building security, and street sweeping.

LGC's biggest study in 1989 was an analysis of the state-owned ports and railroads of North Carolina. Fixler's study found that selling the two state-owned ports and two state-owned railroads could yield $200 million for the state treasury, while shielding taxpayers from future subsidies for these enterprises. The study received extensive statewide news coverage, but went no further.

Also in 1989, we welcomed Bill Eggers, who'd just graduated from UC San Diego, as a one-year LGC Research Fellow, thanks to a grant from the Grover Hermann Foundation. Bill's subsequent career took him to the Heritage Foundation in Washington and later back to Reason Foundation. And in 1990, LGC received a grant from the Howard Jarvis Taxpayers Association to review the State of California's budget for privatization opportunities. The study identified $1.3 billion in annual savings based on competitively contracting certain services and terminating several marginal programs.

By the time *Privatization 1991* was published, in April 1991, the news conference was a large, bipartisan event. Speakers included Assemblyman Richard Katz (D) and LA County Supervisor Mike Antonovich (R), as well as several CEOs of private service providers and the head of California's Business, Transportation, and Housing Agency. The report's findings made news in specialized publications like *City and State*, but also in the *Washington Post* and *Boston Globe*, among other leading newspapers. Sadly, Phil Fixler was not there as the lead author. The previous summer he'd been hospitalized for what turned out to be aggressive cancer. Despite months of chemotherapy (and after making a heroic appearance at our fall 1990 banquet), Phil died in February 1991. He was only forty-four.

Other Policy Research

Fortunately, Research Director Lynn Scarlett had stepped into the breach when Phil got sick, overseeing *Privatization 1991* in addition to directing the Federal Privatization Project, which by that time was winding down. And with environmental issues becoming ever larger nationwide (and in California), Lynn's research interests turned increasingly to such topics as air quality and waste management, where command-and-control policies were the norm but where price signals could make a big difference. Already in 1989, her study "Managing America's Garbage: Alternatives and Solutions," was inspiring a switch to "pay-as-you-throw" policies under which cities charged by the bag or by the can for trash collection, to encourage recycling. Her ideas on this subject were reported in a national AP news story, and later featured in a major *Wall Street Journal* op-ed (January 14, 1991), which the newspaper—not Lynn—titled "Make Your Environment Dirtier—Recycle," which was not her point. In June 1991, she testified on hazardous waste policy before the House Energy and Commerce Committee. That year she also appeared on CNN's *Crossfire* and ABC's *Good Morning America* discussing mandatory recycling laws.

Living in Los Angeles, we all lived with smog most of the time, and as new regulations were put forth, Lynn organized conferences and seminars to draw attention to pricing and incentives as better tools than one-size-fits-all regulations. One 1990 conference featured Gary Bishop of the University of Denver, who documented on-road research finding that less than 10 percent of cars generated more than 60 percent of auto emissions, and showed videos of technology that accurately measured tailpipe emissions of cars on the road. At another conference that year, Lynn contrasted emission fees for stationary sources with one-size-fits-all regulations. In 1991, Lynn authored "A Consumer's Guide to Environmental Myths and Realities" for the National Center for Policy Analysis in Dallas.

Lynn also led us into issues of urban growth and land use, and the overlaps of these areas with transportation policy. In late 1990, we hosted a two-day conference on this subject in downtown Los Angeles. That fall I promoted Lynn to vice president of research, in view of her increased responsibilities and increasingly national profile. And in 1991, to fill the gap left by Phil's death, we added economist David Haarmeyer and political scientist John Guardiano to the research staff.

Becoming Mr. Privatization

Beginning around the time of the move to Los Angeles in 1986, my speaking invitations on privatization shifted from being mostly about *Cutting Back City Hall* service contracting to national asset sales along the lines of what our Federal Privatization Project was focused on. In May 1986, I was one of two overseas experts (along with Madsen Pirie of the Adam Smith Institute in

London) flown in to speak at the first-ever privatization conference in South Africa, held in Johannesburg and sponsored by that
country's Free Market Foundation. About 650 people attended,
the biggest gathering I'd ever spoken to. That event led to a
long-standing friendship with FMF's president, Leon Louw. Later
that year I commented on a paper on privatization by Pirie at
the Mont Pelerin Society meeting in St. Vincent, Italy. I also took
part in a two-day conference on privatization at the Wharton
School and in two panel discussions on privatization at the annual meeting of the National Conference of State Legislatures.

The next year I co-chaired a Heritage Foundation conference
on privatization and was the keynote speaker for a privatization
conference of the Institute of Political Economy at the University
of Utah, and also addressed a congressional roundtable on privatization. Lou came along with me for a two-day Fraser Institute
privatization conference in Vancouver—our first time ever in
that beautiful city. In February 1988, Pirie and I were among the
speakers for the first-ever privatization conference in Greece, held
in a very smoggy Athens. TWA lost my luggage when I changed
planes at JFK, and I ended up having to give my presentation
in flown-in casual clothes. That was the last time I ever did a
speaking trip with checked luggage! Later that year, Lou joined
me for a return to South Africa occasioned by an invitation to
discuss privatization at a Libertarian International conference
in Swaziland. The rest of the trip was vacation, which included
two days in Krueger Park, several days in beautiful Cape Town
riding the famous Blue Train from there to Johannesburg, and
getting a tour of Soweto from one of Leon's staff at the Free
Market Foundation—a very memorable trip.

In July 1989, the Adam Smith Institute hosted a privatization
conference in London; privatized British Airways was one of
the sponsors, and I got to fly there and back in Business Class,
quite a treat. While there, I compared notes with fellow think-
tank people from half a dozen other countries. That September,
I was invited to lecture on privatization at the classical-liberal
summer university held every year at the Universités d'été in
Aix-en-Provence, so that was another trip on which Lou joined

me. We made it largely into a vacation—several days in Paris, the high-speed TGV train to Lyon and Marseilles, then the summer university in Aix, followed by several days relaxing on the Riviera. And December brought yet another overseas adventure: speaking at the Mont Pelerin Society meeting in Christchurch, New Zealand. This took place during the time of radical free-market reforms implemented by Labor Party finance minister Roger Douglas, who was followed by Conservative finance minister Ruth Richardson; both of whom spoke at the conference.

And in November 1990, I went to Stockholm, once again speaking on privatization along with half a dozen other experts from various countries. It was only for a few days, and my lasting memory is of how dark it got by about 3:30 in the afternoon. These trips were all fun and useful in networking with fellow think-tank leaders. But their opportunity cost was high, in terms of time away from managing a growing, and still struggling, Reason Foundation

Building Capacity
Strengthening the Board

Now that we'd relocated to the big city, one of my other priorities was to continue building a stronger board. In 1987, we added Jerry Jordan, chief economist at First Interstate Bank (which was also our bank). Jerry was a good board member, but had to depart after two years when he was appointed to the board of the Federal Reserve Bank of Cleveland.

The next year (1988) saw three strong additions from the business community: Bernie Baltic, Tony Jackson, and Frank Bond. Bernie was an investment manager in Cleveland and had been one of our early National Advisory Council members. He supported a number of other libertarian organizations, including the Mackinac Center, the free-market think tank in Michigan. His interest in them was primarily because they did a lot of training of state think-tank people in how to manage, do PR, and fundraise. He loved *Reason* magazine and thought our privatization work was great. Tony Jackson was an attorney with Baker and McKenzie in Los Angeles and a former radio and television talk show host. His business community connections served us well in gaining support for our annual banquets.

Frank Bond was the founder and president of the Holiday Health Spa chain, an Objectivist, and had been the major donor of the now-defunct Society for Individual Liberty (whose magazine, *The Individualist, Reason* had absorbed). I think it was Manny Klausner who'd made the introduction for me, and it took several visits with Frank in Baltimore before he was sold on Reason Foundation as a good investment. As a trustee, Frank brought a new sense of order and professionalism to the board. In particular, he got us to focus more on developing serious selection criteria, so that candidates for board membership could be assessed comparatively, with scores on a number of factors. (This naturally appealed to me as an engineer.) It was Frank's strong recommendation that we should set a minimum annual contribution of $25K for board members—either to give or to raise. Some members were not at that level, so this was not an easy sell, but it was adopted while grandfathering existing board members. We also decided that new members would serve a one-year, get-acquainted term, and if the relationship worked out, would then be elected to a regular three-year term.

In 1989, board member Joe Coberly introduced us to Joe Coulombe, and we invited him to join the board. Coulombe was the real Trader Joe—the founder and then still CEO of that quirky, wonderful grocery chain that was at the time a California-only phenomenon. He was a great guy to know, but my memory is unclear why Joe served only his initial get-acquainted term. Later that year, in October, Burton Gray—board member, mentor, and friend—died of a massive heart attack at age forty-eight. I was devastated, personally, and it took me a few days for the reality to sink in—he was really gone. We created a Burton Gray Internship fund in his name, and to this day every summer Reason Foundation selects a promising college student as our Burton Gray intern.

In 1990, at David Koch's request, we added Richie Fink of Koch Industries to the board. David did not throw his weight around, but he was not always able to fly out to Los Angeles for the board meetings, so he wanted one of his people to be on the board in addition to himself. This made me a bit uncomfortable, but since Richie and I had a good relationship, I did not see it as a real problem, and it turned out not to be. An event soon thereafter illustrated the wisdom of David having an alternate on our board. In February 1991, David was on a US Airways 737 arriving at LAX Friday night for a Reason Foundation board meeting the next morning. A control tower error cleared the jetliner to land on a runway already occupied by a commuter plane about to start its take-off run. The 737 landed on top of the commuter plane, with significant losses of life. David was able to open the forward exit door and jump out, saving his life, but was hospitalized for smoke inhalation and did not make it to the next day's board meeting. He did not attend many LA board meetings subsequent to that accident.

In 1991, Norm Karlin retired from the board, and to replace him as the academic member (exempt from the $25K requirement) we invited Walter Williams to join, and he accepted. Tony Jackson died and Bob Smiley was unable to renew, so we had at least two vacancies to fill. We found—and added—three strong candidates: Rich Dennis, Neal Goldman, and Harry Teasley.

We'd been courting Rich for several years. A well-known Chicago commodity trader (and part-owner of the Chicago White Sox), Rich is a libertarian Democrat—market-friendly but with his real passion being civil liberties. He was drawn to Reason partly by our principled opposition to the War on Drugs. At that time, he had a home in Los Angeles in addition to Chicago, so he started attending Reason events and meeting senior staff. After he became a donor, it was a no-brainer to invite him onto the board, and he accepted. Neal Goldman is a New York-based investment manager with his own firm, Goldman Capital Management. With many connections in the investment world, he seemed an obvious candidate.

Harry Teasley was a long-time Coca-Cola executive whom Lynn had met and gotten to know at conferences dealing with waste-management, recycling, and related topics. He became a Reason donor, and in 1991 we invited him to join the board. Harry was a tough, hard-headed manager, and his initial impression of our board and management was that both needed a lot of work to become more businesslike. He was right, and during the 1990s he did a great deal to strengthen both.

Financial Support

During our first six years in Los Angeles, our budget grew from $1.4 million in 1986 to $2.2 million in 1991. And in contrast with the struggling years in Santa Barbara—when the majority of years showed operating losses—our revenue and expenditures were within a few percentage points of each other during these years of increasing visibility and credibility. We recruited more individual donors who could make five-figure contributions, we raised money from our annual banquets, and in particular we increased the number of corporate and foundation contributors. In 1986, we had twenty-nine corporate donors; by 1991, that number had grown to fifty-one. And foundation donors had grown from thirty in 1986 to fifty-one in 1991. This was significant growth, reflecting Reason Foundation's increased visibility and credibility.

Several stories illustrate the kinds of unexpected opportunities that turned into larger-scale donor relationships. One day in February 1989, I received a phone call from Mike Milken at Drexel Burnham Lambert. He'd read a column I'd written defending the idea of "junk bonds" as they were being used in those days and wanted to learn more about Reason Foundation. So I made an appointment and drove over to the Drexel offices in Beverly Hills. I spent at least ninety minutes, talking with Milken and several of his staffers. He expressed frustration with financial regulators criticizing investment firms no matter what they did. I laughed and said that reminded me of the classic free-market book *The Incredible Bread Machine*, which relates that if you charge too little, government calls it unfair competition; charge too much and it's price gouging; but charge the same and it's price-fixing. He'd never heard of the book but asked if I could get him a copy. I left his office with a definite "to be continued" and the action item to get him that book.

When I got back to the office I found two copies in the Reason library and figured we could spare one, so I called Milken staffer Mitch Julis and told him we had it. They sent a courier over to get it. And a day or two later Mitch called back and asked where they could buy several hundred copies. Fortunately, I had (LA-based) author Richard Grant's phone number in my address book, and called him to see if he had a supply of them. Fortunately, he did—in a nearby storage room. So Milken's people made a bulk purchase and included the book in the swag bag for all the attendees at that year's junk bonds conference—which turned out to be the last one ever held. Lou and I got comped to attend, and I was very pleased when opening keynote speaker George Gilder held up a copy of *The Incredible Bread Machine* and commended it to everyone.

In the next few months the relationship deepened. We had a shared interest in a truly free, competitive market (including the market for corporate control), and they were also big fans of ESOPs (Drexel Burnham Lambert helped to sponsor our ESOPs and privatization conference). I wrote a *Reason* column about the junk bonds conference, and we discussed having Milken be the honoree at our banquet that fall. We knew it would be controversial. There was already talk of a possible indictment, but Mike and his people could see the PR value in his being honored by an up-and-coming think tank. (Before we could close that deal, I had to meet with their PR firm in New York and convince them of Reason's bona fides.) So we went ahead with the plans. In our banquet "kickoff" event in downtown LA (aimed at potential buyers of entire tables), I remember one oil company CEO telling me flatly that the ability of Milken and others to engage in corporate takeovers was a mortal threat, and that they would have no part of any event honoring Milken.

We stuck to our guns and the October 23, 1989, banquet set a new attendance record of over 450 people. Speakers included Art Laffer, Arnold Schwarzenegger, and Prof. Henry Manne (who noted that "mergers and takeovers have made life far richer and far more meaningful" for millions of Americans and praised the development of the high-yield bond market). The event made local, national, and international media, and was broadcast by

Financial News Network and *PM Magazine*. Alas, Milken was indicted for technical securities law violations and convicted, and Drexel Burnham without Milken folded.[3] But the Milken Foundation continued and became an ongoing supporter of Reason Foundation's work, including our new program on school choice. Lowell Milken became our main point of contact, and we received our first Milken Foundation grant in March 1990.

In September 1987, I attended the Mont Pelerin Society regional meeting in Indianapolis. One of the people I met there was Gordon St. Angelo, a program officer at the Lilly Endowment, one of the largest foundations that supported some free-market think tanks (but not Reason). In talking with Gordon, I learned that he was a member of the governing board of the Indianapolis Airport, and I mentioned airport privatization as an important new phenomenon. Over the next several years, as I wrote several policy papers on the subject, I would occasionally get a call from Gordon, asking questions, since he was intrigued with the idea as a possibility for Indianapolis.

In the summer of 1991, Gordon invited me to Indianapolis to have lunch with the county prosecutor, Steve Goldsmith, who was running for mayor. We talked privatization—both competitive contracting and asset sale/lease ideas—for about two hours, and I was very impressed with Goldsmith (who went on to win election as mayor). While I was in town, Gordon also brought me to Lilly Endowment headquarters where he introduced me to the president and the treasurer. Afterwards, Gordon asked what it would take for Reason Foundation to develop a much larger capability to actively assist mayors and governors who wanted to pursue privatization agendas. I said we would need several dedicated staff members and a travel budget—and he invited me to write up a suitable proposal. Lilly's support, starting in 1992, enabled us to transform the Local Government Center into the Privatization Center, as related in Chapter 9.

In January 1990, we received a visit from Alan Roth and Art

---

3   See Daniel Fischel, *Payback: The Conspiracy to Destroy Michael Milken and His Financial Revolution* (Harper Collins, 1995) for an assessment of Milken that I find persuasive, as did Milton Friedman.

Finkelstein. Alan was Ronald Lauder's senior staffer for politics and policy, and Art was a pollster they worked with. They came to sound us out about Lauder making a sizeable investment in *Reason* magazine and commissioning us to do some privatization research. My initial reaction to the visit was positive—finally a "bail-out" of the magazine to do a major expansion? Virginia, needless to say, was more skeptical, and with good reason. When she and I visited Lauder the next month in New York, it became pretty clear that he wanted significant control in exchange for a major investment. We prepared and submitted a proposal in March, but it laid out editorial independence, and we were clearly in conflict. Lauder made a counterproposal, which we presented to the board for discussion at its April meeting; they turned it down. That was the end of Lauder's *Reason* magazine venture, but as noted previously, we did several projects with the Lauder organization dealing with privatization.

The Business Manager Conundrum

Even though Reason Foundation's finances improved during the early LA years, we still lived from hand to mouth. The only "reserve fund" was our bank line of credit, and it's something of a miracle that First Interstate renewed it annually despite our dicey finances. And if you look through Reason Foundation's annual reports from those years, there's a different business manager in nearly every one. P. K. Lowrey, who started work in Santa Barbara in December 1985 and made the move to LA with us, gave his notice a year later in a disagreement over roles and responsibilities. In this case we lucked out in quickly finding and hiring accountant John Runde, who relocated from Wisconsin with his wife and baby to take the job. John stuck it out for twenty months, but decided he couldn't "take another year of the pressure" and resigned in November 1988. After a gap of two months, I persuaded my old friend Jack Dean, who'd been doing computer work and fundraising for several nonprofits in Orange County, to take the job. Jack stayed for eighteen months, but not being an accountant, needed ongoing outside assistance with that aspect of the job.

Providing that assistance to each new business manager, and filling in during the gaps, was my wife, Lou. With her MBA, accounting experience, and years of work in nonprofit management, she pitched in evenings and Saturdays to keep our systems running and to coach and train each new business manager that came on board. She agreed to provide ten hours per month as a donation, and to be paid an hourly rate for time spent in addition to that. The Reason work was in addition to her work at the UCLA Chancellor's office as a program and budget analyst—a very full-time job.

The board was troubled by this staff turnover, and as early as March 1989, David Koch promised to pay the first three years' salary of a senior vice president who could be in charge of all administrative functions and potentially assist with fundraising—assuming we could find someone qualified for the position. When no good candidates materialized after eleven months of looking, David took two further steps. He agreed to pay for a head-hunter firm to find candidates for us to interview—and, importantly, he reviewed senior staff salaries and got the board to agree to increase them, to make it possible for us to offer a reasonable salary to the new vice president. By July, the headhunters had provided us with two good candidates, and we settled on Bryan Snyder (then with Ernst and Young's Los Angeles office), who started work in September 1990. Lou put in several more months getting Bryan up to speed and preparing files for the annual audit, but she and I were both hugely relieved that this long ordeal of business managers was finally ended.

Joys and Agonies

There were some high points for me personally, in addition to policy successes during those years, despite the stresses of personnel and financial problems.

Besides my Mr. Privatization trips, I started getting invited on junkets. In 1987, the US Air Force invited me to join a group of other Los Angeles business and community leaders on a two-day excursion to two military bases: Kirtland AFB in Albuquerque and Nellis AFB near Las Vegas. Given my love of aviation, I couldn't turn that one down, even though had I been asked to vote on spending taxpayers' money on such things, it would have been an easy NO. We were flown from LAX to Albuquerque on a USAF 737, and I got to spend time in the cockpit talking with the pilots; from them I learned that air traffic control at Albuquerque is provided by USAF controllers, since Kirtland AFB is co-located at that airport. We got tours of the electronic warfare labs there, and had a wonderful dinner of New Mexican food at an Albuquerque restaurant. Next morning, we flew to Nellis, where our tour was of the facility that controls the Red Flag jet fighter exercises. It was a great experience, but I used vacation days for it, since it really could not be justified as work-related.

Also in 1987, the German Consulate offered me a two-week junket in Germany, which I seriously considered accepting. But because Lou could not come along, and because two weeks would have been a huge chunk of time (opportunity cost!), I turned that one down.

For me as an ardent anti-communist, the collapse of communism—first in Eastern Europe and then the USSR—was overwhelming. I could scarcely believe the news reports, and that was one of the few times in my life when I actually watched TV news, seeing for myself people climbing unhindered over the Berlin Wall. The next year (1990), when the Mont Pelerin Society meeting was to be held in Munich, Lou and I made plans to spend two weeks of vacation in Germany, the first week purely as tourists and the second week at MPS (and touring Munich). It was a very memorable trip: Frankfurt, Cologne, then a train to Berlin (passing through the obvious poverty of what had been East Germany). We had several days to explore East and West Berlin. And when we saw that people could chisel their own pieces of the Berlin Wall as souvenirs, we found a hardware store and bought a hammer and chisel. We collected a whole gallon Ziploc full of pieces, and made Christmas gifts for close friends and relatives of a piece of the wall mounted in a picture frame, with photos of us harvesting the pieces. I was wearing my green "Smash the State—and Have a Nice Day" shirt, a gift from the Libertarian Supper Club of San Diego, and Lou wore a Reason T-shirt.

While Marty was still *Reason* editor, Lou and Marty came up with the idea of producing a libertarian cookbook. The idea was to collect recipes from libertarian and classical liberal notables, complete with something personal about the dish from each celebrity. They ended up with a spiral-bound, ninety-eight-page cookbook, divided into the following sections:

- Anarchist Appetizers
- Subversive Soups
- Spontaneous Salads
- Enterprising Entrees
- Voluntarist Vegetables
- Buyer-Beware Breads
- Deregulated Desserts
- Libertarian Libations

They collected a wonderful array of recipes from people that included science fiction authors Poul Anderson and Robert Heinlein, Barbara Branden, Ed and Alicia Clark, Milton Friedman, Karl Hess, John Hospers, Lynn Kinsky, Leon Louw and Frances Kendall, Manny Klausner, Tibor Machan, Dave Nolan, Bob Poole, Ayn Rand, Murray Rothbard, Durk Pearson and Sandy Shaw, Lynn Scarlett, Jack Wheeler, Lou Villadsen, and Marty Zupan, as well as others. *Liberated Cooking* was offered for sale directly by *Reason* and also by Laissez-Faire Books.

Despite all the highs, there were also lows. I started expressing doubts in my journal about whether I wanted to spend the rest of my life running the organization, as early as 1988, such as, "I'll get through this [cash crunch] somehow, but I sure wish there were an easier way to make a living. It gets very wearing." Lamenting yet another Saturday spent at the office later that year, I wrote, "What am I getting out of my life? Yes, my life does produce a lot of rewards, but does it really make sense to continually deny myself time off to do my own things?" After our South Africa trip, I confided to Lou some pangs about going back to the grind. "We talked it out, and I quickly realized how much my identity is tied up in this work—and how I'm able to go to all these places precisely because of what I'm doing with Reason."

Several times over the next few years, Lou and I both resolved to be more disciplined about weekend work, and for me to be more strategic about accepting speaking invitations. I also got several feelers about possible job offers, but never pursued them. Reason Foundation's growing success kept me going, with no serious thought about doing anything else.

Chapter 9

Having Nationwide Impact (1992–2000)

Preview of an Amazing Decade

The decade of the 1990s saw the growth and maturation of Reason Foundation into a serious national think tank, and *Reason* into a respected national magazine. As we moved from our modest office space in a Santa Monica office park into a high-rise tower overlooking the I-405 freeway in September 1991, we gained not only twice the space but a bona fide Los Angeles address.

Shortly after this move, the *Wall Street Journal* did an op-ed page profile of Reason Foundation, including a picture of me and the quotable sentence, "Of all the nation's conservative or free-market policy groups, it may be the most libertarian among them, the Reason Foundation in Southern California, that ends up having the most direct impact on the actual functioning of government." That same year Lynn Scarlett appeared on *Crossfire* talking about how the marketplace minimizes the use of scarce resources like aluminum, which she illustrated by ripping a soft drink can in half. And by 1992, *Reason's* editor-in-chief, Virginia Postrel, had a regular monthly column on the op-ed page of the *Los Angeles Times*, and later a regular column in *Forbes*.

Having achieved significant visibility in the LA metro area, we phased out annual banquets in favor of special-event banquets, and replaced monthly Reason Forums with conferences and seminars focused on specific policy issues—local, state, or national. We also launched annual Reason Weekends for our major individual donors.

By the end of the decade, we had built the policy research division into the Reason Public Policy Institute with six major program areas and full-time professionals researching and writing policy studies, getting op-eds published, testifying before legislative bodies, and appearing on local and national broadcast media. Likewise, *Reason* magazine got into bookstore chains and finally reached my circulation-doubling goal of sixty thousand, while gaining professional recognition in the magazine industry. We were also one of the first think magazines to develop an Internet presence, launching *Reason Online* in 1995.

By the end of the decade, I was very proud. This was the think tank I'd dreamed of, and despite financial vicissitudes and management challenges, it was firmly established as a player in policy and cultural debates.

Building a National Policy Research Program

During the first half of the decade, as our research work expanded beyond transportation, privatization, and environmental policy to include school reform, infrastructure, and urban growth issues, Lynn and I fretted over confusion among policymakers and media people between *Reason* magazine, our policy research, and Reason Foundation overall. As Lynn wrote in Issue 71 of our donor newsletter, *Reason Report*,

> Readers of *Reason* magazine often think that the only activity of Reason Foundation is its magazine. Others more familiar with our research often think that our public policy work is synonymous with the Foundation, while believing that the magazine is either wholly unrelated or only vaguely part of the Foundation. Giving the research department a formal name will provide an organizational symmetry that will allow us to describe the overall mission of the Foundation: the focus, style, and impact of the magazine; and the focus, style, and impact of our public policy research.

By that point in time, Lynn was already vice president of research, and she now gained the additional title of executive director of the newly named Reason Public Policy Institute (RPPI). Its six program areas were:

- Privatization Center
- Infrastructure
- Transportation
- Education Studies
- Environmental Policy
- Urban Futures.

Privatization Center

Thanks to the new support from the Lilly Endowment, we transformed the former Local Government Center into the Privatization Center, recruiting two outstanding young policy researchers: Bill Eggers (our former intern, then working at Heritage Foundation) and John O'Leary (from the Pioneer Institute in Boston), plus research librarian Donna Braunstein. Their mission was to develop extensive material on state and local privatization of services and assets/enterprises, with their "customers" being primarily reform-minded mayors and governors. (Note: as a tax-exempt organization, we were not allowed to do consulting work in competition with tax-paying companies, so our "customers" received our advice and attention at no charge, as part of our overall limited-government mission.)

Our first major customer was Steve Goldsmith, the newly elected mayor of the city/county government of Indianapolis. I took the initial lead, as the one who'd introduced candidate Goldsmith to privatization, and went to Indianapolis at his request to assist in setting up the reform group they called Service, Efficiency, and Lower Taxes for Indianapolis Commission (SELTIC). It consisted of Goldsmith's reform-minded department heads and leading private-sector people from Indianapolis. SELTIC's private-sector co-chair was Mitch Daniels, then a senior executive at Eli Lilly. I soon turned over most of the ongoing relationship to Bill and John, who provided regular assistance to Goldsmith and SELTIC as they went about organizing competitions between existing city workforces and private-sector firms. Over his two terms as mayor, Goldsmith's program competed over fifty services and reduced the cost of those retained in-house, saving taxpayers an estimated $420 million (equivalent to nearly the starting year's annual budget). Indianapolis received national media coverage as a successful practitioner of privatization, giving us a role model to inspire other jurisdictions nationwide. Bill Eggers's 1993 *Reason* magazine article on Goldsmith's revolution was reprinted by *Reader's Digest*, giving it massive nationwide exposure.

The Privatization Center operated a telephone help-line to answer questions from public officials and reporters. While it continued to publish *Privatization Watch* and the *Annual Privatization Report*, its new products included policy research studies on lesser-known kinds of privatization as well as a whole series of how-to-guides on applying privatization to individual services (fire protection, golf courses, park maintenance, street repair, etc.). These guides were much in demand, as measured by the sales volume of these hard-copy reports (in those pre-Internet days).

Another important part of the center's program was privatization conferences. The first one took place in nearby Orange County, September 29, 1992, called "Balancing Budgets without Raising Taxes." One of the speakers was Louis Schimmel, who had served as the receiver for bankrupt Ecorse, Michigan, and had eliminated a $6 million deficit by privatizing numerous city services. Attorney Karen Hedlund explained the new opportunities provided by White House Executive Order 12803 (described below under Infrastructure), which made it easier to sell or lease infrastructure assets that had received federal grants.

The center's first *national* conference occurred in Lake Tahoe, California, in February 1993. Over three hundred people attended, with Mayor Goldsmith as the keynote speaker. During the next several years, the center's high-profile customers included Mayors Richard Daley (Chicago), Ed Rendell (Philadelphia), and Richard Riordan (Los Angeles), as well as Governors Bill Weld (Massachusetts) and Christine Whitman (New Jersey). The center's two-day 1994 "Streamlining Government" conference took place in Chicago, with speakers including Daley, Goldsmith, and Mayors Norquist (Milwaukee), Schundler (Jersey City), and White (Cleveland). And 1995's "21st Century Government" conference in Philadelphia featured Rendell, Goldsmith, Weld, and Whitman as speakers.

Over the years, there were smaller half-day and one-day privatization workshops in other cities, including Honolulu and Pittsburgh, but two major impacts occurred closer to home, in Los Angeles and Orange County.

In spring 1993, we got a call from Prof. William Ouchi at UCLA asking if Lynn and I would be interested in joining a small group of thinkers in coming up with an agenda of policy reforms for LA's next mayor. We said yes, especially since Dick Riordan was running and seemed market-friendly and change-oriented. Maybe we could have our own Steve Goldsmith right here in LA, I hoped. We drafted some position papers on competitive contracting for city services and floated the idea of privatizing major city-run enterprises such as Los Angeles International Airport (LAX) and the Department of Water and Power, the city's giant municipal utility. So we were delighted when Riordan was elected that June on a platform that included contracting out garbage collection and privatizing LAX. Ouchi joined the new administration, heading up efforts to reinvent the city government. We arranged fact-finding visits for Riordan with Mayor Goldsmith in Indianapolis and Mayor Rendell in Philadelphia, and he returned vowing to set up a business/government team along the lines of SELTIC in Indianapolis.

LAX privatization had already been the subject of a Reason policy paper that Vice President of Administration Bryan Snyder and I had researched and written in 1992. Our assessment found serious flaws in a study the city had commissioned by aviation consultants Babcock and Brown—basically a defense of the status quo. Armed with our new study, Riordan was not deterred, and engaged staff to work on the idea and to revive the Airport Commission's previous interest. In parallel, we proposed a "Reinventing LA Project" that would take an arm's-length view of potential savings from Indianapolis-type competitive contracting for city services. Deputy Mayor Michael Keeley spoke at a

Reason fundraising luncheon for the project at the California Club on December 8, 1993, and we received enough local business support to carry out the first phase.

Phase 1 was an overview study during the first five months of 1994, conducted by Privatization Center senior staff assisted by twelve graduate students from the University of Southern California's public policy program. That study estimated $120 million in annual savings from contracting out seven services, including garbage collection, emergency medical services, and five others. The study findings got major publicity in print and broadcast media—but nothing happened. Riordan never did appoint the SELTIC-type committee to oversee such changes, and public employee union opposition swayed a clear majority of city council members against any privatizations. Although Riordan won re-election to a second term, I was frustrated that he did not back council candidates to run against anti-privatization incumbents, so nothing changed on the council. And the major airlines ran a propaganda campaign against LAX privatization, as well as threatening litigation if the city tried to go through with it. So Riordan eventually threw in the towel on that effort, too.

Our other local opportunity was created when nearby Orange County filed for bankruptcy on December 6, 1994, due to risky investments that went bad. A few weeks later, the Lincoln Club of Orange County invited me to a private meeting to discuss a grant under which we would develop a plan to radically downsize the OC government, via privatization, aiming to save enough money each year to enable the county to resume debt service on its bonds. Even before that meeting, the *Los Angeles Times* had raised the prospect of selling the county's John Wayne Airport (and I'd been quoted in that article). We agreed on the basics, a schedule, and a dollar amount. When work began, we got an incredibly lucky break. OC's acting treasurer, hired to manage things during the bankruptcy, was Tom Daxon, who'd read my *Cutting Back City Hall* years before and already had a proposed agenda that included selling the airport, landfills, and parks and outsourcing various services. Tom gave us access to any and all budget and performance data that we needed.

Bill, John, Lynn, and I worked feverishly on our plan, and after a heroic six weeks, we released it on February 15, 1995. I presented our findings before an audience of over two hundred people at the Orange County Forum. Downsizing and outsourcing were estimated to save $233–238 million per year, more than enough to offset the county's $160 million shortfall in ability to pay annual debt service on its bonds. And asset sales could yield $2.5–3 billion in one-time proceeds. It was front-page news in all the newspapers, and my op-ed appeared the next day in the *Los Angeles Times*. I wrote in my journal that this report "probably had had more immediate impact than anything Reason Foundation has ever published."

The major impact was to halt momentum that had been building for a sales-tax increase. We suffered a setback in March, while Lou and I were on vacation in the Florida Keys. I'd designated Bryan to handle any media related to the OC report during my absence, and on a radio talk show, in answer to a question of whether he could rule out a sales tax increase, he said "No." Well—the next day this was front page news in the *Los Angeles Times*, accompanied by an editorial claiming, triumphantly, that even Reason Foundation was now okay with a sales tax increase. From my hotel room on Key Largo, I outlined damage-control media strategies, but the damage had been done. Still, by the time voters were faced with an OC sales tax increase several months later on the June ballot, they turned it down. *Investor's Business Daily* editorialized that this was a victory for OC taxpayers and that "the best package for Orange County remains the plan from the Reason Foundation released in February." The county did work its way out of bankruptcy, with some degree of competitive service contracting, but did not sell or lease any of its major assets.

During 1994–95, Bill and John drew on their firsthand experiences advising innovative mayors and governors to write a book on reinventing government. *Revolution at the Roots: Making Our Government Smaller, Better, and Closer to Home* (Free Press, 1995) was a worthy successor to my *Cutting Back City Hall* from fifteen years before. It reflected the change in privatization from a small, experimental activity to a mainstream tool for innovative mayors and governors of both parties. We paid for them to do a nationwide book tour, which led Free Press to do a second printing to keep up with sales. The book was widely reviewed, and Bill and/or John had op-eds in many leading papers and did more than seventy radio and TV appearances. A number of presentations were hosted by state-level free-market think tanks like the Pioneer Institute in Boston and the Georgia Public Policy Foundation in Atlanta. Their book shared first place in the 1996 Sir Antony Fisher Memorial Awards, given by the Atlas Economic Research Foundation (today renamed Atlas Network) for "the book making the greatest contribution to the free economy during the past two years."

In 1996, Lilly Endowment gave us an additional grant to work with those state think tanks. Specifically, we sponsored a competition, asking them to propose privatization projects, from which we would select the most promising ones, give the winners each a sub-grant from the Lilly money, and provide technical assistance as needed. These think tanks were all members of the growing State Policy Network, on whose board I served from 1998 through 2005.

Following their successful book tour, John O'Leary was wooed away by the Sacramento office of consulting firm KPMG in summer 1996. That fall we hired Adrian Moore, a PhD candidate in economics at UC Irvine, US Army veteran, and co-author of an excellent Brookings Institution book, *Curb Rights: A Foundation for Competition and Entrepreneurship in Urban Transportation*. Adrian started out as associate director of economic studies, but by 1998 he'd advanced to director of privatization and government reform. That occurred after Bill Eggers took a leave of absence to run for the state legislature; after he lost, he decided to move into government, and got a job with the Texas Controller's office, just as Gov. George W. Bush was beginning his second term. Prior to leaving Reason, Bill did a three-week fact-finding tour of Australia and New Zealand in autumn 1996, resulting in an excellent *Reason* article about the radical free-market reforms implemented there; he also briefed Vice President Gore's National

Performance Review on the applicability of these reforms to the United States.

Adrian picked up the reins, continuing the Privatization Center's newsletter, workshops, *Annual Privatization Reports*, privatization how-to guides, and other programs. In late 1998, he organized a four-event LA-area speaking tour for Steve Goldsmith, discussing Goldsmith's new book, *The 21st Century City*. We hoped that his record of success in both improving public services and saving taxpayers money would inspire local officials in the region's more than 120 municipal governments.

Adrian's baptism by fire occurred in September 1998, when he chaired the Second Annual Conference on Privatizing Correctional Facilities, held in New York City. As he recounted in *Reason Report* Issue 75, during lunch on the first day, "a crowd of men with badges and large buttons with 'Privatization' in a circle with a slash through it came barging in," disrupting the proceedings. The correctional officers' union president got on stage and shouted "Privatization will not happen as long as we have breath in our bodies." And he continued, "If you do privatize a prison in our states, we'll burn it down."

Adrian reported that as conference chair, he stood up "and sarcastically thanked them on behalf of taxpayers for their reasoned discussion of the issues." At which point the official "marched over and stuck a finger in my face, yelling, 'You're not a taxpayer; you're a snake oil salesman! And if you want to debate the issue, let's step outside.'" Fortunately for all, they then departed without further incident.

New policy studies continued under Adrian's leadership, dealing with subjects such as privatizing public hospitals, jails and prisons, landfills, and municipal utilities. Another study looked at the deficiencies of typical government cash-based accounting systems. In July 2000, RPPI and the State Policy Network hosted a national conference in Los Angeles on "Shrinking the State in a Time of Budget Surpluses." That year also saw Adrian and recent hire Carl DeMaio launch a project called "Redesigning Government for the 21st Century," aimed at larger-scale reforms of the federal government than had been accomplished by the

Clinton/Gore National Performance Review's reinventing government team. That summer the project hosted a series of workshops in Washington, DC, involving about twenty officials from the Clinton administration and another twenty former Reagan and Bush people. Both *Government Executive* and *Federal Times* closely followed the discussions. The project was aimed at developing recommendations that could be used by whichever administration took over the following January—that of Al Gore or George W. Bush.

Infrastructure

Early in the 1990s, I came across the reports released in 1988 by the National Council on Public Works Improvement (NCPWI), a one-time national commission authorized by Congress. The Council produced the first "report cards" on the far-from-ideal condition of US airports, highways and transit systems, water supply, wastewater treatment, solid waste management, and hazardous waste disposal systems. But instead of being simply a call for more tax money, the main report included some strong market-based recommendations:

- Users should pay a greater share of the cost of infrastructure;
- Greater use should be made of pricing infrastructure services;
- A steady and predictable revenue stream would facilitate not only major capital improvements but also proper ongoing maintenance; and,
- There were opportunities for increased private participation in the provision of infrastructure, at all levels of government.

Reading the summaries of the NCPWI's reports, it occurred to me that an underlying (but never explicitly stated) theme was *government failure* in properly managing infrastructure. And that the same principles we'd been urging for highways, airports, and air traffic control could be applied more widely to other infrastructure systems that were being run far from optimally by political bodies.

That was the genesis of RPPI's Infrastructure Program. One of our first successes occurred late in the administration of George H. W. Bush. In 1991, we had published John Giraudo's legal critique of the barriers to airport privatization embedded in the regulations that accompany federal airport grants. And it turned out similar regulations accompanied nearly all federal grants for infrastructure, including water and waste-disposal systems. A regulation from the Office of Management and Budget applied across the board, requiring that if a facility built in part with federal grants had a change of ownership (such as being privatized), the federal grant money had to be repaid. If privatization is a sound idea, this requirement constituted a penalty tax on doing something good.

Giraudo had been counsel to the President's Commission on Privatization, so he had White House connections. In autumn 1991, he and I visited Al Hubbard who directed the Vice President's Council on Competitiveness, explaining that these grant restrictions were a barrier to private investment in revitalizing US infrastructure via sale or long-term lease. In January 1992, in response to a White House request for ideas that might be included in the State of the Union Address, we suggested removing federal barriers to infrastructure privatization. That led to Lynn and me meeting with White House counsel Boyden Gray (brother of the late Reason board member Burton Gray). Boyden asked us to prepare a concept paper on the extent of state and local infrastructure that might be privatized if the barriers were removed, and the paper we developed was later published as the RPPI policy study "Mining the Government Balance Sheet." We alerted friendly mayors and governors to weigh in with the White House on this, and our friend Ronald Lauder—then finishing up as chairman of the New York State Senate Advisory Commission on Privatization—set up a round-table meeting with Vice President Quayle and the Council on Competitiveness, at which Giraudo and I were two of the presenters.

The result was Executive Order 12803 on Infrastructure

Privatization, which President Bush signed on April 30, 1992. It declared private infrastructure investment and privatization a good thing that federal agencies should facilitate—not hinder—and it reduced (but did not eliminate) the grant repayment requirement. (For my birthday that year, Lou gave me a framed copy of EO 12803, which still hangs on my office wall.)

In subsequent years, RPPI researched and published over a dozen policy studies on topics such as municipal water supply and pricing, wastewater system privatization, port privatization, electric utility deregulation, and the case for competition with municipal utilities. I spoke on the subject at several conferences sponsored by *Forbes* magazine, the National Association of Regulatory Utility Commissioners, the National Council for Public-Private Partnerships, the Canadian Council for Public-Private Partnerships, and at other venues.

When the Clinton administration took office in 1993, I worried that "our" executive order might be rescinded. This was the era of New Democrats, generally market-friendly and pragmatic, and their primary think tank was the Progressive Policy Institute (PPI) in Washington, DC. I managed to get an appointment at PPI with Rob Atkinson, who became a friend and colleague, and through him I made contact with the White House staffer responsible for infrastructure, Michael Deich. I knew that public employee unions wanted EO 12803 killed, so my objective was to explain to Michael its genesis and why it made sense for the federal government not to interfere with state and local efforts at reinventing government.

Michael and I ended up having periodic discussions about infrastructure privatization and public-private partnerships throughout Clinton's first term. I recall that one of his concerns was that a company or a buyout fund might buy an airport and a few years later "flip it" in order to profit from its (presumably) increased value. I tried to explain that investors built portfolios, and their composition needed to change over time. In the end, probably thanks to Vice President Gore's National Performance Review, the Clinton White House not only did not rescind our EO but issued a new one to complement it. EO 12893, issued in

January 1994, called for uniform principles in federal infrastructure programs, including cost/benefit analysis, market-based mechanisms, and "private-sector participation in the ownership, financing, construction, and operation" of infrastructure. Moreover, federal agencies were directed to "minimize regulatory and legal barriers to private sector participation."

We published a follow-up study on the unfortunately modest impact of the two executive orders in 1995, "Revitalizing State and Local Infrastructure: Empowering Cities and States to Tap Private Capital and Rebuild America." Among other recommendations, it proposed eliminating the grant-repayment requirement completely, as long as the facility remained in service to the public. That study caught the interest of Sen. Connie Mack (R-FL), who at that time chaired the Joint Economic Committee (JEC) of Congress. Following my meeting with him in 1995, he had the JEC staff prepare a report based on our study, "The $7.7 Billion Mistake." JEC held a hearing on the subject in early 1996; those testifying included New York governor George Pataki, Ronald Lauder, heads of several leading privatization firms, two union officials, and me. Shortly thereafter former Sen. John Danforth helped organize a coalition of public officials and business leaders seeking changes in these federal barriers, but the only major impact was the Airport Privatization Pilot Program, enacted in 1996, discussed later in this chapter.

Another output of the infrastructure program was an empirical study in 1996 that compared investor-owned and government-owned water systems. It found that investor-owned water utilities provided comparable water services at virtually the same prices as municipal water agencies, yet the latter have higher costs, are less efficient, and receive generous state and local tax subsidies. The idea for this study came from an attorney in the San Francisco Bay Area, Patrick Maloney. He and co-author Kathy Neal were both well-connected moderate Democrats, which may have helped the study to be taken more seriously than it otherwise might have been in increasingly Democratic California. It got serious California news coverage and a major article in *Forbes*, "Socialized Water." The study encouraged a number of efforts to privatize municipal water systems in the years that followed, some of which succeeded. In the next several years, either Adrian or I (sometimes both of us) were called in as experts as a number of cities sought to privatize their water departments, usually being defeated by a combination of public employee unions and status-quo inertia. Some of these campaigns were very heated.

Transportation

Given my previous work on airports, air traffic control, and toll roads, transportation was obviously another core policy area for RPPI. During the 1990s, we continued to work on these areas, making progress at federal, state, and local levels of government.

Airport Privatization

As noted previously, in 1992, our VP Bryan Snyder and I did a policy study that critiqued a Los Angeles Airport Commission's consultant study that basically dismissed the case for privatizing LAX. Our study inspired Riordan to campaign for mayor partly on that issue and to devote a lot of effort to carrying it out once in office, only to be thwarted by airline and city council opposition. Two SPN think tanks—Pioneer Institute in Boston and Wisconsin Policy Research Institute—commissioned us to study the case for privatization of, respectively, Boston Logan Airport (1992) and Milwaukee's Mitchell Field (1994). And we followed up our Orange County bankruptcy rescue plan with a more-detailed study on privatizing OC's airports—proposing to privately finance a larger, less-constrained airport at soon-to-be-closed El Toro Marine base and to gradually transition the small John Wayne Airport into a general-aviation (private planes) airfield.

By 1995, there was a fledgling industry grouping called the Airport Alliance, with firms such as Lockheed Air Terminal (a contract operator of airports such as Albany and Burbank) and a relatively new US division of privatized BAA (BAA USA) seeking to change US policy to remove barriers to airport privatization. We had published two studies on federal barriers to privatization of airports and other infrastructure that had received federal grants, and, as previously discussed, I had worked with the Bush 41 White House on the 1992 Executive Order to reduce such barriers.

Ronald Lauder, who had supported Gov. George Pataki, was appointed to chair the New York State Senate Advisory Commission on Privatization, and I recommended some of the authors who wrote chapters in the commission's January 1992 report, *Privatization for New York*. I also wrote the chapter on privatizing the several state-owned airports, the largest of which was Stewart Airport, about fifty miles north of New York City. Lauder got interested in the federal legal obstacles, and when would-be airport companies came up with the idea of a federal pilot program that would grant exemptions from those obstacles, Lauder encouraged and lobbied for those changes. The eventual result, about which I testified in Congress, was the Airport Privatization Pilot Program, enacted by Congress in October 1996.

The pilot program allowed up to five airports to be long-term leased by granting exemptions from several of the most important federal barriers—especially those that would normally require previous federal grants to be repaid, that would prevent the city or county from using the lease proceeds for general government purposes, and that arguably would have prevented the company that acquired the airport from making a profit. It took the Federal Aviation Administration nearly a year to publish guidelines under which airport operators could apply for slots in the program. As soon as those guidelines appeared, I wrote and we released a policy brief aimed at airport owners explaining the case for privatization, examples of benefits from overseas privatizations, and details about the pilot program and how to use it.

Between 1996 and 2000, the American Association of Airport Executives and other organizations held airport privatization conferences, and I made a number of presentations at them. Although quite a few jurisdictions applied for slots in the program, by the end of 2000, only one airport had actually been leased under the pilot program: state-owned Stewart International in New York, as recommended in the chapter I'd written for Lauder's privatization commission report. It seemed like a pretty meager result for so many years of effort.

Air Traffic Control

The 1990s brought new attention to the shortcomings of the air traffic control system as funded by Congress and managed by the FAA bureaucracy. The Clinton administration appointed a National Commission to Ensure a Strong, Competitive Airline Industry, and its August 1993 report called for pulling the ATC system out of FAA and converting into a user-funded government corporation. Having been consulted by the commission during its work, I knew the contents and the release date, and my op-ed, "How to Break the FAA Bottleneck," appeared in the *Wall Street Journal* on August 19, the day the report was issued. We also issued my new Reason Foundation study, "How to Spin Off Air Traffic Control," that same month.

Vice President Gore's reinventing government policy shop, the National Performance Review (NPR), was inspired in part by David Osborne and Ted Gaebler's book, *Reinventing Government* (1991), and also by the radical reforms undertaken in New Zealand, first by a labor government and continued by a conservative government. I was an informal advisor to the NPR, and when I learned that they were especially impressed by Airways New Zealand—the self-supporting government corporation that had been launched in 1987 taking air traffic control out of the transport ministry—I gave them background information on previous US studies and on developments in other countries. The NPR recommended that the US ATC system be removed from FAA and made into something very much like Airways New Zealand.

To move things along, Reason Foundation held a half-day seminar on ATC privatization in Washington, DC, on December 1, 1993. Former DOT Secretary Jim Burnley and several senior FAA officials were among the speakers, and Burnley was again strongly supportive of Reason's nonprofit corporation approach, as he'd been when he was the Secretary.

The NPR's case made sense to DOT Secretary Federico Pena. He created a high-level study team operating out of the DOT Secretary's Office, the Executive Oversight Committee, to come up with a detailed plan and draft legislation to create what they called the US Air Traffic Services (USATS) corporation. Since my work on the subject was well known by that point, I was one of a number of outside experts from whom the committee sought input and advice. Their detailed two-volume report was released in May 1994, and the accompanying legislation was introduced early in 1995. I testified, largely in favor, but suggesting greater benefits from a nonprofit private corporation before the House Aviation Subcommittee on March 5, 1995. Chairman John Duncan (R-TN) subsequently took me to lunch and videotaped an interview with me on privatization. Unfortunately, airline support was only lukewarm, while the general aviation (private plane) community vociferously opposed the idea, fearing the advent of unaffordable ATC user fees. Few members of Congress supported such a radical change, and the idea never got out of committee.

But we saw a new opportunity the following year, for two reasons. First, due to shenanigans in Congress, FAA reauthorization had stalled, so all the aviation excise taxes (on passenger tickets, fuel, etc.,) were suspended and airlines were newly interested in user fees paid directly to the ATC provider, to replace those politicized taxes. Second, Canada was in the final stages of enacting legislation to create a self-supporting nonprofit ATC corporation very much along the lines of what I'd been advocating since 1981. So, just retired Lockheed Air Terminal CEO Viggo Butler and I set to work writing a new Reason Foundation policy study. "Reinventing Air Traffic Control" was released in May 1996 and included a detailed proposal for ATC user fees so that airlines and private plane operators could see exactly what this would entail.

We unveiled the study at a Washington, DC, news conference and followed up with numerous meetings with stakeholder groups. Media coverage included the *Wall Street Journal*, *Aviation Week*, *Journal of Commerce*, and many others. I was also interviewed on PRI's *Marketplace* and Radio America's *Dateline Washington*. But the airlines were at that point bitterly divided over user fees, with the legacy carriers on one side and rising low-cost carrier Southwest on the other, so their trade association (which require unanimity) could not take a position on the issue. And when Congress finally reauthorized FAA, and the aviation tax revenue began to flow again, interest in ATC user fees and our proposal faded.

Needless to say, the FAA remained sorely underperforming in its ATC task, and the Clinton administration tried again, creating the National Civil Aviation Review Commission chaired by former Rep. Norm Mineta (D-CA). Once again, I was consulted for input, and the commission's December 1997 report called for an almost-government ATC corporation, converting the ATC portion of FAA into a "performance-based organization" that would charge ATC fees to airlines (only) and be able to issue revenue bonds for capital improvement projects. Congress in 2000 adopted a portion of this by calling for FAA to pull together its ATC-related activities into a performance-based organization within the agency—but without any change in funding via aviation taxes requiring annual appropriations by Congress.

In January 1997, I chaired the panel on air traffic control that was part of a new Gore commission dealing with aviation safety and security, and I testified on ATC user fees before the House Aviation Subcommittee that February. My approach to the issue intrigued Southwest's government affairs director, Ron Ricks, and we had a meeting to discuss this further. It turned out that Viggo had known Southwest CEO Herb Kelleher for years, so we managed to set up a meeting with Herb at Southwest's Dallas headquarters in March. What had been planned as a one-hour meeting ended up going two full hours. The result was Herb's challenge to Viggo and me to come up with a revised ATC corporation/user fee plan that would treat all airlines fairly. He also asked for more specifics on how to structure a balanced governing board of aviation stakeholders, and other details—basically a how-to guide on creating a US ATC corporation.

That project took considerable work over the next two years, and would not be released until early 2001. But meanwhile, my critiques of the government corporation approach in studies and again in House Aviation Subcommittee testimony in 1998 apparently circulated fairly widely within DOT and the White House, prompting ongoing discussion. Out of the blue in August 1999, I received a call from White House National Economic Council infrastructure economist Dorothy Robyn, asking when I would next be in DC. NEC and NPR were doing a series of briefing sessions on ATC commercialization with aviation stakeholder groups, and they wanted to pick my brain on the subject. I met with them on September 11, 1999, and afterwards I wrote in my journal, "It went very well, and I'm to keep in regular touch. I'm coordinating with Jim Burnley and supportive airline people. Maybe—just maybe—we're getting close to action on this 20-year crusade." In November, I met with leaders of controllers' union NATCA, with UPS, and once again with Dorothy.

The next year, with the new study's user-fee and revenue model still being tweaked, I testified on ATC reform before the House Budget Committee. And at a DC conference in April, FAA Administrator Jane Garvey said that Reason's Nav Canada-type model would be one of four reform options she would give to the White House by the end of the month. I also appeared on *The O'Reilly Factor*, discussing air travel delays and the case for a more-advanced air traffic control system. And in September 2000, I was the guest of the National Air Transportation Association for its board meeting/retreat at the Greenbrier, for serious discussions on the case for an ATC corporation.

In short, as we looked forward to 2001 and a new administration, I was optimistic that we would finally gain traction for this long-needed change.

Toll Roads and Road Pricing

The transportation area where we had the greatest impact during the 1990s was in highways. In the wake of California's success in getting serious private-sector proposals for new toll road projects in 1991, other states began enacting legislation similar to AB 680, the law that our 1988 policy paper had inspired. Arizona, Minnesota, and Washington State had each enacted private toll road pilot program laws by 1993, and a new toll bridge was privately financed and developed in San Juan, Puerto Rico. Proposals for similar legislation were being debated in half a dozen other states. Thus, when Congress started work on reauthorizing federal fuel taxes and the federal highway and transit program in 1990–91, there was considerable interest in toll finance.

We helped spark that interest by working closely with the Federal Highway Administration's policy staff in 1991. In charge of coming up with new approaches was Steve Lockwood, an outside-the-box thinker who seemed especially intrigued by my concept of express toll lanes that would use variable pricing to reduce or eliminate rush-hour congestion, as was planned for the 91 Express Lanes in Orange County (which would soon break ground for construction). Steve organized an ongoing series of FHWA seminars in 1990–91 looking at road pricing (which came to be called congestion pricing), toll finance, public-private partnerships, and related ideas. The resulting 1991 reauthorization law, the Intermodal Surface Transportation Efficiency Act (ISTEA), partially removed the long-standing federal ban on tolling on any federal-aid highway (which meant nearly all highways of any consequence). While converting Interstate highways to tolling was still forbidden, tolls could now be used to finance all other highways, though with reduced federal matching funds. And ISTEA also created a Congestion Pricing Pilot Program, providing seed-money grants to encourage state and local transportation agencies to experiment with priced lanes. This included what FHWA called "HOV buy-in," under which underutilized HOV (carpool) lanes could allow non-carpool vehicles willing to pay a toll for a less-congested trip to buy their way in. These ideas all came out of Steve's seminars.

These changes spurred our transportation program to action. Our first response was a policy study titled "Private Tollways: How States Can Leverage Federal Highway Funds," released in February 1992. I gave an advance presentation on this at the Transportation Research Board annual meeting that January, and went on from there to address the Michigan Road Builders' annual meeting in Grand Rapids. Later that year we released "The Market for Private Toll Projects in the United States." It estimated that if all states took full advantage of the opportunity, they could generate an additional $19 billion per year in highway investment.

Because of FHWA's new congestion pricing program, we commissioned a set of six policy studies, mostly by outside academics such as Profs. Ken Small of UC Irvine, Genevieve Giuliano of USC, and Martin Wachs of UCLA. Those studies aroused strong interest within FHWA and the Federal Transit Agency. They invited Reason Foundation to work with them on creating the FHWA/FTA Congestion Pricing Symposium, held in April 1992 in Arlington, Virginia, with an overflow attendance of about 150 people from across the country. This level of interest helped inspire FHWA's Congestion Pricing Pilot Program to offer workshops to metro areas interested in implementing demonstration projects. As that effort found takers in more than a dozen metro areas over a decade or so, I was often one of the presenters.

A very important outgrowth of the April 1992 conference began with a side conversation between me and FTA program analyst Fred Williams. I complained to him that the term the agencies were using for an HOV lane converted to pricing—"HOV buy-in"—was clunky and unsexy. To get people interested in the concept of uncongested pay lanes, we needed a better marketing term. Fred suggested HOT (High-Occupancy/Toll) lanes, which I thought was much better. As a federal bureaucrat, Fred confessed, he was not in a position to put this better name into circulation. But Reason, as a public policy think tank, could do so. Fred gave me the term to use and the rest is history.

I commissioned two respected transportation economists at UC Irvine—Pete Fielding and Dan Klein—to write our November 1993 policy study, "High-Occupancy/Toll Lanes: Phasing in Congestion Pricing a Lane at a Time." The study did not make general news—but it was highly influential in the transportation community. Within a year, FHWA had scrapped "HOV buy-in," and "HOT lanes" became widely accepted as the name for this new approach. And after San Diego converted the HOV lanes on I-15 to HOT lanes, the Congestion Pricing Pilot Program started getting a steady stream of proposals from other metro areas to do likewise. Today such lanes are in operation or being planned in nearly all the largest US metro areas.

I was very proud to be at the ground-breaking ceremony for the 91 Express Lanes, on July 27, 1993, to be photographed with my hard hat and Gov. Pete Wilson. As we noted in *Reason Report* Issue 58, it was the first private toll road built in the twentieth century, the world's first toll road without toll booths, and the first highway in the United States to employ variable pricing. It was even more gratifying to be present for the grand opening in late December 1995. Jerry Pfeffer of Kiewit, the leading company in the consortium, recognized me in his remarks as "the intellectual father" of the AB 680 legislation, and Phil Romero of Caltrans asked me to help him write Gov. Wilson's testimony for the upcoming Joint Economic Committee hearing on federal barriers to privatization. It was a great day.

But our high hopes for many privately financed toll projects failed to materialize during the 1990s. The private sector submitted proposals, as requested, for new projects in Arizona, Minnesota, and Washington State. And every single one was shot down by opponents—a combination of NIMBYs, environmentalists opposed to any highway expansions, and people opposed to tolling. A more politically palatable approach than "private toll roads" emerged in Virginia in 1995. Part of the opposition in the three states that had emulated California's pilot program was dismay at the idea that private capitalists might exploit highway users in quest of profits.

Though economically illiterate, there was political wisdom in the idea that the only projects to go forward would be ones on which the state DOT, following legislated guidelines, sought competitive bids from toll road companies, placed conditions on their operation via long-term lease/concession agreements, and in which it was acceptable for the state to invest a portion of the equity so as to reduce the amount that had to be financed—and hence the level of toll rates needed. Virginia's Public-Private Transportation Act (PPTA) of 1995 became the model increasingly followed by other states, mostly after it was proven via several small projects in the late 1990s. Large numbers of state-enabling laws modeled after the PPTA were enacted in the late 1990s and early 2000s, and those laws did lead to dozens of projects in leading-edge states. And the privatization trade group that had been formed in 1985 as the Privatization Council changed its name in 1990 to the National Council for Public-Private Partnerships (NCPPP).

Our transportation work in the latter half of the 1990s followed three tracks. First, I got more deeply involved with important transportation organizations. At the Transportation Research Board, I joined the new Congestion Pricing Committee, writing additional papers and taking part in panels at TRB conferences. I increased my participation with the American Road and Transportation Builders' Association (ARTBA), getting onto the program almost every year at its annual Public-Private Ventures Conference. I also attended and started giving presentations at the conferences of the International Bridge, Tunnel, and Turnpike Association (IBTTA), and chaired its 1997 public-private partnership (PPP) toll roads conference in Santa Monica.

The second track was to try to persuade the big three US auto companies (still the market leaders in the 1990s) that traffic congestion was a serious threat to their continued growth and that PPP toll roads and toll lanes would be positive for "auto-mobility." We had environmental analyst Ken Green write a policy study, "Defending Automobility: A Critical Examination of the Environmental and Social Costs of Auto Use," as an opening shot in this effort. My aim was to persuade key policy people at the three companies to focus more attention on highway infrastructure issues (whereas most of their policy focus was on environmental and safety regulation issues).

During the whole decade of the 1990s, the Ford Motor Company Fund was the only one that contributed to Reason Foundation every year. I had gotten to know chief economist Marty Zimmerman. He understood road pricing and saw increasing congestion as a major problem. GM had been an early corporate supporter, thanks to two free-market people in its Washington, DC, office. But that support disappeared in 1992 once they retired. Fortunately, I managed to connect with senior policy official Lewis Dale at the Detroit headquarters, and by 1995 he was increasingly in sync with our approach, and GM resumed giving. I was far less successful at Chrysler, which gave only once during that decade.

But all those visits and memos eventually paid off, to some extent. After eighteen months of discussion and planning, we put on a workshop for the policy people from all three companies, in Detroit during December 1997. Ford was the most engaged, thanks to Marty Zimmerman, and Ford funded a June 1999 conference on traffic congestion at MIT, at which I gave a presentation. We followed that with a Ford/RPPI highway policy conference in Washington, DC, that October. I don't think any of the big three devoted serious lobbying efforts to these issues in subsequent federal reauthorization battles, but at least their policy people were now up-to-speed on tolling, pricing, and PPPs as part of the answer to better auto-mobility.

The third track was reaching out to state DOTs in states that looked promising for tolling, HOT lanes, and PPPs. I had tried promoting these ideas in California when I served for a year on Gov. Wilson's special Commission on Transportation Investment. Despite being just one of thirty-three members, I worked hard and successfully for our January 1996 final report to include:

- Expanded and institutionalized use of private investment in the highway system,
- Serious research on per-mile charging and direct road pricing for the future,
- Devolution of the federal gas tax to the states (a big idea for several years in the mid-1990s), and
- Removal of barriers to entry for private transit modes such as jitneys and commuter shuttles.

But the political winds were changing in California, and these policies found little support in the state legislature. Florida and Texas looked far more promising. Drawing on contacts I'd made with both Florida and Texas DOTs, I pitched the idea of Reason organizing a workshop for each of them on tolling, PPPs, and congestion pricing—and both liked the idea. The first one took place in Austin in December 1998. It was a day-long event, with senior people from Texas DOT and several other agencies in attendance. And the Florida workshop took place in March 2000, hosted by the Florida Transportation Commission. Unfortunately, I did not save the agendas for either of these workshops, but they were both very well received. In the following decade, Florida and Texas became two of America's leading states for expanded tolling, express toll and/or HOT lanes, and long-term PPP mega-projects.

After a solid decade of work on these issues, I was pleased to see my favorite weekly news magazine, *The Economist*, publish an article headlined, "Tolled You So: Road Pricing in California" in June 2000. It focused on a consensus transportation policy paper from the California Environmental Dialogue, whose members included both General Motors and the Environmental Defense Fund. The paper endorsed the principle that users should pay for road use and that "tolls and congestion pricing should be utilized wherever possible," citing this as a first for auto firms. The article also quoted me advocating the conversion of HOV lanes to market-priced HOT lanes.

Education Studies

RPPI started working on school choice in a modest way, egged on by Public Affairs Director Kevin Teasley, who was an ardent supporter of school vouchers, still a relatively untried idea in 1991. That year our downtown Los Angeles Reason Forums included three education reform speakers in successive months: Sy Fliegel from New York (on a public-school choice program he'd led); Joseph Alibrandi, CEO of Whitaker Corporation and former chair of the California Business Roundtable's education task force; and John Chubb of Brookings Institution, co-author of *Politics, Markets, and America's Schools*. We also landed a grant that year to commission a statewide public opinion survey in California on school choice. And our annual banquet that year featured Polly Williams, author of the landmark Wisconsin law that created the Milwaukee school voucher program.

Kevin departed at the end of 1991 (to work full-time on school choice), but in 1992 we formally launched RPPI's Education

Studies program, hiring Janet Beales from the National Chamber Foundation to be its director. Her first policy study, released in fall 1992, was based on a new public opinion survey on school vouchers within the territory of the huge Los Angeles Unified School District. A majority favored vouchers, with the strongest support coming from minority communities. Janet went beyond the survey results to analyze the budgetary impact on the school district, if such a program were implemented. Since the vouchers would be for less than the overall per-pupil cost, she estimated the taxpayer savings that would result in the district, and then extrapolated the results statewide.

Janet was very creative. Teachers' unions strongly opposed vouchers, and a statewide ballot measure on the subject failed in 1993. So Janet followed up with a series of other studies, aiming to chip away at the public school monopoly. These included:

- Satellite schools—provided on company premises as a perk for employees with children, via public-private partnerships (1993)
- Out-of-control special education budgets in public schools (1993)
- Contracting out school support services (1993, Beales and John O'Leary)
- Nationwide survey of school voucher programs (1994)
- Update on contracting for support services (1994)
- Private-practice teachers (1994)
- Empirical study of Milwaukee voucher results (1995)
- Phony accounting for school bus costs (1995)
- Private schools and disabled students (1996).

As with the Privatization Center, conferences became a feature of the Education Studies program. In 1993, we did a series of seminars in California, conducted jointly with the Claremont Institute and the Pacific Research Institute, featuring school reformer Myron Lieberman and education innovator Lewis Perelman. Our first "Making Schools Work" conference took place in Santa Barbara in 1995 and was followed by a second one in 1999. By the time Janet was hired away by education company Kids 1 in 1997, she had become a nationally recognized expert on school reform, putting RPPI on the map on that subject.

Janet's successor was Rich Seder, formerly a Koch Fellow at the Center for Market Process at George Mason University, who had previously directed the Allegheny County (Pennsylvania) Public Schools Synthesis Project. Rich picked up where Janet had left off; his first policy study was on charter school innovations, followed by another on alternative teacher organizations, both in 1997. When school violence became a national concern in 1998, Rich and co-author Lisa Snell produced an assessment of school-violence prevention programs across the country, which we went all-out to publicize, making the case against one-size-fits-all solutions and arguing for local control and innovation. The study received coverage in the *New York Times* and many other newspapers, and Rich and Lisa did nearly a dozen radio and TV media interviews.

In 1999, building on previous studies, Rich researched a new study, "Satellite Charter Schools," discussing workplaces and other innovative locations for charter school facilities. Our second Making Schools Work conference, again held in Santa Barbara, was larger than its predecessor and included innovators such as the president of the Association of Educators in Private Practice and representatives of a number of school services companies. Ben Lindquist of *The Education Industry Report* wrote that the conference was a rare example of a "level playing field forum bringing together school people and national service providers." Lisa's profile increased in 2000 with a study on reforming remedial education, and Rich authored what was to be his last RPPI policy study that year, on balancing accountability and local control of school systems. He was hired away that year, and Lisa stepped up to become director of education. She would go on to do great things in subsequent decades.

Environmental Policy

As previewed in Chapter 8, Lynn Scarlett had developed a serious interest in recycling and solid waste questions, as well as the very large problem (especially in Los Angeles) of dismal air quality. So as we formalized RPPI program areas, Environment was an obvious choice, and it was Lynn's bailiwick to oversee. During the 1990s, air quality and solid waste received a great deal of study, and climate change was soon added as the program's third focus area.

Air Quality

One of our early efforts was to try to reform California's mandatory vehicle emissions-inspection program. We highlighted the remote-testing work of Donald Stedman and Gary Bishop of the University of Colorado. Using an infrared roadside sensing device, they measured the tailpipe emissions of thousands of vehicles—not idling on a test stand but in actual operation on a highway (often during acceleration on a freeway on-ramp). Their results disproved two common beliefs—that all cars are serious emitters and that every old car pollutes more than any new one. Their on-road data showed that 10 percent of cars produced over 50 percent of the emissions. The implication of these findings was that randomized roadside inspections using Stedman-type devices could be less costly and more effective than requiring every car to show up every other year at a licensed smog-check facility (as was required by California law). *Reason*'s Washington editor Rick Henderson wrote an article about this in the magazine which brought it to the attention of national print and broadcast media. Our biggest media coup was John Stossel, who did an August 1992 segment on ABC's *20/20* featuring Stedman and his remote-sensing team.

Two years later, Gov. Pete Wilson appointed Lynn to chair California's Inspection and Maintenance Review Committee, which had begun to examine remote-sensing as a possible alternative to smog-check inspections. At that point, California was exploring an even more costly version of smog check, one championed by the federal EPA, that would require all checks to be performed in a handful of government facilities, rather than numerous licensed garages and gas stations. In spring 1995, Lynn explained to US House and Senate subcommittees that

California's IMR Committee had "assembled data and analysis demonstrating that EPA has no sound scientific basis for its claim that centralized testing programs outperform programs that use decentralized service stations to test cars." She also told the Senate committee members that "a real innovation would be to use remote-sensing to identify clean cars and exempt them from any further inspection requirements. That would move us toward a free-market concept in which only polluters would pay for cleanup."

Our air quality seminars in Los Angeles in 1994 had focused a lot of attention on using market incentives rather than command-and-control mandates to achieve cleaner air. In my case, that meant reducing traffic congestion via priced lanes and eventually priced freeways, while Lynn focused on the highly centralized smog-check system as opposed to finding and dealing with gross-emitting vehicles. In 1994, the California Air Resources Board (CARB) appointed both of us to its Market-Incentives Task Force, which also included economically literate environmentalists like our friend Tom Graff of the Environmental Defense Fund. And in 1996, Reason Foundation was selected as one of forty-five institutional members of a year-long Southern California study called REACH—Reduce Emissions and Congestion on Highways—funded by the Federal Highway Administration and coordinated by the Southern California Association of Governments. I was the RPPI member of this group, which ended up considering the relative merits of (1) regional market-based transportation [highway] pricing and (2) region-wide HOT lanes. Though the modeling by Wilbur Smith Associates found higher benefits from the former, it was judged politically infeasible, so the primary recommendation (besides more study of highway pricing) was to move forward with HOT lanes.

Two other mid-1990s California environmental policies came in for RPPI criticism. One was the first-ever state mandate that a certain fraction of new cars sold in the state be electric vehicles. Given the primitive state of EV technology in 1995, the vehicles themselves would not be very useful to motorists. (As an "LA opinion leader," I was one of those invited by General Motors to test drive its EV-1 on a hot August day near downtown. I remember that the cars had to be externally pre-cooled before each test drive, because there was not enough on-board electric power to operate the air conditioning on such a hot day.) Our policy study, by two USC professors, noted that Resources for the Future had found that in terms of cost/ton of Volatile Organic Compounds reduced, reformulated gasoline or emissions-based vehicle registration fees would be twenty times more cost-effective than the EV mandate.

The other issue was EPA's proposed mandate that employers of one hundred or more people implement mandatory employee ride-sharing programs, called the Employee Commute Option (ECO), in cities defined as in non-attainment of air quality standards. Since California already had a state version of ECO, RPPI analyst Ken Green was able to document the program's high cost and very small effect on air pollution. His study suggested an array of other policies that would be more cost-effective.

But Ken was just getting started. In 1997, he did a follow-up study on California's smog-check program. Although we had defeated the EPA mandate, the state was still requiring all cars to report to a licensed inspection station every two years for a smog check. Ken cited recent data showing that trying to repair marginal emitters (which just barely failed the test) often led to higher emissions.

In another study, Ken took on the EPA again, this time over its proposed tighter limits on ozone and particulates. Having already been collecting data for about a year, Ken produced three studies challenging both the science cited by EPA and the poor cost-effectiveness of the proposed regulations. The overall message of the three papers was that EPA's science was flawed, they exaggerated the harm from low levels of emissions, and the economic impacts ($90–150 billion per year) would harm many lower-income people. The studies were released in a briefing session at the National Press Club in Washington, and led to Ken meeting with senior members of Congress from both houses. A year later, in May 1999, the US Court of Appeals for the District of Columbia barred EPA from enforcing the new regulations.

Arguments from Ken's studies were cited in oral arguments, written briefs, and in background materials submitted to the court.

Solid Waste and Recycling

Lynn's op-ed articles on sensible recycling led to numerous speaking appearances before groups we hadn't known existed, such as the Solid Waste Association of North America, the Paperboard Packaging Council, and the Polystyrene Packaging Council. She also engaged in debates with advocates of harsher recycling mandates at such venues as the National Recycling Congress and the Oregon Association of Recyclers. After she appeared on *CBS News* in 1993, she also began getting invitations from city public works departments that already knew of RPPI thanks to the high profile of our Privatization Center. After an attack on her as an "anti-recycler" in *Resource Recycling* magazine in September 1992, she was given an opportunity to reply in its December issue. She explained that recycling should not be seen as a panacea, and should be used where there is an actual market for the products recycled. She also defended the many benefits of modern packaging, and urged that local governments should charge for garbage by weight or volume, to give people incentives to recycle.

Lynn fleshed out those points in two 1993 policy studies, "Mandates or Incentives? Comparing Packaging Regulations with User Fees for Trash Collection" and "Variable Rates for Municipal Solid Waste: Implementation, Experience, Economics, and Legislation." A more detailed RPPI study, by outside researchers, appeared in 1995, "Garbage by the Pound: On the Streets," recounting numerous examples of the implemented garbage fees, finding that weight is a better metric to use than volume.

Later that year the EPA itself sponsored two workshops on "pay as you throw" programs, cosponsored by the International City/County Management Association, one in Boston and the other in Washington, DC. EPA also produced a seventy-five-minute satellite video conference on the subject, with Lynn as one of the featured speakers. Lynn and colleagues did a few more recycling policy studies after that, but they had largely won that battle by 1995. At the outset, when Lynn had begun making the case for "pay as you throw" garbage fees, just a handful of cities used this approach. After several years of RPPI studies and EPA endorsement, several thousand US cities had embraced the use of such fees.

Environmental Risk Assessment

The Environment program moved on to more complex topics. In 1996, Ken commissioned an overview paper by George M. Gray of the Harvard Center for Risk Analysis on removing distortions and ensuring fairness in environmental risk comparisons. Gray found that many risk assessments overstated people's actual exposure to environmental contaminants, resulting in overly restrictive and costly regulations. Two other studies commissioned by Ken that year addressed the environmental risks of soil contamination and challenges in enforcement of environmental regulations.

In 1997, Lynn gave an invited presentation to the US Senate Environment Task Force, as well as speaking at a special environmental conference for congressional staffers sponsored by the Center for Market Processes at George Mason University. And in 1998, RPPI launched a national project on state environmental innovations, done jointly with the National Environmental Policy Institute. Phase 1 surveyed all fifty states to identify incentive-based environmental programs. Phase 2 then zeroed in on the more promising examples to document how they work, what they cost, and what kind of results they achieved.

Climate Change

Probably the Environment program's most controversial focus area—at least in hindsight—was policy research on global climate change. In 1993, Lynn commissioned outside researchers Steven Moss and Richard McCann to assess the extent of the problem and review policy options for dealing with it. Though at that point there was not the kind of consensus that exists today on the extent of the problem, Moss and McCann argued that it was enough of a threat that policy measures were warranted. Of the four options they reviewed, they recommended a no-regrets approach focused on improving energy efficiency and reducing previously identified air emissions—a strategy that would produce benefits regardless of how large or small global warming turned out to be. A follow-up study in 1994, again by Moss and McCann, argued that incentive-based approaches were more cost-effective than command and control methods.

That was where we left it, until the 1997 Kyoto agreement focused more political attention on climate change, with the signatory governments all agreeing to reduce greenhouse gas emissions in future years. In response to the second major report of the Intergovernmental Panel on Climate Change in December 1997, Ken Green released a "Plain English Guide to Climate Change," explaining both the complexity of the subject and the difficulty of making costly policy decisions with still-limited information. He followed this in 1998 with a policy brief, "Evaluating the Kyoto Approach to Climate Change," criticizing it for producing negligible benefits during its agreed time period, at fairly serious cost. He argued that its tunnel-vision approach could turn what was intended as a public safety measure into a public health hazard. And in 1999, Ken joined with former authors Moss and McCann to produce "Climate Change Policy Options and Impacts: Perspectives on Risk Reduction, Emissions Trading, and Carbon Taxes," assessing the pros and cons of each.

By 2000, Ken's growing stature as an analyst dealing with climate change was acknowledged in two ways. First, the *MacMillan Encyclopedia of Energy*—a reference book for libraries nationwide—asked Ken to write the entry on climate change. Second, the Intergovernmental Panel on Climate Change announced that Ken had been accepted as an expert reviewer for all three volumes of its upcoming *Third Assessment Report*. He had already reviewed reports on the subject for the US General Accounting Office and an IPCC report on aviation and global climate. Also in 2000, we released an updated "Plain English Guide—Exploring the Science of Climate Change."

From this brief overview, it should be clear that in none of this work did RPPI "deny" the reality of climate change or say that nothing should be done about it. But to this day some environmental groups and their followers review our corporate donor lists from the 1990s and find—horrors!—oil companies listed. I raised much of that money myself, and I have no apologies for having done so. We did environmental policy work because we judged it to be important—and never at the behest of any corporate donor. We called the shots as our analysts saw them, and if an oil company was unhappy about what we produced, they were free to not contribute. (And as I noted in Chapter 8, one CEO of a Los Angeles-based oil company told me to my face that his company would no longer give because we were planning to honor Michael Milken. Well, too bad!)

The same kind of guilt-by-association was thrown at me in 2011 by a local elected official taking part in a workshop on proposed congestion-relief solutions for a large metro area, which we had organized in conjunction with the Federal Highway Administration. Clearly not liking my recommendation for express toll lanes, she tapped away at her laptop searching for dirt on Reason Foundation, while I was speaking, and then announced to the group that Reason was a tool of the auto and oil companies and should not be taken seriously! By that time, we had not received auto company contributions in about a decade, and when we had, the cause and effect had gone the other way. I'd spent years educating them that they should pay attention to traffic congestion and support us in coming up with solutions like express toll lanes. Fortunately, this little tirade had no effect on the FHWA people, who'd been having me speak at their workshops for nearly two decades, nor on the head of the local Metropolitan Planning Organization, in whose facility the workshop was being held. Other Reason analysts have their own stories about opponents using this tactic when facts and logic fail them.

Urban Futures

The sixth RPPI program area was urban growth and land-use policy, which we called Urban Futures. California in the 1990s was already in the forefront of what became known as "smart growth" policies—an effort to centrally plan the urban form according to planners' visions. Going well beyond the original idea of zoning as a way of preventing externalities (such as a factory in the midst of a residential area), this new approach aimed at restricting suburban growth (denigrated as "sprawl"), significantly increasing residential densities in already urban areas, regardless of the desires of those already living there, and linking transportation planning with land-use planning, emphasizing transit as opposed to roadways.

Lynn announced the launch of the program in mid-1997, saying it would be a systematic effort to develop market-oriented solutions to land-use issues. In an article in *Reason Report* Issue 73, she elaborated: "The world is dynamic, and progress means change. You want change and freedom. Regulations and prescriptive laws prevent that. On the other hand, you don't want chaos. So you want to create rules that prevent harmful impacts without interfering in people's lives." She noted that most urban planning schools did not even require basic economics courses, and recounted a recent talk she gave at the League of California Cities where she listened to talk about revamping zoning as a kind of central planning. So, she wrote, "We couldn't have started this program at a better time."

Since "people are policy," the key to getting the program off the ground was finding the right policy analyst to run it. Urban economist Sam Staley was our choice, coming to us from the Buckeye Institute, the free-market think tank in Ohio. During his first six months, in 1998, Sam gave presentations on urban sprawl at two conferences, wrote and had published twenty op-ed pieces dealing with "urban sprawl" issues in various parts of the country, and appeared on more than a dozen radio talk shows—including the syndicated *Bob Grant Show* from WOR in New York. In mid-1998, we also contracted with urban geographer Joel Kotkin as an Urban Futures research fellow. Joel at that time was also a contributing editor to the *Los Angeles Times* Opinion section and a columnist for the *Los Angeles Business Journal*. Joel later went on to a teaching position at Chapman University and created the valuable NewGeography.com website.

Sam's first major policy study appeared early in 1999. "The Sprawling of America: In Defense of the Dynamic City" was an across-the-board challenge to the mantras of "smart growth" and "livability" that were being promoted by planning groups and a Clinton-Gore "livability agenda." Our publicity campaign for the study noted that Sam had already become a respected thinker and speaker on this perspective, including the *Pittsburgh Tribune-Review* dubbing him "the urban planning researcher who's become the most credible voice in the sprawl debate." The study received excellent coverage in a feature article in the *New York Times* by reporter John Tierney, who drew on Sam's paper for details in "Room Aplenty for Sprawl in the Suburbs." The study pointed out that "the new city is decentralized, low-density, neighborhood-based, and highly mobile. Urban and land-use policy should embrace this evolution, using markets as their guide, not adopting top-down planning in vague attempts to mold consumers to an ideology of urban form rooted in the past."

Sam's next big study, in 2000, was "The Vanishing Farmland Myth and the Smart-Growth Agenda." He presented data showing that the amount of crop land has been remarkably stable over time, but that smart-growth advocates repeatedly argue that any land that is now in agriculture is "prime farmland" and must be preserved as such, rather than letting the property owner decide the land's future. Sam unveiled the study at the National Press Club in Washington, DC, that January, and it received impressive media coverage, including both AP and Reuters, and extensive coverage in agricultural media. The news conference included representatives from the US Department of Agriculture and the American Farmland Trust, whose views differed sharply from Sam's.

May 2000 saw Sam's photo and ideas featured in a long article in *Governing* magazine, "The Boys of Sprawl: Free-Market Think Tanks Are Working Hard to Convince Americans that Smart Growth Is a Stupid Idea." A map in the article noted the names and locations of thirteen free-market think tanks, all of which Sam was, of course, networking with. And while somewhat critical of our perspective on the issue, the article was great exposure for what was still an emerging perspective launched by our Urban Futures program.

Making *Reason* Magazine Mainstream

Under Virginia's leadership as editor-in-chief, *Reason* magazine grew in quality, stature, and journalistic credibility during the 1990s. Circulation reached forty-five thousand in 1992, and a new high of fifty thousand in 1993. It took a number of additional years, and several donor-sponsored bulk gift subscription projects (e.g., to every member of Congress), a program with several airlines to include *Reason* on their magazine racks for air shuttle service in the Northeast Corridor, plus several breakthroughs into chain bookstores to finally, in 2000, reach the sixty thousand circulation goal I'd set many years before. Besides spending as much money as we could scrape together on continued direct-mail subscription promotions, a lot of the growth occurred because of Virginia's improvements in content and her growing fame as a public intellectual.

Improved Reason Content

Virginia continued finding interesting people to interview and getting blockbuster articles from provocative authors. When Clarence Thomas was nominated for a Supreme Court opening in 1991, his background and legal views were little-known. So Virginia circulated our 1987 interview with Thomas, which opened many people's eyes to his intellectual bona fides. A penetrating February 1992 article on the Clarence Thomas confirmation hearings, by journalist Edith Efron, was a finalist in the National Magazine Awards that year. Efron followed up with an insightful cover story on President Bill Clinton's psychology. We knew it would be a big deal, so (thanks to contributions from several board members) we took out ads in *The New Republic* and the *Washington Post*, and Virginia did interviews about it on nationally syndicated radio talk shows. Waldenbooks, which normally carried five hundred copies each month, ordered ten thousand more of that November 1994 issue due to customer demand. And when those were gone, it ordered five thousand more.

More journalistic honors came *Reason*'s way in 1996. Glenn Garvin's two-part series on immigration was a finalist for a

National Magazine Award in the Public Interest category. And the same year, Virginia was a finalist in the annual Gerald Loeb Awards for Distinguished Business and Financial Journalism, for selected editorials in *Reason*. And although we did not win a National Magazine Award in either 1992 or 1996, in 1997 Virginia was invited to be a judge in the Award's General Excellence category for magazines under one hundred thousand circulation. From her experience there, she commented that "the most gratifying part of the experience was realizing that if *Reason* had entered this category, our best work would have stacked up extremely well. Even if we hadn't made it to the finals, I think we could have survived the first day's cuts—and that's saying a lot."

We had two more National Magazine Award finalists in 1997: science correspondent Michael Fumento's investigative piece, "Gulf Lore Syndrome," and Jacob Sullum's "No Relief in Sight," chronicling the suffering of chronic-pain patients due to physician fear of running afoul of the Drug Enforcement Administration for prescribing opiods. And in its May 1999 issue, the *Columbia Journalism Review* published a very positive article, "Mainstreaming Reason: How a Libertarian Magazine Elbows Its Way to the Table."

Virginia continued the tradition of publishing interviews with intriguing and often controversial people. During this decade, *Reason* interviews included scholars Ronald Coase, Richard Epstein, and Milton Friedman; humorists Dave Barry, Drew Carey, and Penn Jillette (all three fans of *Reason*); management guru Tom Peters; technology popularizer Esther Dyson; anti-tax advocate Grover Norquist; Green Revolution pioneer Norman Borlaug; journalist John Stossel; the ACLU's Nadine Strossen; and public intellectual Camille Paglia.

Reason's twenty-fifth anniversary issue (May 1993, Vol. 25, No. 1) was another tour de force. It featured original articles by notables including Richard Epstein, Peter Huber, Joel Mokyr, John McClaughry, journalists Jonathan Rauch and also Brian Lamb of C-SPAN, and Donald (later Deirdre) McCloskey, previewing some of the themes of Deirdre's future trilogy on bourgeois values. As HillaryCare was being developed in 1993, *Reason* published an expose on Medicare's broken promises to be a relatively low-cost program, followed by a January 1994 special issue on health care reform whose theme was "Catastrophic Care." With controversy raging over California governor Pete Wilson's anti-immigrant Prop. 187 later that year, we published Ron Unz's conservative case against those kinds of restrictions. Unfortunately, the measure passed, and despite most of its provisions being found unconstitutional, it helped spark the subsequent long-term decline of the Republican Party in California.

On certain hot topics on which *Reason* had published a lot, Virginia and her staff assembled collections, which were made available to interested readers and for use in classrooms. Among these were the *Reason Environmental Reader* (1992) and the *Reason Health Care Reader* (1993).

Aggressive Public Relations

Getting well-known didn't just happen. It took a combination of good public relations and the willingness of Virginia and her editorial team to write op-ed pieces, columns, and make media appearances. Virginia set the pace, as a role model for her team, and they followed suit.

As early as 1991, Virginia began appearing periodically on CNN's *Crier & Co.*, and she made her CNN *Crossfire* debut in 1992, debating FDA policy on breast implants with Dr. Sydney Wolf; she discussed the same issue on *Larry King Live*. The "Opposing View" slot in *USA Today* was one that many Reasoners, including Virginia, took full advantage of. Her debut on public radio's *Marketplace* took place in 1993. She also appeared that year on the *Today* show to discuss a Supreme Court decision on sexual harassment, and on *Fox Morning News* and *CNN & Co.* in 1994.

Virginia began a long presence on the op-ed page of the *Los Angeles Times* in 1993, appearing every month in the "Column Right" slot. In 1996, *Forbes* created a spin-off magazine—*Forbes ASAP*—focused on the high-tech industry, and Virginia became a regular columnist. After that magazine ceased publication, Virginia's columns continued in *Forbes*. In 1997, senior editor Jacob Sullum got a weekly syndicated column with Creators

Syndicate—which continues to this day. (Fellow freedom-oriented columnists represented by Creators Syndicate include Steve Chapman and Walter Williams.) In 1998, Virginia's long, thoughtful piece in *Wired*, "Technocracy R.I.P.," cautioned the high-tech community against falling for this superficially appealing vision of governance by experts. And after handing the editor-in-chief reins to Nick Gillespie at the beginning of 2000 and becoming editor-at-large, Virginia began a monthly economics column in the business section of the *New York Times*. And Nick became something of a regular on National Public Radio starting in 1998.

Reason articles were increasingly picked up and reprinted in other publications. In 1992, the New York Times Syndicate started distribution of selected *Reason* content to subscribing newspapers. We reached a similar deal with Knight-Ridder Financial News Service in 1993.

Books by Editors

Another way we put *Reason* on the map was to move back into book publishing in a modest way. To commemorate the magazine's twenty-fifth anniversary in 1993, Virginia and I compiled a collection of some of *Reason's* greatest hits over those years. *Free Minds & Free Markets: 25 Years of Reason* included the classic interviews with Ronald Reagan (1975), F. A. Hayek (1977), Charles Murray (1985), and Clarence Thomas (1987). Articles that made national news included Reason's Love Canal exposé (1981), and Jan Bellamy's award-winning "Two Utilities Are Better than One" (also 1981). Selected editorials included my "Libertarian Realpolitick" (advice to the fledgling Libertarian Party, 1976) and Virginia's "Fin de Siecle" on the fall of Communism in Europe (1991). Far ahead of its time was Thomas Szasz's case against "Drug Prohibition" (1978). And also notable was Jack Wheeler's "How to Dismantle the Soviet Empire" (1983). With so much really good material to choose from, it was agonizing to have to cope with a 375-page limit, so many worthy pieces ended up not being included. Still the book made a very important statement.

Next up was Jacob Sullum's *For Your Own Good: The Anti-Smoking Crusade and the Tyranny of Public Health*, published in 1998.

For this new volume, we arranged a book tour, with events in New York, Chicago, Cleveland, San Francisco, Los Angeles, and several other cities. In Los Angeles, we garnered a lot of additional publicity for the book by holding a "smoke-in" in West Hollywood, featuring Drew Carey and Penn Jillette making the point that bars and restaurants should be free to make their own decisions on when and where their customers could smoke—or not. Proprietor Irwin Held of Barney's Beanery gladly hosted the event, agreeing with the point we were making.

Late that same year, Virginia's powerful book, *The Future and Its Enemies*, was released, to rave reviews. In the book, Virginia argued persuasively that instead of a liberal/conservative dichotomy, it was more insightful to address the contrast between advocates of *stasis* and advocates of *dynamism*. The book struck a real chord in Silicon Valley and among such thinkers as Esther Dyson, Deirdre McCloskey, and Tom Peters. For this book, the book tour was much larger, encompassing twenty-six cities. Friendly audiences around the country were assembled by think tanks such as the American Enterprise Institute and Cato Institute and a host of SPN think tanks such as the Cascade Policy Institute, the Goldwater Institute, the Heartland Institute, and others. Chapters of the Federalist Society also hosted events in a number of cities. An unexpected event resulting from publicity over the book was an invitation from Florida governor Jeb Bush for Virginia to come to Tallahassee to give a talk on it for his cabinet.

Late in 2000, in the final *Reason Report* of that year, we announced that Associate Editor Jesse Walker had signed a contract with New York University Press for his forthcoming book, *Rebels on the Air: The Death and Life of Great American Radio*. In the following decade, books by *Reason* editorial staffers started coming out fairly often.

Reason Events

To build a stronger relationship with the magazine's readers, Virginia came up with the idea of holding "Evening with the Editors" events. We tested the idea in Los Angeles. The format was a wine and hors d'oeuvres reception in the early evening, centered on the large conference room/library in our Sepulveda Blvd. offices, but with the whole place open for people to visit and talk with staffers. Of course, most of the policy and management staff turned out, as well. The first event, held in August 1992 in Los Angeles, attracted more than a hundred subscribers and supporters—many of whom none of us had met before, but also including people who'd been subscribers for several decades. A second Los Angeles event, the following February, attracted nearly as many, persuading us that the concept was sound. In later years, we did these events in other cities where we had large numbers of subscribers and supporters, including New York, Princeton (Virginia's alma mater), Chicago, San Francisco, and Washington, DC (where anti-tax activist and long-time subscriber Grover Norquist was our host).

But the most consequential Evening with the Editors took place in our LA offices in fall 1996. In addition to science fiction writer Larry Niven (who lives in the San Fernando Valley), the other surprise attendee was Drew Carey. This was during the time period of the weekly TV series *The Drew Carey Show*, set in a department store in Drew's home town of Cleveland, but filmed, of course, in Los Angeles. Drew had been a *Reason* subscriber for several years, and dropped in to meet the people who produced the magazine he enjoyed. In addition to chatting with the attendees, he bought a couple of *Reason* T-shirts, and to our great delight, wore one on an episode of the show the following season. This was the beginning of a long and very productive relationship between Drew and Reason Foundation.

One of our institutional goals, for both the magazine and fundraising, was to develop a stronger following in Silicon Valley. When Michael Rothschild's path-breaking book *Bionomics: Economy as Ecosystem* was published in 1990, I realized that his description of how markets work, and the many parallels with how things evolve in nature, was a powerful new way of understanding Schumpeter's "creative destruction." And since Rothschild was part of the Silicon Valley community, I made a point of meeting him to explore possible ways in which we might work together. But it turns out he had already received such positive feedback on the ideas in the book, that he'd decided to take a five-year sabbatical from his management consulting work to create the Bionomics Institute to further explore the ramifications of this new paradigm, basing it of course in Silicon Valley. I attended all five of the annual Bionomics conferences, and spoke at several, making a number of promising contacts in the high-tech community. And when it came time for the final conference (and termination of the Institute) in 1998, Michael invited Virginia to be the opening speaker. It was an excellent platform for her to preview the ideas in her forthcoming book, *The Future and Its Enemies*.

After that book was published, Virginia came up with the idea of a successor to the Bionomics conferences, which we called Dynamic Visions conferences. The first took place in Santa Clara in February 1999. Speakers included open-source software "evangelist" Eric Raymond, economic historian Joel Mokyr, anthropologist Grant McCracken, futurist Gregory Stock, and a number of Reason and RPPI people. Conference attendees spent Valentine's Day evening at a special reception at the newly opened Tech Museum of Innovation in San Jose. Attendee response was overwhelmingly positive, with a lot of support for this to become an annual event, like the Bionomics conferences had been.

The next year we did a reprise, over President's Day weekend, again in Santa Clara. Several returning speakers were joined by astrophysicist (and science fiction writer) Gregory Benford, my old friend Adam Powell (then at Freedom Forum in DC), *Fast Company* contributor Dan Pink, author Richard Rodriguez, and aerospace engineer Robert Zubrin. Again, there was a great turnout, and very positive feedback. But due to Virginia's evolving interests it turned out to be the last Dynamic Visions conference.

Going Online

In April 1995, I attended a conference at the Hoover Institution about how think tanks can and should make greater use of TV, video, and the Internet. I wrote in my journal that this was "challenging stuff, but still hard to figure out how to do cost-effective things with it." But Virginia and Lynn were already ahead of me on that score. They were starting to think seriously about creating an online presence for Reason Foundation, and by year-end we launched both Reason.org (the Foundation and policy research site) and Reason.com for the magazine, with convenient links between the two. Technical aspects were handled by Ray Ng, our versatile and talented information technology guy, and several Silicon Valley volunteers. With this dual launch, we were among the first free-market think tanks and one of the very first think magazines to go online.

The initial Reason.com site included the full text of back issues from 1995 and, going forward, all future issues. But without any "page limits," the site also hosted things like speeches by editors, links to other interesting sites, notices of upcoming media appearances (such as Virginia's upcoming appearances on Comedy Central's *Politically Incorrect*). In fall 1996, we added an email alert system to let interested subscribers (who had to ask for this service) know of upcoming appearances by *Reason* people. The first implementation of a "news" function on Reason.com took place in July 1998 with the launch of a Breaking Issues feature on the site. Webmaster Brian Taylor and Managing Editor Rick Henderson developed the feature, and we notified online journalists, operators of electronic mailing lists, and other public policy groups about the new feature. Later that year came the launch of *Reason Express*, initially a weekly (Monday) e-newsletter written by DC-based staffer Jeff Taylor. Today its successor provides new commentary five days a week.

We were all very proud in fall 2000 when web directory Top9.com listed *Reason Online* as one of the top nine news magazines online. In this ranking, we beat out the websites of all our principal think magazine competitors except *National Review*, so we topped *The New Republic*, *The American Spectator*, and *The Weekly Standard*, all of which had larger print circulation than *Reason*.

Magazine Ups and Downs

All was not sweetness and light during the 1990s. Several events led to controversies, either internal or external. Part of my job, as president and (for most of this period, publisher) was to deal with these unanticipated events.

In December 1993, a *Reason* reader who was also a successful business entrepreneur came to us with a proposal for him to make a major investment in the magazine. He proposed a significant revamp to make *Reason* more accessible to a much broader audience—including such changes as shorter articles and more stories about people fighting big government. He was thinking of putting in something like $500K per year for three or four years of expansion, but on condition of becoming publisher and having an option to buy the magazine if it turned profitable. Virginia disagreed with his proposed editorial changes, and I was very skeptical about the idea that this man with zero publishing experience could make a think magazine profitable when none of our larger competitors had ever achieved that status. In the end, of course, we turned him down, as we'd turned down Ronald Lauder the previous decade. But there was a good deal of internal debate and discussion before we reached that decision.

A very public flap occurred in 1996. The Libertarian Party had selected noted financial author Harry Browne as its presidential candidate that year, to be formally selected at the nominating convention in DC over the July 4 weekend. I was enthusiastic that Harry was the best-known person the LP had ever had as its presidential candidate, with a large following in "hard-money" investment circles. Many friends of mine (who were long-time *Reason* readers and some of them donors) were part of his campaign effort. Nick, as senior editor, did an interview with Harry that he (and I) assumed would be published as a normal *Reason* interview. But to everyone's surprise (including me), what emerged in the July 1996 issue was an article by Nick, "The Libertarian Party's Dilemma," using quotes from the interview he'd conducted but basically making a case that a Libertarian Party campaign for the presidency was an oxymoron. Today, from the perspective of two decades, the piece (despite some snide comments) was asking serious questions.

But that's not how it was received by huge numbers of activist LP members who were also *Reason* subscribers and donors.

They were outraged that their beloved magazine was attacking the best shot the LP had ever had. We got lots of hate mail and demands that I, as publisher, fire Nick. While that was out of the question, I was angry with both Nick and Virginia for not taking into account that LP members were historically our very best source of new subscribers and that many of our donors (and some of our board members) were LP supporters. I was especially miffed that Virginia, who had recently been made vice president of *Reason* magazine, had not realized the potential negative reactions from a significant portion of our subscriber and donor bases—and had therefore not shown a draft of the article to me before committing it to publication. The response that I was merely overreacting to friends' anger struck me as naïve and wrong.

So my job became to limit the damage. Our former business manager Jack Dean was close to the Harry Browne campaign, and he and I worked out a damage-control effort. I would sign an LP fundraising letter on behalf of the Harry Browne campaign to send to the *Reason* mailing list, have a peace-making meeting with Harry at the convention, and go ahead with the planned Reason Foundation booth at the convention, prepared for the slings and arrows.

Just after working this out, I left on a previously scheduled speaking trip to New Zealand, as guest of the NZ Business Roundtable, followed by trips to Detroit and Toronto. As I wrote in my journal the day before leaving for the LP convention, "All the while [I was traveling], the controversy [over Nick's article] has been raging, and I haven't done enough damage control early enough. We do have internal consensus, and will be handing out [from the booth] a four-page statement, but I'm still dreading the whole thing." Fortunately, the convention didn't turn out as badly as I'd feared. As I wrote in my journal afterwards, "A majority of those who came by the booth had positive things to say, and [during an evening event] I was asked up on stage to recount an early *Reason* anecdote." So I'd managed to rebuild the bridge that Nick had damaged.

Three years later (1999), Virginia told our management

meeting that she was tiring of management and production responsibilities and wanted to step down as editor-in-chief in a year or so to become an editor-at-large. She said she wanted to groom Nick to be her successor, but I was dubious. Nick was clearly very talented and could offer a fresh take on *Reason*'s approach, but the Harry Browne episode still rankled, and I wondered if he would be able to take seriously the responsibilities that went along with becoming vice president of the magazine division. A few months later, she changed the planned date of her transition to the end of 1999, just four months away. In view of my doubts, I wanted to conduct a search, as I'd done when Marty stepped down—but it wasn't clear there would be enough time for a proper search. I talked about this with board chairman Harry Teasley and he advised against doing a search—doing so might risk losing both Virginia and Nick. I didn't like this, but without board support, and with such a short period remaining, I gave in and decided I would have to make sure Nick understood the responsibilities of being vice president in addition to editor-in-chief. And in fact, Nick worked out well in his new role.

Growing the Foundation
Donor Events

When we were having annual banquets, we tagged on a half-day seminar for donors who came to town for the banquet, and those were pretty well attended. But when we contemplated shifting to banquets only for special occasions, we were left with a need for regular relationship-building events, especially with our higher-dollar individual donors.

These were the early Clinton administration years, so I'd read several articles about many Clinton people attending an annual conference for liberals called Renaissance Weekend. Wouldn't it be great, I thought, if we could do a weekend like that aimed at celebrating liberty and free societies? I also learned from several of our board members that Cato Institute had started an annual high-dollar-donor event called a Benefactors' Summit. Far be it from me to be shy of copying an Ed Crane innovation that seemed to work. So we began brainstorming the idea of an annual Reason Weekend in 1993, and held the first one in June 1994 at the Silverado Resort in Napa, California.

Though the planning was collaborative, I took the lead on coming up with an interesting array of speakers. Rather than just picking the usual free-market scholar suspects, I wanted an array of provocative thinkers and doers. The first year's speakers, besides several of Reason Foundation's own stars, included *Bionomics* author Michael Rothschild; nanotechnology pioneer Eric Drexler; technology guru George Gilder; our privatization superstar, Mayor Steve Goldsmith; noted biochemist Bruce Ames; former Reagan White House adviser Chuck Hobbs; and drug policy expert Ethan Nadelman. The setting was great, the speakers were stimulating, and the attendee response was super-positive. The only negative was that the resort was a long drive from the Oakland and San Francisco airports.

The next year we shifted to the East Coast, at the Boca Raton Resort & Club in Florida. This time our speakers included ABC's John Stossel, Judge Alex Kozinski, USC fuzzy-logic expert Bart Kosko, Charles Murray, and Christina Hoff Sommers. With a growing attendance (and an increase in the average size of large-donor contributions), we decided that Reason Weekend was a winning concept. Most years we alternated between east and west coasts (except for one year in Dallas), and we continued to include innovators from industry and technology in addition to policy wonks and academics. Almost a decade before aerospace designer Burt Rutan's Spaceship One was awarded the X Prize for the first privately funded manned flight into space (2004), we featured Rutan as a Reason Weekend speaker, discussing his numerous innovative aircraft designs. Other early speakers included *Washington Post* reporter Joel Garreau discussing his book that put the term "Edge City" into our vocabulary, former astronaut Buzz Aldrin, economist wunderkind Paul Romer, education reformer Lisa Graham Keegan, Mars exploration pioneer Robert Zubrin, legal scholar Peter Huber, and urban geographer Joel Kotkin. Reason Weekend remains a mainstay of Reason Foundation's relationship-building efforts, and as I write, those weekends are into their third decade.

Our shift away from annual banquets meant that each banquet we did thereafter marked a special occasion. In 1993, we celebrated the twenty-fifth anniversary of *Reason* magazine and hence the fifteenth anniversary of Reason Foundation. Held at the Sheraton Grande in Los Angeles, the black-tie event attracted over three hundred people, with Charles Murray as the keynote speaker. Cameo speakers included Peter Huber, Jim Pinkerton, T. J. Rodgers, and Walter Williams; Contributing Editor Tom Hazlett served as master of ceremonies.

Five years later, the thirtieth anniversary banquet in 1998 was even bigger and better. Held at the Miramar Sheraton in Santa Monica, it drew five hundred people. John Stossel was the keynote speaker, and additional thoughts and congratulations were offered by Los Angeles mayor Richard Riordan, talk-show host Larry Elder, former Indianapolis mayor Steve Goldsmith, and Judge Alex Kozinski. Among the many notables attending were three former Libertarian Party presidential candidates (Ed Clark, David Bergland, and Harry Browne), Nathaniel Branden, former *Reason* editor-in-chief Marty Zupan, David Kelley of the Institute for Objectivist Studies, Chip Mellor of the Institute for Justice, and *Wired* founder Louis Rossetto. We devoted the entire next day to donor events: a morning seminar featuring *Reason* and RPPI staffers discussing their recent accomplishments, and, after lunch, the choice of either a trip up to the Mount Wilson Observatory or to the newly opened Getty art museum in the Sepulveda Pass. A good time was had by all.

The next banquet was an opportunity that fell into our lap. Lady Margaret Thatcher was planning a US speaking trip for 1999, and our friend Lew Uhler of the National Tax Limitation Foundation, based in Sacramento, had secured the California franchise, so to speak. But his organization did not have the staff and resources to organize and publicize a gala event on the appropriate scale. So he worked out a deal with me for our two organizations to jointly sponsor the banquet in Los Angeles. It was a somewhat difficult negotiation, since we ended up doing nearly all the work, and the deal gave us a large majority of the net proceeds (if any—and fortunately there were).

That banquet was our largest ever, at that point. We had a nationwide audience and a wonderful evening. This event was a special thrill for me, since I admired Margaret Thatcher more than any other national leader during my adult life. While the pre-dinner reception was going on, a handful of us had a private audience with Lady Thatcher, and she autographed my copy of her book, *Downing Street Years*. Board Chairman Harry Teasley and I sat on either side of her during dinner, after which Harry gave a moving introduction for her speech. After the speech, Lew Uhler and I took to the stage with her to review written questions from the audience and select the ones to ask her. Everything went well (except for Lew's subsequent unhappiness with our final accounting for expenses and his organization's share of the net).

Besides the Dynamic Visions conferences aimed at building relationships in Silicon Valley, we also started developing "show the flag" events to take on the road. Called "Advancing Liberty in Policy, Politics, and Culture," they were launched in 2000 and featured Lynn, Nick, and me explaining how the various parts of Reason Foundation work, and how we seek both policy change and culture change in our efforts to increase liberty in America. The first two events, in June 2000, took place in New York City and in Orange County, California.

Building a Stronger Financial Base

An important part of my job was increasing both the number of donors and the amounts they gave. So, during the 1990s, many of the speaking invitations I accepted in cities such as New York, Chicago, Dallas, Houston, San Francisco, etc., ended up being week-long trips, with as many visits to current and prospective individuals, corporations, and foundations as I could arrange. Occasionally, according to my journal, a multi-city trip would extend as long as ten days. Lou and I used to joke that while we'd been married a nominal twenty years, it didn't seem anywhere near that long because of all the time I'd been on the road. These efforts, combined with the impressive results of *Reason* magazine and RPPI, did succeed over time in increasing Reason Foundation's annual revenue. But with the board encouraging me to continue my effective hands-on policy research, fundraising was still a very part-time effort for me. And that simply was not good enough to build the kind of strong financial base we needed.

So we needed to build a "development" staff. We had pretty good success finding and keeping someone to manage the donor records, get the fundraising letters (which I wrote) organized and sent out, send thank-you letters promptly, etc. But a "development director" who could research prospects, write proposals, and actually go on donor visits proved to be very difficult. We hired the first such person in 1991 and she lasted until 1994 but didn't ever get to the point of making donor visits. After a long search we hired a replacement in 1995, with high hopes. He actually did go out on the road and make visits, but after a year on the job, grants and contributions looked to be less than the year before, so that was the end of his Reason tenure. We did find a promising young woman, Erica Mannard, to work on development; she became our events planner for banquets and Reason Weekends and did excellent work. She had the potential to start making donor visits, but decided to depart at the start of 2000. We replaced Erica with Donald Heath, who had done events management and donor relations for the Institute for Objectivist Studies, later renamed The Atlas Society. Don was a solid addition to the team, but proved to be primarily an inside person, rather than a go-out-and-visit-donors-and-prospects person.

That left the burden still largely on my shoulders. During the dot-com bubble years of the late 1990s, we all thought emerging Silicon Valley millionaires and billionaires would be our salvation. Starting with the Bionomics conferences in the early 1990s, I made numerous trips and met a lot of people. I also became a supporter of Erik Drexler's fledgling nanotechnology-promoting think tank, the Foresight Institute, and attended a number of its conferences, primarily to network with its donors. One of those I met there, Pierluigi Zappacosta (founder of Logitech), became a Reason supporter and board member, as did Palo Alto intellectual property lawyer Sarah O'Dowd. And T. J. Rodgers, CEO of Cypress Semiconductor, became a fan of Virginia's writing and my transportation work, a speaker at one or two of our events, an occasional *Reason* author, and a donor. But generally my hopes far exceeded the reality.

School choice was a cause for some of the Silicon Valley biggies, and I attended a school voucher dinner in a huge tent behind venture capitalist Tim Draper's house—with Milton and Rose Friedman in attendance. My meetings with him failed to make a sale. I also had at least one visit with Reed Hastings, a school choice fan (but opposed to vouchers). He was the CEO of a small start-up that was beginning to rent movie videos by mail. He turned us down, but went on to turn Netflix into a huge success. Then there was a young woman who was only the second or third employee of an Internet search start-up called Ask. com. She was a big fan of *Reason* and was sure it would be only a year or two until she would be an Internet millionaire. That never happened, and she dropped off our radar screen.

Despite these shortcomings in our development efforts, we achieved impressive growth during the 1990s. Total income increased from $2.18 million in 1991 to $5.25 million in 2000. In six of those years, expenses slightly exceeded income (by between one and two percent) but the other four were in the black, with a 3.1 percent net in 1997 and 3.8 percent net in 1998. Nevertheless, the balance sheet was still abysmal. For Reason Foundation's entire history through 2000 we had a negative net worth, for two reasons. First, we operated without a reserve fund, so that each year's revenue was planned to be spent entirely on programs. Secondly, because a magazine inherently has a large subscription liability (people pay up-front for a subscription whose costs are incurred for one or more years in the future), there will be a negative net worth unless the balance sheet has offsetting assets. Since we owned no property and had no reserves, the result was always a negative net worth. This apparently caused us little trouble with donors, since (a) few requested our audited financials, and (b) in any financials that we sent out in such cases, we included an explanation of the subscription liability and the common magazine industry practice of a competitor nearly always being willing to take over the subscription liability of a magazine that was shutting down, to gain access to the subscriber list.

Even so, this basically shaky financial situation weighed on me, and led me to discuss with the board some kind of capital campaign during the 1990s. Actually, David Koch had first suggested we consider an endowment campaign at a board meeting in 1992. But we didn't start serious discussions about such a campaign until 1998–99.

A key player in that discussion was Harry Teasley. At our management meetings early in 1994, Lynn, Virginia, Bryan, and I discussed how we could get the board to be more actively involved in governance and fundraising. For all the years since the Foundation's incorporation, I had served as de-facto board chairman, though having only the title of president. As we reviewed the line-up of board members, Harry appeared to have the most business management experience and was the most interested in improved governance of the organization. I raised the question with him in March 1994, and he agreed to think about it. We brought the subject up at board meetings later that year, and discussions continued in 1995, complicated by another board member expressing interest in the chairmanship. That created a sticky situation, which was eventually resolved in Harry's favor in 1996, with his first meeting as chairman in October of that year.

As I wrote in my journal after that meeting, "Clearly the old order has passed, and it's a whole new ball game. . . . And much rests on me to change my overall M.O. as well as the Foundation's approach overall." Harry was a tough task-master, but he pitched in seriously to help, rather than simply giving directives. In May 1997, he spent a week in Los Angeles with us. He met with each manager individually for two or more hours, discussing roles and responsibilities. He had meetings with the entire team discussing strategic planning. During two of the evenings, he took me with him to have dinner with prospective LA donors. And for that fall's board meeting, he made it an all-day event, with the morning devoted to strategic planning and the meeting itself in the afternoon.

At the fall 1998 board meeting, having briefed Harry in advance, I presented the outlines of a five-year plan, including a capital campaign during the last several years of that period. The board discussed but made no decision about the capital campaign. It turned out that Harry was opposed in principle to free-market groups building endowments, rather than having to sell their program to donors every year. We had been researching capital campaign planning firms at that point in 1999, so this news came as a real shock. Lynn and I discussed the problem, Lynn having had a longer relationship with Harry than I, predating his joining our board. She suggested that raising money to launch new programs, and to build a prudent reserve fund, might well fly with Harry. After some further discussions with him, he agreed that this was something he could support.

Leading up to the November board meeting, we signed a contract with a fundraising consultant firm with a solid track record on capital campaigns. The morning before that meeting, we had a two-hour meeting of the board's new Development Committee, discussing the stages of the campaign with our assigned consultant. Afterwards, I wrote in my journal, "That was very positive. I think we're finally getting board members engaged with fundraising."

Personal Reflections on My 1990s at Reason

On one hand, the tremendous growth and success of the Foundation during these years was very gratifying. We had built a real think tank, and turned *Reason* into a very credible magazine. I also achieved considerable satisfaction seeing some of my transportation policy ideas implemented. On the other hand, these experiences made me realize my strong preference for policy work rather than fundraising and management.

Privatization Consulting

Even though only one US airport had been privatized during the 1990s (Stewart), I had the opportunity to be part of a two-man consulting team in 1992 doing a feasibility study of privatizing the undersized and rather primitive airport at Montego Bay, the prime tourist destination in Jamaica. This was a project of a short-lived for-profit subsidiary of Reason Foundation that Bryan and I created called Reason Associates. The IRS bans nonprofits competing with for-profit consulting firms, but a taxpaying consulting subsidiary was perfectly legal.

The Jamaica study was only the second Reason Associates project. The first was a study commissioned by Bechtel Corp. on the potential US market for PPP toll roads. It was fun doing the Jamaica study, despite strong opposition from the airport consulting establishment and American Airlines, the primary carrier serving the airport. And Lou joined me for a three-day weekend at the Grand Lido resort in Negril. Even better, the airport was eventually privatized, in 2003.

But some of our privatization-related donors made it known that they weren't happy about the competition from Reason Associates in privatization studies. Between that and realizing the large opportunity cost of me spending time on such projects, we terminated Reason Associates by the end of 1992.

Still Mr. Privatization

I also enjoyed continuing to be Mr. Privatization on a global scale. For several years I wrote the US column for a newsletter called *Privatization International*, based in London. And I kept getting speaking invitations from overseas. In 1992, I was invited back to London for the Adam Smith Institute's anniversary dinner—this time, flying JFK to Heathrow on the supersonic Concorde, courtesy of ASI donor British Airways. As a life-long aviation buff, flying on the Concorde was a once-in-a-lifetime experience, and I still have the on-board mementos provided by BA to passengers.

In 1993, I was off to Sao Paulo to speak at a privatization conference and visit a free-market think tank there. In 1994, I was the dinner speaker at the fifth anniversary banquet of the leading free-market think tank in Chile, founded by some of the "Chicago boys" who had privatized and deregulated the country's economy. I turned down a World Bank invitation for a two-week visit to Australia and New Zealand, but did make a return visit to South Africa to speak at a 1995 Mont Pelerin Society meeting in Cape Town. And in 1999, a Reason Foundation donor with business interests in Peru persuaded me to do a set of privatization lectures in Lima—by paying for a week-long trip for both Lou and me that included tour guides and a side trip to see the Inca ruins at Machu Picchu. Besides six or seven university lectures in two days, I gave an address to the national congress that was covered live on cable TV. (I also framed one of the posters that were all over town announcing this event.) Needless to say, all these events had simultaneous translations.

In hindsight, while these trips were all gratifying and educational for me and nice to write about in *Reason Report*, they also had a large opportunity cost in terms of time diverted from fundraising, management, and policy research.

Bush/Cheney Campaign Policy Team

During 2000, our friend Steve Goldsmith (who was heading up domestic policy for the Bush/Cheney campaign) persuaded Lynn and me to become part of policy teams for the campaign: me on the transportation team and Lynn on the environment team. We were supposed to do this on our own time, of course, not on Reason Foundation time. We both found these activities very productive; in my case, working with a team of transportation people that included friends Steve Lockwood, Ken Orski, and Alan Pisarski to craft a whole agenda of policies based to a considerable extent on Reason Foundation work. And Lynn had a similarly good experience on her environment team. I was also made a nominal member of the transportation transition team, but the only thing I had to do was to come to DC in January 2001 for a ceremonial meeting and photographs.

Qualms and Transition Planning

Increasingly during this decade, I began thinking more seriously about what I wanted to do with the rest of my life. Lou and I talked about this from time to time, as I griped about having to deal with what seemed like every-year personnel problems—laying off low-performers, countering outside job offers made to Lynn and Virginia—and the annual trauma of putting together a budget, coping with still-dicey cash flow, and discovering that a nonprofit board can have its share of politics, too.

One trigger for getting more serious about this subject was the Northridge earthquake in January 1994. Lou and I lived in a mid-century modern home on a hillside in Sherman Oaks, overlooking (well, on a smogless day) the San Fernando Valley. The epicenter of the 6.7 magnitude quake was less than ten miles from our house; we were shaken awake at 4:30 a.m., terrified that this was the Big One (the San Andreas fault letting go). Though not the Big One, it killed fifty-seven people, caused a number of apartment buildings to collapse, and put several major freeways out of commission. Our house, fortunately, was on bedrock and suffered no structural damage.

But Lou and I had long discussions over the following weeks. Did we really want to remain in LA for the rest of our lives, and risk being there when the Big One finally occurred? No, we didn't. But moving away would not be compatible with my remaining CEO of Reason Foundation, despite our pretty good success by the mid-1990s in having some of our staffers be virtual employees located in other parts of the country. In autumn 1992, we'd had a vacation in South Florida, where I grew up and still had relatives. At the time, Lou (a native Californian who'd never lived anywhere else) discovered that she really liked the sub-tropical climate and vegetation, and we talked about someday retiring there—especially given the large disparity in housing prices between coastal California and South Florida. But post-earthquake we started having what-if conversations about my shifting from CEO to full-time policy researcher, which I could do as a virtual employee. In March 1994, I wrote in my journal, "In many ways I hate being CEO, as opposed to being a researcher/guru of privatization/transportation."

On a Caribbean cruise vacation in March 1996, Lou and I agreed on a long-range plan for me to phase out as CEO, and Lou to "retire" from UCLA once she had completed the required fifteen years for her pension to vest. At that point, we would relocate to South Florida and build our dream house, etc. Because it would take until 2001 for Lou's pension to vest, I did not disclose this plan to the board or the management team until 1998. That August, I took Lynn and Virginia to lunch and explained my desired change of role, and they took it calmly. Virginia had no interest in becoming CEO, but Lynn did, which seemed fine with me. And at the November 1988 board meeting's executive session, I unveiled the succession plan to them, stressing the need for Reason Foundation to have a full-time CEO committed to growing the organization, and it seemed to go over well.

In January 1999, I visited Harry at his home in Tampa to discuss management roles and responsibilities, given the succession plan. He'd evidently been talking with Lynn about this and said we should start moving sooner on making changes, including getting Lynn comfortable with the idea that as a full-time CEO, she would be giving up hands-on policy research to concentrate on management. We did a fair amount of that management planning during 1999. In parallel with that, another board member who was close to Lynn began lobbying me to, in effect, get out of the way and let Lynn take over several years sooner. The idea was that Lynn could take over as CEO in 2001, leaving me free (as founder) to lead the planned long-term funding campaign.

It took me a while to get comfortable with this accelerated schedule, but by early 2000 I had accepted it, especially since I really wanted the capital campaign to take place. So with the board's concurrence, Lynn and I worked out the details for me to hand over the reins to her the first week of January 2001. And as noted above, we contracted with a consulting firm that specialized in capital campaigns for nonprofits to begin the research and planning for that effort.

We had an all-hands meeting on September 30, 2000, to unveil the plan to the entire staff and got busy planning the announcements to donors and our friends and colleagues in the think-tank community. We sent a confidential letter to all major donors at the end of October, and wrote the December 2000 issue of *Reason Report* with my last President's Letter as the front-page story. The issue also included interviews with Lynn, as incoming president, and with Adrian, as the incoming RPPI executive director.

On December 29, 2000, Lynn and I had office-moving day; she moved into my large corner office and I moved into her adjacent smaller office. In my journal I wrote about my aching back from having lugged full file drawers from one office to the other, and feeling liberated by getting rid of lots of obsolete paperwork and having things somewhat better organized. But I also wrote, "Next week is going to feel strange, though—working in a new place and no longer being in charge." But I was also sure I would feel a great sense of relief at no longer having all the responsibility on my shoulders.

Chapter 10

2001: The Year Everything Changed

I began the first year of the new millennium, 2001, with great expectations. With Lynn Scarlett in place as our new CEO, I reveled in being able, at last, to devote full-time efforts to transportation policy. My work on air traffic control seemed on the verge of producing a major breakthrough with the airlines and the new Bush administration, and I was already working on policy studies to further advance two ideas for specialized toll lanes on highways. Advance work on the long-term funding campaign was underway with our consulting firm, Ketchum, under contract. Lou and I were making our plans to move to Florida in about a year. But circumstances intervened to change almost all of this before the year was over.

Management Transitions

The year started off exactly as planned, with Lynn settling in as the new CEO, penning her first President's Letter in *Reason Report* Issue 88 in February. From my office next to hers, I was available for consultation as needed, but focused hard on my policy work, including a pro-forma meeting of the Bush administration's transition team just after the Transportation Research Board's annual meeting in January. My colleagues and I who'd been on the Bush/Cheney campaign's transportation *policy* team had no actual role on the *transition* team, but as the latter was wrapping up its work, they invited all of us to a final meeting to be thanked for our work and have a group photo taken.

Actually, though I was excited that our friend from Indianapolis, Mitch Daniels, had been appointed as director of the Office of Management and Budget, I was disappointed that former Congressman Norm Mineta was the nominee for Secretary of Transportation. Though highly qualified, he had been only lukewarm on HOT lanes and on ATC corporatization during and after his time on the House Transportation and Infrastructure Committee. I'd been hoping Steve Goldsmith (who'd headed domestic policy on the campaign team) would get that job—and if that had happened, I might have been asked to take a senior policy position at DOT. Lou and I had discussed this possibility, and had agreed that if it were an important enough post, we'd figure out a way to make this work—but that was not to be, to Lou's relief.

As recounted later in this chapter, during the first three months of 2001 I was back and forth to Washington on transportation issues, both ATC and surface transportation, and feeling on top of the world about the progress. After just three months of doing hands-on policy work nearly full-time, without constantly dealing with management and fundraising questions, I could already see the improvement in quality—having time to actually read the reports from the Government Accountability Office and the DOT Office of Inspector General, rather than only their one-page summaries. I was also gradually assembling email lists of contacts in aviation and surface transportation so that I could send them periodic updates about our transportation policy work. I was already spending more time networking with contacts and colleagues in transportation.

But around the first of March, as I wrote in my journal, "Lynn dropped her bombshell." Like me, during the Bush/Cheney campaign, she had also been recruited by Steve Goldsmith, in her case to serve on the environmental policy team. She developed a close working relationship with team leader Gale Norton, who was nominated and confirmed early in 2001 as the new Secretary of the Interior. Lynn's ideas on a "new environmentalism" (based in part on decentralization and property rights) that she'd outlined in a widely circulated paper for the National Center for Policy Analysis, had made a big impression on Gale Norton.

Lynn came into my office that day in March and told me that Gale had sounded her out for a very senior position there: the top policy job with major oversight of the budget. She said she hadn't told board members about this yet. There were still some issues on Gale's end that needed to be clarified before they could actually make an offer, but she thought it was pretty likely to be made. And if so, she would seriously consider taking it.

I was devastated. Just as I had adjusted to my new role of non-CEO and the freedom to do more-serious transportation work, the whole new arrangement looked likely to be overturned. I confided in my journal, "There is no way I'm going back to the status quo ante. Yet what can Reason Foundation do? Adrian is too inexperienced to take over. So that means we'd have to do a national search—and I'd still have to be caretaker president for—how long—6 to 12 months? What a disaster, if this actually happens."

Prior to our upcoming 2001 Reason Weekend, Lynn told me that after our November board meeting, she had talked with Harry and a few other board members about the possibility of a high-level job offer from the new administration, and they'd told her they wouldn't want to stand in her way. In a way, that ticked me off, since Harry and another board member had pushed me to make the transition to Lynn as CEO on a faster schedule than I'd proposed—but they were clearly depending on me to be there in case that didn't work out.

At Reason Weekend in Miami Beach later in March, we said nothing to donors and other attendees, since there was no actual job offer. But at the board meeting that took place during this event, Lynn disclosed the situation to the full board. When we went into executive session, with Lynn absent, I made clear to them that while I'd be willing to step in as interim CEO, I would not go back to the status quo ante, so we'd need to do a search. There was some talk of preparing a counteroffer, but after Harry talked privately with Lynn, he came away convinced that if the position turned out to be as high-powered as she expected, she would take it regardless of any counteroffer from us. So, we decided to create a search committee, to begin work if needed.

And that work soon did become necessary. The first week of April, Lynn got the offer by phone, and accepted. So the next day, we held another all-hands staff meeting to tell everyone and started working on an announcement to donors, to be sent out right after the White House announcement. Lynn was willing to remain full-time CEO through the confirmation process (estimated as six to eight weeks), which took some of the immediate pressure off me. But still, the need for me to step back in hit me pretty hard. I decided not to terminate the contract with Ketchum, figuring that the news of Lynn's appointment to a high-ranking government position based on her decades of Reason Foundation work would be an additional selling point. I spent a day and a half in early April working with our consultant on developing the "infrastructure" for the campaign—materials (not including printing) and prospect lists—so we'd be ready to roll once the new CEO was on board, whenever that would be.

While the board search committee was getting up to speed, I had some discussions with Adrian. As of mid-April, we'd identified very few potential candidates from the free-market think-tank community, so if the choice ended up being to hire a non-movement person or to promote someone from within, I leaned very much toward the latter approach—and Adrian had been thinking along the same lines. Mentoring Adrian, trying to get him up-to-speed, seemed like a prudent just-in-case policy.

By mid-May, Lynn got word that the FBI had cleared her for the nomination (after interviewing many people, including me), so the next step was for the Senate committee to schedule the confirmation hearing, which would take more time. We estimated another four to six weeks of Lynn remaining CEO, which meant I wouldn't have to step back in as interim CEO until sometime in June, and that was a relief.

Meanwhile, the good news was that the Search Committee had come up with an excellent candidate. Board member Jim Lintott suggested David Nott, who at that time was the president of two free-market think tanks at George Mason University: the Institute for Humane Studies (where former *Reason* editor Marty Zupan worked) and the Mercatus Center. Jim and David had been roommates at Stanford University, and as an IHS board member, he'd been the one who had recommended David for the CEO position there. From everything we could determine, David had an outstanding track record at both organizations, growing them in staff, programs, and funding—and he was also an engineer!

Other than Jim, none of us had ever met David. But completely separate from our Search Committee efforts, late in the spring Marty had emailed me to ask if Lou and I could host a reception at our home for IHS, as part of a series of donor events they were holding around the country to celebrate the organization's fortieth year. We agreed, and that event took place on June 9. Lou and I also had dinner with Marty and David, a chance for informal conversation that carefully avoided any talk of a change of employment for David (since Marty was unaware of that possibility). With David being in town for several days—and having already been sounded out about the job opening by Jim—it was a great opportunity for him to visit the office, meet senior staff, and ask numerous questions about our history, programs, funding, future plans, etc. He was definitely interested, and on his way back east arranged to fly via Tampa so he could spend the better part of the day with board chairman Harry.

Lynn's confirmation hearing took place on June 20, but because the GOP had just lost control of the Senate (due to one senator switching parties), the actual vote on her nomination was postponed. Since confirmation looked like a sure thing, based on the results of the hearing, we went ahead with negotiations for David to become Reason Foundation's CEO. It took some time to get to yes, in part because management compensation at Reason was still below that of think tanks of comparable size. But David was the far superior choice, and the board closed the deal on July 19. By coincidence, that turned out to be Lynn's last day as president, because the Senate committee had approved her nomination a few days before, and Gale Norton needed her in place as soon as possible. David agreed to begin work in Los Angeles the first week of September. So that meant I had only six weeks to serve as interim CEO until David arrived and took over—a huge relief.

Those six weeks were not a happy time for me. Though I'd been getting monthly financial reports (as a board member), what I saw was a serious revenue shortfall building up as we moved into the fourth quarter of our fiscal year (July–September). I had worked with Lynn in preparing the FY 2001 budget, and like previous budgets it was based on continuing to grow the organization, which meant that both revenues and expenditures were projected to increase, with little margin for error. Well, the spending had, indeed, increased basically as planned, with several additional staff members and a large *Reason* direct-mailing effort. But revenue was not keeping up. Several recently acquired donors were not renewing, and as of early August, our CFO gave me a projection that showed a $750K loss by the end of the fiscal year. This was a disaster.

I had mid-August meetings with Adrian and Nick, respectively the VPs for RPPI and the magazine division. Clearly the planned $168K September subscription mailing could not go forward, and we needed to look seriously at staff reductions. Around Labor Day, several large contributions that we were not certain would materialize came through, so things didn't look quite as dire. But I dreaded presenting David with the extent of the financial hole we were in. By the end of September, our figures showed a loss for the fiscal year of $388K—an enormous number. This would be David's baptism by fire.

David's number-one challenge was to produce a credible budget to present to the board at his first board meeting in November 2001. And this clearly required staff and program cuts, for which David gave Adrian and Nick their marching orders. David's medium-term priority, of course, would be to change the way we managed, making annual growth secondary to building up financial reserves so that we could get through ups and downs in the economy, and in grants and contributions without having to make drastic cuts.

David's second week on the job was interrupted by 9/11. I was working at home that day, because I had to attend a half-day conference in the San Fernando Valley not too far from our house in Sherman Oaks. Lou was on her way to jury duty in downtown LA when she heard the first news on the radio, and learned that the courthouse would be closed. She immediately pulled over and called me. In response to her call, I went online and actually got real-time updates from a New York City member of the online aviation discussion group (Mifnet) that I had recently joined. In my journal later that week, I wrote, "This was the week the world changed. . . . It still seems almost unbelievable, probably 5,000 people killed altogether. All airline service stopped, the markets closed. I still have a hard time not breaking out in tears when I read or see too much about it."

I also thought about the implications for Reason Foundation. "What was nearly a recession will surely become one now. . . . Reason's already difficult budget for '02 will have to get a lot tighter. In aviation, my ATC donors may not be able to contribute anything next year, or the investment bankers. Aviation looks like it's going to be devastated. So our policy goals re ATC corporatization and airport pricing will be far less of a priority than their sheer survival. It's going to be horrible. And so is flying likely to be, with all the new rules and regulations."

But after the shock wore off, we all buckled down and got back to work. On the last working day of September, several promised contributions had not actually come in the door, but were likely the next week and would be counted if the checks were dated in September. More important, David decided we would go ahead with the previously scheduled reception honoring Lynn Scarlett in New York City. David and Julia Koch had offered to host the event at their new place (formerly owned by Jackie Onassis) overlooking Central Park. Lou and I flew to New York on Sunday, October 1, experiencing the new airport security, which began even in the long-term, economy parking lot at LAX and continued with numerous armed officers in the terminals.

The reception went very well. Despite much of the city still being in a state of shock, we had a good turnout at the Kochs' place. In addition to many loyal New York donors, a number of media stars attended, including our friend John Stossel and others from *Forbes* and the *Wall Street Journal*. David introduced Lynn, and she gave a firsthand account of how her priority starting September 11 had become protecting numerous federal properties and national monuments that were part of the Department of the Interior. After the reception, David and Julia took Lou,

Lynn, and me to a nearby restaurant for a late supper. We talked for several hours, but my only lasting memory is that CBS newscaster Walter Cronkite was seated at a nearby table.

During October and into early November, David continued to struggle with getting the FY 2002 budget to balance. In my journal I noted that he was "having difficulty getting Adrian and Nick to accept the reality of how much change is needed to get out of the financial hole we're in. He comes and talks with me just about every day, as we get prepared for the [November] board meeting." I noted around the end of the year that three people were being laid off in January, and I expected several more would be leaving in 2002.

RPPI in 2001

While all of the above was going on, Reason Foundation continued to function in high gear. RPPI made considerable progress on high-profile issues, in most of our focus areas.

Transportation
Air Traffic Control Reform

My top priority was to build on the progress I'd been making with airlines and the incoming Bush administration, aiming to build airline and administration support for emulating Canada's successful transition of ATC from Transport Canada to a newly created nonprofit corporation, Nav Canada, in 1996. Based on meetings and discussions I'd had with senior people at American, Continental, Delta, FedEx, and Southwest Airlines, Viggo Butler and I had spent nearly two years on a new policy paper, "How to Commercialize Air Traffic Control." It drew on what was, by this time, the experience of a dozen or so countries on how to structure and govern an ATC corporation, what the user fee structure should consist of, how private planes ("general aviation") should be handled, and employee transition issues. We built a quantitative model of the pricing system, and showed how it would affect each of the major carriers, as well as private plane operators.

To build support prior to the study's release in February 2001,

I'd gotten a meeting with Mitch Daniels, now the new OMB director, who seemed quite positive about the idea. I'd also been busy using a network of aviation contacts to recruit nine former FAA officials (including three former Administrators) who were all willing to sign a statement in favor of ATC corporatization. One of these was Langhorne Bond, the FAA Administrator during the Carter administration, to whom I was introduced by his cousin, Jim Haynes, a fan of my aviation work. Langhorne and I hit it off, and he agreed fully with what was laid out in our policy study. I also recruited former CAB chairman Alfred Kahn, the father of airline deregulation, and my friends former DOT Secretary Jim Burnley and former Clinton White House analyst Dorothy Robyn.

Our news conference at the National Press Building in February featured Bond, Burnley, Kahn, Robyn, and me as speakers, and our press package included the statement from the nine former FAA officials. The study generated considerable media coverage, including the *New York Times* and the *Wall Street Journal* and dozens of other papers, as well as the aviation trade press. Both Americans for Tax Reform and the National Taxpayers' Union endorsed the proposal, as did the World Travel and Tourism Council. Langhorne and I also gave an in-person briefing to Rep. John Mica (R-FL), chairman of the House Aviation Subcommittee. He liked the idea, and told us he'd go to bat for it if the White House supported it.

But there was a fly in the ointment. Word had gotten around that some of the major airlines had contributed money to Reason Foundation in support of this study, and that caused a big problem for Carol Hallett, CEO of their trade association, the Air Transport Association. During the 1990s there had been a battle between the "legacy" airlines and "upstart" Southwest over a possible shift from ticket taxes to ATC fees. But ATA could not take sides, due to its policy that the organization would only support policies agreed upon by them all. Since not all ATA members were on board, on March 1, Hallett issued a statement on behalf of ATA saying that the major airlines do not endorse "privatization" and reject the RPPI study.

I could not let that stand, and figured that the best hope for changing the situation was to reach out to ATA board member Fred Smith, founder and CEO of FedEx. In those days, Smith was a member of the board of Cato Institute, so I met with Ed Crane (with whom by that point in time I was on pretty good terms), and Ed arranged a telephone meeting for me with Fred Smith. I explained the extensive inputs his policy and tax people had made to the study and the support from four other ATA member airlines. He told me he'd resolve the problem. And he did.

Shortly thereafter, I received a friendly phone call from Carol Hallett inviting me to make a presentation on the study to the ATA board (all the CEOs) at their June meeting. I thanked her, and got to work on what I considered the most important PowerPoint I'd ever prepared. The resulting session, on June 7, went well. I gave a very focused briefing, which led to some serious discussion. The next day I called my contacts at American and Continental and learned that the CEOs' reaction was largely positive, but that FedEx and Southwest had some points they wanted to work on over the summer and bring back to the next board meeting, in September. In my journal I wrote that the meeting was one of the best days of my whole career, and that our nonprofit/stakeholder board model (like Nav Canada) was becoming the default position of ATA.

Alas, that follow-up board meeting was scheduled for a few days after September 11, and when it was held, the airlines' focus was entirely devoted to aviation security and survival. ATC reform was nowhere in sight.

Florida HOT Lanes

My other main 2001 transportation project concerned HOT lanes. That spring I got a call from the south Florida district office of Florida DOT. They explained that one of their consultants, Craig Miller, had told them of my role in helping bring about the country's first express toll lanes project (the 91 Express Lanes in Orange County) and that I might be able to do a preliminary feasibility study for them on converting the HOV lanes on I-95 in Miami into HOT lanes. Would I be interested? I was, but since RPPI did not do paid government consulting, I would have to do the project as an individual, using vacation days.

With a tentative agreement in hand, they flew me to Miami for an orientation meeting, and we finalized a small consulting contract. They provided me with work done by Miller on the idea, and my task was to provide an objective assessment of present and future traffic congestion and to estimate how much difference HOT lanes would make. During that year I took vacation days here and there to do the analysis, finishing a first draft by the end of the year. In 2002, after their review and my revisions, they paid for several trips to Miami so I could give presentations of the results, which led to me meeting a number of other FDOT people (adding to the contacts I'd made when I did the briefing in Tallahassee in 2000). Since by this time Lou and I were actively looking at where, specifically, we'd move to in South Florida, on some of these trips I was able to add a day of personal time to look at properties.

There were a number of further chapters to this FDOT HOT lanes story, which I will relate in Chapter 12.

Airport Security
The 9/11 catastrophe focused national attention on airport security, and this created a new responsibility for me. As one of the few think-tank analysts who knew much about airports, and with my friend and colleague Viggo Butler whose company had managed airports, we had knowledge that we hoped could promote rational thinking about what to do. In the week following 9/11, Viggo and I wrote a policy brief that we circulated in Washington, DC, arguing that a massive federal takeover of airport screening was ill-advised, because the 9/11 failure was not in using contractors but in (1) having no training requirements or performance standards—an FAA failure documented by the GAO, among others, and (2) forcing airlines to pay for screening as an unfunded mandate, which they naturally sought to do at lowest cost. We pointed out that most large European airports used private security firms, but hired by the *airport* and governed by national

aviation security standards. My first op-ed along these lines appeared in *USA Today* on September 28.

When I was in DC for several days in mid-October, as Congress was debating "federalization" of airport security, I met with two senior people at Heritage Foundation (at their request) who told me that my work on this was right on target, and they wanted to bring me back to DC to work the issue with key members of Congress. That trip occurred at the end of October. I did three intensive days of meetings and briefings—with White House staff and GOP congressional staff, and did two live appearances on Fox News Channel and a bunch of print media interviews. The culmination was a news conference on the Capitol steps with House Transportation Committee Chair Don Young (R-AK) and Aviation Subcommittee Chair John Mica (R-FL). The House ended up rejecting the Senate idea of a total federal takeover, passing instead a bill that called for tough federal standards and shifting the provision of screening to airports rather than airlines (which could contract with private security or hire their own screeners, either approach subject to the new federal standards).

Unfortunately, when the two bills got to the conference committee, the White House admitted that the president would sign a final bill that resembled that of the Senate, which greatly diminished the House's bargaining power in the conference committee negotiations. So the resulting bill created the TSA as the primary provider of screening, but permitted a modest opt-out pilot program for five airports. What a disappointment, especially given the many resulting failures of the TSA.

But that experience proved to be only the beginning for me of more than a decade's work on improving airport security.

Privatization Center

Among the many projects carried out by Adrian, Geoff Segal, and others at the Privatization Center during this tumultuous year, three stand out: the President's Management Agenda, Competitive Cities, and San Fernando Valley Secession.

President's Management Agenda

Early in 2001, Adrian met with OMB Director Mitch Daniels and discussed the potential of using more aggressively a long-standing OMB policy (A-76) that called for competitive contracting for all federal services that were not "inherently governmental." Daniels agreed there was a great deal more potential than previous administrations had made use of. With his blessing, a team of former Privatization Center director Bill Eggers (by then at Deloitte's DC office), RPPI Director of Government Redesign Carl DeMaio, and Adrian developed what became known as the President's Management Agenda. The aim was to develop a factual basis across the federal government for assessing which programs and structures were not delivering good value and should be opened to competition. As Adrian wrote in *Reason Report* Issue 94, "The five areas and goals of the President's Management Agenda are really aimed at creating the institutional change that creates a bottom line and a competitive system. Performance is the common thread."

Competitive Cities

In this innovative project, Adrian along with Geoff Segal and Prof. James Nolan (University of Saskatchewan) sought to compare the public-service performance of America's fifty largest cities. Data limitations led to the study being limited to forty-four cities and analyzing eleven (out of eighteen possible) public services, using a technique called Data Envelopment Analysis. The top five cities, in order, were Phoenix, El Paso, Tulsa, Memphis, and Nashville, with the bottom five being Detroit, San Jose, Seattle, Oakland, and Los Angeles. The study got considerable attention, especially in higher-scoring cities.

A follow-up study applied the same methodology to the ten largest cities within California, reviewing ten public services. San Diego came out on top, followed by Fresno and Long Beach, with Anaheim, Oakland, and San Francisco bringing up the rear. The study also identified the most-efficient and least-efficient city in each of the ten public services.

These two reports were precursors to the Annual Highway Reports we began doing later, which rank the highway systems and state DOT performance of all fifty states.

San Fernando Valley Secession

The most suburban part of the City of Los Angeles is the San Fernando Valley, which includes Van Nuys, Sherman Oaks, Encino, Tarzana, Woodland Hills, and other thriving suburbs. The Valley is separated from the rest of the city by the Santa Monica Mountains. For many years civic and business organizations had complained about the Valley being treated as a kind of stepchild in the allocation of resources by the Los Angeles City Council. One of the movers and shakers in the Valley was attorney David Fleming, whom I'd met when Mayor Riordan had appointed him to the Fire Commission. By 2001, when he joined the Reason Foundation board, David had also been a member of the California Transportation Commission and was currently co-chair of the Economic Alliance of the San Fernando Valley.

As a serious move for the Valley to secede from Los Angeles gained business and political support in 2000, David and I brainstormed what kind of leaner and more cost-effective government might be possible to create, should secession succeed. My colleagues and I introduced David to the work of people like Prof. Ronald Oakerson (Houghton College), who'd done notable decentralization research for the Advisory Commission on Intergovernmental Relations and Prof. Robert Nelson (University of Maryland), whose book manuscript on governance by neighborhood associations I was in the process of peer reviewing. We also discussed the highly decentralized borough system of London as a possible model.

The end result was a one-day Symposium on Rightsizing Local and Regional Government, sponsored by the Economic Alliance of the San Fernando Valley on February 5, 2001. Speakers included Lynn Scarlett, Sam Staley, Joel Kotkin, James Nolan, and me from RPPI; Sam Olivito, executive director of the California Contract Cities Association; the previously mentioned Profs. Oakerson and Nelson plus several other academics; and Jeremy Smith, former chief executive of the London Borough of Camden. There was extensive discussion of research findings, including that *very few* municipal services have significant economies of scale (i.e., lower unit costs with larger units of government). An expert from Florida recounted a wave of incorporations of suburbs of Miami, which gained control of their public services and were able to competitively contract some of them.

It was a heady experience, and there were follow-up events later that year to formulate plans for a kind of local/regional London borough-type governance model, should the San Fernando Valley actually be able to secede. (In fact, on the morning of the 9/11 attack, I was working at home in Sherman Oaks due to needing to attend such a meeting later that morning.) The political committee that was formed, Valley VOTE, did get a measure on the city-wide ballot in November 2002, but under the rules in effect, it needed a majority vote in both the area proposing to secede and the city overall. The measure achieved 50.7 percent in the Valley, but only 33 percent overall. Had it succeeded, the Valley would have formed America's sixth largest city. David Fleming and my RPPI colleagues and I were all very disappointed in the result.

Electricity Deregulation
One of the hot issues in many states in 2000–2001 was deregulation or restructuring of electricity markets. In many states, this was a fairly straightforward process, in which generating electric power was separated from transmission and distribution, with the idea that competition among generating companies would lead to lower prices (and increased investment, as indicated by market forces). In California, however, the government attempt to restructure the electricity market was misconceived and convoluted (but misnamed "deregulation"), so RPPI took on the challenge of explaining the difference to policymakers.

We had published seven studies dealing with federal power authorities, municipal utilities, and related topics in the 1990s, but deregulation was a new subject. Fortunately, just as the California crisis began, at the end of 2000, Adrian had hired economist Lynne Kiesling, and in her first few weeks on the job that January, she and Adrian pulled together a fifty-six-page study, "Powering Up California," summarizing what successful deregulation looked like in other states and critiquing California's centralized approach. That positioned RPPI at the forefront of the California debate, and Lynne wrote or co-authored four more studies in 2002 and 2003. She and Adrian testified, did interviews, and took part in conferences around the country. Her position, unfortunately, fell victim to 2003 budget cuts, and she moved back to Chicago and taught at Northwestern University, later moving on to become the associate director of the Purdue University Research Center in Economics.

Education Studies

Education program director Lisa Snell really came into her own after previous program director Rich Seder was hired away in 2000. Her 2001 policy studies included a case for vouchers in the federal Title 1 program for low-income students, a case study on Florida's workplace charter schools, an assessment of performance-based private schools, and another on school vouchers as legal sanctions.

RPPI had established a solid working relationship with the relatively new organization, the Association of Education Practitioners and Providers—the first national organization for private-practice teachers and private-education contractors. In the summer of 2001, RPPI and the University of Southern California cosponsored what was AEPP's largest conference to date, EDVentures 2001. It drew over four hundred participants. Speakers included Michael Milken discussing the Milken Family Foundation's National Educator Awards; Chris Whittle of Edison Schools, Inc.; Jack Clegg of Nobel Learning Communities; and Jeanne Allen of the Center for Education Reform. Lisa gave a presentation on workplace charter schools and moderated a panel on how the private sector is serving special-ed and remedial-ed students via contracts with public, private, and charter schools. Media coverage included CNN's *Moneyline*, and *Education Week*.

Urban Futures

Sam Staley had an excellent second year as head of the Urban Futures program. In addition to numerous op-eds and speaking appearances, he produced three policy studies, as follows:

- "Market-Oriented Approaches to Growth: Outsmarting Sprawl's Impacts"
- "Smart Growth and Housing Affordability: Evidence from Statewide Planning Laws"
- "Smart Growth in Action: Housing Capacity and Development in Ventura County, California."

In addition, Greenwood Press released the book *Smarter Growth: Market-Based Strategies for Land-Use Planning in the 21st Century*, edited by Sam and Randy Holcombe of Florida State University. The contents were based on a conference the two had organized at FSU in 2000 at which I spoke on urban transportation policy, getting me a chapter in the book.

Environmental Policy

After Lynn Scarlett's departure, the Environmental Policy program continued during 2001 under Ken Green's leadership. He commissioned several studies by outside authors, including one on storm-water utilities by Barrett Walker and another on environmental risk assessment and children by Gail Charnley. With co-author Steven Schroeder he researched and wrote "Reducing Global Warming through Forestry and Agriculture," and a spinoff paper, "Q&A About Forests and Global Climate Change." Also under the environment program was a Carl DeMaio study, "Managing for Results at the US Environmental Protection Agency."

Based on his 1999 RPPI paper, "Seeking Safety in a Dangerous World: A Risk-Reduction Framework for Policymakers," Ken was invited to Washington by the Office of Personnel Management to give three hour-long seminars for federal managers from the Environmental Protection Agency, the National Science

Foundation, the Defense Department, the Transportation Department, and the General Services Administration. OPM sponsor David Ost wrote Ken afterwards that the seminars were a "rousing success," scoring 4.9 on a 5.0 scale.

Reason Magazine Comes of Age

By 2001, Virginia and her husband, Steve, had moved to Houston so Steve could take a teaching position at Southern Methodist University. Out of Virginia's shadow, Nick blossomed as *Reason's* editor, making the content more edgy (with more cultural commentary) and continuing the soaring growth of *Reason Online*. The growth stemmed in part from Nick and Publisher Mike Alissi uploading new content every day, so that people were eager to find out what was new, and they also caught the early wave of young people turning to the Internet for news and information. Given the six- to eight-week time lag of a print magazine, the website was a natural for quick responses to current events and engaging in debates over breaking news and controversies. *Reason Online* page views grew from about 420,000 in January 2001 to over 1.5 million by December.

A big coup occurred that June, when *ABC News* aired a John Stossel special called "Tampering with Nature." Stossel's producers had drawn on work by *Reason* Science Correspondent Ron Bailey and RPPI Environment Program Director Ken Green in researching the program, and that of President Lynn Scarlett on several major environmental issues. For on-camera commentary, Stossel extracted from two hours of interviews with Virginia, drawing on some of the themes in her book, *The Future and Its Enemies* (whose cover was shown several times during the special, leading to a surge in sales on Amazon). Virginia countered the views of several prominent figures who attacked genetic engineering and other uses of technology to improve human life and alleviate suffering.

Continuing this theme later in the year was a three-day *Reason*-sponsored conference in New York City, organized by the Institute of Ideas (UK) and held at the New School on October 26–28. "Science, Knowledge, and Humanity: Debating the Future of Progress," featured Virginia, Nick, and Ron Bailey from *Reason*, along with speakers that included Jean Bethke Elshtain (University of Chicago), our friend biochemist Bruce Ames (UC Berkeley), and political theorist Francis Fukuyama. As *Reason Report* noted, the proceedings were often heated, as participants and audience members disagreed sharply. Nick Gillespie concluded, "We got to talk and argue with some of the sharpest minds at work today on a host of issues that are vitally important: the environment, genetic engineering, and the very concept of progress."

On the occasion of the twentieth anniversary of MTV (August 1), NPR had Nick broadcast a four-paragraph appreciation of the music channel that included the following:

> In the years since "Video Killed the Radio Star," America's become a much looser place. We're less uptight with difference, and we're more interested in customized experiences, whether we're talking about 50 flavors of coffee, built-to-order computers, or highly individualized ways of dress, sexuality, and identity. That trend might bother some, but for most of us it's been both liberating and exciting. To the extent that MTV has contributed to it, may its next 20 years be as rich as its first two decades.

Also noteworthy in 2001 was the publication of Associate Editor Jesse Walker's book, *Rebels on the Air: An Alternative History of Radio in America*, by New York University Press. It followed the 1998 publication of Jacob Sullum's first book, and foreshadowed a future stream of books by various *Reason* editors.

Finally, Nick organized and managed an extensive redesign of the print magazine (as we'd begun to call it), which made its debut with the December issue. The new look was one of Nick's objectives as editor, and it was boosted significantly by the volunteer efforts of *Wired* founder Louis Rossetto, a long-time (since 1968 and Lanny Friedlander) *Reason* reader. Rossetto introduced Nick to designers Erik Spiekermann (who had just finished a redesign for *The Economist*) and Susanna Dulkinys (*Wired* books). This led to a ten-month collaboration. The new design drew considerable media attention—including reviews in the *Columbus Dispatch*, the *San Francisco Chronicle*, and the *Village Voice*, as well as an admiring feature article by Cynthia Greiner in the *Washington Times*. Weighing in a bit later was magazine trade publication *Folio*.

A Sad Note

On April 8, 2001, our founding board member, Clyde Packer, died at Cottage Hospital in Santa Barbara after several years of declining health. Despite his unexpectedly early departure from our board, as noted in Chapter 6, he observed our growth and progress from a distance, I'm sure with at least some degree of pride in having given us our start. I visited him occasionally, and once in a while he sent a modest contribution. But, sad to say, he never attended a Reason Foundation event.

Chapter 11

Reason Foundation 2.0 (2002–2017)

Building a Firmer Foundation
Addressing the Financial Situation

David Nott faced a huge challenge in taking over Reason Foundation. The financial result for FY 2001, which ended September 30, 2001, was a loss of $388K. Not only that, but for its entire history Reason Foundation had had a negative net worth—liabilities exceeding assets. That was because our only assets were whatever cash we might have on hand in any given month, while our liabilities included obligations to fulfill subscriptions (many of them multi-year) for some fifty thousand *Reason* magazine subscribers. So his challenge was not simply to get operations back into the black; it was also to build financial reserves that could see us through a serious recession or the sudden loss of a major donor.

In the near term (2002–03), this required spending reductions as well as efforts to increase revenues. In 2001, Reason Foundation had forty-two full-time employees and two part-time adjunct scholars. RPPI had its own editor (a recent addition), and we had both an IT manager and two webmasters, one for the Foundation/RPPI and the other for the magazine division. Those were all nice positions to have, but several had to be eliminated in 2002. David was very transparent with all staff about the difficult situation we were in, and this probably led to both Ken Green and Sam Staley accepting job offers from other think tanks that year. Their departure added to cost savings, but made it difficult to continue the Environmental Policy and Urban Futures programs without a senior person leading each one. Accepting that reality, David decided to focus near-term on our core strengths: *Reason* magazine and *Reason Online*, the Privatization Center, Transportation, and Education Studies.

Other program areas could be rebuilt once the organization was in better financial shape.

Another early decision by David was to terminate the contract with Ketchum for the planned long-term funding campaign. Given the difficult financial situation and the uncertain post-9/11 giving climate, the timing seemed all wrong for such a campaign. Whether and when to engage in a major effort of this kind was deferred to some point in the future when our finances would hopefully be more solid and we had more successes to tout.

David also made a decision that not everyone was happy with at first, but which proved successful over time: abolishing the RPPI brand in favor of everything being simply Reason. One factor in this decision was that we were showing up rather poorly in studies of think-tank media coverage. With three websites—Reason Foundation, RPPI, and *Reason* magazine—media results for each showed up separately, and were hardly ever combined. So when people reviewed surveys that showed national think tanks' media coverage, AEI, Cato, and Heritage had far higher totals than any one of our *individual* brands. I could see the logic of fixing that problem, but was still somewhat worried about testifying on a complicated transportation policy subject and getting hit with extraneous questions about a *Reason* article on, say, drug legalization. Fortunately, situations like that never occurred, and the single-brand decision worked out well for us.

Fiscal year 2002 was still very difficult. David succeeded in reducing expenses from $5.24 million to $4.76 million. But in the post-9/11 climate, revenue also decreased slightly, from $4.86 million to $4.62 million, so FY 2002 ended up in another loss. The turn-around year was 2003. David managed to reduce spending again, to $4.37 million, while revenue grew to $5.7 million, thanks in part to a major grant from Jacobs Engineering founder and retired CEO Joe Jacobs. This was by far the largest individual contribution in Reason's history, and I was the one who landed it. With that gift secured, I didn't feel as guilty for having turned over Reason to David in such difficult financial straits. And Lou and I could plan our move to Florida in good conscience. (We sold our house in late 2001 and lived in a West LA apartment for fifteen months, prior to heading east in April 2003.)

From 2003 through 2016, Reason Foundation fiscal years ended solidly in the black, except for 2008 (financial markets collapse). That also meant 2002 was the last year we ended with a negative net worth. During the past decade, when I received quarterly financial statements as a board member, I would regularly be blown away by the transformed balance sheet. The audited statements for FY 2016 showed a year-end net worth of $8.21 million, equal to more than three-fourths of that year's $10.72 million operating budget. Lou, who had provided accounting assistance during the 1980s and early 1990s, including working with the auditors, was equally bowled over by these financial statements.

One of the most tangible measures of the success of Reason Foundation 2.0 was the purchase of a headquarters building in Los Angeles in 2013. The campaign to raise funds for the purchase partially fulfilled my long-ago plan for a capital campaign and was enthusiastically supported by our board members. The building we bought is a two-story structure in an up-and-coming part of West Los Angeles on what used to be Hughes Aircraft property. The area is also home to offices of Facebook, Electronic Arts, South Park, and YouTube. The high-bay first floor provides a video studio and event space, with administrative offices on the second floor.

A gala ribbon-cutting party took place in December 2013, with board member (and very long-time donor) Carol Sanders christening the building with the traditional bottle of champagne. The event included noted LA food trucks in the parking area. In addition to numerous donors and friends attending, the event was graced by Judge Alex Kozinski and Reason Foundation co-founders Manny Klausner and Tibor Machan. I'd had a tour of the building a month or so before the event, but schedule conflicts prevented me from attending.

The building includes a large, lighted Reason logo just below the roofline, and for me that was a dream come true. When we'd moved into the previous offices on the fourth floor of the office building on Sepulveda Blvd. in 1991, right next to the 405 freeway, I'd fantasized about someday being housed in a building that was visible from the freeway but had a big sign saying Reason. It turns out that the new building is only a few blocks west of that freeway, and the lighted sign is visible as you drive southbound on the 405 at night. Lou and I did that the next year on a visit to Los Angeles. It was a wonderful moment; Lou cried.

The best news about the new building is that by summer 2016—less than three years after we moved in—the mortgage was paid off. In *Reason Report* Issue 148 we included a photo of CFO Jon Graff torching the mortgage document in the parking lot, as staffers looked on.

A Stronger Board

Another key to greater success was building a larger and stronger board. We took advantage of having an initial one-year "trial" membership to invite promising people whom we hadn't known for a decade or more but who seemed both ideologically compatible and ready to give or get at least the $25K annual minimum (except for academics). One target of opportunity was Silicon Valley, from which I'd recruited IP attorney Sarah O'Dowd, and we subsequently recruited Logitech founder Pierluigi Zappacosta. We also sought out somewhat younger entrepreneurs and investors, over the years signing up investor Stephen "Moz" Modzelewski, real estate attorney Baron Bond (son of former board member Frank Bond), and entrepreneur Kerry Welsh.

Harry Teasley stepped down as chairman at the end of 2002 and long-time board member Bill Dunn took over. Bill was a lower-key chairman than Harry, but by this point everything that Harry had taught us about management and strategic planning had been well learned. Bill served through 2011 and was succeeded by investment manager Tom Beach. Tom agreed to serve six years, and was, in turn, succeeded by Moz Modzelewski in 2017.

In addition to their personal financial support, board members introduced friends and colleagues to Reason's work. And equally important, many of them agreed to serve on board committees to oversee various aspects of the organization. Except for a Nominating Committee, we had not really had functioning board committees before David's tenure. By 2005, we had added a Finance Committee and a Development Committee, supplemented later by an Audit Committee.

New Events to Increase Donor Involvement

David continued our annual Reason Weekend events, held every spring in a different city (generally in warmer locations than the Northeast and Midwest). We established a reputation for a more interesting array of speakers than just the usual free-market economists and policy wonks. Because these events introduced some new people to Reason each year, and developed stronger bonds with existing donors, David was keen to try additional special events to do likewise.

The first of these was 2005's "Reason After Dark" in Las Vegas, headlined by our friend Drew Carey. The event served as the evening entertainment for the two days of our Dynamic Cities Conference, which featured adjunct fellow Joel Kotkin, Adrian Moore, and me, among others. "After Dark" speakers included Christopher Hitchens, who'd written a foreword to our new book, *Choice: The Best of Reason*, in addition to Drew. Other evening entertainment included Penn and Teller's magic show and the award-winning dance show *Fashionistas*.

Since "Reason After Dark" was a big hit, David followed up in 2006 with "Reason in Amsterdam." Headlining the event were "South Park" creators (and *Reason* fans) Trey Parker and Matt Stone, along with commentator Andrew Sullivan, discussing his newly released book, *The Conservative Soul*. The event included visits to the city's famed cafes and an evening cruise on Amsterdam's canals.

In 2007 we offered "Reason in DC." This event featured Fox News's Judge Andrew Napolitano, MTV's Kurt Loder, then Secretary of Labor Elaine Chao, DOT policy whiz Tyler Duval (with whom I'd been working closely), and several Reason people. Though mostly taking place at a hotel's conference facility, the event also included an evening program at Reason's brand-new Washington, DC, offices, within walking distance of the hotel.

Several times in the past we'd rented a one-person office for a Washington correspondent (in the days before it was easy for people to be full-time telecommuters working from home). But Trustee Emeritus Frank Bond the previous year had made a strong presentation to our board on the advantages of having a full-time office in the nation's capital, with ample room for people to work and the ability to hold events. With financial support from Frank and a number of other donors, we found a 3,900 sq. ft. space above a bank, a few blocks north of Dupont Circle. It had been custom decorated by the Hewlett Foundation, which wanted out of its long-term lease, enabling us to make a good deal on a very nice space. Drew Carey served as host for the Reason in DC open house, and the event was covered in the *Washington Post*'s Style section.

The next such event was in 2008—*Reason* magazine's fortieth anniversary—with "Reason in Hollywood." It took place at the historic Roosevelt Hotel, on the Hollywood Walk of Fame. Because we held a gala fortieth anniversary banquet one of those evenings, the banquet has blotted out most of my memories of the Reason Hollywood event. Lou remembers that board member David Fleming brought along a genuine Oscar, and people stood in line for photos with the little gold man. Together the event and the banquet were a terrific occasion. Drew Carey served as banquet emcee, and I gave a five-minute overview of the history of *Reason* magazine and Reason Foundation. Many luminaries attended, including both Nathaniel and Barbara Branden, my old friend and *Reason* advisor Mark Frazier, Ed and Alicia Clark, and of course Tibor and Manny, my original Reason Enterprises partners. One of the younger attendees was Rep. (now Sen.) Jeff Flake (R-AZ) who explained that he'd been reading *Reason* many years before being elected to Congress.

For several years after that, we tried Reason Seminar Cruises. The first was a Caribbean cruise in February 2011, with onboard speakers that included UK science guru Matt Ridley and Seasteading Institute founder Patri Friedman (grandson of Milton Friedman). At a stop in San Juan, cruise members were hosted at the Governor's Mansion by Gov. Luis Fortuno, who went on to privatize several state-owned enterprises, including the San Juan Airport. This was followed by a cruise to Alaska in August 2012, and another to the Caribbean in February 2014. The cruises attracted a less-affluent group, on average, than Reason Weekend and the other events, and barely broke even, so as of this writing they have not been resumed. With the relaxation of travel controls for Cuba in 2016, we offered "Reason in Cuba," featuring, among others, Sen. Jeff Flake.

Another new event was the Reason Media Awards in New York City. For more than a decade, a London-based organization—the International Policy Network—had held a contest for pro-liberty journalism. The Bastiat Prize for Journalism was named in honor of nineteenth-century French economist Frederic Bastiat, who was a highly effective communicator of free-market ideas to non-economists. In 2012, when we hired IPN's Julian Morris as vice president of research, the Bastiat Award moved with him to Reason. Our first Bastiat Prize dinner was held in New York in November 2012, with Judge Andrew Napolitano as emcee and economist Walter Williams as keynote speaker. The dinner was made possible by the Donald and Paula Smith Family Foundation.

We expanded the scope of the dinner in 2013, adding two additional awards, renaming it the Reason Media Awards and moving it to a larger venue (the New York Yacht Club). Winning the new Lanny Friedlander Prize was Louis Rossetto, founder of *Wired* magazine, who had co-authored an article on libertarianism (including *Reason*) in a *New York Times Magazine* cover story in 1969. Winning the new Reason Video Award was Drew Tidwell of CEI for his "I, Pencil" video. And the 2013 Bastiat Prize was shared by Lane Filler of *Newsday* and Ross Clark of *The Times*. Since then, the Reason Media Awards has become a glitzy annual event, drawing a capacity audience (more recently at the Edison Club), and supported each year by the Smith Family Foundation. The Friedlander Prize is not awarded every year, but was presented in 2016 to John Stossel on the eve of his retiring from Fox Business to join Reason Foundation.

Another relatively new event is the annual Savas Award for Public-Private Partnerships. It has been made possible (and named in honor of) privatization and PPP pioneer Steve Savas, author of widely read books on the subject. The first awardee, in 2015, was former governor Mitch Daniels. I was honored to introduce him at the awards dinner in New York, with Prof. Savas presenting the award. Daniels thanked Reason Foundation for ideas and assistance when he worked with Mayor Steve Goldsmith on public-services competitions in Indianapolis, when he served as director of the White House Office of Management and Budget, and during his two terms as governor of Indiana. The 2016 awardee was New York charter school champion Eva Moskowitz, and the 2017 winner was former Indianapolis mayor Steve Goldsmith.

Rebuilding the Public Policy Program

As noted earlier, in David's first several years, the policy research program focused on our most-visible and successful programs: the Privatization Center, Transportation, and Education Studies. As finances improved, other programs were added back to the agenda, including urban land-use and growth issues, a revamped environmental program, public-sector pension reform, and national economic policy (in the wake of the financial meltdown and Great Recession).

In the early 2000s, Reason Foundation's virtual staff spread across the country, allowing us to recruit people whose spouses had established careers or didn't want to live in Los Angeles or Washington. The management challenges of a virtual staff are outweighed by needing less space in LA and DC, and having people on-the-ground in a number of major metro areas. Reason was among the early adopters of telecommuting, dating back to Lynn Scarlett's time as research director.

Privatization Center

In 2002, the center's highest-profile project was the President's Management Agenda. It was announced by the White House Office of Management and Budget in August 2001, with the aim of making far wider use of the long-standing OMB policy A-76, calling for competitive contracting for all federal services that are not "inherently governmental." Vice President of Policy Adrian Moore and Senior Fellow Carl DeMaio worked closely (pro-bono) with Jack Kalavritinos, OMB's director of Competitive Sourcing and Privatization after our participation had been blessed by OMB Director Mitch Daniels.

Working with OMB analysts, Adrian and Carl came up with an estimated 850,000 federal positions that qualified as not inherently governmental, and agencies were directed to engage in competitive sourcing. At a news conference at the National Press Club in autumn 2002, Kalavritinos told reporters that "Reason Foundation is truly one of the leading voices out there on privatization . . . . They have done a great job of educating the public and helping agencies to integrate the president's initiatives."

By early 2003, the program had made significant progress. The process for agency competitions was reformed, based in part on Reason recommendations, to take one year rather than three. An evaluation of the performance of 20 percent of federal programs found that more than half could not show results, and 5 percent were deemed "ineffective." DeMaio helped OMB focus on out-of-control information technology spending, leading to reforms in that area, as well. Unfortunately, bureaucracies tend to passively resist reform, and after Mitch Daniels departed OMB in June 2003, the focus on increased competitive sourcing became far less of a priority. But Reason's policy research profile in Washington, DC, was significantly increased by this project.

Raising our profile in California was also an early focus for the Privatization Center. An out-of-control state budget, with a projected 2004 deficit of $38 billion, led to a recall election of unpopular governor Gray Davis in October 2003. Knowing that whoever succeeded Davis would need big-time budget advice, Reason's Privatization Center and DeMaio's (separate) Performance Institute created the California Citizens' Budget, a 150-page plan to balance the budget without a tax increase. It included very specific recommendations, agency by agency, including abolishing six thousand vacant positions, competitive contracting across an array of agencies, implementing fixed-price performance-based contracts at Caltrans, and divesting unused real estate. The plan was praised by former state comptroller Kathleen Connell and former state treasurer Matt Fong in a *Wall Street Journal* op-ed (August 1, 2003). Adrian, Carl DeMaio, and Public Affairs Director George Passantino went on a statewide traveling road show to explain the plan and gain support.

When Arnold Schwarzenegger replaced Davis as governor that autumn, he named several of the co-authors of the study to his transition team. Soon thereafter, he announced a sweeping project called the California Performance Review (CPR), in effect building on the ideas in our Citizens' Budget report. Schwarzenegger appointed our George Passantino to be a full-time director of the effort, and we agreed to loan George to the project for a number of months. The project's 2,500-page report, released in August 2004 called for slashing bureaucracy, eliminating over one hundred state boards and commissions, and consolidating seventy-nine departments and eleven agencies into a dozen entities directly accountable to the governor. With 34 percent of the state workforce expected to retire within five years, the plan incorporated attrition and retirements as means of reducing the state workforce.

Alas, despite all the hard work that went into the CPR, Schwarzenegger faced strong resistance from state agencies and active opposition in the legislature, which had Democratic majorities in both houses. Despite hard work and good intentions, few of the CPR reforms were actually implemented. But the effort further increased Reason Foundation's profile in California. Some of the recommendations were included in a set of ballot measures the governor's team crafted, but a well-funded media campaign against them by public employee unions resulted in all being voted down.

The Privatization Center continued its yeoman efforts assisting motivated mayors and governors with competitive contracting, privatization, and public-private partnerships. One of the most exciting efforts concerned the newly incorporated (in 2005) Atlanta suburb of Sandy Springs. As an unincorporated suburb, Sandy Springs had received all its public services from the Fulton County government, and residents increasingly chafed at the relatively high cost and mediocre quality, which led to its incorporation as new city. Interim City Manager Oliver Porter called on our Privatization Center for assistance in designing a plan by which all public services except police and fire would be obtained via contracts with the private sector. We dispatched Geoff Segal, the center's director, to help Porter, and they devised a plan that was approved by Sandy Springs' new city council. The city ended up with only seven full-time employees (apart from police and fire) overseeing various service contractors.

Once Sandy Springs' plan was on the way to implementation, Geoff made an invited presentation to a group of other mayors and council members in Fulton County, explaining the Sandy Springs case and advising them how to do likewise. Our friends at the Georgia Public Policy Foundation had been introducing these officials to Reason's "privatization curriculum" for several months. As a result, two more new cities, Johns Creek and Milton, incorporated based on the Sandy Springs model in 2006, and several others did likewise in subsequent years. National media coverage of Sandy Springs led to requests for assistance from other cities and would-be cities in Kentucky, Ohio, Texas, and elsewhere.

Geoff was also our point man for assistance to several innovative state governors. In Jeb Bush's second term, after having *Reason's* Virginia Postrel address his first-term cabinet on the ideas in her book, *The Future and Its Enemies*, Gov. Bush called on our Privatization Center for assistance with his recently created Center for Efficient Government. So we loaned him Geoff Segal for several months in 2004 to help the staff develop systematic procedures for reviewing all state functions for potential competitive sourcing opportunities. After this effort, Geoff told *Reason Report* that, "Florida's work to develop standards, templates, guidelines, and a transparent method of managing outsourcing is on the cutting edge." He subsequently advised Pennsylvania governor Ed Rendell, South Carolina governor Mark Sanford, and Virginia legislators on similar efforts. And when Gov. Bill Owens of Colorado in 2005 proposed exceeding the spending limits in that state's hard-won Taxpayer Bill of

Rights, Geoff drafted a report for the Denver free-market think tank Independence Institute called "Priority Colorado"—similar to the Citizens' Budget previously developed for California. Geoff and George Passantino went to Colorado for meetings and presentations on the proposal.

Alas for us, Geoff's visibility and track record led to him being recruited by infrastructure developer Macquarie in 2007. Senior analyst and urban policy expert Len Gilroy took over as director of Privatization and Government Reform and carried on working with mayors, governors, and legislators on pro-market policy reforms.

One of Len's early successes took place in Utah in 2008. Following discussions, meetings, and invited legislative testimony by Len, the legislature revamped an ineffective Privatization Policy Board, giving it new teeth, including a requirement that the state inventory all "commercial activities" that might be done more efficiently if opened to competition.

The next year, in Louisiana, Gov. Bobby Jindal issued an executive order creating a Commission on Streamlining Government, encouraging competitive service contracting and asset sales. The commission idea was developed after several months of meetings between Len and members of the governor's staff. "The new commission will force policymakers to do a serious review of what services are actually necessary and the most effective and efficient way of delivering them," Len told *Reason Report*. And within a year it had led to privatization of claims management in the Department of Administration and of highway maintenance at the Louisiana Department of Transportation, plus many other privatization initiatives during Jindal's two terms in office.

Len took the commission idea to Arizona where his work, with help from Arizona's Goldwater Institute, led Gov. Janice Brewer to create a Commission on Privatization and Efficiency in 2010. Brewer then appointed Len, by this time a resident of Arizona, as a member of the commission. Also in 2010, Len served as an advisor to New Jersey's new Privatization Task Force, whose report estimated over $210 million in ongoing annual savings if all of its recommendations were implemented. And by 2012, the state had privatized building code enforcement, toll collection, golf courses, horse racing facilities, and the state-run TV network.

Another highlight of the Privatization Center's work was publication of the Twentieth Anniversary Edition of the Annual Privatization Report. For this occasion, we asked former UK Prime Minister Margaret Thatcher for an essay on the global privatization revolution. The resulting cover essay led to a *Wall Street Journal* editorial, "Socialism in Reverse: The Success of Privatization, 30 Years On" (July 31, 2006). And in 2013, our venerable print newsletter, *Privatization Watch*, was replaced by Len's new e-newsletter, *Privatization and Government Reform Newsletter*.

Transportation

I discuss my own work on changing transportation policy post-2001 in Chapters 12 and 13. But one major transportation success story was very much a team effort: the Galvin Mobility Project. It was an effort to focus national attention on the scourge of traffic congestion and to propose large-scale remedies.

The idea came from Bob Galvin, former chairman and CEO of Motorola. In 2004, I received a letter from Bob, who had learned about my work in transportation. He asked if Reason would be interested in a large-scale, multi-year project to "end congestion" in America's metro areas. I followed up immediately, and when he learned that I live in South Florida, he suggested that we meet when he next visited the Motorola plant a few miles from my house. When that trip got delayed, I suggested that Vice President Adrian fly to Chicago to visit Bob and get a better idea what he had in mind. After several such meetings, the Galvin Mobility Project was defined enough for Bob to make a multi-year funding commitment. We would research and write two books on the subject, aimed at local elected officials, transportation planners, and state DOT people, to make the case that chronic congestion should no longer be tolerated—and was fixable. And we would do a half-dozen or more detailed case studies of specific metro areas, crafting and costing out plans based largely on networks of market-priced express toll lanes, coupled with region-wide express bus service.

Adrian and I recruited an advisory board of distinguished transportation thinkers and doers, and we had a half-day brainstorming session at Bob's suburban Chicago home. We agreed on a methodology for selecting the best set of candidate metro areas and discussed many aspects of our proposed solutions. At a follow-up meeting, I presented the methodology and the reasons for selecting six metro areas: five very large ones and one fast-growing medium-size one.

The first book produced by the project was *The Road More Traveled,* by Ted Balaker and Sam Staley (Rowman and Littlefield, 2006). (We'd brought back Sam from Ohio's Buckeye Institute thanks to the funding provided by the Galvin project; he had not enjoyed the stress of being CEO of a state policy think tank.) The book was designed to pave the way for the forthcoming metro area congestion-reduction plans; its subtitle was "Why the congestion crisis matters more than you think, and what we can do about it." The follow-up book was *Mobility First,* by Sam and Adrian (Rowman and Littlefield, 2009). It focused on explaining many of the "how to" ideas from the project, including express toll networks, elevated lanes, and tunnels. The book garnered endorsements from a number of transportation experts.

The six case studies were researched by one or more members of the team. I was the principal researcher and author for Atlanta (2006), Miami (2012), and co-author of the one for medium-size Lee County/Fort Myers, Florida (2009). Sam took the lead on Chicago (2012), and several people did the initial work on Denver (2015) and Los Angeles (2015), both of which were completed by Baruch Feigenbaum, a Georgia Tech graduate who had been the transportation aide to a Georgia member of Congress before we hired him. The greatest impacts so far have been in Atlanta and Miami, with large-scale express toll networks now underway, and with several initial corridors in operation. Both Georgia and Florida DOTs cooperated in the research and have embraced most of what we recommended. In Chicago, our study seems to have been the catalyst for the first two express toll lane projects, which are now in the developmental stage. Our study reinforced trends that had gotten underway in Denver, with Colorado DOT now explicitly talking in terms of a network of express lanes, rather than just individual projects. Take-up has been slower in Los Angeles, where anti-car politics is stronger than in the other metro areas. Still, the Southern California Association of Governments has endorsed a five-county express toll network in its long-range transportation plan, and projects are moving forward in four of the five counties.

Unfortunately, Bob Galvin did not live to see the completion of the project. He died, at age eighty-nine, in October 2011, with the project not yet completed. His heirs continued funding for another year, but their priorities were different from his, so that was it. We finished the remaining studies on our own dime.

Education Studies

Lisa Snell became a prominent voice for school choice during this time period.

A proposal on the June 2006 California ballot, backed by actor/director Rob Reiner, called for a $2.4 billion annual tax increase to pay for universal pre-school—a classic feel-good, for-the-children issue. Lisa and Darcy Olsen of the Goldwater Institute had researched the idea's implementation in Georgia and Oklahoma, finding that any preschool advantages fade away by third grade. In Lisa's follow-up study assessing the California ballot measure, she found that if the measure actually did enroll 70 percent of eligible pre-schoolers, it would cost taxpayers $109,000 per kid, per year. Early polls showed that 60 percent of voters were favorable to the proposal. Lisa and policy analyst Shikha Dalmia had interviews and/or op-eds in the *Washington Post, Wall Street Journal, USA Today, San Francisco Chronicle,* and others. They appeared on twenty-four TV and radio programs, and gave numerous presentations before interested groups. In the end, thirty-eight California newspapers editorialized against the measure, and voters rejected it 60 to 40 percent.

Another big victory occurred in Los Angeles in 2009. Lisa took part in the *Los Angeles Times'* Great Charter School Debate—citing evidence that students in LA's charter schools outperform their nearby counterparts in conventional public schools of the huge Los Angeles Unified School District—and spoke at a number of public events on the subject. On August 25, the LAUSD board voted six to one for a resolution that would allow 250 of its 800 campuses to be sites for future charter schools. On January 2, 2012, Lisa's op-ed, "There Are Simply Too Many Teachers," was published on the op-ed page of the *New York Times*.

Lisa helped organize the first National School Choice Week, January 23–29, 2011. It has since become an annual event, bringing together advocates and practitioners of charter schools, student-based budgeting, vouchers, and other choice concepts. In its seventh year, National School Choice Week 2017 was a huge success with more than twenty-one thousand events, 6.4 million attendees, twenty-seven state capitol buildings rallies, an official proclamation from the President of the United States, along with a resolution, passed unanimously, by the United States Senate, and worldwide trending for #SchoolChoice on Twitter.

Over the past several years, Lisa has worked diligently on a concept called student-based budgeting—essentially public-school vouchers—in which parents select which school they want their child to attend, and the money follows the child. She researched school districts (e.g., in Denver) where the idea had been implemented successfully, so when Louisiana governor Bobby Jindal asked for help, she served as an advisor on this idea for two years. In November 2010, she organized the first of three student-based budgeting symposia for the state board of education. She followed up by assisting the new Student-Based Budgeting Task Force in organizing a conference for two hundred education stakeholders. In March 2011, Jindal announced that a statewide pilot program would begin that fall. Lisa also advised Jindal on the enactment of a "parent trigger" law in 2012 that empowers families to change their children's schools into charters. Drawing on Reason's experience in California, the Louisiana law includes safeguards that ensure that the difficulties encountered in implementing California's parent trigger will be avoided.

Lisa has also worked to implement student-based budgeting in

Nevada, starting with an address to legislators at the Governor's Mansion and a 2007 pilot program. More recently, in September 2016, Clark County, the nation's fifth largest school district, announced that it would implement student-based budgeting beginning in 2017–18. She subsequently met with State Senator Becky Harris, chair of the reorganization committee, Assemblyman David Gardner, who carried the bill, and other Nevada representatives about helping with implementation.

In Arizona, in 2015, Gov. Ducey appointed Lisa to the new Classrooms First Initiative Council, which he created to craft sweeping education reforms. She has also been building the case for reform among a wide variety of stakeholder groups, including the Arizona Chamber of Commerce, Hispanic Chamber of Commerce, and the A for Arizona Coalition. The final report on school finance reform issued by the council in December 2016 included Lisa's recommendations on student-based budgeting. Legislation to that effect was introduced in the 2017 legislative session. The bill passed and was signed into law by Gov. Ducey in April 2017.

One of Lisa's most recent successes to date occurred in 2016, when President Obama signed the "Every Student Succeeds Act" (ESSA). The Reason policy study "Federal School Finance Reform" in 2014 noted many deficiencies in the federal Title 1 program for low-income students. It argued that the program would be more effective if the money could follow the child, based on the parents' choice of school. Sen. Lamar Alexander (R-TN) expressed interest, so Lisa advised him on inclusion of a pilot test of weighted student funding in the ESSA bill. It was included, and allowed fifty local school districts to implement this approach. ESSA also included a long-time Reason recommendation that requires school districts to report school-level spending, so parents and taxpayers can see how much each school gets.

Federal Economic Policy

When the financial crisis struck in autumn 2008, and the government responded by bailing out Wall Street, there was a clear need to commit resources to the impending financial regulatory expansion. Economist Anthony Randazzo, a recent hire for the Privatization team, was made director of Economic Research. Randazzo produced one of the first comprehensive analyses of the Obama administration's stimulus, with "A Taxpayer's Guide to the American Recovery Act" that detailed every component of the new law and how it was based on a misunderstanding of the true source of the Great Recession.

In 2010, in response to a request for comment on housing finance reform from the US Treasury, Anthony produced "A Framework for Reforming Fannie Mae, Freddie Mac, and the Housing Finance System," which was subsequently cited by the *New York Times* DealBook blog, and which formed the basis for his testimony before the House Committee on Financial Services. Building on this new research program's work, he co-authored a paper commenting on the new post-crisis monetary policy debate, "The Hayek Rule: A New Monetary Policy Framework for the 21st Century." He expanded his work on post-crisis housing policy with "Rethinking Home Ownership: A Framework for 21st Century Housing Finance Reform."

In late 2010, Anthony formed a working group of think tanks in Washington to develop a consensus framework for housing policy reform that could guide congressional responses to the regulatory problems that contributed to the housing bubble and subsequent collapse. This work culminated in a series of bills in the House Committee on Financial Services.

In early 2011, the Tea Party movement flipped the balance of power in Congress. That February, Anthony testified before the House Financial Services Subcommittee on near-term reforms toward restoring a viable housing sector. The next day the *Wall Street Journal* published his op-ed, "Ten Arguments Against a Government Guarantee for Housing Finance." The following week, the *Washington Times* published his op-ed endorsing the Treasury's option for a fully privatized housing finance system. Ultimately, House leadership decided to pursue efforts to defund Obamacare rather than take on a major housing policy debate.

Anthony subsequently developed further housing policy work, including "Restoring Trust in Mortgage-Backed Securities" (co-authored with Marc Joffe) and "Unmasking the Mortgage Interest Deduction" (with Dean Stansel). He has also delved into issues such as crony capitalism ("Crony Capitalism and Community Development Subsidies" and "Sallie Mae and Uncle Sam: Cronyism in Higher Education Finance"), tax policy ("The Effect of Cigarette Taxes on Illicit Trade"), and the federal debt ("America's Debt and Deficit").

Pension Integrity Project

The great majority of public sector pension funds are seriously underfunded, but little attention was paid to this problem until about around the time of the Great Recession. Reason's first foray into this field was released in 2005, "The Gathering Pension Storm: How Government Pension Plans Are Breaking the Bank— and Strategies for Reform," by George Passantino and Adam Summers. It got some, but not much, media attention.

We returned to the subject in 2010, focusing on California's increasingly serious problem, at both state and local levels, with Adam Summers' "How to Fix California's Public Pension Crisis." Board member David Fleming wrote a hard-hitting piece for the *Los Angeles Business Journal* on the need for California to begin the switch from defined-benefit to defined-contribution plans. When the grossly corrupt and mismanaged city of Bell, California, declared bankruptcy, its unfunded pension system provided a new focal point for attention to this growing problem.

Former Reason staffer Carl DeMaio had resigned in 2008 in order to run as a reform candidate for the San Diego City Council. That city had previously had a major pension scandal, and the system was still seriously underfunded. Once on the council, Carl led an ultimately successful effort for sweeping pension reform that was approved by nearly two-thirds of the electorate in June 2012. After his one term on the council, Carl partnered with Reason in 2013 to help lead a California Pension Reform Agenda, statewide, drawing on lessons from his San Diego reform and a similar effort that had succeeded in San Jose.

By autumn 2013, the scope of the project was broadened to nationwide, thanks to a grant from the Laura and John Arnold

Foundation in Houston. The initial effort included webinars with successful reformers, including Carl, San Jose's Pete Constant, and Utah's Dan Liljenquist; a pension reform "boot camp" for would-be reformers, and plans for policy briefs and how-to guides. The next year saw the publication of case studies of pension reform in a number of jurisdictions, a Pension Reform Handbook for those just getting started, a best-practices guide based on six Reason case studies, and studies of the pension problems of Omaha and Tulsa. That year the Oklahoma legislature enacted a pension reform plan, drawing in part on Reason's work, that will enroll all new state employees in a defined-contribution pension system. In 2015, the Reason pensions team worked with Tulsa mayor Dewey Bartlett on proposed reforms to its municipal pension system, and that reform plan was adopted by the city council in September.

One of the Pension Integrity Project's greatest successes to date occurred in Arizona in 2016. The Arizona Public Safety [police and fire] Personnel Retirement System was less than 50 percent funded. In 2015, State Senator Debbie Lesko created a stakeholder group charged with fundamental reform—and invited Reason's Len Gilroy and Pension Project director Pete Constant to be part of it. Over the next year Gilroy and Constant ended up doing the bulk of the reform design, and negotiated an agreement with the public safety unions, on behalf of the legislative leadership. Reason's director of Economic Research, Anthony Randazzo, led the actuarial work to determine the impacts of various reform scenarios. The measure received the support of the principal public safety unions, and based on that kind of consensus, the legislature passed the measure overwhelmingly, on a bipartisan basis, and Gov. Doug Ducey signed it on February 16, 2016.

Because it required a change to the state constitution, the measure had to go before the voters, and in the May 2016 referendum they approved it by a 70–30 margin. The complete package is projected to save Arizona taxpayers $1.5 billion over thirty years, while cutting financial risks borne by state and local agencies (and hence, taxpayers) in half. Gov. Ducey, in a letter to David Nott, wrote that "Reason's Len Gilroy, Pete Constant, and Anthony Randazzo were instrumental in the process. Their deep subject knowledge, pragmatic approach, and ability to forge consensus . . . was critical to the success of the reform effort." Added *Arizona Republic* columnist Bob Robb, "Politically, public employee unions and libertarian wonks blazed new ground on a difficult and emotional topic that is producing paralysis around the country. Reform doesn't come much bigger than that."

Len and Anthony took over as managing directors of the Pension Integrity Project in July 2016 when Pete Constant departed to become executive director of the Retirement Security Initiative, a pension reform advocacy group that continues to work closely with Reason on reform efforts across the country. And in January 2017, the Project signed a consulting agreement with Rich Heller, long-time senior vice president at retirement firm TIAA and head of its government-markets program. His decades of experience with defined contribution plans will be very valuable in coming years.

Overall, the first three years of the Project made major progress in building Reason's name as go-to pension-reform experts. Besides knowledge and expertise, we provided pro-bono consulting assistance to policymakers, as well as the ability to do actuarial modeling of proposed reforms, and to design policymaker education and stakeholder outreach campaigns. The team continues to be in great demand, with recent pension reform successes in Kentucky and Michigan.

New Environment Program

One of Julian Morris's priorities after coming on board as vice president of research was to revive the expansive environmental studies program that had flowered under Lynn Scarlett and Ken Green. He brought with him from his previous organization, IPN in London, an ongoing research program on climate change.

Studies dealing with greenhouse gases and climate change began appearing again in 2011. In "Weathering Global Warming in Agriculture," Julian and Douglas Southgate explained that ending farm subsidies and employing modern technologies could minimize the risks to agriculture from increased temperatures. A second study by Indur Goklany and Julian analyzed 110 years of data (1900–2010) to document the long-term decline in deaths from extreme weather events. The following year, Julian and Goklany teamed up again with a report on how the Intergovernmental Panel on Climate Change has exaggerated the impacts of climate change, especially on poor countries, and that economic growth would be a better way to shield them than constraints on energy use. In 2013, Julian and William Korchinski assessed the limitations of wind power as an alternative to conventional power generation. In 2014, Julian and Victor Nava produced a highly critical assessment of federal subsidy programs for "green" energy. And in 2015, Thomas Tanton and Julian produced a report called "Assessing the Costs and Benefits of Renewable Portfolio Standards: A Guide for Policymakers."

Julian's 2015 study on the "Social Cost of Carbon" offered an overview of existing literature and added some important insights that most observers were unaware of. For one thing, the "benefits" factored into the Obama administration's derivation of a US social cost of carbon figures were global, contrary to standard US benefit/cost assessments, which are limited to costs and benefits within the United States. Second, the procedure ignored the standard Office of Management and Budget rule that the discount rate used to calculate the present value of future costs and benefits should be 7 percent. And third, the procedure used by the administration's working group relied on three integrated assessment models of climate change that MIT energy economist Robert Pindyck concluded "have crucial flaws that make them close to useless as tools for policy analysis." As a result, Julian reached the startling conclusion that the most realistic value for a properly evaluated social cost of carbon is zero. The paper received significant comment and Julian thinks it may contribute to a change in how federal agencies deal with the cost of carbon (which would have a significant impact on future benefit/cost assessments).

Several policy studies were joint efforts of the Environment and Transportation programs. In 2012 a team headed by David

T. Hartgen studied "The Impact of Transportation Policies on Greenhouse Gas Emissions in US Regions." Their conclusion was that trendy "transportation control measures" such as attempting to shift people from cars to mass transit lead to far less CO_2 reduction than ongoing improvements in vehicle fuel economy. A related study, by Wendell Cox and Adrian Moore, "Reducing Greenhouse Gases from Personal Mobility," demonstrated that encouraging denser neighborhoods is more costly and far less effective than improving motor vehicle technology.

Criminal Justice Reform

In 2013, the Research division hired Lauren Krisai as director of criminal justice reform. Her work has focused on over-criminalization and over-sentencing. Her policy studies and blog posts have focused on mandatory minimum laws, reform of pre-trial systems, sentencing reform, and removing barriers to former inmates' rejoining society. Some of her work has focused on individual states, including Connecticut, Florida, Mississippi, and Pennsylvania, often in collaboration with the relevant state free-market think tank.

Reason in the Mainstream

The success of *Reason* magazine in the 1990s was a tough act to follow, but in the subsequent decade and a half, the magazine division went on to new heights. One of its biggest hits was publishing the world's first personalized magazine cover, and that was but one of a number of uses of new technology

Making Increased Use of Technology

In November 2002, *Reason* launched the group blog *Hit & Run*, which allowed us to provide instant commentary and analysis on news events in the form of blog posts by *Reason* writers throughout each day. Blogging was just starting to take off as an accepted new form of commentary and journalism. *Hit & Run* put *Reason* in the mix, providing a libertarian alternative to the conventional left-wing and right-wing perspectives that dominated the early blogosphere. The blog quickly grew into the main center of activity at Reason.com and currently accounts for 60 percent of the pages viewed on the site.

One of Reason Foundation's supporters is Rodger Cosgrove of Entremedia, a company specializing in direct mail. He told David Nott about an idea for demonstrating a new technology called variable data printing, which allows for personalizing mass-produced print publications. He had software that could match a subscriber's address with a GoogleMaps aerial photo of the person's house or apartment/condo building. What about giving every subscriber a magazine with a cover personalized in this way? The idea was not to creep people out but to illustrate what technology was making feasible in the emerging "database nation." David gave the okay and Rodger worked with Publisher Mike Alissi on the logistics of actually producing the covers and integrating them with the rest of the issues for printing and mailing.

With the personalized issue planned for June 2004, Editor Nick Gillespie persuaded *Wired*'s Declan McCullagh to write a cover story for that issue titled "Database Nation," and Nick wrote an Editor's Note explaining how this new technology would give us better products at lower prices, while also raising new questions about its possible use by governments. Nick's Note also included information about the reader's neighborhood that we drew from the US Census database.

Mike also worked with two *Reason* advertisers to take advantage of the technology to personalize their print ads. The Institute for Justice, a long-time *Reason* advertiser and close ally, developed an attention-grabbing ad opposing eminent domain abuse featuring a bulldozer and a condemnation notice listing the subscriber's address. We also linked subscriber addresses to congressional districts. This enabled the Marijuana Policy Project to run a customized ad urging subscribers to contact their named members of Congress to support legislation prohibiting federal interference with states that legalized medical marijuana.

We left nothing to chance in making sure the June issue (which comes out around the first of May) would be noticed. We gave advance notice to media writer David Carr of the *New York*

Times; he saw the potential and asked for an exclusive, which we granted. The *Times* broke the story on April 5, and it was immediately picked up by Matt Drudge. *Reason Online* got two thousand visits an hour that day. The *Times* article was great, with commentary not only from Nick but also from Marc Rosenberg of the Electronic Privacy Information Center and others. Reporter Carr wrote, "In some respects, *Reason*'s stunt is less Big Brother than one more demonstration that micromarketing is here to stay." He noted that Nick's Editor's Note included three open slots, so that the message itself could be customized to information about that individual reader.

More coverage emerged after the personalized issues hit readers' mailboxes. A *Newsday* story interviewed a half dozen surprised subscribers, and also included comments from Nick and from Publisher Alissi. That included owning up to glitches, such as the case of subscribers whose addresses were post office boxes, whose cover showed that location. We got tons of email including a nice note from Sen. John Sununu and another from the *Ft. Worth Star-Telegram*'s Jill Labbe. All in all, it provided a new high in national media exposure.

Reason Online grew like wildfire, fueled by attention-getting stories posted there and strong traffic from search engines to *Reason*'s deep archives (now over 150,000 published articles). In 2008, we launched a digital edition of *Reason* magazine for the newly released Amazon Kindle, becoming one of the first fourteen magazine titles available on the Kindle. We added a free app for Android phones in 2011, following up on one for the iPhone introduced in 2010. That same year Drew Carey suggested to David that *Reason Online* would attract a lot more traffic if it began serving as a 24/7 news aggregator along the lines of *Huffington Post*. After considerable research, the board approved going forward with the project at its autumn 2011 meeting. The comprehensive redesign of Reason.com went live in summer 2012. Reason podcasts were added in 2016.

Overall, by the end of election year 2016, Reason.com was garnering nearly five million visits per month, up from about one million per month a decade earlier.

Reason TV / The Drew Carey Project

In 2006, Drew Carey contacted David Nott with an idea. Those were the days of Al Gore's film, *An Inconvenient Truth*, and a stream of left-wing propaganda films from Michael Moore such as *Bowling for Columbine* and *Fahrenheit 9/11*. Drew explained to David that he was angry that only liberal/left celebrities were making films to promote their ideas. How would we like to work with Drew to produce videos championing *our* kinds of ideas? David's immediate response was positive, so the next task was to figure out what it would take to implement the idea.

This was the birth of what became *Reason TV*. Drew offered to produce and star in the initial batch of videos and to help us raise money for the new program. The initial response from key donors Ken and Frayda Levy, Rich Dennis, and the Donald and Paula Smith Foundation was very positive, giving David the basis to greenlight the project. Drew introduced us to photojournalist PF Bentley, who produced the original set of debut videos that we called the Drew Carey Project. As we recruited an initial batch of young video journalists, PF trained them.

The Drew Carey Project went public on October 15, 2007. The first three videos dealt with LA traffic congestion ("Gridlock: Hell on Wheels"), medical marijuana in California, and "Redevelopment: a Tale of Two Cities." These were not boring documentaries; they were short (about ten minutes), punchy, engaging stories, narrated by Drew in his inimitable style. The Gridlock video's producer had worked with a popular Los Angeles drive-time radio program to find someone who claimed to have the worst commute in LA—with the prize being a helicopter commute with Drew, instead of his usual freeway hell. But the video also had a serious side: it introduced millions of viewers to the privately financed express toll lanes in Orange County that offer harried commuters an uncongested alternative.

In its first month, *Reason TV* drew over 1.2 million visits, and its videos were embedded in 2,100 outside pages on 330 different sites. They got national attention from the *New York Times*, *Washington Post*, CNN, E!, CBS, and MSNBC, as well as over sixty local news programs around the country. In an interview with *Time* magazine (August 20, 2007) Drew explained, "I never thought I was a libertarian until I picked up *Reason* magazine and realized I agree with everything they had printed."

Once the initial twenty Drew Carey Project videos were completed, *Reason TV* graduated to a self-sustaining operation, with a staff of now-experienced producers and editors and ongoing funding from several foundations, including the Searle Freedom Trust. Drew joined the Reason Foundation board toward the end of 2007, where he continues to this day.

Under Nick's guidance, *Reason TV*'s offerings expanded to include very brief jabs at political inanities, mini-documentaries like those of the Drew Carey Project, interviews with thinkers and opinion-makers (up to an hour in length), and even song parodies critiquing a government policy or current event. In 2011, we discovered Remy Munasifi, a gifted comic and musician affiliated with Comedy Central who has become a mainstay of *Reason TV* with his short, barbed music videos on current affairs.

Audiences for *Reason TV* proved to be wide-ranging. For example, Jeff Shane, under secretary for policy at the US Department of Transportation, told me that he made sure to show the "Gridlock" video to the members of the National Surface Transportation Infrastructure Policy and Revenue Commission in 2007.

In early 2009, our friend John Stossel created an ABC special called "Bailouts and Bull." It included an interview with Drew Carey and excerpts from six videos from our Drew Carey Project, plus an interview with Reason Foundation Education Studies director Lisa Snell. Its broadcast on March 13 drew 6.5 million people and tied for the most-viewed program in its time slot for the young adult demographic.

One of *Reason TV*'s greatest hits was another Drew Carey idea. Drew hails from Cleveland, and his 1990s television comedy series was set in that city. Our six-part "Reason Saves Cleveland" series, narrated by Drew, debuted in March 2010. Drawing on Reason Foundation policy research, it examined Cleveland's economic decline, falling population, troubled schools, and burdensome regulations, offering fresh thinking on how to revitalize the city.

The episodes contrasted Cleveland with more successful cities such as Indianapolis and Houston—and even some successes from Chicago and Oakland. The series got rave reviews—and led to an invitation for Drew and Editor Nick Gillespie to meet with the city council on May 27 to discuss the proposed reforms. The series, and the video of the special three-hour session with the council, garnered extensive media coverage, including on the new Fox Business *Stossel* program, which featured Drew, Nick, and former Cleveland mayor Dennis Kucinich.

"Reason Saves Cleveland" was a finalist for the American Society of Magazine Editors Digital National Magazine Award in 2011, the second year in a row that *Reason TV* made the finals. *Reason TV* also figured in one of the 2011 court cases challenging the individual mandate in Obamacare. US District Judge Roger Vinson found that provision to be unconstitutional, drawing on our interview with USC law professor Erwin Chemerinsky, who said that under his reading of the individual mandate section of the law, "Congress could use its commerce power to require people to buy cars."

By early 2018, *Reason TV* had reached a record of 4.2 million monthly views on both YouTube and Facebook. Over three hundred thousand people had subscribed to the *Reason TV* channel on YouTube by the end of 2017.

Editorial Changes

One reason for the success of *Reason TV* was a change in magazine division leadership. With the growth of the television project and continued growth of *Reason Online*, overseeing both of those as well as the print magazine began spreading Nick too thin. So we recruited back to *Reason* from the *Los Angeles Times* op-ed page Matt Welch, as the magazine's new editor-in-chief as of the April 2008 issue. Matt became vice president of the magazine, and Nick became vice president of *Reason Online*.

Nick had had a great run as editor-in-chief. During his leadership, *Reason* won the 2005 Maggie Award for excellence in print and electronic publishing from the Western Publications Association, besting other finalists including *Mother Jones, Sierra,* and *The Advocate*. The award was based on the June 2004 issue with the "Database Nation" cover story and personalized covers. Later that year, *Reason* received three Southern California Journalism Awards from the Los Angeles Press Club. Thereafter, awards from the LA Press Club seemed to occur just about every year, a real tribute to Matt and Nick's work. *Reason* won another Maggie from WPA in 2009, two more in 2014, and another in 2016—this one for Elizabeth Nolan Brown's "The War on Sex Trafficking Is the New War on Drugs."

Both Nick and Matt scored interviews on PBS's *Bill Moyers' Journal*, Nick in 2007 and Matt in 2008. In introducing Nick, Moyers said, "Month in and month out, you won't read a smarter magazine, and I'm not alone in that opinion. *Reason* has been named one of the fifty best magazines three out of the last four years, and it's widely acknowledged to have one of the best political blogs on the web."

In 2011, Matt and Nick co-authored a powerful book, *The Declaration of Independents: How Libertarian Politics Can Fix What's Wrong with America*. It got numerous reviews, and they did a nationwide book tour. Columnist George Will named it the summer read of the year, and John Stossel did a Fox Business special on the themes of the book. One or both of them did appearances on C-SPAN, Fox's *Red Eye*, CNN's *In the Arena,* and many other programs. They also had jointly written op-eds in the *Los Angeles Times*, *Wall Street Journal*, and *Washington Examiner*.

Matt gained further visibility for Reason in 2013 when Fox Business launched a four nights a week program called *The Independents*, anchored by former MTV VJ Kennedy and co-hosted by Matt and Freethink Media's Kmele Foster. Kennedy had previously appeared in more than fifty *Reason TV* videos and was widely identified as a libertarian. The show appeared in the same time slot as the once-a-week Stossel program, meaning that the 9 p.m. EST time slot had libertarian content five nights a week. *The Independents* was only broadcast for one year, but it was great while it lasted. Kennedy turned out to be the star, based on the ratings, and her contract was renewed for what is now the *Kennedy* show, where she still showcases *Reason* stories and authors.

For the 2016 election year, Matt delegated many editorial duties to Managing Editor Katherine Mangu-Ward in order to focus on the election campaigns, providing in-person coverage of the Libertarian, Republican, and Democratic conventions. This resulted in extensive *Reason* magazine, *Reason Online*, and *Reason TV* coverage of this strange and unprecedented election year. By late spring, Matt expressed his desire to shift away from running the magazine, opting to become editor-at-large. Katherine was then promoted to be the magazine's ninth editor-in-chief. As Matt described her, "Katherine is a talented journalist and strong libertarian who combines *Reason* co-founder Bob Poole's rational, can-do optimism with former *Reason* editor Virginia Postrel's sense of wonder at what free markets will dream up next." To give donors and subscribers a sense of their new editor, we had Virginia interview Katherine before a live audience in the TV studio at Reason's Los Angeles headquarters that summer. The interview was live-streamed and then posted on *Reason TV*.

Books by Editors

During this period that I'm calling Reason Foundation 2.0, various *Reason* editors wrote and published a dozen books with major publishers. I've already discussed Matt and Nick's book, which generated the most publicity. But the other books all got reviewed and talked about.

The first of these was Jacob Sullum's second book. Following up his successful book challenging the anti-smoking crusade, he wrote the provocatively titled *Saying Yes: In Defense of Drug Use* (Tarcher/Putnam, 2003). Hardly a call for being stoned all the time, it was a thoughtful discussion of the use of chemicals to achieve an altered state of consciousness, and a critique not only of drug laws but of propaganda campaigns that go well beyond factual information. It won kudos from both Thomas Szasz and ACLU president Nadine Strossen and a respectful review in *The New Yorker*.

Nick edited *Choice: The Best of Reason* (Ben Bella Books, 2004), a second anthology covering primarily articles since the anthology Virginia and I had edited in 1993. This one included an introduction by Drew Carey and a foreword by Christopher

Hitchens. It includes many wonderful articles and interviews.

My contribution to the book business during these years was only a chapter in the book *Time It Was: American Stories from the Sixties*, edited by Karen Manners Smith and Tim Koster (Pearson Prentice Hall, 2007). It discussed my "libertarian awakening" during my student years at MIT, my involvement in the Goldwater campaign, and subsequently getting involved with the Lanny Friedlander's *Reason* magazine. David Nott liked the chapter so much that he arranged for reprints to be made and sent to Reason Foundation donors. In a way, writing that brief memoir planted the seed for what would become this book.

That same year, Matt published *McCain: The Myth of a Maverick* (St. Martin's, 2007), something of an exposé of the conservative senator as one whose politics are far more authoritarian than many realize. Given McCain's presidential run in 2008, Matt's timing was excellent.

Jesse Walker published his second book, *The United States of Paranoia* (Harper Collins, 2013), focused on the long history of conspiracy thinking and paranoia in this country. Damon Root published his hard-hitting book on Supreme Court decisions, *Over-Ruled* (Palgrave Macmillan, 2014).

Reason Science Correspondent Ron Bailey published two books during this period. The first was *Liberation Biology: The Scientific and Moral Case for the Biotech Revolution* (Prometheus Books, 2005). He followed up with another blockbuster, *The End of Doom: Environmental Renewal in the Twenty-first Century* (St. Martin's Press, 2015). Both were books I recommended to friends.

But the publishing champion of this period was Senior Editor Brian Doherty with four books. He wrote the first serious book on a previously little-known cultural phenomenon, *This Is Burning Man* (Ben Bella Books, 2004), followed by *Gun Control on Trial* (Cato Institute, 2008), as well as *Ron Paul's Revolution* (Broadside Books, 2012). But the book I think will have the greatest long-term impact is Brian's masterful *Radicals for Capitalism: A Freewheeling History of the Modern American Libertarian Movement* (Public Affairs, 2007). At 741 pages, this meticulously researched volume stands as the most detailed history of this important phenomenon.

The Gag Order

We received unexpected and unwanted publicity in 2015, thanks to the US Department of Justice. The US attorney for the Southern District of New York sent us a grand jury subpoena to identify people who had engaged in hyperbole in the comments section of Reason.com. It was accompanied by a "voluntary" request for confidentiality. On advice from counsel, we informed the US attorney not only that we would not reveal the commentators' identities, we would also notify said individuals of their right to respond. Within hours of our doing so on June 4, the US attorney delivered a gag order to Publisher Mike Alissi, forbidding us from acknowledging either the existence of the subpoena or the gag order. But the commentators had already been advised and others were free to speak and write.

On June 8, former federal prosecutor Ken White broke news of the subpoena and posted the grand jury document online on *Popehat*. The attempt to bully *Reason* aroused a flood of outraged commentary from other media, including Bloomberg, CNN, Fox News, NPR, the *New York Post*, the *Wall Street Journal*, the *Washington Post*, and others. The gag order was lifted on June 19. Editor-in-Chief Matt Welch published an op-ed in the *Los Angeles Times*, and *Reason TV*'s Nick Gillespie did a *Daily Beast* column, quickly linked to by Drudge Report. "Gag orders are un-American and should be applied only as a last resort, not as a boilerplate action rubber-stamped by a judge," Matt wrote. And Nick wrote, "We're in a better place in terms of free speech than we've ever been as a country. It's harder and harder for the government to shut down the conversation."

Thus, this ham-handed attempt to squelch online freedom of speech ended up as a failure for the Department of Justice and a PR bonanza for *Reason*.

Anniversary Issues

As things worked out, Matt got to conceive and produce both the fortieth and forty-fifth anniversary issues of *Reason* magazine.

Although Vol. 40, No. 1, was actually the May 2008 issue, Matt's anniversary issue appeared in December of that year, celebrating forty years of *Reason*. The main features included Brian Doherty's oral history of *Reason*, based on interviews with Manny, Tibor, and me (along with late-1960s photos and some historic magazine covers), plus former editors Marty Zupan and Virginia Postrel and other editors. Ron Bailey wrote about the magazine's forty years of covering and speculating about science and technology. Doherty also produced "the inside story of how a gang of libertarian lawyers made constitutional history" by convincing the Supreme Court to restore the original meaning of the Second Amendment. And Nick and Matt made their case for the country being on the verge of a "libertarian moment."

Matt's forty-fifth anniversary issue was dated August/September 2013 (Volume 45, No. 4). Its most talked-about article was the cover story, "45 Enemies of Freedom." Besides such obvious monsters as Idi Amin, Osama Bin Laden, and Fidel Castro, those making the list included Paul Ehrlich, Sheriff Joe Arpaio, Michael Bloomberg, Leon Kass, Jenny McCarthy, and John Rawls. Science Correspondent Ron Bailey contributed another tour-de-force, "Seven Surprising Truths about the World," busting a number of myths. And Matt did an insightful interview with Ninth Circuit Court of Appeals Judge Alex Kozinski. The issue also included a poster of seventeen historic *Reason* covers, spanning the entire forty-five years.

I'm looking forward to what Katherine will do for *Reason*'s fiftieth anniversary issue, scheduled as the December 2018, due out in late October.

Miscellaneous Foundation Efforts

There were several developments during this Reason Foundation 2.0 period that cut across the magazine and policy research divisions: our several-year venture into public opinion polling, the filing of an increasing number of amicus briefs before higher-level courts, and the deaths of people who'd played important roles in the organization's history.

Reason-Rupe Polls

At the end of 2010, David Nott announced the receipt of a three-year, million-dollar grant from the Arthur N. Rupe Foundation. Its purpose was to underwrite the Reason-Rupe Poll, an ongoing public opinion polling project. The idea was to help policymakers and the media to better understand public opinion and a less-and-less-satisfied independent electorate. As David explained in *Reason Report* Issue 126, "Rather than 'testing messages,' we will use open focus questions to shed light on people's core values," via quarterly public opinion polls.

As polling director, David hired Emily Ekins, a PhD candidate in political science at UCLA, from which she had earned her MA in that field. She had also worked as a research associate at the Harvard Business School. The first poll took place in late spring 2011 and found that Americans seemed dissatisfied with politics as usual. Among other findings, it revealed that 96 percent of respondents believed it is important to reduce the national debt, and 45 percent favored reducing spending rather than raising taxes to do that. This initial poll generated nationwide media coverage, and helped inspire Rep Jack Kingston (R-GA) to introduce a bill to cap federal spending. The second 2011 poll focused on entitlement reform. It found that 61 percent of respondents were open to cuts in Social Security benefits and 59 percent to cuts in Medicare if they were guaranteed to get back what they and their employers had contributed to the two programs. These were findings nobody had seen before—because nobody had asked voters these questions. After just the first two polls, Atlas Economic Research Foundation awarded the project a Templeton Freedom Award for Excellence in Promoting Liberty in the category of "initiative in public relations."

Having our own public opinion polling was useful to both the magazine and the policy research divisions. For one of the upcoming polls, Emily asked the transportation policy team for proposed questions that would be helpful in teasing out public opinion on things like fuel taxes and tolls. Likewise, once the Pension Integrity Project was being planned in 2012, Emily included questions about pension reform in one of the Reason-Rupe polls. As she reported in *Reason Report* Issue 133, the polling data showed that support for public pension reform transcends partisanship, with over 70 percent of respondents favoring increased public employee contributions toward their future pension benefits, and 57 percent saying that police and fire employee pension plans should not be excluded from reforms (as they often are). Later in 2012, with a large array of policy changes on the November ballot in California, the Reason-Rupe Poll conducted a survey of California voters.

In 2014, two Reason-Rupe Polls explored the views of the Millennial generation. The first of these found that half of those in this generation self-identify as politically independent, the largest share ever recorded for any generation. A majority opposed being required to buy health insurance (via Obamacare), and a similar share expected that Social Security would be out of money by the time they reached retirement. The second poll, which focused entirely on Millennials, found that 78 percent viewed the national debt and annual budget deficits as major problems, 73 percent prefer to invest their own Social Security taxes, 70 percent view competition positively, 66 percent view government as wasteful, and 64 percent prefer free markets over managed economies (contradicting other surveys finding negative opinions about "capitalism" and positive opinion about "socialism" among Millennials). These findings made news in, among other media, the *Wall Street Journal*, the New York *Daily News*, and the *Washington Examiner*.

Alas, for reasons internal to the Rupe Foundation, their grant funding was not renewed, and our other large donors had other priorities, so the Reason-Rupe Poll was discontinued at the end of 2014. Emily finished her PhD at UCLA, and was hired by the Cato Institute as a research fellow and director of polling.

Amicus Briefs

At the urging of founding board member Manny Klausner, Reason Foundation began to actively seek out court cases with significant implications for liberty, in order to submit friend-of-the-court (*amicus curiae*) briefs. Since 2003, Reason has filed over fifty briefs in significant cases in the US Supreme Court, federal circuit courts, and several state supreme courts.

In 2003, Reason filed a notable brief in two companion cases in the US Supreme Court involving the use of racial preference in admissions by the University of Michigan. Our brief included a detailed discussion of *academic mismatch* and its adverse impact on minority students who were admitted based on race, despite academic credentials significantly lower than their classmates. As noted in the book *Mismatch*,[4] no Supreme Court justice had ever mentioned academic mismatch before Justice Thomas's opinion in Grutter, and "none of the briefs filed on Barbara Grutter's side mentioned mismatch, with the exception of Reason Foundation's amicus brief, which contained an excellent discussion of the literature" (p. 330). Although academic mismatch is controversial and has not yet been a winning argument in the US Supreme Court, the counterproductive impact of a significant disparity in qualifications has become more widely understood and has been a factor in the success of initiatives in several states that now prohibit racial preferences in admissions to state universities and colleges.

In 2004, Reason Foundation filed a notable brief in *Gonzales v. Raich*, asking the US Supreme Court to uphold the California law allowing doctors to recommend, and patients to use, medical marijuana, because there was no evidence showing that such use had a substantial effect on the commercial market for recreational marijuana, and was therefore not subject to federal regulation under the Commerce Clause. The Supreme Court ruled against *Raich* by 6–3, with two dissenting opinions that supported our position. Ultimately, the rationale of our position—that there are meaningful limits to federal Commerce Clause authority—was accepted, by a 5–4 vote in the 2012 Obamacare opinion of Chief Justice Roberts that the mandate was not constitutional under the Commerce Clause.

---

4   Richard Sander and Stuart Taylor, Jr., *Mismatch: How Affirmative Action Hurts Students It's Intended to Help, and Why Universities Won't Admit It*, Basic Books, 2012

In 2006, notable amicus briefs include two filed in state supreme court cases (Hawaii and Ohio) dealing with property rights issues, and in California on free speech on television, one before the Ninth Circuit Court of Appeals in the *Raich* case (on federal prosecution over marijuana grown for one's own use, in violation of the Ninth Amendment), and one before the US Supreme Court (supporting First Amendment protection for grassroots lobbying). Our position was vindicated in both the California and US Supreme Court cases, but was unsuccessful in the Ninth Circuit.

Increasingly with such briefs, Reason Foundation partnered with other organizations. For example, in a 2011 case before the Eleventh Circuit Court of Appeals, we joined with FIRE (Foundation for Individual Rights in Education) in challenging a state college's expulsion of a student for criticizing new student fees. In a US Supreme Court case that year, we partnered with Cato and CEI in supporting a challenge to a medication patent—our position prevailed. In 2012, we joined with the Center for Constitutional Jurisprudence, the Individual Rights Foundation, and others in challenging the University of Texas's race-based affirmative action policy in a Supreme Court case, *Fisher v. University of Texas*. The Supreme Court ruled that racial preferences were subject to strict scrutiny and remanded the case back to the Fifth Circuit. Ultimately, in *Fisher II*, the university's policy was upheld, in a ruling that went against the argument in our *Fisher II* brief.

And in 2016, the Seventh Circuit Court of Appeals rejected Milwaukee taxi monopolists' claim that allowing Uber and Lyft to operate constitutes a "taking" of their property. The ruling by Judge Richard Posner quoted at length from what he termed "an excellent *amicus curiae* brief filed by the Reason Foundation."

Losing Key Pioneers

Earlier in Reason Foundation's history, we lost a number of the pioneers who had inspired me and other members of the team. Among those were Ludwig von Mises (1973), Ayn Rand (1982), Robert Heinlein (1988), F. A. Hayek (1992), and Barry Goldwater (1998).

That pattern continued during the Reason 2.0 years chronicled in this chapter, as more of our heroes reached an advanced age. Milton Friedman died in 2006, at age ninety-four. He remained intellectually active to the end, writing and still making occasional speaking appearances. He'd been a *Reason* reader from the very early years, given us wonderful endorsement quotes, spoken at our 1986 banquet as we made our debut in Los Angeles, and taken a serious interest in my own research on transportation policy.

In 2011, we were surprised to learn of the death of *Reason* founder Lanny Friedlander, at age sixty-three. At that point in time we were not certain he was even still alive, since none of us had seen or heard from him in over three decades (though Ron Bailey the previous December had received a handwritten note from someone who claimed to be Lanny, and probably was). Given *Reason*'s national visibility, the *New York Times* researched and published a long obituary on May 7, 2011, including some details about Lanny's life that none of us knew, and including two *Reason* covers that Lanny had designed. We reprinted the obituary in *Reason Report* Issue 128.

Later that year John Hospers died, at the age of ninety-three. Like Milton Friedman, John had kept writing and publishing, primarily in a now-defunct magazine called *Liberty*, nearly until the end. When we first got to know him, during the Reason Enterprises days in the 1970s, John would sometimes bring us home-cooked food during our marathon "paste-up" sessions once a month in a typesetting shop in the San Fernando Valley of Los Angeles. I had last spoken with him, by phone, in autumn 2008, inviting him to be our guest at the fortieth anniversary banquet in Los Angeles. He told me he'd like to do it, but was unsure if his health would permit it—which it did not.

In 2015, we received the sad news that Nathaniel Branden had died, aged eighty-four. His popularization of Ayn Rand's philosophy during the 1960s was a key influence on the early growth of the libertarian movement. His early help in getting Reason Enterprises off the ground in 1971—his hugely popular *Reason* interview and allowing us to rent his large mailing list—very likely made the difference between *Reason* surviving or not. He was a friend for all the years thereafter, and I was very glad he attended our fortieth anniversary banquet in 2008, at which point I recounted his early role and its contribution to our success. I saw him again, briefly, at a conference in Las Vegas in mid-2009, and would occasionally get emails that he sent out to his list. He'd been frail even in 2008–09, so I was not surprised that he made no further speaking appearances.

The last of the pioneers who left us during those years was Tibor Machan, a co-founder of Reason Enterprises and later Reason Foundation, and very possibly the most prolific book author of the modern libertarian movement. His vision of Reason Foundation ended up being different from mine, which ultimately led to his leaving the board in the late 1980s. But we remained friends, and I would see him occasionally when our travels ended up with us being in the same city. Fortunately for posterity, we had a wonderful event at Reason Weekend 2015 in Santa Barbara, where both Reason Enterprises and Reason Foundation had their beginnings. Matt Welch conducted an after-dinner on-stage interview with Tibor, Manny, and me about the history of the magazine and the foundation. Tibor also took part in a special session of the Foundation's board meeting the next afternoon, advising a board committee on ideas for infusing more moral-vision ideas into our magazine, online, and TV content. Several months before his death in March 2016, I'd had a phone conversation with Tibor, telling him of David Nott's plans for Reason's fiftieth anniversary year, 2018. We joked about him needing to take good care of himself, so he could take part in those events. But that was not to be.

Chapter 12

Reinventing America's
Surface Transportation Infrastructure

Becoming a Full-time Transportation Expert

Once I settled into my new position as full-time director of transportation policy, I began to appreciate that without administrative and fundraising responsibilities, I could do a far more serious job of research, writing, and networking than had been possible during all those years when I was trying to do policy in addition to managing Reason Foundation. My funding worries were relieved when the Searle Freedom Trust began funding Reason's transportation program in 2001, and soon thereafter named me the Searle Freedom Trust Transportation Fellow at Reason Foundation.

One of the first changes I made was to communicate regularly with colleagues, allies, and others. In 2000, I had created initial email lists of aviation and surface transportation contacts, including friendly reporters and columnists, so I could alert them whenever I had an op-ed in print or a new policy study to be released. Over the next year or so, these lists expanded, and I came up with the idea of sending out regular e-newsletters. The first one on air traffic control was sent out in autumn 2001, trying to keep interest in ATC reform alive in the post-9/11 chaos. I began a surface transportation e-newsletter in 2002, and in 2003 decided that airport security had a large enough constituency for an e-newsletter devoted to that topic. That one later evolved to also cover airport policy questions, such as runway pricing and airport privatization. As of early 2018, *Airport Policy News* was going to nearly 3,000 subscribers, *ATC Reform News* to 3,000, and *Surface Transportation Innovations* to over 10,300.

And I also found that I had the time to read a lot more transportation material. During my CEO years, I was aware of the very useful reports issued by the Government Accountability Office (GAO) and the US DOT's Office of the Inspector General (OIG). But the best I could do then was to read the brief summaries of their most relevant reports. Being able to download and read the full reports gave me far greater insight into what was really going on than was conveyed by the generally bland summary pages. I also began subscribing to a larger array of transportation newsletters and magazines—*Engineering News Record* for general infrastructure news, *Journal of Commerce* for all modes of freight transportation, *Aviation Daily* in addition to my long-time favorite *Aviation Week*, and an increasingly wide array of online (free and paid) transportation newsletters.

Networking proved to be very valuable for gaining acceptance and credibility for our new transportation policy ideas. I had long since joined the Transportation Research Board (TRB) of the National Academy of Sciences, and had also joined its fledgling Congestion Pricing Committee in the 1990s. I had accepted speaking invitations from the Public-Private Ventures division of the American Road and Transportation Builders' Association (ARTBA) and the International Bridge, Tunnel, and Turnpike Association (IBTTA), the trade association for toll roads, both public and private. I got more involved with those organizations in my new role, and got elected to the board of ARTBA's PPP division in 2001. I also joined the Air Traffic Control Association and began going to its meetings and writing articles for its quarterly *Journal of Air Traffic Control*. This led to invitations to speak at its big annual conference of aviation policymakers, FAA people, industry players, and transportation reporters.

Thanks in part to my higher profile via the e-newsletters and policy studies, I am periodically asked to speak at the annual convention of the American Association of State Highway and Transportation Officials (AASHTO), the membership organization for state DOTs.

I am also invited to speak at conferences of both US airport groups, Airports Council International-North America (ACI-NA), and the American Association of Airport Executives (AAAE).

It was only some years later that it occurred to me that nobody doing transportation policy at any of the other free-market think tanks was participating in the events of these transportation organizations. It seemed pretty obvious to me that if you want to introduce new ideas aimed at changing policy, you don't just write op-eds and try to get invited to testify before congressional committees (which is mostly theater); you have to be part of the policy discussions that take place among those directly involved. As you will see in this chapter and the next, these kinds of involvements have played a very important role in the success of Reason's transportation program.

This chapter focuses on my work since 2001 in surface transportation. In Chapter 13, I discuss my work dealing with airports and air traffic control.

During the 1990s, Reason's transportation program had succeeded in introducing long-term PPPs for priced highways as well as High-Occupancy/Toll (HOT) lanes as an improvement over carpool (HOV) lanes. We had also published a number of policy studies by outside researchers questioning the cost-effectiveness of a new generation of rail transit projects. My efforts starting in 2002 built on that base of work.

Priced Lanes for Cars, Buses, and Trucks
HOT Networks

Thanks partly to Reason's work in the 1990s, a number of projects were underway in large metro areas to convert HOV lanes to HOT lanes. For the most part, HOV lanes were either too full or too empty, yet elected officials were leery of political backlash if they increased the required occupancy from the usual two persons to three per car. Most of those being converted were ones with lots of unused capacity.

Observing this landscape, it occurred to me that the benefits of priced lanes would be greater if they constituted a seamless network, encompassing most or all of the freeway system (or at least all of it that experienced rush-hour congestion). I brainstormed this idea with two transportation colleagues in Denver, who agreed that it made sense. But we couldn't come to an agreement under which they would research and write a Reason policy study to put the idea into circulation.

I then turned to my friend Ken Orski, a veteran of the Nixon/Ford DOT, who'd been a fellow member of the 2000 Bush/Cheney transportation policy team. We agreed to collaborate on a study that would not only explain the idea but would sketch out what such networks might look like in the eight most-congested US metro areas (Atlanta, Dallas/Ft. Worth, Houston, Los Angeles, Miami, San Francisco, Seattle, and Washington, DC). We also made ballpark estimates of the cost to construct each network, and how much of the cost could be financed based on projected toll revenues. We pitched the idea as a win-win for both motorists and transit users, since the network would provide an uncongested guideway for region-wide express bus service, without the expense of building separate, mostly empty bus-only lanes.

We sent the draft study out to about two dozen peer reviewers in autumn 2002 and made revisions accordingly. During the TRB annual meeting in Washington in January 2003, Ken and I managed to get one-on-one meetings to preview the study with Federal Highways Administrator Mary Peters and Federal Transit Administrator Jennifer Dorn, as well as the number two policy person in DOT Secretary Norm Mineta's office, Emil Frankel. And we had coffee with the head of the American Public Transit Association, Bill Millar, to brief him on the benefits for bus rapid transit.

With this groundwork laid, we released the HOT Networks study at a DC news conference in March 2003. Besides Ken and me, supportive speakers included Lon Anderson of AAA, Michael Replogle of Environmental Defense Fund, and Rob Atkinson of the Progressive Policy Institute, indicating the broad appeal of the idea. The publicity included a long article in the *New York Times* by reporter John Tierney, a very positive syndicated column by Neil Peirce, and news articles in each of the eight metro areas for which we'd proposed such networks. It's gratifying to note that as this book is being written, networks like those we proposed are in the long-range transportation plans of all eight of those metro areas, and initial express toll lanes are also in operation in all of them.

Several years later, the free-market Wisconsin Policy Research Institute (WPRI) commissioned Reason Foundation to do a study of adding such lanes to the Milwaukee freeway system. Working with Milwaukee-based transportation consultant Kevin Soucie, we carried out a detailed assessment, with cooperation from the metropolitan transportation planning body and Wisconsin DOT, estimating traffic levels, toll revenue, and the cost of doing this portion of a planned modernization of the metro area's freeway system as a HOT network. Our revenue projections estimated the project could support a $1 billion bond issue, a significant contribution to the projected $6.2 billion cost of the planned reconstruction of the entire freeway system. Unfortunately, this idea was ahead of its time for Milwaukee, and it was not implemented.

I'm especially proud of my role in bringing about the network that is now well underway in the three-county Miami metro area, where I live and drive. As noted in Chapter 10, I'd done a preliminary study for Florida DOT's Miami office in 2001, which found that converting the HOV lanes on I-95 in Miami to HOT lanes would be feasible.

I recommended they take the next step: an investment-grade traffic and revenue (T&R) study. When they learned this would cost $500,000 or more, they asked if I knew where they could get a grant. Since I'd been taking part in TRB Congestion Pricing Committee meetings, and had been speaking at HOT lane workshops organized by the Federal Highway Administration (FHWA), I told FDOT about FHWA's Value Pricing Pilot Program, which had grants available to assist in getting pricing projects implemented. FDOT gave me a small contract to draft a grant proposal for an investment-grade T&R study. They won the grant, and hired Wilbur Smith Associates (WSA) to do that study. By this time, Lou and I had relocated to South Florida, which made working with FDOT a bit easier. They gave me another small consulting contract to review drafts of the WSA study in 2005.

The final WSA report (2006) evaluated four alternative ways in which the HOT lanes on I-95 could be implemented; all looked too costly in the near term. But in 2007, the US DOT, with Mary Peters now serving as Transportation Secretary, announced an Urban Partnership competition for implementing innovative ideas in road pricing. FDOT's central office in Tallahassee identified the I-95 project as their best bet—so the Miami office gave me yet another small consulting contract to help write its proposal. Since a plain-vanilla HOT lane would not be innovative enough, I urged the proposal to include three new features:

- Eliminate "fam-pooling" by granting free access only to carpools of *three or more* people;
- Simplify enforcement by permitting only carpools *registered with the local ride-sharing agency*; and,
- Identify this project as the first step in a *region-wide network* of priced lanes.

All three ideas were included in the proposal, and the Miami I-95 project was selected as one of six Urban Partnership Agreement winners.

During the January 2008 TRB meeting in Washington, while the initial I-95 project was under construction, Aileen Boucle of the FDOT Miami office invited me to breakfast to discuss next steps. Since I had suggested a region-wide network, would I be available for a consulting project to sketch out that network, analyze its cost to construct, and estimate how much of it could be financed by toll revenues? I thought it over and decided this was too good to pass up and that I had enough unused vacation days that I could do it. My "Managed Lanes Vision for Southeast Florida" was published as an official FDOT document in January 2009 and became the basis for the network that is well underway in Miami-Dade and Broward Counties. Whenever we drive from our home in Broward County to events in Miami or to Miami International Airport, we use what Lou calls "the Bob lanes" on I-95.

The work involved in developing the plan for that network was similar to the activities the Reason project teams used for the

Galvin Mobility Project case studies in Atlanta, Chicago, Denver, Miami (an expansion of my 2009 FDOT report), and Los Angeles, as discussed in Chapter 11. Of these, my Atlanta study was the first, and provided the basic template for the others.

Toll Truckways

By taking part in meetings of the Trade and Transportation Task Force of ALEC (American Legislative Exchange Council), I got to know Ted Scott of the American Trucking Associations. During the ALEC sessions, we'd sparred over the expansion of tolling on US highways, but he seemed to respect Reason's transportation work. On a visit with Ted at ATA headquarters in Alexandria, Virginia, in 2001, he briefed me on the benefits of higher-capacity trucks (long doubles and triple-trailer rigs) that are legal only in a handful of Western states and on selected Eastern turnpikes. Both railroads and highway safety groups have lobbied strongly against any use of these longer-combination vehicles (LCVs) on other highways. Yet Ted presented both a safety and fuel-economy / emissions case for hauling more freight per driver and more freight per gallon using LCVs.

I asked Ted, "What if LCVs were legalized on long-distance Interstates in barrier-separated truck-only lanes?" We discussed the idea at some length, and he liked it enough to promise co-operation if Reason did a serious study of it. I leveled with him that the cost of adding these lanes would require trucks using them to pay tolls, but that I guessed the productivity gains would make such tolls worth paying. Ted said he would like to see such an analysis.

I put together a project team that included *Toll Roads News* editor Peter Samuel (an economist who'd authored several other transportation policy studies for us and was very familiar with LCV use in Australia and Canada) and José Holguin-Veras, a civil engineering professor at City College of New York, whom I knew via TRB meetings. José came up with a high-strength pavement design and did most of the technical calculations. Peter estimated productivity gains and described how LCVs are used in Australia and Canada. Our analysis assumed that trucking companies would be willing to pay a toll equivalent to one-half the productivity gains from using the dedicated lanes for LCVs; we also called for rebates of the fuel taxes accounted for by the miles they drove on the tolled lanes.

Our peer review process for the study included not just the trucking companies that had provided input (and ATA) but also a contact at the National Safety Council. Former Transportation Secretary Jim Burnley liked the study, and talked about it with Rep. Don Young (R-AK). Young was then chairman of the House Transportation and Infrastructure Committee, and because he liked the idea, he agreed to provide a meeting room in one of the House office buildings for us to hold our news conference. At that event, Young introduced me to summarize our findings; offering supportive comments were both Burnley and the National Safety Council's Chuck Hurley. ATA chose not to appear, but later that day posted a mildly supportive comment on its website.

Because there was a lot of interest, Peter Samuel and I did a follow-up study in which we went back to the trucking companies that had cooperated on the 2002 report and asked their inputs on specific Interstate highway corridors that, if toll truckways were added, would make sense for them to use to operate LCVs. We also used data from a FHWA goods-movement database to identify high-volume truck freight corridors. The study, released in February 2004, identified ten corridors, including I-81 in Virginia.

We weren't the only ones to see I-81 as a candidate. A private consortium made an unsolicited proposal to Virginia DOT in 2003 to rebuild all 325 miles of I-81 in Virginia with two truck-only toll lanes added in each direction. Unfortunately, ATA went into all-out opposition mode. Rep. Young had become a big booster of the idea, and saw the I-81 project as a test case for the idea going national. But opponents cited the tolls as likely to cause large diversion of trucks to a parallel state highway, more accidents, environmental impacts due to widening, etc. The battle went on for years, and the companies finally gave up in January 2008.

There were other plausible candidates, and in a major 2005

study (discussed further below) of public-private partnership ideas for California highways, Peter and I proposed and analyzed *urban* toll truckways to serve the ports of Los Angeles and Oakland. The problem faced by both was that containers offloaded from ships at those ports needed to be trucked to distribution centers well inland—up to seventy-three miles in the case of Los Angeles and up to eighty-one miles in the San Francisco Bay Area. A version of this concept had already been studied by the metropolitan planning organization in Los Angeles, but we added a detailed analysis of the productivity gains that would make those truckways viable for truckers and shippers. Neither project has materialized, though the Los Angeles one remains an option in the region's long-range transportation plan.

I did a similar Reason project in 2007, analyzing a much shorter urban truckway in Miami, linking the port of Miami to a railroad yard west of Miami International Airport and the distribution centers to its west. A short, non-tolled elevated truckway was later built west of the airport, but an improved rail connection to the port has relieved some of the previous truck congestion on Miami's roadways, thereby dampening interest in the truckway.

I don't think the idea is dead, even though it has still not been implemented. More recently, it was included as a key component in a study of the reconstruction of I-70 (a major truck route) from Kansas City on the west to the Ohio/Pennsylvania border on the east. Funded by FHWA under a Corridors of the Future grant, it involved the state DOTs of Missouri, Illinois, Indiana, and Ohio, as well as the participation of the state trucking association of each state. The preferred alternative that emerged from the study was to replace the aging four-lane I-70 (two lanes each way) with eight lanes, of which four would be dedicated truck lanes open to LCVs. And because the cost of this massive project was far beyond what could done with projected fuel-tax revenues, tolling of all the lanes was recommended as the funding source. The study was completed in 2010, but the project has not begun, despite Missouri DOT's strong interest. Tolling remains politically difficult in Missouri and some other states, as discussed later in this section.

From HOT Lanes to Express Toll Lanes

As the private sector got more interested in variably priced lanes as congestion relievers (see next section), my involvement on the TRB Congestion Pricing Committee led me to see that two different philosophies were at work among those operating priced lanes. Most projects that converted HOV lanes to HOT lanes are still operated primarily as carpool lanes, allowing some tolled vehicles in, to the extent that there is excess capacity. By contrast, the private-sector lanes (like the original 91 Express project I'd helped bring about in Orange County) are operated as congestion-relievers for paying customers, which might (if required by the state DOT) also be open to certain types of higher-occupancy (three or more people) vehicles at a reduced rate or no charge. My vision of the future was clearly with the latter model.

To get people to understand the difference and to favor the latter, I began to write about this in my *Surface Transportation Innovations* e-newsletter and in my monthly column in *Public Works Financing*. I took part in panel discussions at meetings of the Transportation Research Board, the International Bridge, Tunnel and Turnpike Association (IBTTA), and the ARTBA Public-Private Partnerships Division. I also joined the TRB Committee on HOV and HOT Lanes at the time when there were discussions underway about changing its name to the Managed Lanes Committee. The term "managed lanes" was put into the vocabulary by researchers at the Texas Transportation Institute and soon gained wide acceptance in transportation circles. (I supported the name change, and it took place in 2012.) In public discussions, managed lanes soon came to refer mostly to priced lanes, and the committee's name change focus moved in that direction, as well, with gentle prodding from me.

At a 2010 FHWA road pricing conference in Houston at which I spoke, I met Craig Stone, who was in charge of toll projects for Washington State DOT. He told me of their plans for a managed lanes mega-project for I-405, the other major north-south Interstate (besides I-5) in the Seattle metro area. It was facing political opposition, and he asked if I would be interested in being part of an Expert Review Panel to review and critique their methodology, assumptions, etc. I said yes, and soon found myself joining with four other outside experts, all but one of whom I already knew. (We were paid modest stipends plus travel expenses.)

Our panel made three or four trips to Seattle to meet with the WSDOT project team and attend meetings with policymakers and community groups to discuss the proposed project. We produced a solid report that basically supported what the agency had done, but made a number of suggestions for improvement, including the need to require at least three persons per car for free passage in the new managed lanes, to issue toll revenue bonds to finance the project, and to consider making use of Washington State's public-private partnership law to shift some risks to investors and potentially get the project completed and into operation sooner.

After the report was submitted in December, Craig asked me to be the team member to brief elected officials on our findings and recommendations. So I flew out to Seattle again in early February 2011 and spent a day with Craig, meeting with four individual legislators and then doing a presentation to the House Transportation Committee. I'm happy to say that WSDOT went ahead with the project, and its first two years in operation (2016-17) have been successful.

At the Fourteenth International Managed Lanes conference in Oakland, California, in 2012, I was honored with the TRB Managed Lane Committee's Leadership Award. Four years later I was on the committee that planned the fifteenth conference, held in Miami, and I gave the opening keynote presentation.

As I write this, the majority of lane-miles of US priced managed lanes are still of the HOT lanes kind, but the number of planned express toll lanes continues to increase, thanks in part to growing interest by private-sector firms in developing and operating such projects. Because most of these projects involve newly added lane capacity, they rely largely on toll revenue to finance the project's construction. The typical HOT lane that allows two-person carpools (and sometimes alternative-fuel vehicles) free passage generally has freebies accounting for 60 to 80 percent of total use—which means revenue is typically far too low to cover debt service on toll revenue bonds. Moreover, if the large majority of vehicles are exempt from pricing, the impact of variable pricing to control congestion will be small. Accordingly, I think planned networks of *HOT* lanes are likely to be big disappointments, since their pricing power will be small; hence, they will provide little long-term congestion relief. The *Express Toll Lane* model seems likely to win out.

Sometimes recognition outside the small world of transportation policymakers takes a long time, if ever. So it was gratifying that NPR, in a national feature on managed lanes (developed by NPR's Miami affiliate), identified me as the man who invented "and helped set up market-priced lanes all over the country." This was broadcast in mid-2014, some nineteen years after the 91 Express Lanes in Orange County opened.

Highway Public-Private Partnerships
California Efforts

During the 1990s, four or five other states passed private toll roads-enabling legislation, inspired by California's landmark law AB 680, that had come about due to my 1988 Reason policy paper. But none of those other laws led to any actual projects being implemented, due to political opposition, partly against new tolls but also because of the private, for-profit aspect. I came to the reluctant conclusion that the concept of privately *owned* toll roads was a step too far. But when Virginia enacted its Public-Private Transportation Act (PPTA) in 1995, companies submitted proposals *and projects actually started getting built*. Under this public-private partnership (PPP) approach, the new toll project would be structured as a long-term lease, with actual ownership staying with the state DOT. And unlike California's AB 680, which required 100 percent private funding, Virginia's approach permitted the state to provide a portion of the equity investment (akin to a down payment)—which enabled a much wider array of projects to be done as long-term PPPs and also reduced the amount of the project cost that had to be financed based on toll revenues—meaning tolls could be somewhat lower.

Since California had pioneered private investment and express toll lanes in the early 2000s I still considered the Golden State—with its massive traffic congestion—as the most promising site for long-term PPP toll-lanes and toll-roads projects. But what we needed was a replacement for AB 680, more along the lines of Virginia's PPTA. Gov. Schwarzenegger favored the idea, and I took part in numerous conferences and workshops with private-sector and public-sector advocates of the idea between 2002 and 2009.

Despite Republican Schwarzenegger being governor, the legislature was increasingly dominated by Democrats, most of whom were opposed to "privatization" of highways. One of our best Democratic allies was ex-governor Jerry Brown's sister, Kathleen Brown, in those years working as a senior attorney for Goldman Sachs. A number of very limited bills were introduced, including one in 2006 that allowed only four projects, limited to truck toll lanes, and under which any negotiated deals would have been subject to legislative veto. The latter provision would have created unacceptably high risks for would-be project developers. Needless to say, no projects resulted.

To build support for comprehensive legislation—no limit on the number of projects, open to all kinds of tolled projects, no approval or veto by the legislature of deals negotiated by Caltrans, etc.—I conceived and led a large-scale 2005 Reason policy study, "Building for the Future: Easing California's Transportation Crisis with Tolls and Public-Private Partnerships." It described and provided preliminary cost and revenue estimates for four mega-projects: two major tunnels to fill in missing links in the greater Los Angeles freeway system and two urban truck tollways, one in Los Angeles and the other in Oakland. The study also explained the risk-transfer benefits that are especially important with megaprojects, identified PPP best practices from elsewhere, and outlined needed legal and policy changes. Our public affairs director George Passantino and I did a statewide media tour, with presentations in Sacramento, San Francisco, Orange County, and San Diego. We garnered considerable media coverage, and Schwarzenegger that year introduced his GoCalifornia legislative package that included PPP authority for HOT lanes and toll truckways—but it did not pass.

We finally got a limited transportation PPP law in 2009, thanks to continued efforts by the governor. SB 4 allowed an unlimited number of transportation PPP projects for the next seven years, allowed tolls to be charged to all types of vehicles, and avoided legislative approval requirements for negotiated lease deals. Instead, it created a Public Infrastructure Advisory Commission (PIAC) to devise procedures and best practices for Caltrans, and only to *advise* Caltrans and the legislature on negotiated deals. This was good news, and even better, my Reason colleague Adrian Moore, by then vice president of policy, was appointed as a member of PIAC.

Alas, during the seven years that followed, only one transportation PPP project was developed, thanks in part to the obstructive role of the militant Caltrans engineers' union, Professional Engineers in California Government (PECG). They had fought against this bill and all previous PPP bills. And when the Presidio Parkway project was approved, PECG used its members' role as overseer of the design and construction to second-guess the selected contractor team. This sent a message to the private sector that California was a relatively hostile environment for long-term PPP projects. Other states have done much better.

Leasing Existing Toll Roads

Long-term PPP leases started attracting overseas investors in 2005–06, stimulated by two unprecedented transactions. First, Chicago Mayor Richard Daley offered a ninety-nine-year PPP lease of the Chicago Skyway, an elevated toll road that had a troubled history of inadequate toll revenue. When the final bids were in, the winning consortium of Spanish toll-road operator Cintra and Australia's financial powerhouse Macquarie offered $1.83 billion for the lease, and agreed to a very detailed long-term concession agreement. The deal was finalized in January 2005.

When Mitch Daniels was running for governor of Indiana in 2004, he called me to ask about doing a similar long-term PPP lease of the much larger Indiana Toll Road, which had not had a toll rate increase in nearly two decades and was not well managed. I told him about the widespread use of such long-term toll concessions in France, Italy, Spain, and Portugal, and that the idea made fundamental sense—though it would be controversial. Shortly after he was elected, and before actually taking office, he announced that he would seek to lease the facility and use the proceeds to fully fund a statewide highway improvement program.

During 2005, at Gov. Daniels's request, I made two trips to Indianapolis. The first was as one of half a dozen experts to speak at an all-day briefing session for transportation companies, state officials, and other interested parties on the case for the Indiana Toll Road lease. Later in the year, when the measure was being fiercely debated in the legislature, I flew back to testify. The measure passed by a narrow margin, and Daniels's public approval rating sank. But when the bids came in, the result was similar to that of the Chicago Skyway. Again, the high bidder was Cintra/Macquarie, offering $3.8 billion for a seventy-five-year lease. The Indiana Finance Authority asked me to review the Chicago long-term concession agreement and make suggestions on how they could do better, some of which they followed. The deal reached financial close in June 2006.

These two transactions shined a spotlight on the United States as a friendly environment for long-term transportation PPPs. Even before the Indiana transaction was completed, Reason published a long policy paper by Peter Samuel, "Should States Sell Their Toll Roads?" I spoke on this topic at a number of conferences, including a session at the International Bridge, Tunnel, and Turnpike Association and an investors' conference in New York. Proposals started floating around for possible leases of the New York Thruway, the Illinois Toll Highway Authority's many toll roads, the Harris County, Texas (Houston) toll roads, the Florida Turnpike, and several others. None of those came close to being offered for lease.

But one that did—and sparked a huge battle—was Gov. Ed Rendell's plan to lease the Pennsylvania Turnpike, America's first superhighway, dating back to the 1940s. The Turnpike Authority was well known as a source of cushy jobs for friends of legislators of both parties, so there was bipartisan opposition in the legislature. Opposition also came from a segment of the tax-exempt municipal bond community, which saw changes of this kind as a threat to their comfortable financial status quo. To counter opponents' flawed arguments, I commissioned Peter Samuel and Geoff Segal to write a working paper, "Leasing the Pennsylvania Turnpike: a Response to Critics of Gov. Rendell's Plan," released in June 2007.

After failing to get legislative support for his initial lease effort, Rendell decided to up the ante, offering a longer lease term and officially seeking bids. The hope was that if a significantly large bid were offered, the legislature would be seduced into passing the enabling legislation. A trio of academics went to bat for the status quo in a report titled "For Whom the Road Tolls." Peter Samuel and I took it apart in a Reason policy brief in April 2008. Among our findings was a table comparing the high overhead costs of state-owned US toll roads, compared with much lower overhead of eight representative long-term toll concession projects. The winning bid of $12.8 billion was submitted by Spanish toll-road operator Abertis—but the legislature was not moved, and Abertis subsequently withdrew its bid. The only other long-term lease of an existing toll road took place in 2011 in Puerto Rico, where reform governor Luis Fortuno leased PR 22 and PR 5 for forty years to Abertis.

The Chicago Skyway and Indiana Toll Road leases caused heartburn for some Democratic members of Congress. One of the most vociferous opponents was Rep. Peter DeFazio (D-OR), who chaired a hearing on PPP leases in February 2007. My friend and colleague Karen Hedlund (a PPP expert attorney with the Nossaman law firm) and I were among the witnesses defending the concept as good for transportation and not in conflict with any federal laws or regulations. Several congressional attempts were made over the next several years to restrict such transactions, but none succeeded.

Also getting into the fray was Lou Dobbs, the populist, foreigner-bashing commentator on CNN. I taped an interview for the program with one of Dobbs's staffers, but as I pointed out in a subsequent *Wall Street Journal* op-ed, my best points were left on the cutting-room floor, so that Dobbs could rant on about highways being "sold" to the highest bidders who were—think of it—"foreigners."

New PPP Toll Projects: Texas and Virginia Lead the Way

Fortunately, the case for using long-term PPP lease transactions for needed *new* highway infrastructure was easier for politicians and media people to understand. With fast growth producing horrible congestion on freeways in Texas metro areas, Gov. Rick Perry appointed an advocate of tolling and PPPs to head the state's Transportation Commission. In 2003, that body carried out a major public information campaign about Express Toll Lanes and more highway capacity to provide congestion relief, with toll-based financing as the way to pay for it. They persuaded the legislature to enact a sweeping transportation PPP law (HB 3588) that enabled widespread use of toll financing and long-term PPP concessions. I like to think that the workshop I'd organized for TxDOT leadership back in 1998, and a subsequent visit with Rick Perry, helped to lay the basis for these measures. And in October 2004, Texas DOT brought me to Texas A&M to give a guest lecture on PPP concessions at its annual Short Course for their highway engineers.

These efforts led to significant interest in Texas from infrastructure finance providers and from overseas toll road developer-operators. One of the first projects financed as a new PPP toll road was an extension of TxDOT-built SH 130, from the southern outskirts of Austin to the northern outskirts of San Antonio, for which the winning bidder was the team of Cintra and local construction firm Zachry. Most of the other Texas projects were Express Toll Lanes in Dallas, Fort Worth, and Houston—the metro areas most in need of serious congestion relief.

One case generated considerable controversy. In 2007, TxDOT held a competition for a long-term PPP concession for SH 121, a planned new toll road in the Dallas suburbs. Since this seemed like a very high-traffic project, TxDOT decided to select the winning bidder primarily on the size of the up-front lease payment. Cintra, the winning bidder, offered a $2.1 billion up-front payment. *After* the winner was declared, the local toll agency, NTTA, came forward with a counter-proposal for an even larger up-front payment—basically to protect its turf from the private-sector interloper. The arguments in favor of its proposal ignored the huge toll increases NTTA would have to impose on all its existing toll roads to service the debt on the several billion dollars of new bonds it would have to issue in order to provide the up-front payment.

In response, I wrote a working paper taking apart the flimsy case made by NTTA and its allies, "Tolling and Public-Private Partnerships in Texas: Separating Myth from Fact." I also wrote several op-eds and blog posts on what was going on there. The Federal Highway Administration sent TxDOT a letter pointing out the unfairness of letting a public agency subvert an already completed competition—but offered no threat of any action. In the end, local politics won out, and the project was awarded to NTTA.

Later that year, I got an award for my efforts in defending highway PPPs. The ARTBA Public-Private Partnerships division named me its 2007 Private Sector Entrepreneur of the Year, at that year's annual PPP conference. By that time, I had also been writing and speaking about the proposal from Fluor and Transurban to add Express Toll Lanes to the western half of the chronically congested Capital Beltway in northern Virginia. Finally approved after several years of study and public hearings, the two new express lanes each way opened to traffic in November 2012, bringing welcome congestion relief to that roadway (I-495)

PPP toll projects remained controversial in Texas after the NTTA controversy, so the legislature authorized a Study Committee on Private Participation in Toll Projects. Several of the members were appointed by Gov. Rick Perry—and one of them was me. Nearly all the others were members of the legislature, so it started out as a strange experience for me. Over the course of 2008 we had four public meetings in the largest

Texas cities, hearing testimony from various experts and interest groups.

I got an amazingly lucky break, however, in that the academic who was appointed to lead the drafting of the committee's report was Elizabeth Jones, a former McKinsey consultant and visiting professor at the UT-Dallas School of Management. It turns out she knew my writings on tolling and PPPs and was largely in agreement with them. This led me to devote considerably more time to this project than I otherwise would have, and we ended up writing a report that laid out a smarter way forward for tolling and PPPs in Texas. First, we debunked the idea that new urban toll roads were pots of gold that bidders would pay billions for in lease payments up-front—and still have to pay for building and operating the road! (SH 121 was an aberration in that respect.) Second, we argued that a wiser approach in the case of unexpectedly high future toll revenues was to build in revenue-sharing with TxDOT, to occur in such cases. This would align the incentives of the agency and the company as long-term partners.

While several committee members submitted exceptions to several of the points in the report, I think it helped to prevent repeal of PPP and tolling legislation. And TxDOT accepted and made use of the revenue-sharing approach on major PPP projects in Dallas and Fort Worth. These days, a list of the projects to be offered as long-term PPP concessions must be approved by the legislature in its biennial sessions. And such projects continued to be authorized through 2016.

Unfortunately, grassroots populist opposition to both tolling and PPPs in Texas helped to elect new governor Greg Abbott on a "no more tolls" platform in 2014, along with some like-minded state house members. In the 2015 legislative session, nearly all proposed anti-toll measures were defeated, and PPP projects were allowed to proceed. But in the 2017 legislature, with more populist legislators in office, Texas DOT's list of eighteen planned PPP toll projects (valued at $30 billion) was rejected, and several anti-tolls measures were passed. Local officials in Austin, Dallas/Ft. Worth, and Houston expressed great dismay, but this new status quo will remain at least until the next legislative session in 2019.

Twenty-first Century Tolling

Embracing Tolling as a Better User Fee

Even back in the 1980s when I came up with the idea of privately developed Express Toll Lanes, tolling appealed to me as a far better user fee than fuel taxes. Fuel taxes are supposed to be user fees to support the roadways we drive on. But they are hardly real user fees. With fuel taxes, we pay the same rate per mile whether we drive on a two-lane dirt road or an eight-lane freeway—yet the cost to build and maintain the latter is vastly greater. In 1995, I'd commissioned economist Randy Pozdena to analyze California's fuel-tax-based highway-funding system. Besides identifying diversion of gas tax revenues to non-highway uses, Pozdena also found extensive cross-subsidies among highway users, with rural highway users overpaying and urban highway users significantly underpaying ("Where the Rubber Meets the Road: Reforming California's Roadway System," August 1995). And these days, 20 to 30 percent of this highway user fee is spent on non-highway purposes, undercutting the original idea of users-pay/users-benefit.

When I started attending and then speaking at the toll road conferences put on by IBTTA, I was pleased to see that its membership included not only state toll agencies but also most of the global toll-road companies in the private sector. I also got to know an academic who seemed to be a regular speaker at IBTTA events—Joseph Giglio of Northeastern University, with a previous background at several investment banking firms. Although Joe made some strong defenses of tolling as far superior to fuel taxes as a highway user fee, and was also positive about highway PPPs, some of his ideas in the early 2000s were troubling to me.

In 2005, the Hudson Institute published his book, *Mobility: America's Transportation Mess and How to Fix It*. While I agreed with much of it, I found one of his major themes to be very unwise. In the book's introduction, and in talks and articles, he urged that future roadway pricing (to replace fuel taxes) should be implemented "in a way that effectively converts the roadway system into a basic funding source for all [surface] transportation modes." To me, this was a prescription for converting a nearly pure user fee into the same kind of general public works tax that fuel taxes had become by the end of the twentieth century—to the detriment of highway users.

Several transportation colleagues and I were so distressed by IBTTA's promoting this idea that we arranged to have a private lunch with the organization's excellent CEO, Patrick Jones. I think we must have made some impression on Pat that day, because over subsequent years Joe gradually faded from view at IBTTA events, while I increasingly got invited to make presentations and to be on panels.

At about the same time, the Transportation Research Board appointed me to a special committee to study the long-term viability of fuel taxes. It was quite a high-powered group, including one of my mentors in transportation, Prof. Marty Wachs of UCLA, and a toll-finance expert named Jim Taylor, who today works for Mercator Advisors and has advised me on several projects. We spent about a year, with support from TRB staffers, reviewing trends in vehicle fuel economy and federal regulation thereof, as well as periodic political efforts to reduce petroleum use for various reasons, and concluded that in the long term, fuel taxes should be replaced by a true user fee. One of our major recommendations was that the federal government should encourage states to make greater use of toll roads and toll lanes, and should also seriously explore (with state DOTs) road-use metering and mileage charging.[5]

Several years later, Congress authorized creation of a National Surface Transportation Infrastructure Financing Commission, and a friendly California member of Congress appointed my Reason colleague, Adrian Moore, as a member. I took part as an invited expert at one of its working sessions, and already knew seven of the fourteen members. They produced an excellent report, building on our TRB committee's work and reviewing the pros and cons of a number of alternatives to per-gallon fuel taxes. The final report in 2009 selected mileage-based user fees as

---

5 *The Fuel Tax and Alternatives for Transportation Funding*, Special Report 285, Transportation Research Board, 2006

the best alternative. Adrian went on to help found the Mileage-Based User Fee Alliance, which has worked hard to stimulate a growing number of state DOT-managed MBUF pilot projects. Adrian today serves as vice president of MBUFA.

Interstate 2.0

The fiftieth anniversary of the Interstate Highway System, first authorized by Congress in 1956, led to numerous articles on its history. As I delved into the history of US highway finance, I saw the progression of fuel taxes (begun in Oregon in 1919) from pure user tax at the state level to, initially, a dedicated funding source to build the Interstate Highway System at the federal level. But once the Interstate system was largely completed, Congress gradually watered down the original users-pay / users-benefit principle. Congress was faced with a growing pot of highway revenue each year, and instead of reducing the tax rates, looked for more things to do with it.

Of all people, it was Ronald Reagan's DOT Secretary Drew Lewis who breached the dam, promising big-city mayors that one cent out of a proposed five cents/gallon federal fuel-tax increase would be dedicated to urban transit systems. After doggedly opposing the gas tax increase, Reagan eventually gave in, and users-pay/users-benefit was destined for the scrap-heap. By the time Adrian and I wrote our 2010 Reason study, "Restoring Trust in the Highway Trust Fund," we found that more than 23 percent of all federal highway user tax money was being spent on non-highway purposes. We contrasted this with the aging of the Interstates, many of which would exceed their original fifty-year design life in the coming decade, and suggested refocusing the federal program on infrastructure needed for interstate commerce, rather than the ever-growing array of public works programs it has become. We dubbed the needed second-generation Interstate highway network "Interstate 2.0."

Alas, the political prospects for such a dramatic revamp of the federal program appeared to be close to zero, though we gave numerous presentations on it in 2010–11. But then, out of the blue, I was contacted by the head of the Wisconsin Policy

Research Institute about growing interest in that state in toll-financed reconstruction of its aging Interstates. Over the years, I'd done several previous transportation policy studies for WPRI, always with the cooperation of the relevant agencies. So we negotiated a deal in which WPRI would make a grant to Reason Foundation and I would do a pretty detailed study for them, with the promised cooperation of the Wisconsin DOT.

The first meeting, at WisDOT's headquarters in Madison, went very well. Toll-financed reconstruction and modernization was not an idea they'd actually considered seriously, but a free study by a credible researcher and policy institute was hard for them to pass up. To my surprise, they agreed to generate a large mass of detailed data on every Interstate corridor in the state, and got me access to planning that was underway by the Milwaukee area transportation planning body on a desired reconstruction and widening of the Milwaukee freeways, nearly all of which are Interstates.

The WPRI grant also paid for a research assistant for the project, who developed the tolling spreadsheets and did other tasks. The Wisconsin Transportation Builders Association (WTBA), which I'd gotten to know doing previous WPRI transportation studies, was also very helpful. I found that toll-financed reconstruction and widening was definitely feasible for the less-costly rural Interstates, and might be feasible for (or could at least contribute a lot towards rebuilding of) the urban (Milwaukee) Interstates. When the study was released in September 2011, it was well received by the local media, and I presented it at the next WTBA conference. I was surprised that audience response to my half-hour interview on the Wisconsin NPR station was largely positive (in a state with no history of toll roads). Evidently the study had an impact, because the legislature several years later authorized $1 million for a more-detailed feasibility study of toll-financed Interstate modernization in Wisconsin. The largely favorable set of reports was completed by engineering firm HNTB and released in December 2016.

Since we were getting nowhere on gaining traction for our 2010 proposal to refocus the federal program on Interstate reconstruction, the favorable results of our Wisconsin study led me to the idea of doing a somewhat less detailed study of all fifty states. If Congress could not come up with the huge sums needed for this purpose, how many states would be able to finance Interstate reconstruction and widening based on toll revenues?

That was the genesis of what became our Interstate 2.0 project. FHWA was very helpful, providing data more detailed than what it publishes in its widely used highway statistics tables. I also managed to obtain newly analyzed projections of highway travel growth rates, separately for cars and for trucks (important since truck traffic is expected to grow about twice as fast) from the DOT's Volpe Center in Cambridge, Massachusetts. I used FHWA unit-cost data for Interstate reconstruction and for Interstate lane additions, but adjusted those numbers state-by-state to take into account differences in construction costs among states.

Since urban Interstates cost a great deal more than rural ones, I analyzed each state's rural Interstates separately from its urban Interstates. The first step was to estimate reconstruction costs, urban and rural, for each state. Next, I used a starting set of toll rates for rural Interstates, 3.5 cents/mile for cars and 14 cents/mile for trucks, adjusted annually by an expected annual increase in the consumer price index. This enabled forty-year projections of traffic and revenue for each state's rural Interstates. The computations were more complex for urban Interstates, because I assumed peak and off-peak toll rates would be employed, to reduce peak-period congestion. The results for reconstruction showed that the net present value of revenue exceeded the net present value of costs in most states.

But that did not account for widening. Some of that projected revenue was based on more traffic volume than the existing number of lanes could handle. To figure out where widening was needed—and how many lanes—I needed to examine each specific Interstate in each of the fifty states. That led to identifying ninety-six rural corridors needing one or more lanes each way and ninety-seven urban corridors likewise. And twenty-nine of the long-distance rural corridors had so much projected truck traffic that we recommended dedicated truck-only lanes as their lane additions.

Nationwide, the net present value (NPV) of the cost of reconstruction plus widening was $983 billion, and to my surprise, the NPV of revenue was 99 percent of that. So we were very close on the first ballot. Looking at individual states, thirty states were revenue positive with the basic toll rates or slightly lower. Nine states needed slightly higher rates, and six urban states (including California and New York) needed even higher rates. Only six rural states were not really toll-feasible.

These were very positive results; they differed sharply from the situation in the early 1950s when tolled Interstates were only feasible in the Northeast and Midwest. And the results showed that most states could do these megaprojects on their own, without the need for a (highly unlikely) massive new federal program. Our DC news conference received excellent coverage, including by the *Washington Post*. And I started giving presentations on these findings to transportation organizations, including at the annual meetings of the state DOT's organization (AASHTO) and at IBTTA. I also did a version of the Reason policy study as a paper for the 2014 TRB Annual Meeting; it not only passed their peer review but also was selected for publication in their journal, *Transportation Research Record*.

The "Interstate 2.0" paper had not included much about political feasibility, though I had designed the methodology with that in mind. So the next year I did a follow-up paper called "Value-Added Tolling." It emphasized the importance of designing the toll-financed replacement of Interstate 2.0 to avoid what had happened over the years to federal fuel taxes. Thus, if Congress gave permission for states to embark on this, it should mandate that the new tolls be used solely for the capital and operating costs of the replacement Interstates. Tolls on a corridor should not be charged until the replacement was finished and open to traffic. Of course, tolling should be all-electronic, to hold down the costs of collection that plagued twentieth-century cash toll roads. And taking account of AAA and trucking industry concerns about "double taxation" (those who use current toll roads must pay both tolls and fuel taxes), the state should provide rebates of the calculated amount of fuel tax paid for the miles driven on the tolled replacement corridors.

The response to this follow-up was positive, especially from those it was aimed at. AAA and IBTTA both invited me to present this approach to their governing boards, and the response in both cases was positive. I presented Value-Added Tolling to AAA's national board in September 2015—and they endorsed this approach. In addition, the study at least opened the door to serious, off-the-record discussions with senior officials of the American Trucking Associations, which identified additional industry concerns, such as avoiding an array of transponders from different states, the need for consolidated monthly bills, and confidentiality of routing. This led me to do further research in 2015, resulting in "Truck-Friendly Tolling." Unfortunately, before follow-up discussions on the new report could take place, a major leadership change at ATA led to the departure of those I'd had the discussions with, so ATA is not on board with truck-friendly Interstate tolling as this is being written. But I see some signs of increased openness at ATA to alternatives to their wished-for but non-existent large increases in fuel taxes for Interstate modernization.

In its 2015 federal surface transportation reauthorization law (the FAST Act), Congress authorized several million dollars for TRB to create a special committee on the future of the Interstates. That committee was appointed in 2016 and got underway late that year. I gave an invited presentation on Interstate 2.0 at the second of the committee's field hearings, in March 2017, and it seemed to go well. We'll see.

Rethinking America's Highways Book
During the last year of the G. W. Bush administration, I had meetings with several of the senior policy people at US DOT to discuss what they had accomplished and what they had left undone, so that my Reason colleagues and I might focus on some of this during the next administration. In my lunch with Under Secretary of Transportation for Policy Jeff Shane, I suggested that

he'd had so many interesting aviation policy experiences that he should write a book. His response to me was: "When are you going to write *your* book?"

That got me thinking about my evolving vision for the future of the US highway system. The gradual conversion of fuel taxes from a pretty good proxy for a user fee into an unpopular tax spent on politically favored projects had led me to contrast the battles over *highway* revenues and policy choices with the relatively robust model used for *other* vital public utilities (whether investor-owned or government-owned): electricity, natural gas, water supply, telecommunications, etc.). In each case, the consumer gets a regular bill itemizing the amount and type of services used and pays only for that usage. The revenues all go directly to the provider to cover the capital costs and the operating and maintenance costs of the infrastructure used to provide the service. What we need this century, I decided, is a paradigm shift: rethink and reorganize limited-access highways as network utilities.

It took me several years to carve out enough work time to do the research and writing to produce the book. To make the case as thoroughly as possible, I had to research the early history of highways and how they were paid for, the evolution of US highways from the nineteenth-century private turnpikes to a twentieth-century set of state-owned enterprises funded by taxes. Next I reviewed the post-World War II emergence of investor-owned toll road networks in much of Europe, the migration of this model to Australia, Latin America, and Australia in the late twentieth century, and its reemergence in this country mostly after the turn of the new century. With all that as context, I explained how long-term highway PPPs actually work; the governance mechanism implemented in detailed, long-term concession agreements; and the benefits such as shifting major risks from taxpayers to investors; avoiding pork-barrel projects by the requirement of a return on investment; and how the public interest is protected. I also had to discuss the various kinds of opposition, from left- and right-wing populists, status quo interests, and ideologues of various sorts. And then I developed scenarios for how the transition might come about, and what twenty-first century highways as network utilities might be like.

Altogether, the book encompassed twelve chapters, and it proved to be difficult to find the right publisher. Several agents advised that it would not have large enough sales potential for them to take me on as a client, and that I should go directly to publishers that focus on public policy books or academic presses that also publish serious non-academic books. I finally succeeded with the University of Chicago Press, and the book is scheduled for June 2018 release.

High-Speed Rail

As a lifelong rail fan and model railroader, I really wanted to like high-speed rail and see it become successful. Riding the original TGV line from Paris to Lyon in 1989 was exhilarating. But my engineering and economics background led me to be skeptical of proposals that started cropping up in the United States in the 1990s. Most were purportedly some kind of PPP, but when you looked more closely it was pretty clear that ridership projections were very optimistic, and the extremely high costs of land acquisition and construction seemed likely to require mostly taxpayers' money, in order for the lines to have any hope of covering merely their operating costs from ticket revenues.

But our transportation team did not see much value in challenging any of the early proposals—an allegedly private HSR line between Los Angeles and San Diego in the early 1980s (abandoned after large-scale public opposition to proposed property takes), a proposed HSR connection among the Texas triangle of Austin, Dallas, and Houston (defeated after Southwest Airlines funded critical studies of its viability), and two attempts at state-sponsored, PPP HSR projects in Florida (1996 and 2002). Both of those were cancelled after highly critical studies by our friend Wendell Cox, done for the Florida free-market think tank, the James Madison Institute.

But as a California taxpayer in the mid-1990s, I got worried when I learned that the legislature had created the California High-Speed Rail Authority in 1996, after three years of work by an Intercity High-Speed Rail Commission. It had done studies allegedly showing that a north-south HSR system would be a sound investment. This seemed like enough of a risk to California taxpayers that I wanted Reason to do an independent study of the subject. But we were up to our ears in projects, and my attempts to find a funding source came up dry. (It also didn't help that the chairman of the new authority in the late 1990s was an investment banker friend of board chairman Harry Teasley, who'd recently made his first general-support contribution to Reason Foundation.)

Over a period of years, I read whatever serious research I could find on California HSR proposals. There were already academic studies from UC Berkeley raising serious questions about the early cost and ridership estimates being generated by the authority's consultants. Fairly representative was a paper by David Levinson and colleagues at the Institute of Transportation Studies, UC Berkeley, in 1997.[6] The paper compared the full costs of a proposed LA-to-San Francisco HSR line to the full costs of expanding either airline service or automobile travel. The paper concluded that "high-speed rail is significantly more-costly than expanding existing air service, and marginally more expansive than [expanding] auto travel." More such academic research followed in subsequent years, but despite the growing array of negative academic studies, the HSR Authority continued making plans, including a major federal environmental study in the early 2000s. I obtained and read large sections of this document and found its comparison of HSR with the alternatives of north-south highway additions, or airport gate and runway additions, to be full of holes. I urged Adrian (by this point, my boss as VP of policy) to pursue a Reason study to critique the HSR plans, but HSR still looked like a pipe-dream, and there were no obvious funding sources.

All that changed early in 2008, when we learned that the legislature would put on the November ballot a proposal to authorize

---

6 David Levinson, Jean Michel Mathieu, David Gillen, and Adib Kanafani, "The Full Cost of High-Speed Rail: an Engineering Approach," *The Annals of Regional Science*, Vol. 31, pp. 189–215, 19

$10 billion of taxpayer-supported bonds for the HSR project. With a real threat on the horizon, Adrian assembled a project team of Wendell Cox and Joseph Vranich, a former president of the (US) High-Speed Rail Association who had seen the light. Adrian also raised funding for the study from Citizens Against Government Waste and the Howard Jarvis Taxpayers' Association.

The study, "The California High Speed Rail Proposal: A Due Diligence Report," was released in September 2008, about six weeks before Election Day. At 196 pages, one of our longest policy studies ever, it was a blockbuster. It made a solid case that the projected cost of $45 billion was a gross underestimate, and would likely be in the $65–81 billion range. It also found the ridership projections to be "dramatically inflated" at 65 to 98 million riders per year by 2030; more likely would be 23 to 31 million. And on my point about the bloated costs of the airport and highway alternatives, the study concluded that these were "highly exaggerated," and went into detail as to why. The study got extensive statewide publicity, and may have influenced a number of newspaper editorials opposing the HSR bond measure, but the influential *Los Angeles Times* urged the measure's passage. And it won, by 53 to 47 percent.

Adrian had been project director of that study, and became our chief spokesman on the subject in subsequent years. By 2012, the authority had doubled the original price-tag, halved the ridership estimates, and postponed the planned completion date by thirteen years—vindicating many of our study's findings. The legislature's own Peer Review Group that year recommended that the bonds not be issued. Several organizations filed suit against the authority; among their points were contentions that the conditions included in the bond measure of no operating subsidies ever, and guaranteed trip times between Los Angeles and San Francisco, *could not* be met. Adrian agreed to be an expert witness in one of those suits. Although the project has begun construction on a starter segment in the Central Valley, its future funding is highly uncertain.

Meanwhile, the Obama administration sought to implement its vision of a national HSR network, and offered grants to a number of states for starter lines, including California, Florida, Ohio, and Wisconsin. The latter three had Republican governors. Seeing that the Florida project was for a ridiculously short route between Tampa and Orlando—less than a hundred miles, so short that there is no scheduled air service—I urged Adrian to commission a due-diligence study by Wendell on this latest Florida proposal, and he agreed. Wendell did yeoman work under my direction, on a very tight schedule, because new governor Rick Scott (on whose transition team I had served) would have to make a decision very soon to accept or reject the proffered $2.4 billion grant.

We released "The Tampa to Orlando High-Speed Rail Project: Florida Taxpayer Risk Assessment" in January 2011, Scott's first month in office. On March 4, he announced that he was rejecting the federal money, because the risks of both construction cost overruns and a need for operating subsidies were simply too great. Scott cited our findings as having provided the basis for his decision, and this was widely reported statewide. Both Gov. Scott Walker of Wisconsin and Gov. John Kasich of Ohio also rejected federal HSR grants, but theirs were considerably smaller ($400 million and $800 million, respectively).

I recruited Wendell the next year to debunk another huge boondoggle, an allegedly private HSR line between Las Vegas and (of all places) Victorville, California, supposedly to serve Los Angeles. "The XpressWest High-Speed Rail Line from Victorville to Las Vegas: A Taxpayer Risk Assessment," was released in August 2012. In this case, the major subsidy was not to be a federal grant (Congress had by this time cut off further HSR grants) but a $5.5 billion federal loan under the Railroad Rehabilitation and Improvement Financing program (RRIF). Since Wendell showed that the project was not a viable business, the odds that the company would default on the loan were high. Moreover, simply expanding the capacity of I-15 across the desert to Las Vegas would be far more cost-effective than building a new rail line from a desert town eighty-five miles from downtown Los Angeles.

Early the following year, Sen. Jeff Sessions and Rep. Paul Ryan sent an open letter to DOT Secretary Ray LaHood urging the administration to turn down the loan request, citing the Reason study. And that summer, the Federal Railroad Administration did just that. Another one bites the dust!

I made several other contributions to more-careful thinking about HSR, starting in 2010. The National Conference of State Legislatures invited me to address its Transportation Committee on this subject that April. My presentation was titled "Look Before You Leap: Questions Legislators Should Ask About High-Speed Rail." Among the questions were (1) what is HSR supposed to accomplish, and what evidence is there that it can do any of those things in the United States? and (2) what are the alternatives (increased airport and/or highway capacity)? Perhaps because of this, I was invited to testify before the House Transportation and Infrastructure Committee in May 2011 on the potential for high-speed rail in the Northeast Corridor. My answer was that in principle this was the one place in the United States where HSR might be able to succeed, but the cost of all-new right of way and track would be enormous. And indeed, in 2016 Amtrak came up with a grandiose *$160 billion* plan for HSR in that corridor!

I did identify one proposed higher-speed rail project that might succeed, unsubsidized. All Aboard Florida is a project currently underway by a sister company of Florida East Coast Railway to provide service from Miami, Ft. Lauderdale, and West Palm Beach to Orlando. The distance seems sensible to compete with both driving and flying, the company owns real estate adjacent to the South Florida stations which it is developing into mixed-use commercial, and it can use existing FEC right of way for 83 percent of the route, significantly reducing its construction costs. Also, it will save money on operating costs by limiting top-speed in non-urban areas to 120 mph, not the planned 200+ mph of true HSR. After several semi-favorable articles about the project in my newsletter, the James Madison Institute commissioned me to write a policy brief for them, which came out in January 2017. The first phase—Miami to West Palm Beach—is to be completed in spring 2018, with the remaining link to Orlando expected several years later.

———

With PPPs and tolling moving forward across the country and tax-funded HSR at least largely dead, the future looks pretty good for twenty-first century surface transportation infrastructure to be rebuilt on a users-pay / users-benefit basis.

Chapter 13

Rethinking US Aviation Infrastructure Policy

As noted in Chapter 12, I began an email newsletter on air traffic control reform in 2001 and another on airport security in 2003; the latter evolved into covering airport policy issues across the board—including security, runway pricing, and airport privatization. As with my work in surface transportation, I took an active role in joining aviation organizations and speaking at aviation conferences, developing networks of contacts who were operating airport and ATC infrastructure or advancing industry goals via trade associations. These contacts proved to be critically important in working to change various policies.

Airport Security

In the months following 9/11 as I related in Chapter 11, with help from former Lockheed Air Terminal CEO Viggo Butler, I drew on my airport knowledge to become a kind of instant expert on airport security. In creating the Transportation Security Administration, I judged that Congress had made two fundamental mistakes. First, it combined aviation security *regulation* and airport screening *operations* in a single agency, a serious conflict of interest. Second, it treated all air travelers as equally likely to be a threat to airplanes by insisting that everyone must go through the identical screening process whenever they flew on an airline. My policy-change goals, therefore, were to (1) remove the screening function from TSA, refocusing it on policymaking and regulation, and (2) implement some form of Trusted Traveler policy that would allow pre-vetted travelers to bypass most of the normal airport screening.

My earliest research in autumn 2001 found that screening at most European airports was carried out either by trained airport staff or by airport-hired private security firms. In either case, screening had to meet standards prescribed by an agency of the national government. And when Canada created its own post-9/11 airport security agency, the new CATSA did not do screening; instead, it hired qualified security companies, with compensation of screeners tailored to market conditions and living costs in different parts of the country, as any business would do.

My case for Trusted Traveler began with reflecting on my first two jobs after MIT, when I'd held a security clearance in order to work at my employers' companies, some of whose work was classified. Why should someone who had passed that kind of vetting and had no later problems be treated as a potential terrorist upon arriving at an airport? Or a police officer, or an active-duty member of the military? Two aviation colleagues, Rich Golaszewski, whom I knew from my work on airport privatization, and my friend Professor Michael Levine, co-authored a journal article soon after 9/11 arguing for a Trusted Traveler program. My own initial contribution was an op-ed in the *Wall Street Journal* in January 2002, noting that a Trusted Traveler program had been in operation at Ben Gurion Airport in Israel for four years by then.

Viggo and I then collaborated on a Reason policy study, "Rethinking Checked-Baggage Screening," released in July 2002. In addition to pointing out serious problems with first-generation explosive detection system (EDS) machines, we argued that TSA should shift its focus from detecting bad objects to detecting high-risk people.

That September I followed up with another Reason policy study, "Improving Airport Passenger Screening," whose focus was on significantly expanding the pilot program in the 2001 legislation that allowed just five airports to use TSA-certified security companies to provide their screening. The study cited data from a survey of airport directors we'd conducted which found that 25 percent of them would be interested in joining an expanded pilot program. Basically, the idea was to turn the tables on TSA. If forty or more opt-out airports could be gotten underway quickly, using approved contractors during the first two years when TSA was struggling to staff over four hundred airports with all-new employees, there would be a large demonstration effect that might lead Congress to change the law about TSA being the near-monopoly screening provider. Appendices to the report included (1) the full text of the longer-term opt-out provisions of the 2001 legislation (which few people knew about), (2) details about the widespread use of contract screening at major European airports, and (3) a summary of the numerous federal facilities where security is provided by private firms. House Aviation Subcommittee Chair John Mica (R-FL) and Sens. Richard Shelby (R-AL) and Larry Craig (R-ID) said positive things about our proposal, but it went nowhere in Congress.

The next year, 2003, I collaborated with our Public Affairs director George Passantino on a longer study, "A Risk-Based Airport Security Policy." It laid out in some detail how a system based on separating passengers into three groups would work: pre-vetted Trusted Travelers about whom much is known, ordinary travelers about whom little is known, and known high-risk passengers, who would get additional screening. The report also described existing US risk-based programs, including APIS, NEXUS, SENTRI, and Known Shipper.

That report got little support, but a few years later I tried again. "Airport Security: Time for a New Model" (2006) called for both risk-based separation of passengers, with different levels of screening for each, and devolution of screening to the airport level. For the latter point I analyzed TSA's chronic problem of allocating the right numbers of screeners to each airport (done only once a year) in a dynamic airline industry that adds and drops flights both seasonally and for strategic reasons. I gave a presentation along these lines at both American Enterprise Institute and Heritage Foundation, and also testified about this proposal before the House Subcommittee on Economic Security, Infrastructure Protection, and Cybersecurity, but nothing seemed to result from that.

Then, in mid-2008, I got an email from one of the economists at the International Transport Forum in Paris, an entity of the Organization for Economic Cooperation and Development (OECD). They were planning a symposium on transportation security in December. Having read my 2006 paper, the economist asked if I would be interested in using that frame of reference to compare the aviation security systems of Canada, Europe, and the United States—and present the paper at the symposium in Paris in December. They would pay €4000 and cover travel and lodging. Without realizing how much additional work this would require, I agreed.

What I learned in researching this paper, "Towards a Risk-Based Aviation Security Policy," reinforced my view that the US system was the worst of the three. But I also learned that while the rhetoric of senior aviation security officials in all three regions claimed their policies were "risk-based," none really took those words seriously. The paper was well received at the Paris symposium, resulting in an invitation for me to revise it a bit and present it again at ITF's annual conference in Leipzig, Germany, in May 2009. That was a large-scale event where I became acquainted with a number of fellow researchers and policymakers. ITF published the proceedings of the Paris Roundtable as *Terrorism and International Transport: Towards Risk-Based Security Policy* in 2009.

I continued critiquing TSA shortcomings in my e-newsletter *Airport Policy News*. And by the time of John Pistole's tenure as TSA Administrator (2010–2014), the ideas I had been championing had become more prominent in policy discussions. On the negative side, Pistole's regime began denying requests from individual airports to opt out from TSA-provided screening, as airports had been allowed to do starting in 2004 under the original legislation. In early 2011, while denying a request from the Springfield, Missouri, airport to opt out, Pistole announced that no more airports could participate. A few weeks later, Sen. Roy Blunt (R-MO) got a unanimous vote through the Senate to continue the opt-out program. It required the TSA to respond to an airport's request within thirty days and to report back to Congress the reasons for denial of any application. TSA rescinded its decision, and a number of additional (mostly small) airports opted out in subsequent years.

Things changed positively regarding Trusted Traveler under Pistole's administration. When I spoke on a panel at the annual convention of the Airports Council International—North America in autumn 2010, all four of us on my panel on airport security agreed that a risk-based approach featuring a Trusted Traveler program was a real need. One of the articles in my January 2011 newsletter was "Momentum Builds for Risk-Based Trusted Traveler Program." I noted news articles in major publications like the *Washington Post* citing security experts such as Brian Jenkins of Rand Corporation and law professor John Banzhaf, as well as the endorsement of the idea by the US Travel Association. A few months later, a Blue Ribbon Panel for Aviation Security released a heavyweight report calling for a three-tier checkpoint approach including a Trusted Traveler component. By mid-year, Pistole himself was giving speeches promising that such a program was coming.

That autumn, TSA rolled out a preliminary version of PreCheck, at Miami and DFW (for American Airlines frequent flyers) and at Atlanta and Detroit (for Delta frequent flyers). Since Miami is my home airport, I was among the very first to use the program, and wrote about it extensively. It's been expanded widely over subsequent years and is very popular with frequent flyers. Ten years after the 9/11 legislation was enacted, with language calling for some kind of Trusted Traveler program, we finally got one. I was proud to have played a part in giving the idea visibility over that decade.

Outsourced screening remained a largely unrealized goal. The idea continued to have fans in Congress, and in July 2012 I testified before the House Homeland Security Subcommittee on TSA's conflict of interest as a prime reason for getting TSA out of the screening business, devolving the responsibility to the airport level as in Europe. We followed up the next year with a Reason policy brief, "Overhauling US Airport Security Screening," including updated data on how screening is provided at most major European airports.

Two more-recent developments spurred increased interest in screening opt-out. One was the leak of a DHS Inspector General "Red Team" report on testing passenger checkpoints in 2015, in which screeners failed sixty-seven of seventy tests. And during the

2016 spring break travel season, when screening delays reached unprecedented levels, a number of major airport leaders seriously considered applying to opt out of TSA screening—including Atlanta, Charlotte, Minneapolis/St. Paul, San Jose, and Seattle. That was the first time airports of that size went public with the idea of opting out. But TSA and the airlines pulled out all the stops in time for Memorial Day weekend and Independence Day, and those airports decided not to go through the hassle of applying, especially since TSA screeners were now unionized and had defeated an attempt several years earlier by the Sacramento Airport to opt out.

So as this is written, ending TSA's built-in conflict of interest and improving both security and the passenger experience are still unfinished business for me.

Airport Pricing and Privatization

After all the various US calls by mayors to privatize their airports during the 1990s, that interest seemed to have dried up in the early 2000s. While I continued to chronicle the worldwide growth in airport privatization in my newsletter (and in the aviation chapter in Reason's *Annual Privatization Report*), there was no apparent market for new Reason policy papers on the subject. But with a team of market-oriented people running aviation policy during the George W. Bush administration, especially when Mary Peters was Transportation Secretary, we got an opportunity to advance the idea of airport runway pricing.

Runway Pricing

By 2007, congestion at the major New York airports (Kennedy, LaGuardia, and Newark) had reached horrendous proportions, and the US DOT created what is called an Aviation Rule-making Committee (ARC) to bring stakeholders together to brainstorm a solution. My friend D.J. Gribbin had rejoined the government when Mary Peters became Secretary of Transportation, becoming DOT Chief Counsel. And one day he called out of the blue to ask if I could help with the ARC's work.

By coincidence, earlier that year Reason had hired a young

Canadian economist, Ben Dachis, and he and I had been working on a possible runway pricing system for those three airports. When D. J. called me that autumn, we already had much of the work done—me doing the policy part and Ben creating a simulation model of pricing's impact on airport operations. Because we knew how controversial the proposed system would be, I had reached out to three aviation colleagues for assistance—and ended up commissioning each of them to write a supporting policy brief:

- George Donohue (George Mason University) had helped a university consortium develop a "war-game" exercise to test the responses of airport managers and airline schedulers to a hypothetical pricing system for LaGuardia Airport, whose positive results we applied in our study.
- Mike Levine (NYU Law School) drew on his extensive airline and airport experience to suggest tests that a real-world pricing system would need to pass.
- David Plavin (former aviation director of the New York airports) offered creative ideas for recycling the revenues from runway pricing.

Much of their material was already in hand by the time D. J. called, requesting my help.

So I flew to DC and took part in a long ARC meeting at DOT headquarters, with senior airline and airport people as well as senior FAA and DOT people. I offered only a few brief remarks on runway pricing, but the airline people were immediately hostile, rejecting the idea out of hand. In my journal, I wrote, "What a debacle!" about this meeting. The next week one of those airline people asked me to come back to DC for a kind of summit meeting, whose purpose was evidently to talk me out of going forward with our runway pricing study. When I told them my schedule did not permit another trip that soon, they agreed to a several-hour conference call in which they heatedly argued that pricing would not work, that it would be grossly unfair to incumbent airlines that had made major investments in terminal facilities (which suggests they thought it *would* work, and that new-entrant airlines might outbid them!), on and on for about two hours. I eventually called a halt, leaving them unhappy and worried about what might happen when our report came out.

Ben and I continued working, getting the report nearly finished by Thanksgiving weekend. When I returned to work the next Monday, Ben informed me that he'd decided to resign and move back to Canada. Fortunately, all that remained to do was some editing. Because I knew DOT was expecting the study, I got it on a fast track to be copyedited, formatted, and published.

"Congestion Pricing for the New York Airports: Reducing Delays while Promoting Growth and Competition," was released in mid-December. At seventy-one pages, it was the longest aviation policy study we'd ever done, but it was very comprehensive, and backed up by the three policy briefs by Donohue, Levine, and Plavin. The DOT was not in a position to mandate that the three airports implement runway pricing, and DOT ended up re-imposing some degree of slot controls at the airports (which did ease the congestion somewhat).

Both D. J. and Mary Peters liked the runway pricing idea, and in 2008, their last year in office, they drafted revisions to the DOT's "airport rates and charges policy." The changes made it legal for airports to use runway pricing to deal with congestion, instead of, or in addition to, traditional weight-based landing fees. The Air Transport Association filed suit to overturn the new policy, but after several years of litigation, they lost. So we won that battle—although no US airport has so far implemented runway pricing. Privatized London airports Heathrow and Gatwick *have* done so.

The Return of US Airport Privatization

Between 2000 and 2006 only four small airports applied for slots in the federal Airport Privatization Pilot Program, and all eventually withdrew due to some combination of local political opposition or a change of government priorities. But when Chicago mayor

Richard Daley applied for a slot to privatize Midway Airport in late 2006, the airport community and infrastructure investors perked up. The significance of the Midway transaction was two-fold. Not only was it a "large hub" commercial airport, but in addition, the city engaged in ultimately successful negotiation with its major airline, Southwest, over the terms and conditions of the planned long-term lease, and the other airlines then agreed. This was critically important, because the Pilot Program law requires 65 percent of the airlines serving the airport to approve, as well as airlines representing 65 percent of the annual landed weight—and at Midway, Southwest met both tests.

The credibility of the Midway deal led to serious consideration by leaders of New Orleans of privatizing its Louis Armstrong International Airport (which needed a major terminal modernization). I gave an invited presentation on airport privatization to the airport board in January 2009, and they commissioned an outside study on going forward. But local politics intervened, and New Orleans withdrew its application to the Pilot Program after fourteen months.

The winning bidder for Midway was unable to finance its aggressive offer, due to the financial markets collapse of 2008, and the city terminated its draft lease agreement in 2009, while retaining its slot in the Pilot Program. Meanwhile, under reform governor Luis Fortuno, the government of Puerto Rico applied for a slot in late 2009 for the San Juan International Airport. A new PPP agency created by Fortuno's administration analyzed a number of state-owned assets, and also did a long-term lease of two toll roads in Puerto Rico. The airline lease agreement template developed for Midway was adapted for the San Juan transaction, and won the approval of principal airlines American and JetBlue. Still, the approval process lasted longer than Fortuno's term, and his successor (from the opposite party) came under pressure to cancel the deal. Because this would have given Puerto Rico a black eye with the financial community, the deal ultimately went through in early 2013, thirty-eight months after Puerto Rico had applied for its slot. San Juan's now-privatized airport has a new terminal, and world-class shopping and restaurants.

This rebound in airport privatization led the American Association of Airport Executives (AAAE) to begin a new round of annual airport privatization/PPP conferences starting in 2011. I was the luncheon speaker for the 2012 conference in Miami and the 2013 conference in Washington, DC. As these events were taking place, Chicago's new mayor, Rahm Emanuel, restarted the process for Midway Airport in 2011. This time the city received two responsive bids, but at the eleventh hour, one of the bidders withdrew. Facing a skeptical city council, already unhappy over an unpopular parking privatization deal, Emanuel decided not to negotiate with the sole bidder, and surrendered its slot in the Pilot Program in spring 2013.

The renewed interest in airport privatization led Congress to revise the Pilot Program in 2012, increasing the number of slots from five to ten. I had strongly urged other reforms to make the process less of an obstacle course for airport owners and bidders, but the increase in slots was the only significant change in the FAA Modernization and Reform Act of 2012.

Since 2010, there have been four more slots granted, three for relatively small airports and one for a major one:

- Gwinnett County, Georgia's Briscoe Field, a general aviation (GA) airport near Atlanta that hoped to attract medium-range airline service (2010);
- Hendry County, Florida's Airglades Airport, a GA airport eighty miles north of Miami International, whose intended privatizer aims to expand it into an air-cargo reliever for MIA (2010);
- Westchester County, New York's White Plains Airport, with both GA and scheduled airline service (2016); and,
- St. Louis's Lambert International Airport (2017).

Gwinnet County withdrew its application in mid-2012 due to local political opposition, partly orchestrated by dominant Atlanta carrier Delta Airlines. Airglades and Westchester County remain active, with the former having already selected its private partner and the latter with a competitive procurement completed late in 2017 (but with the deal still to be negotiated with the winning bidder). The St. Louis filing took place as this chapter was being revised. If it goes forward to completion, it would be the largest US airport privatization to date, with passenger numbers nearly twice that of San Juan International.

The three major airports of the New York metro area—Kennedy, LaGuardia, and Newark—are widely recognized as among the worst US airports. In 2016, the Manhattan Institute commissioned me to research and write a policy study on rethinking the Port Authority of New York and New Jersey, which operates the airports, seaports, and major bridges and tunnels. As part of the research, I assembled data on recent sales and long-term leases of major airports, seaports, and tolled highway assets worldwide. My mid-range estimate of the market value of the three airports was $16.5 billion. "Reinventing the Port Authority of New York and New Jersey" was released in January 2017 as a joint Manhattan Institute/Reason Foundation policy study, and it received considerable media attention, especially in the New York metro area.

Overall, while we have not yet seen the major US airport privatization trend that I foresaw in the 1990s (which *has* taken place in most of the rest of the world, recently including France and Japan), the idea is finally gaining traction here in the United States. I outlined my thoughts on US prospects in an invited column in *Eno Transportation Weekly* in March 2017, "Does Airport Privatization Have a Future in the US?" My answer was a qualified yes.

Air Traffic Control Corporation

In the wake of the 9/11 disruption of aviation, I faced a challenge in keeping interest in serious ATC reform alive. I continued to hammer away on this via my monthly *ATC Reform News*; there was some interest from the Bush White House (especially OMB Director Mitch Daniels); and I could count on continued reports from the DOT Inspector General and the GAO to highlight deficiencies and failures at FAA. But I realized that in addition to putting out a steady stream of ideas challenging the status-quo

ATC paradigm, I would also have to find allies. As was the case with my work on surface transportation, I needed to get better plugged into the relevant industry organizations and get better acquainted with key players, beyond simply the airline people who'd been supportive prior to 9/11.

There had been a lot of media attention on ATC "privatization" during the last few years of the Clinton administration and the first year of the Bush administration, so organized opposition to the idea was building. The controllers' union, NATCA, was at that point headed by a populist firebrand, John Carr. As far as he was concerned, anything called "privatization" meant one of two things, both bad: either selling an existing agency to the highest private bidder or outsourcing its function to the lowest bidder. Either way, Carr portrayed this as wiping out union jobs.

In response to a 2002 NATCA White Paper opposing "privatization" of ATC, I authored a detailed Reason Foundation rebuttal, released in March 2003. Their piece attacked outsourcing of ATC (which none of us were advocating), never considered our actual 2001 proposal of "corporatization" (converting the existing ATC system into a user-funded non-profit corporation), seriously distorted the track record of overseas ATC corporations, and contained little or no analysis, just rhetoric. My rebuttal paper included as appendices (a) a bibliography of serious reports that called for structural and financial reform of the US ATC system, and (b) the statement by former FAA officials endorsing corporatization that we had released at our February 2001 news conference.

In those years NATCA was engaged in long-running litigation attempting to have FAA's successful and cost-effective Federal Contract Tower program declared illegal, on the grounds that ATC is "inherently governmental" and therefore, under OMB rules, cannot be contracted out. If they were to win, it would doom the existing contract towers, but even worse, make it impossible to convert the ATC system to a private, nonprofit corporation. I had gotten to know Carlos Bonilla, an attorney on the White House staff, and discussed the problem with him.

He drafted Executive Order 13264, declaring ATC to be *not* inherently governmental, and President Bush signed it on June 4, 2002. The next year, NATCA conducted an all-out campaign to include language overturning that EO as part of that year's FAA reauthorization bill. After months of infighting, chronicled in my newsletter, the White House issued a veto threat, and the NATCA language was removed from both House and Senate bills. As she had done with "my" previous Executive Order, Lou had a copy of EO 13264 framed, and it now hangs beside EO 12803 on my office wall.

Viggo Butler remained eager to help, and in May 2003 he invited me along as his guest for the spring outing of Conquistadores del Cielo, an organization for top aviation executives. At the event, held at a golf resort near Atlanta, I met and talked with the CEOs of four or five airlines and two former FAA Administrators who had signed our 2001 statement. It was a good networking event. Later that year, Dorothy Robyn (the infrastructure economist from the Clinton White House staff) and I published a full-page Viewpoint in *Aviation Week*, arguing that political squabbling over FAA reauthorization (due to NATCA lobbying to end the Contract Tower program) showed how ill-suited a tax-funded, politically controlled agency was to operating a high-tech service business. Already by that time there were twenty-nine ATC corporations in operation worldwide, including in Australia, Canada, Germany, and the UK, and we said the USA should do likewise. Our pairing was important to illustrate that ATC reform could and should be a bipartisan concern.

One of the few results of the 1997 Mineta Commission report was congressional action in 2000 to reorganize the FAA, pulling together into a "performance-based organization" all the portions of the agency that dealt with ATC operations, facilities, training, and technology development and procurement. This was intended to be a quasi-corporation, but headed not by a CEO but only by a Chief Operating Officer, reporting directly to the FAA Administrator—in other words, *reporting* to the safety regulator, instead of being *regulated* at arm's-length by the safety regulator. After three years of planning and recruiting, the "Air

Traffic Organization" made its debut at the end of 2003, with Russ Chew hired as its COO.

I had met Russ in late 2000, when former DOT Secretary Jim Burnley arranged a briefing session for Rep. Don Young (R-AK), who would take over as chairman of the House Transportation and Infrastructure Committee in January 2001. Jim arranged for three presenters: Russ Chew of American Airlines, someone on surface transportation, and me discussing ATC problems. Russ and I had not spoken again between that meeting and his appointment as the new COO, but I quickly added his email address to my ATC newsletter list.

After he'd been reading my newsletter for his first six months or so on the job, trying to convert an assemblage of bureaucratic fiefdoms into some semblance of a business organization, I began to get emails from Russ, and, later on, evening phone calls. He needed someone to vent to about the travails of reorganizing a vast bureaucracy. By 2004, we both thought it would be useful to meet up in person, but did not want to do this in any public place in DC where we might be spotted and set tongues wagging. We ended up meeting at a model railroad convention at a hotel in Crystal City, Virginia (across the river from DC). It turns out that Russ was a fellow model railroader, and in the same scale as me (O scale), so the venue had an added attraction for him besides talking with me. This relationship continued until Russ resigned in frustration in February 2007. (He was replaced by another former airline executive, Hank Krakowski, whom I also got to know.) I still have a folder of emails and notes from many phone conversations with Russ. I learned a lot about the inner workings of the FAA from these communications, making me even more determined to de-politicize the ATO.

I also signed up as a member of the Air Traffic Control Association (ATCA, not to be confused with NATCA), and attended its technical conference in Atlantic City and its large annual conference in Washington, DC. This was also an excellent networking opportunity. At the Atlantic City conference in March 2004, Russ shared the stage with the CEOs of corporatized (independent, user-funded, and hence de-politicized) ATC provider DFS of Germany and Canada's ATC provider, Nav Canada. Both CEOs told of their staffs' transition from lifelong civil servants to company employees; both had brought in senior executives from industry, and both mentioned that over the first few years they'd had to replace about 50 percent of senior managers who just could not cope with a performance-driven organization. Poor Russ knew that he had far less freedom of operation than those CEOs.

From that year onward, I attended the ATCA annual conference every fall, in later years speaking on or chairing panels on ATC reform and authoring articles in ATCA's *Journal of Air Traffic Control*.

Paying far closer attention to FAA and the ATO than I ever had before (and aided by exchanges with Russ), my newsletter kept up steady criticisms, as well as reports on successes of overseas ATC corporations. In September 2004, I highlighted how the House Appropriations Committee was still making the key decisions on procurement of advanced technologies, instead of Russ Chew. My piece concluded that, "Sad to say, in functional terms, the ATO's actual customers are the members of those congressional committees. Until that changes, it's not going to be much of a business."

By 2005, it was clear that the FAA was in a serious budget crunch, as airline ticket tax revenues (based on a percentage of the ticket price) were not keeping pace with the growth of travel and ATC activity. Airline financial analyst Vaughn Cordle, had seen this coming, so the May 2005 Reason policy study we co-authored, "Resolving the Crisis in Air Traffic Control Funding," quantified the recent decline and projected a worsening future. It called for shifting from ticket taxes to ATC fees, and included a table showing that all but a handful of the world's countries charged ATC fees, generally based on the charging principles specified by the International Civil Aviation Organization (ICAO).

This report caught the attention of FAA Administrator Marion Blakey, whose senior staff had begun looking into the idea of shifting from taxes to user fees. The agency held a "Trust Fund

Forum" in April 2005, at which Vaughn summarized our proposal, and I followed up with a full-page Viewpoint in *Aviation Week* the next month. By that summer I was having meetings with Blakey's policy director, Sharon Pinkerton (whom I'd met in 2001 when she was a senior staffer for Aviation Subcommittee Chair John Mica), and that October Sharon arranged an hour-long session with Administrator Blakey to discuss strategy and tactics for these reforms.

The airline trade group, Air Transport Association, seized on the idea of replacing ticket taxes with ATC fees, and asked me in to brainstorm the idea with its staff on several occasions. Unfortunately, however, they decided that a shift to ATC fees could give them a major advantage over competition from business jets and relatively new services such as NetJets. That was because under the long-established user-tax funding system, business jets paid only a small fuel tax. Even though they accounted for more than 10 percent of ATC-controlled flight hours, their contribution to the system's revenue was only around one percent. But the airlines ignored the ICAO charging principles, used worldwide, under which a controlled flight from A to B is charged a fee based on the weight of the plane and the distance flown. That means a small Learjet pays a modest fraction of what a 757 pays, due to the larger plane's weight. ATA's mantra was "a blip is a blip"—i.e., it costs the ATC system the same to control any plane, regardless of weight. But charging such high fees would be a huge cost increase to private aviation. ATA ignored this, and began a TV ad campaign maligning business jets as free-loaders.

The bizjets trade group, National Business Aviation Association (NBAA), began lobbying heavily against both ATA and FAA over user fees. I saw a good cause being sabotaged by the airlines going overboard, and decided to try setting the record straight via a new policy study. I purchased detailed information from an aviation data company on fifteen popular bizjets of all sizes. The data included fuel consumption and the average annual miles and hours flown for each one. This enabled me to calculate what each one would pay per year:

- In current FAA fuel taxes;
- In ICAO-type weight-distance charges using Nav Canada's charging formula; or,
- In ATA's proposed "a blip is a blip" approach, disregarding aircraft weight.

The results showed that for most bizjets, a Nav Canada-type fee would cost more than the fuel tax, but nowhere near as much as the ATA-type fee that ignored weight. I also showed that if a shift to user fees facilitated a more efficient, modernized system that reduced delays by eliminating non-direct routes and holding patterns, it would take only a few percent reduction in annual flight hours to make up in operating cost savings the extra cost of shifting to weight-distance charges.

I thought this report, with hard numbers, would really change the debate. But politics is seldom decided by facts, as opposed to emotional rhetoric. ATA and NBAA continued their war of words. FAA released its detailed user-fee funding proposal in February 2007, which included the ability for the agency to issue revenue bonds for modernization, backed by the user-fee revenue stream. In my newsletter, however, I pointed out that under the proposal the revenues would still be paid into the US Treasury (just like the aviation taxes) and could only be spent when and as Congress approved. So congressional micromanagement would remain, and it's doubtful that bond-buyers would consider the fees as a dependable revenue stream, given periodic lapsing of taxing authority and government shut-downs. Moreover, FAA caved on user fees for bizjets: all turbine-powered aircraft would have continued to pay the existing fuel taxes. The FAA's proposal was dead on arrival in Congress, and the agency eventually threw in the towel on shifting from user taxes to user fees.

With this failure impending, the Heritage Foundation asked me to do a new report, restating the case for real corporatization. I agreed, as long as Reason could publish it as well. By this time, there were several serious international studies providing before and after comparisons of ATC performance in countries that had corporatized, and they were all positive. "The Urgent Need to Reform the FAA's Air Traffic Control System," March 2007, summarized this evidence and also cited the divestiture during the Reagan administration of Washington National and Dulles Airports (which had previously been owned by the federal government and paid for as line items in the FAA's annual budget). That, too, had been politically difficult, but those difficulties had been overcome, and the devolved airports—now with revenue-bonding authority—had made major improvements.

Norm Mineta had stepped down as DOT Secretary in 2006, and Mary Peters took his place. I'd gotten to know Mary and her senior people when she'd been Federal Highways Administrator during the Bush administration's first term. In discussing my frustrations with my friend, former FAA Administrator Langhorne Bond, he suggested that we meet with Mary to make the case for going beyond the FAA's user fees and bonding proposal, to actually divest the ATO, converting it into something like Nav Canada. We got our wish, and met with Mary and top officials Jeff Shane, Tyler Duvall, and Andy Steinberg in November 2006, having a substantive discussion for nearly an hour. Unfortunately, the November 7 election resulted in Democrats gaining majorities in both House and Senate, which did not bode well for a major market-oriented reform.

My next target was the White House policy staff. I knew Karl Zinsmeister, chief domestic policy advisor (and a former *Reason* magazine author). I met with him periodically about ATC reform. With FAA Administrator Blakey's five-year term due to expire in September 2007, I talked with Karl about finding a market-oriented successor. Karl invited Langhorne and me to breakfast, and we recommended Mike Levine, who as far as we knew was a Democrat and might be confirmable despite being nominated by President Bush. Mike had a sterling reputation in aviation circles for his role in helping bring about airline deregulation at the Civil Aeronautics Board in 1978, for having been a senior executive at several post-deregulation airlines, and for having encyclopedic knowledge of aviation law.

I discussed the idea with Mike (whom I'd known since the

1970s when he taught at Caltech and USC in Los Angeles), and he was willing to spend a few days in Washington meeting key people, which he did that July. But nothing ever came of it. The White House never put forward a nominee for Administrator, and Deputy Administrator Bobby Sturgell served as Acting Administrator for the remainder of Bush's second term.

One fan of my newsletter turned out to be Ken Mead, the DOT Inspector General during both the Clinton and Bush administrations. After Ken stepped down in February 2006, he would send occasional emails responding to newsletter articles, and occasionally call to talk about one point or another. He seemed quite friendly toward ATC corporatization. By the first year of the Obama administration, we would occasionally get together for a meal when I was in DC. At a lunch meeting in December 2009, we discussed a possible pro-corporatization coalition.

In February 2010, Ken (who by then was doing legal work for private pilots' group AOPA) arranged to come visit me in my Florida home office, bringing along new AOPA president Craig Fuller, whom I'd never met. What had been intended as an hour-long meeting ended up as about two and a half hours. Craig was a veteran of the Reagan White House, and though a long-time private pilot, was relatively new to DC's aviation politics. Though under previous CEOs, AOPA had fiercely opposed ATC corporatization or privatization, Craig was willing to be educated on the subject, and we had a great meeting. (He and Ken also enjoyed seeing my large, under-construction model railroad layout.)

My Reason colleague Shirley Ybarra earlier in her career had helped DOT Secretary Elizabeth Dole get through Congress the legislation to divest National and Dulles airports. In January 2010, Shirley and I visited former governor John Engler, then CEO of the National Association of Manufacturers, to discuss possible NAM interest in Reason's approach to impending *surface transportation* reauthorization. To our surprise, Engler steered the conversation to ATC reform. He'd evidently been reading my newsletter, and also remembered the privatization ideas we'd provided him in the 1990s when he was governor of Michigan.

I left that meeting with an assignment: produce a paper for him on the business case for converting the ATO to a self-funded ATC Corporation.

That paper went through several drafts (being vetted by one of his staffers), and he liked the end product. But it wasn't until April 2011 that Shirley and I had a follow-up meeting with Engler—and by then he'd changed jobs and was CEO of the Business Roundtable (BRT). He was now ready to devote serious time and BRT resources to advancing ATC reform. His new challenge to me was to recruit a team of ATC experts who could develop a business plan and build a coalition to corporatize the ATO.

By mid-June I had assembled that group, and we had our first meeting. They included Russ Chew (former COO of the ATO), Langhorne Bond (former FAA Administrator), Ken Mead (former DOT Inspector General), Jeff Shane (former DOT Under Secretary for Policy), Rich Golaszewski (FAA number-cruncher for GRA, Inc.), John Strong (academic, co-author of *Managing the Skies*), David Schaffer (former counsel, House Aviation Subcommittee), Shirley Ybarra (former assistant to DOT Secretary Elizabeth Dole), and me.

We had meetings about every other month, debating whether the Clinton USATS model (government corporation) or the Nav Canada model (private, nonprofit) was better and discussing which aviation stakeholder groups might support or oppose a corporatization effort. We developed an increasingly detailed "term sheet" outlining the corporation's features and attributes, including a balanced governing board of aviation stakeholders, but left open the question of which type of corporation—government or private nonprofit. We planned to decide that based on stakeholder feedback. We kept the project under wraps, pending briefings of the principal stakeholder groups.

During the second half of 2011, with Ken Mead's encouragement, I had two dinner meetings aimed at wooing Ed Bolen of NBAA. The first involved just Craig Fuller, Ed, and me and did not get into ATC reform, per se, but I emphasized to Ed how off-base and foolish the airlines' anti-bizjets campaign had been. The second dinner added Ken and Jeff Shane; we discussed an array of aviation issues, including the BRT project. Ed was on his best behavior, simply taking in information rather than disputing any of it.

Also that autumn, Jeff Shane and I were invited to brief the FAA Management Advisory Council (MAC) on ATC reform. I'd been asked specifically to discuss the case for separating aviation safety regulation from ATC service provision, as had been ICAO policy since 2001 (but which the USA has never adopted). That seemed to get a largely positive hearing from most of the members, with the exception of NATCA president Paul Rinaldi and (ex-officio) FAA Administrator Michael Huerta. Unknown to me at the time, MAC chairwoman Gina Marie Lindsay and member Steve Van Beek had been driving an agenda on the MAC that both the funding and governance of FAA were broken and needed to be replaced, and which resulted in a strong final report proposing ATC corporatization at the end of their terms on the MAC, in January 2014.

In April 2012, the BRT group did its first stakeholder briefing, in the conference room at Airlines for America (A4A, the new name of the former ATA). By this point, A4A had new leadership, and its senior policy person was Sharon Pinkerton. Engler, Rich Golaszewski, and I gave the briefing. The response was mildly positive, though it seemed to me that Sharon was leery of getting back into battles with the bizjet people. We briefed AOPA's Craig Fuller in July, and that seemed to go well. We were very nervous about briefing the other major stakeholder, NATCA, and held off doing that for the rest of the year. Meanwhile, I discussed the BRT project with Steve Van Beek, whom I'd known for years, because of his long background in the airport community, as well as his role at the FAA MAC. I brought him to meet our BRT project coordinator, former Senate staffer Matt Sonnesyn, and we added Steve to the project team.

The next year, 2013, proved to be a major breakthrough. In February, I spoke at the first World Air Traffic Management Congress in Madrid, sponsored by the membership organization for ATC providers, CANSO and our own ATCA (which sponsored my trip). Former ATO CEOs Russ Chew and Hank

Krakowski were both there, and I was invited to the *Jane's Airports* annual awards dinner, where I met the deputy COO of the ATO, Terri Bristol—who told me she was a regular reader of my ATC newsletter.

In March 2013, the federal government budget sequester went into effect, imposing serious cuts on FAA and most other agencies. For air traffic control, the consequences were furloughs for controllers of one day off without pay every two weeks, and the threatened shutdown of several hundred contract towers unless Congress provided an emergency budget fix. On the second day of the furloughs, I got a call from *Huffington Post*, inviting me to take part in a half-hour live-streamed discussion of the impact of the sequester on air traffic control. They could use the video camera in my laptop to connect me with both audio and video. I agreed, and they set up the connection.

There were three or four participants besides me, and one of them was NATCA president Paul Rinaldi. I should explain that since the John Carr days, NATCA members had elected two very sensible union presidents, of which Paul was the second. I took advantage of the opportunity to state, several times during the half hour, that such an outrageous interference in ATC operations could not happen in most other developed countries, because they had all *de-politicized* their ATC systems, insulating them from government budgets. I think I mentioned Australia, Canada, Germany, and the UK in this regard.

The next day NATCA headquarters in DC called to ask how often I got to Washington, because Paul wanted to meet with me. As luck would have it, I was scheduled to be there the following week, so they set up an appointment. Matt Sonnesyn from BRT joined me for the hour-long meeting at NATCA headquarters, with Paul and his VP, Trish Gilbert. Given my previous history with NATCA in the John Carr days, and NATCA's long history of being anti-privatization, both Paul and I recognized the irony of the situation. But we had a very engaging discussion of the case—not for sale or outsourcing—but for conversion of the existing ATO into something like Nav Canada. They had already done a bit of research, talking with their ATC union counterparts in Canada and the UK, and had gotten positive reports. So Matt and I explained the BRT project, and apologized for our long delay in arranging a briefing about it—but now they'd just had it.

A few weeks later, on May 22, we gathered the top people of the three main stakeholders in the conference room at BRT headquarters: Nick Callio and Sharon Pinkerton of A4A, Paul Rinaldi and Trish Gilbert of NATCA, and Craig Fuller and Ken Mead (now general counsel) of AOPA. Engler, Matt, Russ Chew and I handed out the latest version of the ATC corporation term sheet and walked them through it. When we got to the general discussion part, one of them asked if we really thought a government corporation was preferable to a private, nonprofit like Nav Canada. We all said no, but we thought a government corporation would be easier to get through Congress. Their response—all three groups—was that we should go for what we thought would work best, and we all agreed that Nav Canada was the better model.

And they were genuinely on board. NATCA invited me to be on a panel to discuss ATC reform at its July conference held jointly with airline union ALPA, and I agreed. Craig was interested in joining Matt and the governor in private briefings for the heads of the relevant House and Senate authorizing committees—Senate Commerce and House Transportation and Infrastructure. We were still uncertain about Ed Bolen of NBAA, and strongly suspected that based on past behavior, he would all-out oppose corporatization (as proved to be the case).

That summer the Eno Center for Transportation decided to launch an ATC reform project of its own. The idea (not knowing about the BRT project) was to create a working group of all the aviation stakeholders to study the problems plaguing the ATC system (as highlighted most recently by the sequester). Eno recruited as co-chairs former DOT Secretary Jim Burnley (R) and former Senator Byron Dorgan (D), and had Russ Chew address the first meeting.

Meanwhile, with interest in corporatization heating up, I'd launched two new policy research efforts. One had been suggested by friend and FAA consultant Gary Church: a quantitative study of the case for consolidating and modernizing FAA's aging facilities. The other was commissioned by Chris DeMuth at the Hudson Institute: a study by me documenting FAA's resistance to serious innovation and contrasting that with the best of the ATC corporations overseas. On the latter study, when I finished the draft, Hudson convened a half-day workshop at which twenty transportation and aviation experts provided feedback; they generally agreed with my basic thesis that the Air Traffic Organization was conservative and status-quo oriented because it is embedded within the aviation safety regulator, rather than being regulated at arm's-length as is the case for innovative firms like Boeing, Honeywell, Saab Sensis, and others.

Former DOT Secretary Burnley, who'd attended the Hudson workshop, recommended to Eno CEO Joshua Schank that I make a presentation on my findings at the next ATC reform meeting. It shifted opinion within the group toward corporatization. They ended up having working group meetings just about every month, and invited me to become a member. I decided this was important enough to do so, and participated either by telephone or (most of the time) by flying to DC for these monthly meetings.

That fall I published the first of several invited articles on ATC reform in *Professional Pilot* magazine (aiming to reach business jet pilots), and also began a regular column for the quarterly international magazine *Air Traffic Management*. And my panel at the ATCA annual meeting in October, which included Nav Canada CEO John Crichton and NATCA president Paul Rinaldi, was the talk of the event. Having the controllers' union publicly support corporatization was a very big deal.

Several more developments wrapped up the year. Engler and one or two other members of the BRT task force briefed House T&I Committee chair Bill Shuster, and Shuster's subsequent speech on ATC reform was very positive. The COO of the Air Traffic Organization, David Grizzle, announced his retirement effective December 31 and (privately) asked if he could join the BRT task force, which we were glad to agree to. Both GAO and the DOT Inspector General's Office launched new studies on the issues that would be involved in ATC corporatization.

The year 2014 proved to be a big one for air traffic reform. In January, the outgoing FAA Management Advisory Council released its unanimous report titled "FAA and Aviation Policy Reform: Now Is the Time." It laid out the FAA's dire funding situation and called for reform of the structure of FAA and the funding and governance of the ATC system, including the replacement of the current array of aviation taxes with "transparent schedules of cost-based fees" to fund ATC. It included a table of organization models, including Australia, Canada, Germany, and the UK—all of which have ATC corporations.

At the 2014 Transportation Research Board annual meeting, Steve Van Beek chaired an excellent panel that included people from A4A, Paul Rinaldi of NATCA, and a senior person from Boeing. In April, at the US Chamber of Commerce's annual aviation summit, I was on a panel chaired by former American Airlines CEO Bob Crandall (a long-time advocate of ATC corporatization), along with Van Beek and opponent Ed Bolen of NBAA. Both David Grizzle and Dorothy Robyn joined the ongoing Eno project.

In July, David, Dorothy, and I did an invited briefing for senior staffers of the House Aviation Subcommittee on ATC corporatization. Accompanying us was David Weingart, former FAA chief of staff who'd been recruited by GRA, Inc., to do detailed analysis of FAA data on ATC revenue, cost, and flight activity for a funded BRT study. That August I brainstormed with Matt Sturges of the House T&I Committee ideas for its initial hearing on ATC reform, for that September. Given that BRT's role was now public knowledge, thanks in part to a long *Wall Street Journal* article, they wanted Engler to testify, so I discussed that with Matt Sonnesyn, who asked me to do a first draft of testimony for the former governor. In November, the House T&I Committee held its context-setting hearing on ATC reform as part of the next FAA reauthorization. Engler did well, and his testimony was pretty close to my first draft. The BRT group, whose leader by this point was David Grizzle, was refining a more-detailed ATC corporation "term sheet" during the autumn months.

December included a visit by Eno working group members to Nav Canada headquarters in Ottawa, for those (including me) who had never been there. CEO John Crichton and several others gave us very useful briefings in the morning, followed by a visit to the development center and the control tower at the Ottawa Airport. Even though I knew a great deal about Nav Canada, I learned new things, and was even more impressed by seeing the facilities and talking with various officials, engineers, and controllers.

Early 2015 brought more progress. BRT convened an aviation stakeholder briefing session, with GRA presenting results of a study on the impact of alternative ATC fee structures. In February, I took part in two more House T&I Committee events. The first was a private briefing by Dorothy, David, and me for Chairman Shuster and Ranking Member DeFazio. The latter asked many good questions, and we briefers all viewed the meeting as very positive. That afternoon Chairman Shuster hosted a "Roundtable Policy Discussion" on ATC reform for T&I Committee members, at which I spoke along with senior people from A4A, AOPA, NATCA, the DOT Inspector General's Office, and aerospace company Honeywell. That was followed in March by a formal hearing, at which I again testified, and American Airlines CEO Doug Parker declared that the airlines wanted the ATO separated from FAA and converted into a user-funded nonprofit corporation. Major media coverage resulted.

We expected a House corporatization bill by mid-summer, so that spring TRB asked me to help organize a July symposium on ATC reform. I recruited Jeff Shane (now chief counsel for International Air Transportation Association in Montreal) to provide opening remarks. That event went very well, and I helped a TRB staff member edit the summary of proceedings. I also did several briefings for staffers of the Senate Commerce Committee and its Aviation Subcommittee. The final meeting of the Eno working group took part in May 2015, approving the final report (recommending either a government corporation or a private nonprofit).

The Senate Commerce Committee, on the same day, held its first hearing on ATC reform, at which the Eno group's co-chairman, former senator Dorgan, testified in favor of corporatization, as did NATCA's Paul Rinaldi. At the end of the month, *Aviation Week* published my guest editorial on the subject. By June, the House subcommittee had a draft outline of its corporatization proposal, and several of us gave feedback. And TRB's July symposium on ATC reform went very well, with an outstanding opening keynote by Jeff Shane.

But all was not sweetness and light, as DC awaited the release of Chairman Shuster's FAA reauthorization bill with its expected ATC corporation section. First, senior FAA officials took a defensive stance, variously asking what problem reformers were trying to solve, defending progress on ATC modernization, and stating that if major reform were to occur, there must be unanimity among all the stakeholders—which would hand NBAA veto power. And the naysayers by this point included Delta Airlines, which had figured out a way to tweak its flight times (in real time) to attain the best on-time record in the industry, and did not really want to spend a small fortune adding new technology to the oldest fleet of planes in the US airline industry. As A4A began to take a strong position in favor of corporatization, Delta quit the organization.

And, to my dismay, Craig Fuller, whose contract as CEO of AOPA had not been renewed, became chairman of a new FAA Management Advisory Council that began walking back the previous MAC's unanimous support for corporatization. It released drafts of a vague plan to take the entire FAA off-budget, a position that ranking member (of House T&I) DeFazio seemed to be embracing in remarks at a September 2015 aviation conference. He called for converting the FAA itself into a federal government corporation funded by aviation user taxes. I explained in my newsletter that keeping ATC and safety regulation together would fail to produce arm's-length safety regulation and would therefore not fix the ATO's status-quo culture.

The year 2016 dawned with the promise that Shuster's ATC reform proposal would finally be introduced. It was released in early February, apparently without being shared in advance with DeFazio or Aviation Subcommittee Ranking Member Rick Larsen. At the introductory hearing on the bill, at which I testified alongside Paul Rinaldi, DeFazio came out with guns blazing. Gone was his alternative proposal for an FAA corporation. Instead, he attacked corporatization as "privatization," thereby conjuring up the ghost of former NATCA populist John Carr—either selling the system to the highest bidder or contracting it out to the lowest bidder. Testifying a few seats over from me, Ed Bolen argued that Shuster's bill would give "taxing" power to a small group of aviation insiders, the major airlines. The chair recognized me to respond that even a government utility such as TVA does not tax: it sends *bills* to its customers for the service they have used. In this polarized environment, Shuster called for a vote on the corporatization section of the FAA bill for the very next day, and it passed on a strictly party-line vote, after a few amendments. Not an auspicious start.

NBAA created and funded an Alliance for Aviation Across America (Ed Bolen, chairman), which bamboozled small-city mayors and rural-state congress members into believing his mantra that ATC "privatization" meant turning over the ATC system to the major airlines, and that this threatened the continuation of control towers at small airports across the country. These efforts (which never mentioned NBAA's real motivation—to continue allowing its bizjet members to get ATC services practically for free) sufficiently worried Senate members from rural states that the Senate FAA reauthorization bill avoided an ATC reform section altogether. And in the House, the tax-writing Ways and Means Committee did not prepare the needed provision to reduce the large majority of aviation excise taxes starting in the year that the ATC corporation would begin charging users for ATC services. Without that provision, airspace users would end up paying both the existing aviation taxes and the new ATC fees. Consequently, by the time the House bill reached the floor, the ATC corporation section had been dropped. In the end, the two houses simply voted to extend the current legislation to September 30, 2017, leaving ATC reform to be debated anew in 2017.

In the months since then, I continued to write and speak in various forums, and BRT, Eno, A4A, and NATCA remained committed to this reform. We picked up editorial endorsements from *Aviation Week,* the *Boston Herald,* the *Chicago Tribune, Miami Herald, Orlando Sentinel, Wall Street Journal,* the *Washington Post,* and *USA Today.* The only major editorial dissent came from the *New York Times.* I also had to do battle with a small set of conservative groups that misinterpreted the Shuster bill provisions for a smooth transfer of ATO staff to the new corporation as "a give-away to unions." I'm pleased to say that think-tank transportation experts from Brookings, Cato Institute, Competitive Enterprises Institute, Heritage Foundation, Hudson Institute, and the National Taxpayers Union were all on board. So were many former senior officials of FAA and DOT.

I had several meetings with T&I Committee senior staff to discuss how to counter the arguments made against the 2016 bill. First, to defuse the claim about the corporation being "dominated by the big airlines" (based on four out of thirteen board members to be nominated by A4A), I suggested only one or two nominated by A4A, one by *regional* airlines (which serve smaller airports), and another for *cargo* airlines. Next, I said they needed strong language about ensuring access to ATC services for small airports and reassurance about continuation of contract towers. Third, the *airport* community should also be recognized as a key stakeholder that would nominate a board member. Finally, to deal with conservative union concerns, a more direct no-strike provision was needed (and I'd already been assured by Paul Rinaldi that this would be no problem for NATCA). All these changes were made, producing a much stronger 2017 bill.

The resulting bill was such an improvement that Rep. Sam Graves (R-MO), co-chair of the General Aviation Caucus in the House, who had voted against the 2016 bill, endorsed and voted for the improved 2017 version in June. This time around, the new Trump administration had announced support for ATC corporatization, with D. J. Gribbin as the White House point man on infrastructure. New DOT Secretary Elaine Chao also strongly endorsed the idea, as did House GOP leadership (Reps. Paul Ryan and Kevin McCarthy). Delta Airlines, under a new CEO, switched sides to favor corporatization. When the T&I Committee voted on the 2017 version in June, the bill passed again, with more votes than the previous year.

To my shock and dismay, despite being given everything they had asked for, AOPA joined with NBAA and other general aviation groups in all-out opposition. And due to the concerns expressed by rural officials over alleged threats to small-city airports, there was still no ATC reform provision in the corresponding Senate committee's FAA bill. Chairman Shuster promised to bring the FAA bill to the House floor after Labor Day, this time including a revenue title, and OMB's 10-year budget projection showed the reduced FAA spending starting in the projected year that the cut-over would take place. But tax reform and potential government shut-downs took up most of the remaining legislative time through the end of 2017.

In early February 2018 the word was quietly passed to supporters that the House FAA bill would be on the floor for a vote by the second week of March. But to everyone's surprise, on February 27, Shuster announced that he was giving up and would remove the ATC corporation provision from the bill. As *Politico* subsequently reported, the decision to go forward had been based on President Trump having committed to House Leadership at the end of January that he would lobby wavering House Republicans to support the bill, ensuring enough votes to pass it. But the weekend before Feb. 27th, the White House informed the T&I Committee that Trump would not lobby for the bill after all. Shuster and the Leadership apparently decided that pulling ATC from the bill was less bad than having it defeated.

I've gone into this much detail simply to illustrate that bringing about large-scale public policy change can be very difficult. Those who are wedded to a mediocre status quo have considerable inertia on their side—what Milton Friedman called "the tyranny of the status quo." And those who benefit from that status quo, such as business jet owners and private pilots, will fight doggedly to preserve their interests. Despite this early 2018 loss, I will pick myself up and continue the battle.

———

To sum up, of my goals for changing US aviation policy, there have been wins and losses. In aviation security, we've won on Trusted Traveler but have only whittled away at TSA's built-in conflict of interest in both operating and regulating airport security. In airports, we kept the flame of US airport privatization alive, and it is seeing a new level of interest from hard-pressed airport owners like at St. Louis. Airport runway pricing has been legalized, but it will likely take privatization of a congested airport to bring about its first US implementation.

And on air traffic control, my vision of a self-supporting ATC corporation has been realized in more than sixty countries, since the creation of Airways New Zealand in 1987. We've made major progress in this country discrediting the old paradigm. There is widespread understanding of the case for separating air safety regulation from the provision of ATC services. There are endless reports from the GAO and the DOT Inspector General showing that the "reforms" Congress has imposed on FAA have not solved its large problems. And there is growing understanding within aviation that corporatization is a better model than the politicized status quo. The key question is how long it will take to overcome opposition from those who benefit strongly from the status quo—mostly owners of private planes and those in Congress who don't want to give up their ability to micromanage ATC legislatively. So this battle has a few more rounds to go.

Chapter 14

Reflections on Past and Future

As I write this concluding chapter, it's November 2017. Next year will mark the fiftieth anniversary of Lanny Friedlander creating *Reason* magazine. And it will be my forty-ninth year of being involved with this venture. This seems like an appropriate time to reflect on the institution that I helped create—what it's accomplished, where it's tried but not yet succeeded, and where it hopes to go in coming decades. I'm still a Reason Foundation staff member and board member, but these are my personal views, as founder.

To begin with, today's Reason Foundation is successful beyond anything I imagined when we created Reason Enterprises or its successor, the Foundation itself. Yes, we needed to give the magazine a more sustainable home, and I had vague ambitions for the organization to evolve someday into something like RAND Corporation, but no clear idea on how to do this. But thanks to the support of thousands of individuals and dozens of foundations, we've made this upstart into a serious player on a national scale.

Reason's journalism division—the print magazine, Reason.com, and *Reason TV*—is now a serious participant in the national conversation on politics, public policy, and culture. A few examples from 2017 include:

- A few weeks after Donald Trump's inauguration, *Vanity Fair* sought out Editor-in-Chief Katherine Mangu-Ward for a piece examining media difficulties in covering the new president.
- Robby Soave's online commentary attributing Trump's victory to a backlash against political correctness was cited by *The Washington Post*, *The Wall Street Journal*, other leading newspapers, Bloomberg, *The Daily Beast*, InstaPundit, and many others.

- Peter Suderman's scoop that the IRS would not reject tax returns that lacked an answer to the question on health insurance was covered in *all the major media*, both print and broadcast.
- The *Washington Post* cited C.J. Ciaramella's finding that asset forfeiture in Chicago affected mostly people in poor, black neighborhoods.
- And when Trump's border wall became a focus of debate, the *New York Times* editorial board recommended *Reason's* cover story explaining why such a wall would not work.

Our public policy work also scored impressive media hits in 2017.

- My own work on air traffic control reform was cited in a number of editorial endorsements of the House bill, including those of the *Wall Street Journal*, the *Chicago Tribune*, and the *Orange County Register*, and my op-eds appeared in dozens of papers. My *Reason* cover story on the battle over ATC reform was distributed by the staff of the House Transportation and Infrastructure Committee.
- Reason Foundation's links to the Trump transportation transition team also received extensive media coverage, and I became a fairly regular source for media such as Bloomberg, *Bond Buyer*, and *Congressional Quarterly* on the evolving Trump infrastructure plan.
- The foundation's Pension Integrity Project's successes in getting serious reforms adopted in Arizona, Michigan, and South Carolina (so far) attracted significant positive media coverage in those states.

Overall, our journalism and policy work was cited or mentioned in 8,238 print and online media stories in FY 2017, reaching a circulation of 900 million readers. There were 1,200 television and radio appearances, a 12 percent increase over FY 2016.

It's also gratifying that many Reason interns over the years have gone on to build careers in media or public policy. In the public policy world, my 1989 intern, John Hood, went on to create and run the John Locke Foundation in North Carolina, and more recently became president of the John William Pope Foundation. My 1990 intern, Bill Eggers, went on to a job at Heritage Foundation, but we hired him back in 1992 to help staff our new Privatization Center. He's had a thriving career since his Reason years at Deloitte's Washington, DC, office, from which he's produced several books and numerous policy papers. Former magazine interns Rob Pollock and James Taranto went on to the *Wall Street Journal*, where Rob became a member of the editorial board and James first helmed the Best of the Web feature and is now the op-ed page editor. And my 1990 summer intern, David Rhodes, went into journalism, and by 2011 was named president of CBS News.

On the premise that success leads to success, over the years Reason donors have responded positively to our increasing effectiveness. In fiscal year 2017, revenue was $13.3 million, up from $11.8 million the previous year. Expenses totaled $12.5 million, compared with $10.7 million the year before. At the November 2017 board meeting, I learned that the organization has seventy-three full-time people plus some part-timers and contractors. The board approved a record-high budget for FY 2018 of $13.8 million.

Changing the World?

As noted in Chapter 8, for the magazine's twentieth anniversary in 1988, I wrote a *Reason* article called "Things Are a Lot Groovier Now," comparing the status of economic and personal liberty then with the dismal state of things in 1968 (which included assassinations, campus takeovers, the military draft, and an amazing array of restrictions that had been done away with by 1988). Is liberty more secure thirty years later?

On a global level, the most dramatic change since 1988 was the collapse of the Soviet Union and the liberation of what my generation grew up calling the "captive nations" of Central and Eastern Europe. The Cold War and the threat of nuclear annihilation were over. Almost as monumental has been the transformation of "Red China" into a still repressive but far more open state-capitalist regime and the emergence there of a huge and growing middle class. In the post-Cold War glow of the 1990s, the "Washington consensus" for free markets and less-statist governments gained widespread acceptance in a large swathe of developing countries, especially in Latin America. I was among many Americans who thought that socialism was dead and buried (apart from a handful of outliers such as Cuba and North Korea).

But the new century has thrown cold water on that naïve optimism. The 9/11 attack on the United States was a brutal wake-up call, which led to massive and costly invasions and failed nation-building efforts in Iraq and Afghanistan. And a new wave of what *The Economist* dubbed "personalized authoritarian rule" swept Latin America, encompassing Argentina, Bolivia, Ecuador, Nicaragua, and (in its most extreme form) Venezuela. Asia saw new authoritarian regimes emerge in Malaysia, the Philippines, and Thailand. And newly assertive Russia and China—defying long-established international law—made aggressive forays beyond their borders, notably in Ukraine and the South China Sea. As the late political scientist (and contributor to the Reason Foundation book *Defending a Free Society*) Rudy Rummel had predicted, a multi-polar world turns out to be less stable and more conflict-filled than the world dominated by the two Cold War superpowers.

These are sobering developments for any advocate of liberty and limited government. What gives me cause for some degree of optimism is the amazing growth of free-market think tanks around the world, most with assistance and encouragement from Atlas Network, an organization started by the late Antony Fisher (who was inspired by economist F. A. Hayek to start the first such think tank—the Institute of Economic Affairs, in London, in 1955). As of 2017, the network of Atlas Network think tanks encompasses 484 such organizations, in 92 countries.

Meanwhile, in this difficult and unstable world, how should free countries deal with threats such as nuclear-armed rogue states like Iran and North Korea, with illegal extra-territorial grabs of territory by China and Russia, and with international terrorism? While I agree with the general libertarian opposition to nation-building efforts and an endless global "war on terror," I despair over naïve libertarian isolationist views that would renounce mutual defense alliances such as NATO, downsize the US military across the board, and assume that two oceans are still ample protection to ensure the survival and prospering of the United States. In a world full of threats, for example, somebody has to defend and keep open the sea lanes, on which most international trade (a huge force for good) depends. And today there is no realistic alternative to US leadership in that task. I certainly don't have all the answers to these complex questions, but advocates of free markets and limited government need to devote more serious attention to these problems.

Turning to the status of freedom here at home, in some ways things are even groovier now than when I wrote that 1988 *Reason* article—and Reason Foundation has played a role in these changes.

In general, personal liberty here is in better shape than ever before. Reason's longstanding efforts to get Americans to see that prohibition of drugs (especially marijuana) is as ineffective and as harmful to personal liberty as alcohol prohibition, has really borne fruit in recent decades. There has been a steady increase in acceptance of gay and transgender people as citizens with the same individual rights and dignity as other Americans. And the very large increase since 1988 of women in management and the professions is very encouraging.

Technology has given us opportunities and options that were confined to science fiction in 1968. Lou and I refer to the Internet as the *Encyclopedia Galactica* (as in Isaac Asimov's *Foundation* trilogy), making a treasure trove of information instantly available to us. Phones have evolved from hard-wired devices fixed in place to all-purpose communications and information-access devices that go with us everywhere. Tech-based business models have created new options in retail trade, travel arrangements, hotel booking, and personal transportation. Autonomous vehicles, though overhyped by mass media, will definitely change how we travel, though no one really knows which scenarios will prevail over the next thirty years or so.

A couple years ago, I was a commentator at an invitation-only seminar at the Hudson Institute. The two presenters were Charles Murray, offering a rather dim view of America's future, and Peter

Thiel, presenting a more optimistic picture. Though Charles is one of my heroes, I was dismayed at his glass-half-empty perspective. In particular, he ignored the accelerating progress in biotechnology (regularly reported on by *Reason* science correspondent Ron Bailey and also by former *Reason* contributor Patrick Cox in his *TransTech Alert* newsletter). Gene editing and induced pluripotent stem cells offer amazing breakthroughs for longer lives and better health—and potential easing of the impending Social Security/Medicare debacle. This is a very exciting time to be alive.

The public school monopoly has been breached, step by step, with ongoing support from *Reason* magazine (over its entire fifty years) and in recent decades by our education program's policy studies and hands-on work with "customers" at state and local levels of government. Public-sector vouchers, private-school vouchers, charter schools, and home schooling have all made significant progress, and it's encouraging that a number of thoughtful Democrats have embraced charter schools, despite the all-out opposition of the powerful teachers' unions.

Privatization/competitive contracting of public service delivery—one of my earliest causes with the 1980 book *Cutting Back City Hall*—has become a bipartisan, mainstream tool for better government at city, county, and state levels across the country, with ongoing support from Reason Foundation's Privatization Center. We have also played a key role in introducing long-term public-private partnerships for large-scale infrastructure —for highways, bridges, and tunnels; for municipal water and wastewater systems; and in some cases for new public buildings.

Our policy research efforts have also tried to introduce pricing into areas where it has largely been ignored—such as congestion on urban freeways and airport runways. We've made great progress on the former, with networks of market-priced express lanes under development in the majority of the top-twenty most-congested urban areas. On airports, however, our sole victory has been to change federal airport policy to include market-based runway fees—but no US airport has chosen to make use of this new freedom. The only airports I know of that have switched are privatized London airports Heathrow and Gatwick.

Those are all important gains for markets and liberty. But there are also growing threats that none of us anticipated in the post-Cold War euphoria. The most disturbing of these threats has evolved out of the growth of identity politics (a form of collectivism) and its attendant extremes of political correctness. By 2017, this had devolved to university administrations banning Halloween costumes and allowing the shut-down of politically incorrect speakers by vociferous and sometimes violent student (and non-student) protesters. The idea that universities are supposed to be "safe spaces" shielding students from ideas they may disagree with is inimical to free inquiry and learning. Reason's journalism team has become a leading voice in defense of the First Amendment and of restoring universities to being places of free inquiry and learning. Our friend Mitch Daniels, as president of Purdue University, has emerged as a role model for other university leaders on this. And our friend Jonathan Haidt of New York University has done great work creating the Heterodox Academy project to encourage administrations (and alumni) to restore civilized discourse to colleges and universities.

Despite all the positive developments of recent decades, the federal government has expanded inexorably, under administrations of both parties. It's hard to believe that during the last year of the Clinton administration (2000), there was actually a small federal budget surplus. But spending exploded under the George W. Bush administration, due not just to the military buildup and creation of the Transportation Security Administration as part of the "war on terror," but also to the creation of the new prescription-drug entitlement in the Medicare program. And despite Bush's personal interest in some form of partial privatization of Social Security, no reforms were enacted to that or any other entitlement program.

The Obama administration continued the expansion of government spending, with massive increases in annual budget deficits, leading to almost doubling (up 95 percent) of the national debt in its eight years. There were no serious efforts to reform federal entitlements, which operate entirely on autopilot, expanding year after year based on the number of eligible recipients. The Obama years were the last opportunity to make substantive changes before the start of several decades when retiring baby boomers will greatly expand the number of those "entitled" to payments under Medicare, Medicaid, and Social Security. And of course, Obamacare's expansion of Medicaid made the problem even larger.

During the 2016 presidential race, *none* of the leading contenders offered anything on entitlement reform, and the national debt was absent from the debates. Both Democratic candidates actually campaigned on *expanding* Social Security, and Donald Trump promised no changes in the entitlement programs.

The other troubling federal change has been the continuing growth of the administrative state. That term refers to the inexorable expansion of what some have termed the fourth branch of government: federal regulatory agencies. Each of these myriad entities combines legislative, executive, and judicial functions under the same roof: enacting costly and convoluted regulations, putting them into practice, and using its own "administrative law judges" to adjudicate objections to those regulations. A handful of Supreme Court decisions in recent years have chipped away a bit of these agencies' almost untrammeled power, but their total size and scope continue to expand, regardless of the party in power.

I'm also dismayed by the growing populist trend in political thinking over the past decade. When the late David Nolan first put forth what became known as the Nolan Chart, with a horizontal axis of personal liberty and a vertical axis of economic liberty, it clarified that there are four main political orientations: conservative (higher on economic, lower on personal liberty), liberal (higher on personal, lower on economic liberty), libertarian (high on both) and populist (low on both). Public opinion surveys in the 1980s and 1990s generally showed that populism was the least prevalent of the four, with libertarian (broadly defined) encompassing 20–25 percent, which we libertarians found very encouraging.

The Tea Party movement last decade combined libertarian and populist tendencies, and this decade the populist mindset seems to be wining. Right-wing populism is hostile to immigration and free trade, and also to market pricing in many cases.

In my own work in transportation policy, it has been populist conservatives that have opposed both express toll lanes and public-private partnerships that bring in large-scale private investment for needed highway and bridge projects. Unfortunately, the Trump campaign drew on and helped legitimize right-wing populism, splitting the Republican Party, which still has pretensions of being the best vehicle to further limited government, individual liberty, and free markets. A number of libertarians (including Lou and I) are involved with the Republican Liberty Caucus, in an effort to counteract the populist influence in the party by backing freedom-oriented candidates over populist ones.

So, as we enter Reason's fiftieth year, are things groovier now than in 1968? In many ways, yes. But I see far greater challenges ahead today than I did in 1988.

Where Do We Go From Here?

As a young libertarian in the 1960s, I often heard colleagues refer to their objective as "freedom in our time." They thought that a strong enough movement could undo all the growth of government beyond a very limited "night watchman state," within our lifetimes. During my long career of working for personal and economic liberty, free markets, and limited government, I have learned that it *is* possible to change minds, debunk and discredit bad ideas, overturn long-established paradigms, and bring about real change.

But I have also learned that big policy change (like getting air traffic control out of the clutches of politicians in Congress) is very hard, because it must overcome what Milton Friedman called "the tyranny of the status quo." Public Choice Theory offers important insights into what its pioneers James Buchanan and Gordon Tullock called "the economics of politics"—that those engaged in making and changing public policy are strongly motivated by their own self-interest, whether they are bureaucrats, legislators, or interest groups affected by both the status quo and any alternative.

In answer to those who may ask, "When will Reason Foundation be able to declare victory and disband?" my short answer is "Probably never." The reason for this is a line often attributed (mistakenly) to Thomas Jefferson: *"Eternal vigilance is the price of liberty."* Statements along these lines have been traced back as far as 1790 (in Ireland), but regardless of whether Jefferson ever penned those exact words, they certainly reflect his classical liberal thinking. We have restrictions or prohibitions on market pricing not simply because some people don't understand economics; we also have them because those who benefit from the status quo have powerful incentives to defend it (or to reintroduce it after it has been reformed).

As Reason embarks on a second fifty years, there will be no shortage of work to take on. The challenge facing the organization will be to select from among the wide array of possible efforts the ones where Reason has (or can build) a comparative advantage. As both a senior staffer and a member of the board, I am involved in ongoing discussions about this question. The answers and priorities will inevitably change over time (as my own quickly did when Congress proposed a complete federal takeover of airport security in the wake of 9/11). But I can share with you some of what we are thinking about in preparation for Reason's fiftieth anniversary.

One obvious priority is to assess current core programs for their continued relevance. It's pretty clear that the goal of dismantling the near-monopoly of public schooling has a long way to go, and that Reason Foundation's Education Studies program is a credible and respected player in this endeavor. Likewise, our core strength in privatization, while it has legitimized competitive service contracting, has a lot more work cut out for it in advancing large-scale public-private partnerships for transportation and other infrastructure, as well as potential privatization of government enterprises at all levels (e.g., airports, municipal utilities, water systems, federal electricity providers, and the aging locks on federal inland waterways).

Several of our newer policy programs have had impacts already but could do a lot more given the wide array of opportunities. The criminal justice program can ally with the growing Right on Crime movement, partnering with many of the state-level free-market think tanks on subjects like sentencing reform and asset forfeiture reform. A related area is the need for serious work on developing sensible policies to implement the decriminalization of drugs. If we believe the rhetoric that drugs should be treated comparably to alcohol, what does that actually mean in terms of state laws and policies and how do we find and work with "customers" to bring about those reforms?

Another major target is the administrative state. There is budding legal scholarship on this subject, typified by Columbia University law professor Philip Hamburger's masterful book *Is Administrative Law Unlawful?* The target here is the massive array of federal regulatory agencies and their usurpation of what should be functions of the three branches of the federal government defined and authorized by the Constitution. Reason's prior work in this area dates back to the 1982 book *Instead of Regulation*, a critique of a set of high-profile federal regulatory agencies. More recently, aspects of our environmental program have critiqued federal overreach, and the journalism division has done extensive work on ambitious over-expansion of public health and land-use ("sustainable development") regulations.

My Personal Unfinished Business

I've had an exciting career thus far, initially building a national magazine and public policy think tank, and since 2001 working hard to change paradigms and implement change in transportation infrastructure. Knowing my age, some people ask me if I'm ready to retire. To me, that question misunderstands the difference between a job and a career.

On a number of occasions during the past twenty years, people I've worked with in transportation policy (and whom I saw as sharing much of my policy agenda) reached some arbitrary age and "retired." And they seemed to drop off the map—no email address, no letters to the editor on issues they'd dealt with, not attending conferences where they'd been regulars—and each case made me wonder: did they really care about the things we were working on, or were they just doing a job?

For me, the work that I've been doing, especially since 2001, is far more than a job—it's a calling. I'm proud to have accomplished a lot of change, but I still have a long agenda of unfinished business in the infrastructure field:

- Pursuing the highways paradigm shift from state-owned enterprises to investor-owned businesses (*Rethinking America's Highways*, 2018);
- Finishing the job of removing the Air Traffic Organization from the federal safety regulatory agency (FAA) and converting it into a nonprofit, user-funded ATC corporation;
- Having the United States join the global trend of airport privatization and runway pricing;
- Privatizing numerous state and municipal businesses;
- Enlarging the emerging synergy between pension fund investment needs and PPP infrastructure investors;
- Commercializing the aging locks on the federal Inland Waterways System via lock tolls and PPPs; and,
- Shifting space transportation from NASA to private companies (such as Blue Origin and SpaceX).

This is an agenda for several decades, and will require added staff to carry it out. After my 2018 book tour, my near-term plans do include cutting back from my current fifty-hour week to more like a forty-hour week, and at some point probably cutting back to part-time. But as long as there is breath in my body, I can't imagine not participating in the ongoing debate on these topics.

When Lou and I moved from Los Angeles to South Florida in 2003, some of my ideological opponents cheered, assuming that this meant I was retiring. To their dismay, my transportation policy work became much better and more influential, as summarized in Chapters 12 and 13. Tau sigma, you guys!

I do want to have more time to spend with Lou—traveling, enjoying our Florida lifestyle and continuing to build my very ambitious model railroad. But that will not preclude my vigorous participation in the ongoing debates about improved, market-based infrastructure. Stay tuned!

Index